**BRITISH ARMOURED
FORMATIONS
1939 – 1945
A
BIBLIOGRAPHY**

BRITISH ARMOURED FORMATIONS
1939 – 1945
A
BIBLIOGRAPHY

Annotated and Illustrated,
incorporating Armoured Regiments,
Brigades and Divisions in Service
during World War Two

JOHN A. SMITH

Published by
TANK FACTORY

First published in Great Britain in 2014 by
Tank Factory
www.tankfactory.co.uk

Copyright © John A. Smith 2014
Illustrations © by author.

ISBN 978-0-9930228-0-7

John A. Smith has asserted the moral right to be identified as the author of this work.

All rights reserved. No part of this book may be reproduced, stored in a retrieval system, or transmitted, in any form or by any means, electronic, mechanical, photocopying, recording or otherwise, without the prior permission of the copyright holder.

A CIP Catalogue record for this book is available from the British Library.

Printed and bound in Great Britain by CPI Antony Rowe.

To the men in the green fields;
And those who served with them

In memory of Corporal Reg Spittles, 2nd Northamptonshire Yeomanry and 1st Bn, Royal Tank Regiment, veteran and friend, 1918 – 2013.

Contents

List of Illustrations	xvi
Acknowledgements	xix
Introduction	1
Abbreviations and Glossary	9
Section I - Household Cavalry	11
1st Household Cavalry Regiment	14
2nd Household Cavalry Regiment	16
Section II - Royal Armoured Corps: Heavy Cavalry	18
1st King's Dragoon Guards	19
The Queen's Bays (2nd Dragoon Guards)	21
3rd Carabiniers (Prince of Wales's Dragoon Guards)	23
4th/7th Royal Dragoon Guards	26
5th Royal Inniskilling Dragoon Guards	28
Section III - Royal Armoured Corps: Light Cavalry	32
1st The Royal Dragoons	33
The Royal Scots Greys (2nd Dragoons)	35
3rd The King's Own Hussars	38
4th Queen's Own Hussars	42
7th Queen's Own Hussars	43
8th King's Royal Irish Hussars	45
9th Queen's Royal Lancers	47
10th Royal Hussars (Prince of Wales's Own)	49
11th Hussars (Prince Albert's Own)	50
12th Royal Lancers (Prince of Wales's)	53
13th/18th Royal Hussars (Queen Mary's Own)	55
14th/20th King's Hussars	59
15th/19th The King's Royal Hussars	60
16th/5th Lancers	63
17th/21st Lancers	64

Section IV - Royal Armoured Corps: War-raised Cavalry	66
22nd Dragoons	67
23rd Hussars	68
24th Lancers	70
25th Dragoons	71
26th Hussars	72
27th Lancers	72
Section V - Royal Armoured Corps: Royal Tank Regiment	73
1st Bn, Royal Tank Regiment	76
2nd Bn, Royal Tank Regiment	79
3rd Bn, Royal Tank Regiment	81
4th Bn, Royal Tank Regiment	87
5th Bn, Royal Tank Regiment	89
6th Bn, Royal Tank Regiment	93
7th Bn, Royal Tank Regiment	93
8th Bn, Royal Tank Regiment	95
9th Bn, Royal Tank Regiment	95
10th Bn, Royal Tank Regiment	97
11th Bn, Royal Tank Regiment	98
12th Bn, Royal Tank Regiment	98
Section VI - Royal Armoured Corps: Reconnaissance Corps	99
1st Reconnaissance Regiment	102
2nd Reconnaissance Regiment	102
3rd Reconnaissance Regiment	103
4th Reconnaissance Regiment	105
5th Reconnaissance Regiment	105
15th Reconnaissance Regiment	105
18th Reconnaissance Regiment	106
38th Reconnaissance Regiment	108
43rd Reconnaissance Regiment	108
44th Reconnaissance Regiment	111
45th Reconnaissance Regiment	112
46th Reconnaissance Regiment	112

49th Reconnaissance Regiment	112
50th Reconnaissance Regiment	113
51st Reconnaissance Regiment	114
52nd Reconnaissance Regiment	114
53rd Reconnaissance Regiment	116
54th Reconnaissance Regiment	116
56th Reconnaissance Regiment	116
59th Reconnaissance Regiment	117
61st Reconnaissance Regiment	117
80th (Holding & Training) Reconnaissance Regiment	118
161st Reconnaissance Regiment	118
1st Airborne Reconnaissance Squadron	120
6th Airborne Armoured Reconnaissance Regiment	121
GHQ Liaison Regiment (Phantom)	123
Section VII - Royal Armoured Corps: Supplementary Reserve	**130**
North Irish Horse	131
Section VIII - Royal Armoured Corps: TA - Yeomanry	**133**
The Royal Wiltshire Yeomanry (Prince of Wales's Own)	135
The Warwickshire Yeomanry	136
The Yorkshire Hussars (Alexandra, Princess of Wales's Own)	137
The Nottinghamshire (Sherwood Rangers) Yeomanry	137
The Staffordshire Yeomanry (Queen's Own Royal Regiment)	146
The Cheshire (Earl of Chester's) Yeomanry	148
The Yorkshire Dragoons (Queen's Own)	148
The North Somerset Yeomanry	149
1st Derbyshire Yeomanry	150
2nd Derbyshire Yeomanry	151
Royal Gloucestershire Hussars	152
1st Royal Gloucestershire Hussars	152
2nd Royal Gloucestershire Hussars	153
Lothians & Border Horse Yeomanry	154
1st Lothians & Border Yeomanry	155
2nd Lothians & Border Horse	155

The Fife & Forfar Yeomanry	157
1st The Fife & Forfar Yeomanry	157
2nd The Fife & Forfar Yeomanry	157
2nd County of London Yeomanry (Westminster Dragoons)	158
County of London Yeomanry (Sharpshooters)	159
3rd County of London Yeomanry (Sharpshooters)	161
4th County of London Yeomanry (Sharpshooters)	161
The Northamptonshire Yeomanry	165
1st The Northamptonshire Yeomanry	166
2nd The Northamptonshire Yeomanry	168
East Riding Yeomanry	168
1st East Riding Yeomanry / East Riding Yeomanry	169
2nd East Riding Yeomanry	171
The Inns of Court Regiment	171
Section IX - Royal Armoured Corps: TA – Royal Tank Regiment	**174**
40th Bn, Royal Tank Regiment	175
41st Bn, Royal Tank Regiment	175
42nd Bn, Royal Tank Regiment	176
43rd Bn, Royal Tank Regiment	177
44th Bn, Royal Tank Regiment	177
45th Bn, Royal Tank Regiment	179
46th Bn, Royal Tank Regiment	180
47th Bn, Royal Tank Regiment	180
48th Bn, Royal Tank Regiment	181
49th Bn, Royal Tank Regiment / 49th Armoured Personnel Carrier Regiment	182
50th Bn, Royal Tank Regiment	184
51st Bn, Royal Tank Regiment	185
Section X - Royal Armoured Corps: TA – Royal Armoured Corps Regiments	**186**
107th Regiment, Royal Armoured Corps (King's Own)	187
108th Regiment, Royal Armoured Corps (The Lancashire Fusiliers)	190
109th Regiment, Royal Armoured Corps (The Lancashire Fusiliers)	191
110th Regiment, Royal Armoured Corps (The Border Regiment)	192
111th Regiment, Royal Armoured Corps (Manchester)	194

112th Regiment, Royal Armoured Corps (Sherwood Foresters)	195
113th Regiment, Royal Armoured Corps	196
114th Regiment, Royal Armoured Corps	196
115th Regiment, Royal Armoured Corps	198
116th Regiment, Royal Armoured Corps (Gordon Highlanders)	200
141st Regiment, Royal Armoured Corps (The Buffs)	201
142nd Regiment, Royal Armoured Corps	205
143rd Regiment, Royal Armoured Corps	206
144th Regiment, Royal Armoured Corps	207
145th Regiment, Royal Armoured Corps (Duke of Wellington's)	209
146th Regiment, Royal Armoured Corps (Duke of Wellington's)	211
147th (Hampshire) Regiment, Royal Armoured Corps	213
148th Regiment, Royal Armoured Corps	214
149th Regiment, Royal Armoured Corps	216
150th Regiment, Royal Armoured Corps (York and Lancaster)	217
151st Regiment, Royal Armoured Corps	218
152nd Regiment, Royal Armoured Corps	219
153rd Regiment, Royal Armoured Corps	220
154th Regiment, Royal Armoured Corps	221
155th Regiment, Royal Armoured Corps	222
156th Regiment, Royal Armoured Corps	223
157th Regiment, Royal Armoured Corps	224
158th Regiment, Royal Armoured Corps	224
159th Regiment, Royal Armoured Corps (The Gloucestershire Regiment)	226
160th Regiment, Royal Armoured Corps	227
161st Regiment, Royal Armoured Corps	228
162nd Regiment, Royal Armoured Corps	230
163rd Regiment, Royal Armoured Corps	231
Section XI - Corps of Royal Engineers	**232**
5th Armoured Engineer Regiment, R.E.	235
26th Assault Squadron, R.E.	235
82nd Assault Squadron, R.E.	236

Section XII - Foot Guards	237
Grenadier Guards	239
2nd (Armoured) Battalion, Grenadier Guards	241
4th Tank Battalion, Grenadier Guards	243
Coldstream Guards	244
1st (Armoured) Battalion, Coldstream Guards	245
4th Tank Battalion, Coldstream Guards	246
3rd Tank Battalion, Scots Guards	247
2nd (Armoured) Battalion, Irish Guards	249
2nd (Armoured Reconnaissance) Battalion, Welsh Guards	252
Section XIII - Royal Marines	256
Royal Marines	257
Section XIV - Armoured Brigades	261
1st Armoured Brigade	262
4th Armoured Brigade	262
8th Armoured Brigade	264
22nd Armoured Brigade	265
23rd Armoured Brigade	265
26th Armoured Brigade	266
31st Armoured Brigade	266
34th Armoured Brigade	266
35th Armoured Brigade	267
1st Assault Brigade, RE	267
6th Guards Armoured Brigade	268
Section XV - Armoured Divisions	269
1st Armoured Division	270
2nd Armoured Division	271
6th Armoured Division	271
7th Armoured Division	272
8th Armoured Division	279
9th Armoured Division	280
10th Armoured Division	280
11th Armoured Division	280

42nd Armoured Division	283
79th Armoured Division	283
Guards Armoured Division	286
Section XVI - Miscellaneous	**289**
Miscellaneous	290
Appendix A - Theatres of Operations	**299**
Appendix B - Regiments Operating Funnies	**303**
Appendix C - Cavalry and RTR Regimental Titles Post-war	**304**
Index of Authors	**307**
Addenda	**315**

List of Illustrations

1. **The Household Cavalry at War** Section I
    The Story of the Second Household Cavalry Regiment
    Orde, R., Aldershot; Gale & Polden Ltd; 1953

2. **Second To None** Section III
    The Royal Scots Greys, 1919 - 1945
    Carver, C.B.E., D.S.O., M.C., Lt-Col R. M. P.; Glasgow; The
    Regiment; n.d. [1954]

3. **"Push On 20"** [15/19 H] Section III
    Butler, M.C., Capt. K .F.; London; Holbrook & Son Ltd – printers;
    n.d. [c.1945]

4. **B Squadron 23rd Hussars** Section IV
    No imprint; 1945

5. **The Story of the Twenty-Third Hussars 1940 – 1946** Section IV
    Written by members of the Regiment; No imprint; 1946
    Illustrating the dust-jacket.

6. **The Story of the Twenty-Third Hussars 1940 – 1946** Section IV
    Written by members of the Regiment; No imprint; 1946
    Illustrating the leather binding with cartouche.

7. **Seconds Out!** Section V
    A History of the 2nd Royal Tank Regiment
    Volume Two The Second Round
    Chadwick, 14483488, Sgt K.; No imprint; n.d. [c.1969]
    Illustrating the smaller draft edition.

8. **Seconds Out!** Section V
    A History of the 2nd Royal Tank Regiment
    Volume Two The Second Round ‡
    Chadwick, 14483488, Sgt K.; No imprint; n.d. [c.1970]
    Illustrating the larger official edition.

9. **The Gods Were Neutral** [3RTR] Section V
    Crisp, Robert; London; Frederick Muller Ltd; 1960

10. **Wardrop of the Fifth** Section V
    The Diary of Sgt J. R. Wardrop (Jake) of 5th Royal Tank
    Regiment Nov 1940 - Jan 1944
    Wardrop, Jake; Garnett, Jack (Ed.); No imprint; 1968

LIST OF ILLUSTRATIONS xvii

11. **'A' Squadron Diary** Section V
    7th Royal Tank Regiment
    [*Joscelyne, Maj. R. A.*]; Krefeld, Germany; Scherpe; 1946

12. **Bivvy Broadcast Omnibus NW Europe 1944-5** [49RTR] Section IX
    Celle, Germany; Regiment; 1945

13. **This Band Of Brothers** Section VI
    A History of the Reconnaissance Corps of the British Army
    Taylor, Jeremy; Bristol; The White Swan Press Ltd; 1947

14. **History Of 3rd Reconnaissance Regiment (N.F.) in the** Section VI
    Invasion and Subsequent Campaign in North West Europe
    1944 – 1945
    No imprint; n.d. [1946]

15. **It's The Same Brush…** Section VI
    A History of the 12th Battalion Green Howards and its and X
    Successors The 161st Regiment Royal Armoured Corps
    (Green Howards) and The 161st Reconnaissance Regiment
    Royal Armoured Corps ‡
    Sylvester, Fred (Vic); No imprint; Private self-published; 1997

16. **Sherwood Rangers** Section VIII
    The Story of the Nottinghamshire Sherwood Rangers
    Yeomanry in the Second World War
    Lindsay, T. M.; London; Burrup, Mathieson & Co Ltd; 1952

17. **A Short Account of the 1st Lothians & Border Yeomanry in** Section VIII
    the campaigns of 1940 and 1944-45
    Woolward, W. A.; Edinburgh; The Lothians & Border
    Regimental Association; n.d. [1946]

18. **The Story of the Westminster Dragoons** Section VIII
    In North West Europe from June 6th 1944 - May 8th 1945 ‡
    [*Ravensdale, Keith S. T.*]; Germany; Lüneburger Landeszeitung;
    n.d. [1945]

19. **Men and Sand** [4CLY] Section VIII
    The Earl of Onslow, K.B.E., M.C., T.D.; London; The Saint
    Catherine Press Ltd; 1961

20. **Europe Revisited** Section VIII
    The East Riding Yeomanry in the liberation of Europe and
    the Defeat of Germany
    Ellison, V. C.; Hull; A Brown & Sons Ltd; n.d. [c.1946]

21. **"We Were There!"** Section VIII
    The Story of a Journey Made by C Squadron The Inns Of
    Court Regiment 1941 – 1945
    Various, Flensburg; Emil Schmidt Söhne; n.d. [1946]

22.	**The History of "A" Squadron 141st Regiment R.A.C. (The Buffs)** **June, 1940 – November, 1945** [*Storrar, Maj. George*]; Cupar; J. & G. Innes, Ltd (Printers); 1946	Section X
23.	**Blue Flash** **The Story of an Armoured Regiment** [144RAC/4RTR] *Jolly, Alan*; London; The Solicitors' Law Stationery Society Limited; 1952	Section X and V
24.	**5 Armoured Engineer Regiment, H Hour D Day to VE Day** No imprint; n.d. [c.1945]	Section XI
25.	**A Short History Of The Seventh Armoured Division** **October 1938 - May 1943** *Carver, Lt-Col R. M. P.*; 'In the field'; The Printing and Stationery Services, M.E.F.; 1943	Section XV
26.	**A Short History Of The 7th Armoured Division** **June 1943 - July 1945** *Lindsay, Capt. Martin & Johnston, Capt. M. E.*; 'In the field'; Printing and Stationery Service; 1945 (Note damage to spine, prevalent on these bindings.)	Section XV
27.	**The First Official Account of the Royal Armoured Corps, Through Mud & Blood to the Green Fields Beyond** *Owen, Frank & Atkins, H. W.*; His Majesty's Stationery Office; 1945 – with cover.	Section XVI
28.	**The First Official Account of the Royal Armoured Corps, Through Mud & Blood to the Green Fields Beyond** *Owen, Frank & Atkins, H. W.*; His Majesty's Stationery Office; 1945 – without cover.	Section XVI

Regimental newspapers, newsletters

29.	**The Blue Flash. The Weekly Newspaper of the 4th Royal Tank Regt.** ‡	Section V
30.	**VeRiToR. The Fortnightly Review of The Fifth Royal Tank Regiment**	Section V
31.	**Sharpshooter's Gazette. Journal of the 3rd/4th County of London Yeomanry**	Section VIII
32.	**Milestone. News and Views of 141st Regt. RAC (The Buffs)** ‡	Section X

The illustrations are reproduced at one of two constant scales. Those of larger publications, marked ‡, are smaller again by approximately fifteen percent. Detailed dimensions are given in each book's entry.

Acknowledgements

A book of this nature is more complete due to the help and assistance given by many people. I have spent numerous hours at the shelves of several major libraries studying many of the books listed here and would like to thank the staff of those establishments for the assistance and advice they have provided – Janice Tait and Stuart Wheeler at The Tank Museum, Bovington; Tim Ward at the Prince Consort's Library, Aldershot; Andrew Orgill at The Royal Military Academy, Central Library, Sandhurst; and the staff at the Imperial War Museum, the National Army Museum, the Royal Engineers Museum, Gillingham, and the British Library, London.

I would like to express my thanks to the book dealers who have helped me over the years and in respect of this project. In particular they are, Tim Harper, Martin and Robert Garwood, Christopher Slade, and Philip Austen.

For his help and immense knowledge of all things Recce, I would like to thank Brigadier (Retd) Clive Elderton, CBE. He helped open doors and this work owes a debt of validity as a result of Clive's support.

Lt-Col (Retd) Bob Wyatt, MBE, TD was most generous in assisting with the scope of the project. His significant book collection, which ranges across the history of the British Army, helped me to establish books or editions not found elsewhere.

For his knowledge and generous help on the subject of Tom Chadwick, 3rd Hussars, my thanks go to Julian Francis, a significant collector and authority on engraved prints.

I must fully acknowledge the inspiration and substantial help I gained in the early days from White's Bibliography and more recently from Victor Sutcliffe's bibliographical volumes.

I owe a debt of creativeness to several bibliographies which have helped to confirm certain approaches, alter others and introduce some new ones. They are, in order of my association with them: *A Bibliography of Regimental Histories of the British Army* by Arthur White; *Regiments of the British Army. A handbook with book lists. Part 2 - Cavalry and Armour* by Victor Sutcliffe; and *Regiments. Regiments and Corps of the British Empire and Commonwealth 1758 – 1993* by Roger Perkins.

Were there to be a bibliography at the end of this book, it would include two titles – *A New Introduction to Bibliography* by Philip Gaskell, and *Methods of Book Design* by Hugh Williamson. Both have been valuable references, providing an insight into the technical aspects of book production and demystifying many of the obscure terms of the trade.

I am grateful to the following organizations and people who have provided permission to quote or reproduce:

Bill Bellamy's quotation from *Troop Leader, A Tank Commander's Story*, used by permission of The History Press. All other quotations are Crown Copyright - *History of C Squadron 9th Lancers - World War 1939 – 1945* ~ © 1945; *'A' Squadron Diary, 7th Royal Tank Regiment* and *"We Were There!", The Story of a Journey Made by C Squadron The Inns Of Court Regiment 1941 – 1945* ~ © 1946.

Reproduction of the covers of the following books: *The Gods Were Neutral*, Crisp, Robert, Frederick Muller Ltd, 1960 - used by permission of The Random House

Group Limited; *It's The Same Brush...*, Sylvester, Fred (Vic), self-published, 1997 - used by permission of Mrs A Sylvester; *Sherwood Rangers*, Lindsay, T. M., Burrup, Mathieson & Co Ltd, 1952 - used by permission of St Ives Holdings Limited; *Men and Sand*, The Earl of Onslow, The Saint Catherine Press Ltd – used by permission of the Countess of Onslow; *The Blue Flash*, Jolly, Alan, The Solicitors' Law Stationery Society Limited - used by permission of Elsevier, and *Second To None, The Royal Scots Greys, 1919 – 1945*, Carver, Lt-Col R. M. P., The Regiment, c.1954 – used by permission of the Regimental Secretary, The Royal Scots Dragoon Guards.

Any errors or inaccuracies are my responsibility alone. If any reader has details of a history, biography or memoir that is not included I would of course be delighted to hear from you.

Two people deserve especial thanks. My father, John, for his unstinting support, as unpaid proof reader, and whose computer expertise provided technical inspiration just when it was needed. My greatest thanks go to Christina, my wife, for putting up with overflowing book shelves and as unpaid proof reader and constant reference point, without whose help, support and encouragement, this book would not have been published.

John A. Smith,
September 2014

Introduction

The regimental history as a concept will soon be approaching its 200th anniversary. In 1836, under King William IV, the Adjutant-General's office was commanded to create an account for each regiment of the British Army. The mandate was:

'His Majesty has been pleased to command that, with the view of doing the fullest justice to Regiments, as well as to individuals who have distinguished themselves by their bravery in action with the enemy, an account of the services of every Regiment in the British Army shall be published under the superintendence and direction of the Adjutant-General;...'

Starting in the 1830s, those histories were written almost exclusively under the direction of one man, principal clerk Richard Cannon. The development of warfare into a global affair meant that by the end of the Second World War the scope of such an undertaking required the involvement of many authors in the production of hundreds of histories, now covering not only the army but also the navy and the air force.

The regimental history, however, is only part of the story. There, the official account of a regiment can range from a bald development of its war diaries to a full, expansive telling of men, machines, and the range of actions they saw. The other significant part of the story is told through the memoirs that soldiers have published. This bibliography is the first to record these. They provide the personal, the comment on daily life, the reasons a civilian fought, their reactions to combat. Put together, the two parts enhance the readers understanding of the battles and the men.

It would be some years before the government published its vast multi-volume *History of the Second World War*, and in comparison to many regimental histories, they would be dry versions born of officialdom. However, these would take many years to produce and there was a need and an acknowledgment that regiments and higher formations could produce less rigid, more personal records relatively swiftly after the war. The army had the mechanisms to gather authors and to canvass the men involved while so many were still in uniform, before demobilisation took them away and diminished the pool of immediate knowledge. Within four years of the war's end, approximately 120 histories, summaries and memoirs had been published.

Maj. R. A. Joscelyne wrote in the foreword to 7RTR's *'A' Squadron Diary*, 'I hope the shortcomings of amateur historians will be overlooked, as also the inevitable omissions of which, I fear, there are many.' The army had a ready supply of such 'amateur historians', officers working in headquarters, usually with an NCO clerk, used to writing up the squadron's or regiment's doings. They were ready to write up their version of events and had one eye on why they had fought, '... I hope that these few [incidents] may serve to remind you of the others and also enable you to bore your grandchildren in years to come!' - Maj. D. E. C. Steel, 9th Lancers.

These more immediate works also provided the regiments with the opportunity to honour their dead with rolls of honour, often at squadron level. (A note for researchers: the date of publication of these RoH should be borne in mind. Full investigations were often yet to be carried out and the records used were mostly those of the regimental admin which had the exigencies of war to contend with when compiling and retaining them. The Commonwealth War Graves Commission has these records under continual review.)

All histories include an element of opinion and create the difficult task of selecting as many representative events as possible. The men who took part do not always agree on what was written about events germane to them. An example of history in print not pleasing all readers comes from a copy of the Royal Scots Greys' newsletter of October 1945, 'The issue of the History of the 4th Armoured Brigade caused quite a few arguments. Some of the beribboned authorities seem to think that the Brigadier is a little out in his facts!'

A handful of authors wrote of their personal experiences almost immediately, for example, Roy Farran's *Winged Dagger* in 1948. (Memoir or biography? A useful way to distinguish them is that a biography is the person's life history, and therefore naturally includes an autobiography, and a memoir is a recollection from a narrower period or set of events.) Works of pure fiction are excluded from this bibliography. However, where an author has written a novel based on their factual experiences, then it has been included. An example of that being *Warriors for the Working Day* by Peter Elstob, it would be remiss to exclude such a work.

A study of the quantities of titles produced per decade reveals a gentle waxing and waning reflecting the interests and the ages of the veterans and the audiences. The 1960s had the lowest quantity of titles. The veterans were in their late 30s, early 40s, and focused on families and jobs; the country as a whole had a naturally evolved distance from the war. Unsurprisingly the 1990s witnessed the greatest number of books published and re-published. The late 1980s saw men of serving age reaching retirement and the following decade burgeoned with memoirs from veterans. An apposite quotation comes from *Troop Leader* by Bill Bellamy: 'For the first forty years or so, I didn't want to think about the war, but some time after I had retired the box came out of the attic and down to my office.' The D-Day 50th Anniversary commemorative events in 1994 raised the profile of the Normandy campaign in the minds of the general public. This coincided with the veterans reaching retirement age and many starting to talk about their experiences for the first time, very often prompted by their children or, more effectively, grand-children.

British veterans often display an ethos of self-deprecation. This is both charming and frustrating - charming in the way horrors can be summed up in a phlegmatic phrase and frustrating because those horrors are often glossed over, providing a cosier view of what it is to be a soldier. There has been a definite poignancy for me in collating the memoirs. The heyday of veterans publishing their recollections is sadly gone; these men are getting fewer and fewer and are now at an age where writing a book would be too onerous. Thankfully so many did put their memories into print.

It was during the very late 1940s and the 1950s that the bulk of the major histories were published. One publisher synonymous with the regimental history is Gale and Polden Limited. They could be described as publishers to the military, printing not only traditional books, but short histories, pamphlets, training manuals, and official army forms. Such a business relationship has almost certainly passed into history itself and after a proliferation of different publishers during the 1970s-1990s, the modern printing business means that there are only a handful of regular publishers now printing specialist military titles. Of the publishers listed in this bibliography, the top five by volume are: Leo Cooper Limited, Gale & Polden Limited, Malcolm Page Limited, Pen & Sword Books Limited (born of the Leo Cooper imprint), and Sutton Publishing Limited.

INTRODUCTION

Whilst the 1990s saw the greatest increase in the quantity of books published in one decade, the subject matter was heavily biased to the North West European campaign. The further away from the Normandy coast, the less familiar the terrain and the cultural references, the fewer titles there are.

The passing of time is part of the distillation process of writing history. Prejudices diminish, records are released and fresh minds applied. The corollary of too much time passing is that it leads to a divorce from people and the events surrounding them. This does not mean that the writing of good history stops but it leaves a gap in the primary evidence that can be used by future authors. However, such authors do have a very valuable unpublished resource. In several of the libraries that I visited there are memoirs deposited by veterans which for one reason or another have not, to date, been published.

My research and study of the Royal Armoured Corps over the last twenty years brought me to realise that my list of wants was in effect becoming a reference list. This book was born, therefore, from the commonest of reasons – one like it did not exist. Two major bibliographies exist which deal with works covering the Second World War – Arthur White's and Victor Sutcliffe's. (Refer to 'Section XVI – Miscellaneous' for details.) Each covers most branches of the British Army and as such could not go into the detail that I ultimately desired. By focusing on one branch of the British Army, I have been able to include more titles and to expand the scope to include brigades and divisions, as well as memoirs.

The objective of the book is to collate an inventory of publications relating to the armoured regiments, brigades, and divisions of the British Army operating during World War Two, covering the publication period from 1939 to the present day. As supplementary information, it also lists the regimental periodicals: journals, newspapers and newssheets.

It would be rash to claim that every single book on this topic has been catalogued here. By virtue of itself being printed, this book has to conclude with publications printed up to mid-2014. There are many self-published books, several with abstruse titles which do not lend themselves to even intense searching out. For those which have slipped through the net I hope the reader will appreciate the difficulties and accept my apologies.

There are exclusions from the scope of this bibliography - print on demand publications (in their 'specialist handful of copies' sense rather than the increasing modern use by large publishers of re-issuing titles on a print on demand basis); general ephemera (such as orders of service, or celebratory menus which many regiments printed during and immediately after the war); campaign histories and titles on particular models of tank. A handful of exceptions warrant inclusion because they contain sufficient unit specific information.

The Book Entries

Each book has its own table which provides not only all the bibliographical information that one would expect, but also a set of notes providing an overview of the book together with any ancillary information which may be informative.

The table below shows the format for each entry and below that, explanations of the components and the terms used. This Key table is repeated at the end of each Section for handy reference. For an explanation of all of the abbreviations, please refer to the 'Abbreviations and Glossary'.

Key to Book Entries
Book Title and Sub-title(s)
Author   Museum Holdings
Place of Publication; Publisher; Date of Publication; ISBN; Pages/Illustrations; Binding; Indexed; Glossary; Appendices; Bibliography; Size (in mm); Availability
NOTES:

Book Title and Sub-title(s)	A book's title can vary between the title page, front board, spine, and dust-jacket. That from the title page is noted here, with reference to case.
Author	Taken from the title page where they are usually fully credited. Editors and compilers duly noted. Where Author equals 'Not stated [See Notes]' the author is known from other sources rather than being credited in the traditional way on the title page.
Museum holdings	An entry denotes a holding by one of the following military libraries: TM – The Tank Museum, Bovington IWM – Imperial War Museum, London NAM – National Army Museum, London RMAS – Royal Military Academy, Central Library, Sandhurst PCL – Prince Consort's Library, Aldershot RE – Royal Engineers Museum, Gillingham (RE specific only)
Place of publication	The publisher's address town as per the title page.
Publisher	As per imprint page. If no publisher is listed but a printer is, the printer is noted in parentheses. Establishing the publisher is not always as straightforward a task as may at first appear. Even with self-published memoirs, it is not necessarily the author who has acted as publisher. Where there is sufficient doubt, the entry is marked as No imprint or Not stated dependent upon what information has been printed.
Date of publication	As per title page. Although some books are undated, an approximate date is noted where this can be assessed from clues in the book's production – binding or typographical style, dates in the preliminaries, narrative, or appendices; estimated and interpreted dates noted in square brackets.
Pages/Illustrations	Page count taken from the printed numbers – usually Roman numerals for the preliminaries and Arabic numerals for the main content and back pages. Very occasionally, a second run of Roman numerals is used for the final back pages. The quantity and type of illustrations are noted. This may

INTRODUCTION

assist the reader in gauging the style of the book and potentially some of its merit as to whether to consult. It will also assist collectors to ensure that all illustrations are present.

Binding	Three main categories: hardback, softback and paperback. The distinction here between paperback and softback is that the traditional mass-market thin paper covers are described as p/b, the stouter card covers are described as s/b. Other bindings are noted such as comb - used by some self-publishers. The term cloth has been used for generic simplicity. Older books may have their boards covered in a natural cloth but most modern books utilise a synthetic equivalent, still referred to as cloth. The colour has been based on a simple palette rather than a complication of shades.
Indexed; Glossary; Appendices; Bibliography	Denoted by a Y or N. Their existence, or lack of, may assist a researcher.
Size – H x W	The book's overall external dimensions; for case-bound (hardback) books this is to the extremities of the boards and spine. Otherwise for soft and paperbacks it is to the extremities of the cover. The actual paper size, octavo, duodecimo, etc., is the trimmed paper size and due to the variations in original sheet size and printer trimmings, this is provided as a guide. The millimetre dimensions are of more practical use when gauging a book's size.
Availability	The availability of a title is based on experience and is, therefore, a subjective value. It will assist collectors or researchers to establish the ease with which a title may be obtained outside of any listed museum holding. Ratings are:

No rating:	The item is either commonly available or appears frequently in on-line listings.
Uncommon	The item can be obtained with modest effort.
Rare	The item can be obtained only with a degree of determined searching.
V Rare	The item is extremely difficult to find and may take many years to source.

NOTES	Additional information such as print runs, amount of content relating to WWII, confirmation of RoH, honours and awards, etc., plus my own comment on the content. 'Not physically inspected' is entered where a book is known of but a hands-on inspection has not been possible.

The rarity of an item is influenced by several factors. The first, naturally, is how many were produced, next, how ephemeral the item is considered to be. Some items are less popular leading to greater attrition. The counters to that are popularity or desirability and the influence they have on how often an item is released to the collector's market.

Many of the official histories were intended for ex-members of the unit and many veterans intended their memoirs only for family and close friends. Print runs, therefore, were often modest, frequently just a few hundred or one or two thousand rather than many thousands. Surviving numbers of some of these books have reduced through natural wastage, disposal through bereavements, and a lack of appreciation of their worth. With the rise in the number of collectors, the available stock has a different feed to the sales market. Many of the books coming to market over the years have been from the very veterans they were aimed at, now sadly dwindling in number.

Overview of the listings

The scope of the listings is primarily the Royal Armoured Corps. In addition the Household Cavalry, armoured Engineers, Foot Guards, and Royal Marines are included; a realistic limit to the scope was to exclude the Commonwealth forces.

All regiments that served in the Royal Armoured Corps are listed. Some came into the RAC for as little as eight months and the prospect of any published work mentioning such a fleeting existence is remote indeed. A lengthy period of service was no guarantee of being written about either; some of the converted infantry regiments served as armour for several years and yet no specific history or substantial mention can be found.

The RAC evolved several ad-hoc units during the war including those which were termed 'Dummy Tanks'. Units such as 38RTR, 60RTR, 102RTR, and 4NY were among the many dummy unit titles employed. Amongst the non-regimental units utilising real armoured vehicles were – 'A', 'B', and 'C' Special Service Squadrons; 400 and 401 Independent Scorpion Squadrons; No. 1 Independent Troop, RTR; Malta Tanks; Gibraltar Tank Squadron; and 52 Tank Squadron. Articles describing them have been published in various journals and magazines but there is no evidence that either formal or informal histories have been published.

The book is structured to start with the regiments, followed by brigades and divisions. The regiments are listed in order of precedence according to the Army List, taken as at 1944 after the Reconnaissance Corps had been absorbed by the RAC. The year 1944 was chosen because by that time the order had settled to its final status for the remainder of the war, the only differences thereafter being where regiments ceased to exist by being disbanded. Reprints and new editions are included as discrete entries. Publications which incorporate more than one unit are included under each unit for convenience.

A concept that I have applied is that it may be as useful to know that a title has no, or very little, pertinent information as it is to know that one is full of information. This can be most applicable to books with titles that imply they have relevant content when in fact they cover other topics.

INTRODUCTION

The bibliographical entries are contained within sixteen sections, each of which is structured thus:

- An introductory page provides some of the background to the branch in question, highlighting certain aspects of the complex formation of tank regiments in WWII.
- A title bar shows the unit's full title followed by its official abbreviation as per War Office instructions of the period. The abbreviations are as set out in *Field Service Pocket Book Pt I Pamphlet No. 3 Abbreviations, 1944*. Due to the proliferation of units during the war, not all of them had an abbreviation listed in this pamphlet; where these have been interpreted by me they are noted by square brackets.
- Following the title bar are notes on the dates of mechanization and service within the RAC where relevant. For the infantry converted Reconnaissance and RAC regiments, a list of the infantry battalions from which they were raised is also shown here.
- If applicable, there is a list of the unit's journals and newspapers. A word of caution regarding the numbering of unit journals - these were often produced in-house rather than by professional publishers and a not too uncommon fault, particularly at a change in editorship, is that the volume or edition numbering goes awry. As an example, *The Tank* ran consistently until the late 1970s when April, July and October 1977 editions were all printed as edition number 680. Other regiments have similar anomalies. (An interesting regulation appears in the 1940 King's Regulations for the Army. Paragraph 1731 states 'C.O.s are invited to send copies of all historical records and regimental magazines and newspapers that may be printed privately to the principal librarian of the British Museum, and the Librarian, The War Office.' It is outside the scope of this book to investigate how closely this instruction was followed but it provides an interesting view of the official attitude to retaining these items for future reference.)
- In some sections, the Royal Tank Regiment and Reconnaissance Corps for example, there have been generic books published where several or all of the regiments of a branch are represented. These are listed first, followed by the regiments, in their order of precedence. Within each unit, the books are presented in chronological order by date of publication. This results in reprinted titles being separated but it does provide a landscape of the unit's historiography.

Also included in the listings are some of the official documents which have recently gained public circulation through the disposals made by some libraries. Examples include the *79th Armoured Division Final Report* and *23rd Armoured Brigade, Operations in Greece October 15 1944 - January 7 1945*.

The bibliographical entries have been set out with reference to *British Standard 5605 Recommendations for citing and referencing published material*. The main departures from the standard are for the purpose and legibility of this book. A publication's title is listed first, rather than the author and at the end of each entry is a notes field. Because they were not introduced until 1967, ISBN numbers are absent from many of the entries here. ISBNs were a 9, then 10 digit string and from 1 January 2007 all ISBNs are 13 digits long.

Three appendices provide the reader with some quick reference tables summarising the following topics:
- Appendix A lists all of the armoured regiments and provides a Y/N entry against the major Theatres of Operations. Supplementary annotation provides more detail on service in some of the sub-theatres.
- Appendix B lists the 22 regiments which employed specialized Funnies and notes the brigades in which they served.
- Appendix C will assist readers to sort through the name changes of the cavalry regiments through the various amalgamations that have taken place since the war. It also lists the post-war RTR regiments and charts which regiment they merged with over the same period.

The scope of this book does not lend itself to a pithy one line title, nor could that title encompass all of the books covered. For example, the Household Cavalry and the Foot Guards were administratively separate from the Royal Armoured Corps. However, the RAC supplied the training and some of the men, so to exclude these on such a technicality would be discourteous. They are by virtue of their tactical employment, wholly suited to inclusion.

Inclusion is based on being specifically unit focused. This leads to some titles being omitted which the reader may otherwise have expected. For example, *Nine Lives To Berlin, with a tank brigade 1939 – 1946* would appear to be an obvious candidate for inclusion in this bibliography. However, the author served with a signals regiment and so his book is outside the scope of this work. 'Home-made' memoirs which have been deposited with a library such as at The Tank Museum have not been catalogued. They have been included where there is evidence that the author sold or distributed them outside the family group.

The views and opinions on the books listed here are my own, as an interested observer both of the content and the way it is presented. I hope the reader will share my views but in any case appreciate that they may help in identifying the volumes of most or particular interest. The value of one book over another will very often be influenced by the needs of the reader; one key fact or phrase may be all that is needed to make the reading of one book worthwhile.

Whether a history was written for a squadron or a division, they were produced for two essential reasons, summed up perfectly in the foreword to "*We Were There*", C Squadron, Inns of Court – 'In producing this publication, we had two main ideas in mind. Firstly, to give you some sort of souvenir of the Squadron which you could keep in the days to come. Secondly, to provide a record of some of the Squadron's achievements and activities in the days that have gone by.'

Abbreviations and Glossary

Book sizes: Name / Dimensions up to

64mo	76mm/3in.	8vo (aka 'Octavo')	248mm/9.75in.
48mo	102mm/4in.	4to (aka 'Quarto')	305mm/12in.
32mo	127mm/5in.	Folio	380mm/15in.
24mo	146mm/5.75in.	Elephant Folio	585mm/23in.
16mo (aka 'Sextodecimo')	171mm/6.75in.	Atlas Folio	635mm/25in.
12mo (aka 'Duodecimo')	197mm/7.75in.	Double Elephant Folio	1270mm/50in.

Armd	Armoured
AVRE	Armoured Vehicle Royal Engineers
Bde	Brigade
BEF	British Expeditionary Force
Bn	Battalion
BAOR	British Army of the Rhine
Brig.	Brigadier
bw	Black and white
Capt.	Captain
CDL	Canal Defence Light – specialist tanks ('Funnies') mounting a high powered searchlight.
clr	Colour
CO	Commanding Officer
Col	Colonel
Comb	Plastic spiral binding typically found on self-published works.
Coy	Company
Cpl	Corporal
DD	Duplex Drive – one of Hobart's 'Funnies', a 'swimming' tank.
d/j	Dust-jacket
Ed.	Editor
f	Folding
fep	Front end paper
Fr	Frontis
Fw	Foreword
GSGS	Geographical Section, General Staff
GSO	General Staff Officer
h/b	Hardback
Hon.	Honourable
i/c	In command (2 i/c – second-in-command)
Illus.	Illustration
IO	Intelligence Officer
ISBN	International Standard Book Number. Introduced in 1970.
IWM	Imperial War Museum
L/Cpl	Lance Corporal

LO	Liaison Officer
Lt-Col	Lieutenant-Colonel
Lt-Gen	Lieutenant-General
LVT	Landing Vehicle Tracked
M	Map
Maj.	Major
Maj-Gen.	Major-General
Mbds	Map – on boards
ME	Middle East
Mep	Map – end papers
Mf	Map – folding
NA	North Africa
NAM	National Army Museum
n.d.	No date
ne	Not established (used in context of presence of dust-jacket and colour of binding cloth.)
NWE	North West Europe
OC	Officer Commanding
OCA	Old Comrades Association
OCTU	Officer Cadet Training Unit
OoB	Order of Battle
OR	Other Ranks
p/b	Paperback
PCL	Prince Consort's Library
PI	Photographic illustration
POW	Prisoner of war
pp	Pages
PRO	Public Record Office – now The National Archives
QM	Quartermaster
RAMC	Royal Army Medical Corps
RE	Corps of Royal Engineers / Museum library
rep	Rear end paper
RMAS	Royal Military Academy Sandhurst
RMASG	Royal Marine Armoured Support Group
RMO	Regimental Medical Officer
RoH	Roll of honour
RSM	Regimental Sergeant Major
s/b	Softback
Sgt	Sergeant
SI	Sketch illustration
SOE	Special Operations Executive
Sqn	Squadron
TA	Territorial Army
TM	The Tank Museum, Bovington
Tp	Troop
Tpr	Trooper
WD	War Department
WE/WET	War Establishment/War Establishment Table
WO1	Warrant Officer Class 1

Section I

Household Cavalry

The Household Cavalry consists of the most senior, and some of the oldest, regiments of the British Army. Following the evolving unit titles of the Household Cavalry can be confusing; therefore a family tree is shown on the following page to assist the reader with the lineage of the regiments.

During the Second World War the Life Guards and Royal Horse Guards combined to form two armoured car units. The two regiments, 1HCR and 2HCR, did not convert to armour until 1942 and 1941 respectively. 1HCR went to Palestine with its horses in 1940 and converted to armoured cars relatively late, in February 1942. It took part in the battle of El Alamein and then operated in Syria before arriving in Italy in April 1944. It left Italy at the end of 1944, moving to NWE in March 1945; the two regiments met briefly mid-April 1945, the first time they had done so during the war. 2HCR landed in NWE in July 1944 and operated in that theatre through to VE-Day.

The close relationship of the two regiments is demonstrated by the mix of officers and men in each of the armoured car units. 1HCR was commanded by Life Guards officers with a split of sabre squadrons of 2 x LG and 1 x RHG. 2HCR was commanded by Royal Horse Guards officers with a split of 2 x RHG and 1 x LG sabre squadrons.

The Household Cavalry was kept outside the scope of the Royal Armoured Corps when that was formed in 1939 and remains a separate, although symbiotic, corps today. However, personnel for both regiments received their training through the RAC and both adopted the black beret (1HCR in 1942 and 2HCR in 1941), official headgear of the RAC.

In 1969 The Royal Dragoons (1st Dragoons) were amalgamated with The Royal Horse Guards to form The Blues and Royals (Royal Horse Guards and 1st Dragoons), hence books written about the Household Cavalry after that date should include reference to the Royal Dragoons/Royals. For the period of World War Two and this bibliography the Royal Dragoons will be found in 'Section III – Royal Armoured Corps, Light Cavalry'.

Summary Lineage Table 1922 - Present

The Life Guards can trace their history back to 1658 and The Blues and the Royals back to 1661. The Blues became part of the Household Cavalry in 1820 and the Royals in 1969. For a brief period after World War Two, both regiments appended 'Armoured Car Regiment' to their titles. 1922 has been selected for the following table as a modern starting point to reach World War Two and follow on to the modern day.

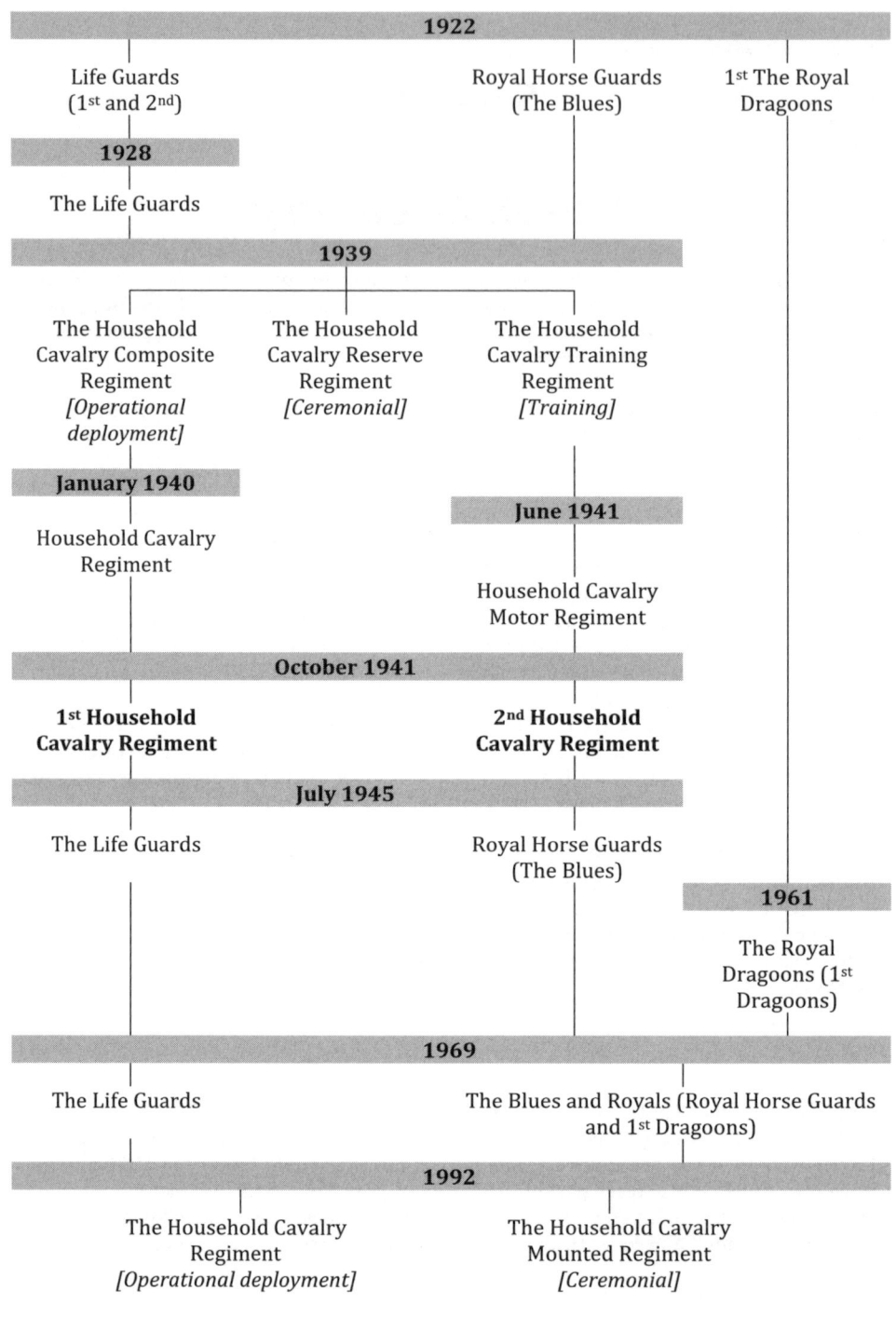

Household Cavalry

Regimental publications:
The Household Brigade Magazine
Pre-1900 to Spring 1968. (Quarterly)
Hector. The Household Cavalry Training Regiment's News-Letter
August 1943 – unknown. Reproduced typescript.

The Story of the Guards
Paget, Julian   IWM; NAM; PCL
London; Osprey Publishing Ltd; 1976; ISBN 0 85045 078 0; 304pp/17 x clr PI/12 x clr SI/46 x bw PI/38 x bw SI/11 x bw M; h/b / d/j Blue cloth; Indexed Y; Glossary Y; Appendices N; Bibliography Y; 292 x 218 (4to)
NOTES: A general history of the Household Division (Household Cavalry and Foot Guards) presented in chronological order. Summary of 1HCR and 2HCR within the narrative. Reprinted 1977.

All the Queen's Men
The Household Cavalry and the Brigade of Guards
Braddon, Russell
London; Hamish Hamilton Ltd; 1977; ISBN 241 89431 X; 288pp/Various clr & bw illus.; h/b / d/j Red/black cloth; Indexed Y; Glossary N; Appendices N; Bibliography N; 252 x 196 (4to)
NOTES: An overview history of the Household Division with a brief 6pp on the Household Cavalry and Foot Guards in WWII.

All the Queen's Men
The Household Cavalry and the Brigade of Guards
Braddon, Russell   TM; NAM
Not stated; Book Club Associates; 1977; ISBN None; 288pp/Various clr & bw illus.; h/b / d/j Red/black cloth; Indexed Y; Glossary N; Appendices N; Bibliography N; 250 x 192 (4to)
NOTES: Reprint of 1977 first edition.

A Short History of the Household Cavalry
Not stated
No imprint; Regiment; n.d. [c.1980]; ISBN None; 13pp/No illus.; s/b (card); Indexed N; Glossary N; Appendices N; Bibliography N; 252 x 165 (4to); Uncommon
NOTES: Chronological summary of LG, RHG and 1RD with 4pp covering all three in WWII.

Through Fifteen Reigns
A Complete History of the Household Cavalry
Watson, J. N. P.   NAM; RMAS; PCL
Staplehurst; Spellmount Limited; 1997; ISBN 1-873376-70-7; xiv + 192pp/15 x clr PI/20 x clr SI/66 x bw PI/31 x bw SI/43 x bw M; h/b / d/j Red cloth; Indexed Y; Glossary N; Appendices Y; Bibliography Y; 283 x 225 (4to)
NOTES: The first chapter provides an excellent summary of the evolution of the Household Cavalry and its constituent regiments. The book traces the history of three

regiments: Life Guards, Royal Horse Guards and Royal Dragoons through a chapter per monarch; George VI's is 22pp. The last two regiments were amalgamated as The Blues and Royals in 1969. Extremely good summary accounts of the three regiments in WWII.

Horse Guards
White-Spunner, Harvey TM; RMAS; PCL
London; Macmillan; 2006; ISBN 978-1-4050-5574-1; xiv + 626pp/1 x clr SIfep/20 x clr PI/122 x clr SI/77 x bw PI/33 x bw SI/25 x clr M; h/b / d/j Black cloth; Indexed Y; Glossary N; Appendices N; Bibliography Y; 266 x 200 (4to)
NOTES: Written to provide a history of all four regiments of the Household Cavalry to coincide with the relaunch of their museum in 2007. It spans the years 1600 – 2006, concentrating on the period up to 1939 with WWII covered in 54pp. A few proofing errors have slipped through the editorial net but a very readable brief history which includes several veterans' quotations.

1st Household Cavalry Regiment — 1 HCR

Date of mechanization: March 1941 (Armd cars March 1942)

Regimental publications:
The Acorn: the Regimental magazine of The Life Guards
Vol. 1, No. 1 Spring 1965 to not established. (Annual)

The Household Cavalry at War
First Household Cavalry Regiment. The Story of the First Household Cavalry Regiment
Wyndham M.C., Col the Hon. Humphrey TM; IWM; NAM; RMAS; PCL
Aldershot; Gale & Polden Ltd; 1952; ISBN None; xiii + 189pp/1 x bw PIfep/65 x bw PI/2 x bw SI/2 x PIM/11 x bw Mf; h/b / d/j Blue cloth; Indexed Y; Glossary N; Appendices Y; Bibliography N; 247 x 157 (8vo); Uncommon
NOTES: Part one of a two part history, appendices include casualty lists and officers in WWII. Good narrative, although does tend to jingoism in areas.

The Life Guards
Short Regimental History
Meakin, W.O.1 D. TM; IWM; PCL
Windsor; Luff & Sons Ltd; n.d. [c.1954]; ISBN None; 23pp/No illus.; s/b; Indexed N; Glossary N; Appendices Y; Bibliography N; 153 x 122 (16mo); Uncommon
NOTES: Summary 2pp on WWII.

The Life Guards
(Famous Regiments)
Hills, R. J. T.; Horrocks, Lt.-Gen. Sir Brian (Ed.) TM; IWM; NAM; RMAS; PCL
London; Leo Cooper Ltd; 1971; ISBN 0 85052 087 8; iv + 128pp/17 x bw PI/15 x bw SI; h/b / d/j Red cloth; Indexed N; Glossary N; Appendices N; Bibliography N; 222 x 140 (8vo)
NOTES: Brief account of WWII service; 13pp cover WWII.

Irregular Regular
Smiley, David IWM; NAM
Norwich; Michael Russell (Publishing) Ltd; 1994; ISBN 0 85955 202 0; 218pp/1 x bw PIfep/4 x bw M; h/b / d/j Blue cloth; Indexed N; Glossary N; Appendices N; Bibliography N; 240 x 158 (8vo)
NOTES: In the first third of this book the author describes his early service with the RHG and, upon the Household Cavalry's reorganisation, with 1HCR. He served with 1HCR in the Middle East but was also attached to other units: firstly with the Middle East Commandos 1940/41 and secondly, with 101RTR operating dummy tanks, in 1942. After 1HCR's withdrawal following the battle of El Alamein, he volunteered for the SOE and the remainder of the book deals with his experiences in Greece, Albania and Thailand.

Balkan Blue
Family and Military Memoirs
Redgrave, Roy IWM
Barnsley; Leo Cooper; 2000; ISBN 0 85052 755 4; 250pp/36 x bw PI; h/b / d/j Blue cloth; Indexed Y; Glossary N; Appendices N; Bibliography N; 240 x 160 (8vo)
NOTES: Born in Romania, of Anglo-Romanian parents, the author commuted to England for his education and was sent to England when war became imminent. He completed his education and served in the Home Guard before joining the Household Cavalry. RR recounts aspects of his training and in late 1943 he signed up to a commission with the RHG, following which he was posted to 1HCR in late 1944. After a brief summary of 1HCR's war, he recalls his experience as an armoured car troop leader at the end of the war in NWE from March 1945. Whilst lacking in much regimental detail, these eloquent memoirs are evocative of the period. 47pp on WWII.

Balkan Blue
Family and Military Memoirs
Redgrave, Roy
Barnsley; Pen & Sword Select; 2003; ISBN 978 1 84468 000 9; 250pp/Illus. (See Notes); h/b / d/j Blue cloth; Indexed Y; Glossary N; Appendices N; Bibliography N
NOTES: New hardback edition published 2003. (Not physically inspected.)

The 1st Household Cavalry 1943-44
In the Shadow of Monte Amaro
Taken from the war diaries of 1HCR officers
O'Connor, Gary RMAS; PCL
Stroud; Spellmount; 2013; ISBN 978 0 7524 8857 8; 192pp/24 x bw PI/7 x bw SI/1 x bw M; h/b / d/j Black cloth; Indexed Y; Glossary N; Appendices Y; Bibliography Y; 240 x 160 (8vo)
NOTES: The author has used the diaries of several ex-officers of 1HCR (predominantly A Squadron and RHG) together with interviews to produce a story of the regiment in Italy. Each of the main contributors is introduced in chapter two. Useful detail from the war diaries included. A view into officers from a distinct tranche of English society. Appendix lists officers who served with the regiment in Italy including their squadron.

2nd Household Cavalry Regiment	2 HCR

Date of mechanization: September 1941

Regimental publications:
The Blue: the journal of The Royal Horse Guards (The Blues) Past and Present
Vol. 1 1964 to Vol. 6 1969. (Annual)

His Majesty's Royal Regiment of Horse Guards (The Blues)
Not stated IWM
Aldershot; Gale & Polden Ltd; n.d. [c.1946]; ISBN None; 24pp/1 x clr SI; s/b; Indexed N; Glossary N; Appendices N; Bibliography N; 183 x 123 (12mo); Uncommon
NOTES: Pocket history, 6pp on WWII.

The Household Cavalry at War
The Story of the Second Household Cavalry Regiment
Orde, R. TM; IWM; NAM; RMAS; PCL
Aldershot; Gale & Polden Ltd; 1953; ISBN None; xxi + 624pp/1 x clr PIfep/1 x clr PI/1 clr SI/108 x bw PI/35 x bw SI/2 x bw Mbds/8 x clr M/9 x bw M; h/b / d/j Blue cloth; Indexed Y; Glossary N; Appendices Y; Bibliography N; 247 x 163 (8vo); Uncommon
NOTES: Comprehensive and well regarded part two of a two part history. Appendices include casualty lists and officers in WWII. The author served in D Sqn as rear link officer. (Drawings are by Cpl Eric Meade-King.)

The Royal Horse Guards (The Blues)
(Famous Regiments)
Hills, R. J. T.; Horrocks, Lt.-Gen. Sir Brian (Ed.) TM; IWM; NAM; RMAS; PCL
London; Leo Cooper Ltd; 1970; ISBN 85052 027 4; v + 116pp/17 x bw PI/11 x bw SI; h/b / d/j Blue cloth; Indexed N; Glossary N; Appendices N; Bibliography N; 222 x 140 (8vo)
NOTES: Includes an overview of their wartime history which is more complicated than this book covers. 13pp cover WWII.

The Story of The Blues and Royals (Royal Horse Guards and 1st Dragoons)
Watson, J. N. P. TM; IWM; NAM; RMAS; PCL
London; Leo Cooper; 1993; ISBN 085052 238 2; viii + 328pp/1 x bw PIfep/6 x clr PI/121 x bw PI/22 x bw SI/8 x bw M; h/b / d/j Blue cloth; Indexed Y; Glossary N; Appendices N; Bibliography Y; 234 x 158 (8vo)
NOTES: A history of The Blues and Royals from 1945 on. One chapter on their respective histories during WWII covered in 9pp. The author's book, *Through Fifteen Reigns*, q.v., provides coverage of WWII.

Dangerous Liaison
Cooper, Derek; Maxse, A. J. (Ed.) IWM
Norwich; Michael Russell (Publishing) Ltd; 1997; ISBN 0 85955 229 2; 151pp/16 x bw PI/13 x bw M; h/b / d/j Red cloth; Indexed Y; Glossary N; Appendices N; Bibliography N; 222 x 143 (8vo)
NOTES: Uses author's diary interspersed with editor's comments. Interesting account of a liaison officer. See also, the biography *For Love of Justice*.

For Love of Justice
The Life of a Quixotic Soldier
Baynes, John IWM
London; Quartet Books Limited; 1997; ISBN 0 7043 7109 X; x + 302pp/26 x bw Pl/8 x bw M; h/b / d/j Black cloth; Indexed Y; Glossary N; Appendices N; Bibliography Y; 240 x 156 (8vo)
NOTES: A biography of Derek Cooper who joined the Irish Guards in 1936 and volunteered to join 2HCR upon the creation of the Guards Armoured Division in late 1941; this required him to transfer to the LG. The book concentrates on his post-war life. WWII is covered in 28pp, mainly comprising selected entries from DC's diary covering 30 July 1944 – 27 April 1945; many of these are recorded in DC's own memoirs *Dangerous Liaison*, q.v.

Key to Book Entries
Book Title and Sub-title(s)
Author Museum Holdings
Place of Publication; Publisher; Date of Publication; ISBN; Pages/Illustrations; Binding; Indexed; Glossary; Appendices; Bibliography; Size (in mm); Availability
NOTES:

Section II

Royal Armoured Corps: Heavy Cavalry

The distinction between Heavy and Light Cavalry was anachronistic by World War Two. However, it is a useful device to sub-divide the regular cavalry regiments of the Royal Armoured Corps. In 1927 the War Office had issued instructions that the Corps of Dragoons, Corps of Lancers and Corps of Hussars be merged to a single corps named the Cavalry of the Line. When created, the RAC absorbed most of the Cavalry of the Line but specifically excluded two Light Cavalry regiments, 1st The Royal Dragoons and The Royal Scots Greys.

The list of 'heavy cavalry' regiments below indicates the main types of armoured vehicle that they employed. These included armoured cars for reconnaissance, cruiser tanks, medium battle tanks, and fast armoured reconnaissance tanks. With the advent of tank-borne cavalry units, the traditional distinctions of heavy or light became redundant.

1st King's Dragoon Guards	- Armoured cars
The Queen's Bays (2nd Dragoon Guards)	- Crusader/Sherman
3rd Carabiniers (Prince of Wales's Dragoon Guards)	- Lee/Grant
4th/7th Royal Dragoon Guards	- Light Tank/Sherman
5th Royal Inniskilling Dragoon Guards	- Light Tank/Cromwell

A recurrent theme in all their stories is the delay and intransigence in adopting armour and leaving the age of the horse behind. The war naturally forced the issue and these regiments became highly trained, effective armoured units which fought in North Africa, Italy, North West Europe and Burma.

With the exception of the 1980s and 2000s, each post-war decade witnessed one or more regimental amalgamations. Refer to 'Appendix C - Cavalry and RTR Regimental Titles Post-war' to see when they amalgamated and the titles they adopted.

Royal Armoured Corps: Heavy Cavalry

1st King's Dragoon Guards   KDG

Date of mechanization: January 1938
RAC service: 04/04/1939   Post-war.

Regimental publications:
The K.D.G., The Regimental Journal of The King's Dragoon Guards
Vol. 1, No. 1 May 1930 to Vol. 3, No. 3 1939 (Varies); suspended between 1940 – 1944
Vol. III, No. 4 Winter 1945/1946 to Vol. V, No. 5 1958. (Varies)

History of the King's Dragoon Guards 1938 - 1945
McCorquodale, O.B.E., Col D.; Hutchings, Maj. B. L. B.;   TM; IWM; NAM; PCL
Woozley, Maj. A. D.; Woozley, Maj. A. D. (Ed.)
Glasgow; Regiment (McCorquodale & Co. - printers); n.d. [1950]; ISBN None; xv + 403pp/1 x clr SIfep/36 x bw PI/18 x clr M/2 x clr Mf; h/b (d/j - ne) Black cloth; Indexed Y; Glossary N; Appendices Y; Bibliography N; 222 x 142 (8vo); Uncommon
NOTES: Well written chronological account although not especially detailed. RoH, tipped in RoH additions and errata.

1st King's Dragoon Guards
A brief pictorial record of the regiment 1685 - 1958
Not stated   TM; RMAS; PCL
Aldershot; Gale & Polden Ltd; n.d. [c.1965]; ISBN None; 31pp/1 x clr PI/35 x bw PI/5 x clr SI/5 x bw SI; s/b (card); Indexed N; Glossary N; Appendices N; Bibliography N; 189 x 249 (12mo); Uncommon
NOTES: Published as a brief history at the time of the amalgamation with The Queen's Bays to form 1st The Queen's Dragoon Guards. 4pp pictorial, and one paragraph on WWII. There are two editions; one has '1st The Queen's Dragoon Guards' printed on the front cover and inside the cover, a brief comment on the amalgamation with the Bays. It is, though, a pictorial record of 1KDG only. RMAS copy has been rebound in hardback.

The Queen's Dragoon Guards
Belfield, Eversley   TM; NAM; RMAS; PCL
London; Leo Cooper Ltd; 1978; ISBN 0 85052 242 0; 114pp/9 x bw PI/10 x bw SI/2 x bw Mbds/1 x bw M; h/b / d/j Red cloth; Indexed N; Glossary N; Appendices Y; Bibliography Y; 222 x 143 (8vo)
NOTES: Incorporates good summary of KDG and Bays in WWII. 19pp on WWII. This title is one of the Famous Regiment series in all but title page; format is the same but in this instance the cover is an illustrated dust-jacket and the title pages contain no reference to the series.

A Brief History of 1st The Queen's Dragoon Guards
No imprint   TM; NAM; PCL
No imprint; No imprint; n.d. [c.1980]; ISBN None; 18pp/No illus.; Paper; Indexed N; Glossary N; Appendices N; Bibliography N; 210 x 147 (8vo); Uncommon
NOTES: Typewritten pamphlet. 4pp on WWII précising the service of KDG and Bays.

1st The Queen's Dragoon Guards 1685 – 1985
No imprint   IWM
No imprint; No imprint; n.d. [1985]; ISBN None; 24pp/11x clr PI/13 x clr SI/12 x bw PI/1 x clr M; s/b Blue string tasselled marker; Indexed N; Glossary N; Appendices N; Bibliography N; 181 x 248 (12mo); Uncommon
NOTES: Pictorial booklet produced for the Tercentenary in 1985. Lists COs of 1KDG and Bays, two photographs, one per regiment, no narrative.

A Brief History of 1st The Queen's Dragoon Guards
No imprint   PCL
No imprint; No imprint; n.d. [c.1988]; ISBN None; 24pp/No illus.; Paper; Indexed N; Glossary N; Appendices N; Bibliography N; 210 x 147 (8vo); Uncommon
NOTES: Typewritten pamphlet. 4pp on WWII précising the service of KDG and Bays.

The Regimental History of 1st The Queen's Dragoon Guards
Mann, Michael   TM; RMAS; PCL
Norwich; Michael Russell (Publishing) Ltd; 1993; ISBN 0 85955 189 X; x + 589pp/1 x clr PI/39 x bw PI/15 x clr SI/23 x bw SI/59 x bw M; h/b Blue cloth; Indexed N; Glossary N; Appendices N; Bibliography N; 253 x 178 (4to)
NOTES: Well written account of KDG's and Bays' histories throughout the war. Essentially a blending of the major histories and each regiment's War Diaries; 84pp on WWII.

A Rat of Tobruk Returns
A diary of a journey to Tobruk organised by Lady Avril Randell
Gardiner, Gilbert Alec
Lincoln; Century Books; 1998; ISBN 1-897684-38-X; iv + 49pp/14 x bw PI; s/b; Indexed N; Glossary N; Appendices N; Bibliography N; 197 x 141 (12mo); Uncommon
NOTES: A diary of the author's trip to Egypt and Libya in May 1997; no wartime reminiscences.

Sermons for Soldiers
Mann, KCVO, Rt Revd Michael   NAM
Norwich; Michael Russell (Publishing) Ltd; 1998; ISBN 0-85955-240-3; 112pp/No illus.; s/b; Indexed N; Glossary N; Appendices N; Bibliography N; 216 x 139 (8vo); Uncommon
NOTES: A collection of 30 sermons and three prayers. The author served in the KDG in WWII and was ordained in 1957.

History of the King's Dragoon Guards 1938 - 1945
McCorquodale, O.B.E., Col D.; Hutchings, Maj. B. L. B.;
Woozley, Maj. A. D.; Woozley, Maj. A. D. (Ed.)
Doncaster; D. P. & G. Military Publishers; 2000; ISBN None; xv + 403pp/Illus.; h/b Blue cloth; Indexed Y; Glossary N; Appendices Y; Bibliography N; 215 x 154 (8vo)
NOTES: D. P. & G. facsimile reprint of 1950 first edition. (Not physically inspected.)

Recollections of a Junior Officer in the KDG 1939-1945
Memories of 'Old Unhappy Far-off Things and Battles Long Ago'
Fraser, W. G. P.
Norfolk; 1st The Queen's Dragoon Guards; 2002; ISBN None; 59pp/No illus.; s/b; Indexed N; Glossary N; Appendices N; Bibliography N; 228 x 154 (8vo); Rare
NOTES: Brief summary account of the author's time from going out to the ME with the regiment in 1940 through Libya, Greece and back to the ME. The author served in C Sqn which stayed behind in the Tobruk garrison in 1941.

The Queen's Bays (2nd Dragoon Guards) — BAYS

Date of mechanization: 1936
RAC service: 04/04/1939   Post-war.

Regimental publications:
The Queen's Bays Regimental magazine "Rusty Buckles"
Vol. 1, No. 1 Sept 1948 (Annual) Suspended 1949. Replaced by
The Regimental Journal of the Queen's Bays (2nd Dragoon Guards)
Vol. 1, No. 2 Dec 1950 to Vol. 2, No. 2 Dec 1958. (Annual)

A Short History of the Queen's Bays
From the Outbreak of The Second World War, 3rd September, 1939, to the Capitulation of the German Armies in Italy, 2nd May, 1945
In Three Parts I France, II North Africa, III Italy
Not stated   IWM; PCL
Aldershot; Gale & Polden Limited; 1947; ISBN None; 49pp/2 x bw Pl/4 x bw M; s/b; Indexed N; Glossary N; Appendices Y; Bibliography N; 179 x 117 (12mo); Rare
NOTES: Published by the Comrades Association for those who served. Very detailed compact history, awards are referenced within the narrative.

The Story of the Queen's Bays (2nd Dragoon Guards) 1685 - 1950
Not stated   PCL
Fallingbostel; Adolf Zech; n.d. [c.1950]; ISBN None; 6pp/No illus.; s/b (card); Indexed N; Glossary N; Appendices N; Bibliography N; 192 x 134 (12mo); Rare
NOTES: Pocket history, five paragraphs on WWII.

A History of the Queen's Bays (The 2nd Dragoon Guards) 1929 ... 1945
Beddington C.B.E., Maj-Gen. W. R.   TM; IWM; NAM; RMAS; PCL
Winchester; Warren & Son Ltd; 1954; ISBN None; xiv + 271pp/1 x bw Plfep/2 x clr Pl/29 x bw Pl/2 x clr Mbds/14 x clr Mf/3 x bw Mf; h/b / d/j Red cloth; Indexed Y; Glossary N; Appendices Y; Bibliography N; 222 x 145 (8vo)
NOTES: Routine regimental history, few quotations but good reference on the tanks employed by the regiment.

The Queen's Dragoon Guards
Belfield, Eversley NAM; PCL
London; Leo Cooper Ltd; 1978; ISBN 0 85052 242 0; 114pp/9 x bw PI/10 x bw SI/2 x bw Mbds/1 x bw M; h/b / d/j Red cloth; Indexed N; Glossary N; Appendices Y; Bibliography Y; 222 x 143 (8vo)
NOTES: Incorporates good summary of KDG and Bays in WWII. 19pp on WWII. This title is one of the Famous Regiment series in all but title page; format is the same but in this instance the cover is an illustrated dust-jacket and the title pages contain no reference to the series.

A Brief History of 1st The Queen's Dragoon Guards
No imprint TM; NAM
No imprint; No imprint; n.d. [c.1980]; ISBN None; 18pp/No illus.; Paper; Indexed N; Glossary N; Appendices N; Bibliography N; 210 x 147 (8vo); Uncommon
NOTES: Typewritten pamphlet. 4pp on WWII précising the service of KDG and Bays.

1st The Queen's Dragoon Guards 1685 - 1985
No imprint IWM
No imprint; No imprint; n.d. [1985]; ISBN None; 24pp/11x clr PI/13 x clr SI/12 x bw PI/1 x clr M; s/b Blue string tasselled marker; Indexed N; Glossary N; Appendices N; Bibliography N; 181 x 248 (12mo); Uncommon
NOTES: Pictorial booklet produced for the Tercentenary in 1985. Lists COs of 1KDG and Bays, two photographs, one per regiment, no narrative.

A Brief History of 1st The Queen's Dragoon Guards
No imprint PCL
No imprint; No imprint; n.d. [c.1988]; ISBN None; 24pp/No illus.; Paper; Indexed N; Glossary N; Appendices N; Bibliography N; 210 x 147 (8vo); Uncommon
NOTES: Typewritten pamphlet. 4pp on WWII précising the service of KDG and Bays.

Shots In The Sand
A Diary of the Desert War 1941 - 1942
Halsted, O.B.E., J. Michael G. TM; IWM; NAM
East Wittering; Gooday Publishers; 1990; ISBN 1-870568-19-2; 248pp/42 x bw PI/7 bw x SI/2 x bw M; h/b / d/j Black cloth; Indexed Y; Glossary N; Appendices Y; Bibliography N; 222 x 140 (8vo)
NOTES: The author's diary of the time forms the bulk of the book. Contains many fascinating minutiae of daily life in the desert for an officer. The last third of the book deals with the author's time working on the British Army's Staff in the USA (including the social scene in the States) administering Lend-Lease; he specialised in tank advice as a former 'end-user'. Finally there are his reflections on life in the desert and the equipment used.

Fear No Foe
Pollock, John TM; IWM
London; Hodder & Stoughton; 1992; ISBN 0-340-55806-7; xviii + 173pp/12 x bw PI/1 x bw M; p/b; Indexed N; Glossary N; Appendices N; Bibliography N; 197 x 127 (12mo)
NOTES: Written by Michael Pollock's brother, this book is actually a religious work propounding the Christian message and the act of conversion to it; the first half provides

ROYAL ARMOURED CORPS: HEAVY CAVALRY   23

that message. The second half deals with Michael Pollock's service in North Africa and has interesting anecdotes about life as an officer in the desert.

The Regimental History of 1st The Queen's Dragoon Guards
Mann, Michael   PCL
Norwich; Michael Russell (Publishing) Ltd; 1993; ISBN 0 85955 189 X; x + 589pp/1 x clr PI/39 x bw PI/15 x clr SI/23 x bw SI/59 x bw M; h/b Blue cloth; Indexed N; Glossary N; Appendices N; Bibliography N; 253 x 178 (4to)
NOTES: Well written account of KDG's and Bays' histories throughout the war. Essentially a blending of the major histories and each regiment's War Diaries; 84pp on WWII.

To War with The Bays
A Tank Gunner Remembers 1939 - 1945
Merewood, Jack   TM; IWM
Cardiff; 1st The Queen's Dragoon Guards; 1996; ISBN 0 9522141 1 3; 209pp/19 x bw PI/3 x bw M; h/b / d/j Red cloth; Indexed Y; Glossary N; Appendices N; Bibliography N; 236 x 160 (8vo)
NOTES: Good description of basic training and barrack life. One of the best personal memoirs of tank life in the desert and Italy, one that takes you to the moment.

A History of the Queen's Bays (The 2nd Dragoon Guards) 1929 ... 1945
Beddington C.B.E., Maj-Gen. W. R.
Doncaster; D. P. & G. Military Publishers; 2000; ISBN None; xiv + 271pp/Illus.; h/b Red cloth; Indexed Y; Glossary N; Appendices Y; Bibliography N; 215 x 154 (8vo)
NOTES: D. P. & G. facsimile reprint of 1954 first edition. (Not physically inspected.)

3rd Carabiniers (Prince of Wales's Dragoon Guards)   3 DG

Date of mechanization: 01/01/1938
RAC service: 04/04/1939   Post-war.

    Regimental publications:
    The Feather and Carbine: Regimental Journal of the 3rd Carabiniers (Prince of Wales's Dragoon Guards)
    Vol. 1, No. 1 1936 to Vol. 1, No. 4 1939 (Annual) Suspended 1940 – 1946
    Vol. II, No. 1 June 1947 – Vol. VI, No. 3 May 1971 (Annual)
    3rd Carabiniers P.O.W. Dragoon Guards Newsletter
    Dates unknown but example viewed from Autumn 1945 which includes a Roll of Honour.

Third Dragoon Guards
Regimental History 3rd Carabiniers (Prince of Wales's Dragoon Guards)
Not stated
No imprint; 1957; ISBN None; 12pp/See Notes; s/b; Rare
NOTES: Not physically inspected.

3rd Carabiniers (Prince of Wales's Dragoon Guards) and Cheshire Yeomanry, T.A. Regimental Recruiting Handbook
Not stated
London; Malcolm Page Limited; 1961; ISBN None; 63pp/10 x bw PI/18 x bw SI; s/b; Indexed N; Glossary N; Appendices N; Bibliography N; 212 x 136 (8vo); Uncommon
NOTES: 1960s regimental recruiting booklet. Two page specific detail on battle honour of Nunshigum, April 1944. Passing sentence reference to general WWII history plus list of battle honours.

I Serve
Regimental History of the 3rd Carabiniers (Prince of Wales's Dragoon Guards)
Oatts, D.S.O., Lt-Col L. B.   TM; IWM; NAM; RMAS; PCL
Not stated; [Regiment] (Jarrold & Sons Ltd – printers); 1966; ISBN None; 333pp/1 x clr PIfep/4 x clr SI/32 x bw PI/11 x Mf; h/b / d/j Red cloth; Indexed Y; Glossary N; Appendices Y; Bibliography N; 252 x 192 (4to)
NOTES: Short section on WWII, mainly because the regiment was not actively engaged until January 1944. Contains a 7pp summary history of the 25D, raised from a 3DG cadre. Privately published via subscription with a limited quantity sold to the public. 39pp on WWII. d/j is polyester ('Glassine/Mylar/Melinex') variety.

The History and Traditions of the Royal Scots Dragoon Guards (Carabiniers & Greys)
Not stated   TM; IWM; NAM
Aldershot; The Forces Press (Naafi); n.d. [c.1972]; ISBN None; 29pp/4 x clr SI covers/2 x clr PI/9 x bw PI/15 x bw SI; s/b (card); Indexed N; Glossary N; Appendices N; Bibliography N; 228 x 152 (8vo); Uncommon
NOTES: Brief booklet history of RSDG formed from amalgamation of 3Carbs and RSG. 5pp on WWII, summary history of each regiment.

The History and Traditions of the Royal Scots Dragoon Guards
Not stated   PCL
Yeovil; Edwin Snell (Printers); n.d. [c.1978]; ISBN None; 28pp/2 x clr SI/9 x bw PI/15 x bw SI; s/b (card); Indexed N; Glossary N; Appendices N; Bibliography N; 209 x 147(8vo); Uncommon
NOTES: Reprint of pocket regimental guide.

The History and Traditions of the Royal Scots Dragoon Guards
Not stated   NAM
Yeovil; Edwin Snell (Printers); n.d. [c.1986]; ISBN None; 36pp/2 x clr PI/6 x clr SI/13 x bw PI; s/b (card); Indexed N; Glossary N; Appendices N; Bibliography N; 209 x 147(8vo); Uncommon
NOTES: Reprint of pocket regimental guide. This edition is updated to 1985.

In the Finest Tradition
The Royal Scots Dragoon Guards (Carabiniers & Greys) Its History and Treasures
Wood, Stephen TM; IWM; NAM; RMAS; PCL
Edinburgh; Mainstream Publishing Company (Edinburgh) Ltd; 1988; ISBN 1 85158 174 X; 160pp/1 x bw SIfep/14 x clr PI/80 x bw PI/26 x bw SI; h/b / d/j Blue cloth; Indexed Y; Glossary N; Appendices N; Bibliography Y; 252 x 193 (4to)
NOTES: The regiments' (3DG & RSG) histories are told through the association with their regimental possessions.

The Reminiscences of Four Members of "C" Squadron 3rd Carabiniers (Prince of Wales's Dragoon Guards) Burma Campaign 1943-45
Morgan, Maj. I. E.; Scott Dickins, Maj. G. L.; Connolly, M. & Hobson, C. H. TM
No imprint; No imprint; 1989; ISBN None; 39pp/12 x bw PI/3 x bw M/3 x Mf; s/b; Indexed N; Glossary N; Appendices N; Bibliography N; 293 x 208 (4to); Uncommon
NOTES: Provides some daily details of tank actions in Burma from June 1944. Privately printed in March 1989 with immediate reprint April 1989.

The History and Traditions of the Royal Scots Dragoon Guards
Not stated NAM
Yeovil; Edwin Snell (Printers); 1995; ISBN None; 40pp/4 x clr PI/4 x clr SI/12 x bw PI/10 x bw SI; s/b (card); Indexed N; Glossary N; Appendices N; Bibliography N; 209 x 147(8vo); Uncommon
NOTES: Reprint of pocket regimental guide. This edition updated with 4pp insert covering 1985-1995.

Nunshigum
On the Road to Mandalay
Freer, Arthur F. IWM
Bishop Auckland; The Pentland Press Ltd; 1995; ISBN 1-85821-264-2; 262pp/1 x bw PI/32 x bw SI/5 x bw M; h/b / d/j Black cloth; Indexed N; Glossary N; Appendices Y; Bibliography N; 240 x 160 (8vo)
NOTES: The author tells of his part in the remarkable battle of Nunshigum where Lee/Grant tanks were manoeuvred up a mountain ridge to attack well dug-in Japanese. Written in diary form. Provides an insight into tank combat tactics in the jungle of Burma and how oppressive and messy it was, how the enemy was only part of the battle, and the relationships inside a tank. Amongst the appendices the author has provided a far more expansive glossary than the norm, explaining many of the unusual terms used in the Far East.

Third Carabiniers P.O.W. Dragoon Guards
Second World War 1939 - 1945
Connolly, M. L. NAM
No imprint; No imprint; n.d.; ISBN None; 37pp/10 x bw PI; s/b (card); Indexed N; Glossary N; Appendices N; Bibliography N; 207 x 148 (8vo); Uncommon
NOTES: A short history of the regiment. RoH. Dot-matrix print on glossy paper.

4th/7th Royal Dragoon Guards　　　　　　　　　　　　　　　　4/7 DG

Date of mechanization:　　　　1938
RAC service:　　　　　　　　　04/04/1939　　　　　Post-war.

Regimental publications:
4th-7th Dragoon Guards magazine
Vol. 1, No. 1 June 1925 to Vol. 8, No. 32 Sept 1936 (Quarterly) Replaced by
IV-VII Royal Dragoon Guards Regimental Magazine
Vol. 8, No. 33 Dec 1936 to Vol. 11, No. 43 June 1939 (Varies) Suspended 1940 – 45
4th/7th Royal Dragoon Guards Regimental Magazine
New Vol. 1, No. 1 Dec 1946 – Vol. XLII, Apr 1991 (Latterly annual) (Regiment amalgamated with 5th Inniskilling Dragoon Guards in 1992.)
Dragoon Diary – 2pp typescript newssheet from approx. Oct. 1944 to mid-1945.

Actions of the 4th/7th Royal Dragoon Guards May-June, 1940
Not stated　　　　　　　　　　　　　　　　　　　　　　　　　　　　IWM
No imprint (Dorking); No imprint (Rowe's Printers); n.d. [c.1941]; ISBN None; 55pp/1 x bw Pl/5 x bw M; s/b; Indexed N; Glossary N; Appendices N; Bibliography N; 211 x 135 (8vo); Rare
NOTES: Compilation of various diaries from the regiment during the French campaign of 1940. Extremely well detailed - officer's posts, vehicles employed plus extracts from the squadron war diaries. Compiled and published a year after the events, the authoritative immediacy is tangible. In addition to the RoH, the narrative provides further details of all the casualties. Awards. Printed for private circulation - pasted in letter at front from the Lieutenant-Colonel introducing the book, 'It is quite unofficial and is being distributed privately.'

The First and The Last
The Story of the 4th/7th Royal Dragoon Guards 1939 - 1945
Stirling, Maj. J. P. D.　　　　　　　　　　　　　　TM; IWM; NAM; RMAS; PCL
London; Art & Educational Publishers Ltd; 1946; ISBN None; xv + 193pp/1 x clr SIfep/39 x bw Pl/4 x bw SIf /13 x bw Mf; h/b Black cloth; Indexed N; Glossary N; Appendices N; Bibliography N; 216 x 137 (8to); Uncommon
NOTES: Employs the useful device of notes in each margin providing a running calendar with highlighted events, including casualties. Includes a full CO to Tp Ldr named listing for May 1940, June 1944 and May 1945. The author was 2 i/c A Sqn, later OC B Sqn. Very good for detail of squadron experience. Just over two-thirds of the book deals with D to VE-Day. Honours/Awards. No RoH but all casualties are noted in the margins. The book was also sold directly by the author.

Short History of the 4th Royal Irish Dragoon Guards 1685 - 1922, 7th (Princess Royal's) Dragoon Guards 1688 - 1922, 4th/7th Royal Dragoon Guards 1922 - 1939
d'Avigdor-Goldsmith, Maj. J. A.　　　　　　　　　　　　　　　　　　TM; IWM
Aldershot; Gale & Polden Limited; 1949; ISBN None; 66pp/1 x clr SIfepf; s/b; Indexed N; Glossary N; Appendices N; Bibliography N; 189 x 126 (12mo); Uncommon
NOTES: The author was the regiment's Adjutant from 1937 to 1940. The booklet provides a pocket history from its formation up to mechanization in 1938.

A History of the 4th/7th Royal Dragoon Guards and their predecessors 1685 - 1980
Brereton, J. M. TM; IWM; NAM; RMAS; PCL
Catterick; By the Regiment; 1982; ISBN 0 9508331 0 X; 494pp/1 x clr SIfep/1 x clr PI/55 x bw PI/18 x clr SI/12 x bw SI/2 x clr M/17 x bw M; h/b Red cloth; Indexed Y; Glossary N; Appendices Y; Bibliography N; 255 x 190 (4to)
NOTES: Extremely well written and authoritative. Takes the regiment's history right back to King James II. Only 54pp dedicated to WWII, appendices include regimental music, customs and traditions, colonels, COs, etc. RoH/Honours/Awards. (Also provides an insight into the early days, machinations, and progress of Britain's cavalry formations.) Issued with card carton and polyester ('Glassine/Mylar/Melinex') type dust-jacket, 3000 copies printed and later 1000 paper dust-jackets were produced and added to the existing stock.

Evacuation Tarbat Peninsula 1943-4
Fallon, Dr, James A. TM
No imprint; No imprint; n.d. [c.1985]; ISBN None; 29pp/2 x clr PI/4 x clr SI/12 x bw PI/3 x clr M; s/b; Indexed N; Glossary N; Appendices N; Bibliography N; 210 x 147 (8vo)
NOTES: A local heritage booklet that tells the story of the area's evacuation for use as DD tank training, 6pp summarise the use of the area by 4/7DG, 13/18H, SY & ERY.

A Trooper's Tale
Newton, Cecil IWM
Marlborough; Cecil Newton; 2000; ISBN None; xiii + 76pp/16 x bw PI/2 x bw SI/5 x bw M; s/b; Indexed N; Glossary N; Appendices Y; Bibliography Y; 210 x 148 (8vo); Uncommon
NOTES: The author served in 4 Tp, B Sqn (1942 - 1944) and his memoirs cover that period, primarily 6 June 1944 – 19 November 1944 when he was seriously wounded. Starts with 7pp listing actions between those dates. Contains some gritty detail. (IWM copy held with C. Newton's private paper archive.)

The First and The Last
The Story of the 4th/7th Royal Dragoon Guards 1939 - 1945
Stirling, Maj. J. P. D.
Doncaster; D. P. & G. Military Publishers; 2000; ISBN 1-903972-20-5; xv + 193pp/1 x clr SIfep/39 x bw PI/4 x bw SIf /13 x bw Mf; h/b Black cloth; Indexed N; Glossary N; Appendices N; Bibliography N; 216 x 151 (8vo)
NOTES: D. P. & G. facsimile reprint of 1946 first edition. (The introductory pages have been bound out of order.)

A Trooper's Tale
Newton, Cecil TM; IWM
Marlborough; Cecil Newton; 2001; ISBN None; xiii + 77pp/18 x bw PI/2 x bw SI/5 x bw M; s/b; Indexed N; Glossary N; Appendices Y; Bibliography Y; 217 x 148 (8vo); Uncommon
NOTES: Reprint of 2000 first edition with minor updates. (IWM copy held with C. Newton's private paper archive.)

Chariots of the Lake
The Story of Britain's Secret Weapon during the Second World War. From Fritton Lake to D-Day and Beyond
Jarvis, Robert B. TM
Lowestoft; The Heritage Workshop Centre; 2003; ISBN 1-904413-04-8; 131pp/5 x clr PI/56 x bw PI/4 x bw SI/1 x bw M; s/b; Indexed Y; Glossary Y; Appendices N; Bibliography Y; 260 x 210 (4to)
NOTES: Tells the story of the DD tank through the Suffolk training area at Fritton Lake and includes information on the DD equipped regiments: 4/7DG, 13/18H, ERY, SRY, and SY contained in 29pp.

A Trooper's Tale
Newton, Cecil PCL
Marlborough; Cecil Newton; 2004; ISBN None; xiii + 78pp/19 x bw PI/2 x bw SI/5 x bw M; s/b; Indexed N; Glossary N; Appendices Y; Bibliography Y; 210 x 148 (8vo); Uncommon
NOTES: Reprint of 2001 second edition.

Actions of the 4th/7th Royal Dragoon Guards May-June, 1940
Not stated
Uckfield; Naval & Military Press Ltd; 2013; ISBN 978 1783310258; See Notes; s/b; Indexed ; Glossary ; Appendices ; Bibliography ;
NOTES: Facsimile reprint by NMP of 1941 first edition, available in s/b.

Reflections of a Tank Trooper (Retd)
Johnston, Eric
Brighton; Pen Press; 2014; ISBN 978-1-78003-756-1; 91pp/3 x clr PI/3 x bw PI/1 x clr M; s/b; Indexed N; Glossary N; Appendices N; Bibliography Y; 215 x 140 (8vo)
NOTES: Eric Johnston provides a concise summary of the experiences of a tank trooper in NWE; he served in the Reconnaissance Troop as co-driver of a Stuart tank. EJ landed on D-Day and recounts his time through to VE-Day with the focus on the men he served with and reflections on certain mores over 70 years.

5th Royal Inniskilling Dragoon Guards — 5 DG*
* 5 INNIS DG in the early part of the war.

Date of mechanization: 1938
RAC service: 04/04/1939   Post-war.

Regimental publications:
5th Inniskilling Dragoon Guards Journal
Vol. 5, No. 1 June 1928 to Vol. 6, June 1935 (Varies) (whilst in India)
Vol. 7, 1936 to Vol. 7, No. 6 June 1939 (Varies) Suspended 1940 – 1945
Vol. 7, No. 7 June 1946 - unknown
Off the Square (B Squadron newspaper)
Vol. 1, No. 1 Jan 1946 to Vol. 1, No. 10 Sept 1946 (Monthly)
Shufti (C Squadron newspaper)
Vol. 1, No. 1 Jan 1946 – Vol. 2, No. 2 Feb 1947

Squadron Handbook
Legard, Maj. C. P. D.
Northampton; Captain Keith Fraser, Royal Tank Regiment; n.d. [Wartime]; ISBN None; 256pp/2 x bw Plfep/11 x bw PI/53 x bw SI; s/b (card); Indexed N; Glossary N; Appendices N; Bibliography N; 198 x 124 (8vo); V Rare
NOTES: 'I intend this book to be used as a Handy Reference Book which will enable all members of the Squadron to have in emergency some knowledge of all the essential subjects.' C. P. D. Legard served with 5RIDG during the war and commissioned this compilation reference guide which contains reproductions of many training notes and pamphlets for tank troops. It is not clear from the book how widespread its use was outside 5RIDG although its publishing by an RTR officer would indicate it may have been taken up elsewhere.

5th Royal Inniskilling Dragoon Guards
Queen, Harry
Aldershot; Gale & Polden Ltd; n.d. [c.1946]; ISBN None; 24pp/6 x bw PI; s/b; Indexed N; Glossary N; Appendices N; Bibliography N; 215 x 139 (8vo); Rare
NOTES: Formally published newsletter in booklet form covering the regiment's actions from December 1944 to May 1945. RoH.

First In - Last Out
Pilborough, J.
Kirkburton; North Road Printing Works; 1947; ISBN None; 100pp/7 x bw PI/31 x bw SI/1 x bw Mbds; h/b Blue leatherette; Indexed N; Glossary N; Appendices N; Bibliography N; 250 x 188 (4to); V Rare
NOTES: Very engaging narrative which provides the reader with a 'ringside seat'. Reprinted 1986.

The Story of the Fifth Royal Inniskilling Dragoon Guards
Together With a Short Account of Their Illustrious Parent Regiments. The Fifth Princess Charlotte of Wales's Dragoon Guards and The Sixth Inniskilling Dragoons
Evans, Roger   TM; NAM; RMAS; PCL
Aldershot; Gale & Polden Limited; 1951; ISBN None; xiv + 445pp/1 x clr SIfep/1 x clr SI/18 x bw PI/1 x clr Mbds; h/b / d/j Green cloth; Indexed Y; Glossary N; Appendices Y; Bibliography Y; 221 x 145 (8vo)
NOTES: Very well written narrative, weaving more of a story than the average regimental history. Whilst the narrative is engaging, it sadly does not reference the men of the regiment by name often enough and is sparse on technical details. Book draws heavily on *First In - Last Out*, q.v. 145pp on WWII. Appendices contain full lists of officers and WOs in service at September 1939 and May 1940. Curiously there is no RoH or Honours/Awards.

Soldier in the Saddle
Modern Men of Action
"Monkey" Blacker   IWM
London; Burke Publishing Co Ltd; 1963; ISBN None; 191pp/28 x bw PI; h/b / d/j Red cloth; Indexed N; Glossary N; Appendices N; Bibliography N; 201 x 133 (8vo)
NOTES: Horses dominate the memoirs of this author, who was both a cavalryman and a horseman. He joined 5RIDG in 1936 serving in France, 1940, as Adjutant. A year later he

was C Sqn commander in the newly formed 23H and shortly after landing in France in 1944 he was promoted to 2 i/c. His memoirs display a genial tone until he recounts 23H's part in Operation Goodwood, July 1944, where the regiment suffered heavy casualties. (This battle is expanded upon in his later book *Monkey Business*, q.v.) Indeed his military recollections end abruptly after the Goodwood pages with no reference to the rest of the NWE campaign; he went on to command 23H after the war. 48pp on WWII.

Change and Challenge
The Story of the 5th Royal Inniskilling Dragoon Guards 1928-1978
Together with a short account of their parent regiments The 5th Princess Charlotte of Wales's Dragoon Guards and The 6th Inniskilling Dragoons
Blacker, G.C.B., O.B.E., M.C., Gen. Sir Cecil, and Woods, TM; NAM; RMAS; PCL
M.B.E., M.C., M.A., Maj-Gen. H. G.
London; William Clowes and Sons Ltd; 1978; ISBN None; xxix + 210pp/2 x clr SIfep/18 x bw PI/5 x bw M; h/b / d/j Green cloth; Indexed N; Glossary N; Appendices Y; Bibliography N; 223 x 142 (8vo)
NOTES: The men of the regiment are well represented, their names and actions. 58pp on WWII, RoH at the end of the WWII section.

First In - Last Out
Recce Squadron 5th Royal Inniskilling Dragoon Guards 1942 - 1946
Pilborough, J. TM; NAM; PCL
Chester; W.H. Evans & Sons Ltd; 1986; ISBN None; 120pp/4 x bw PIfep/53 x bw PI/27 x bw SI/1 x bw M; s/b; Indexed Y; Glossary N; Appendices N; Bibliography Y; 208 x 148 (8vo)
NOTES: Expanded reprint with an 11pp index/précis biography of the squadron's members at the back of the book, plus 8pp of late-war and modern photographs. (Also seen hardbound with gold embossed title and regimental badge - personal rebinding or special run?)

Tracks In Europe
The 5th Royal Inniskilling Dragoon Guards 1939 - 1946
Boardman, Capt. C. J. TM; NAM; PCL
Salford; City Press Services; 1990; ISBN 0 9515822 0 8; 263pp/23 x bw PI/1 x bw SI/7x bw M; h/b / d/j Green leather; Indexed N; Glossary N; Appendices N; Bibliography N; 227 x 150 (8vo)
NOTES: The author, who served in Recce Tp/Sqn, recounts his own memoirs plus the story of the regiment 1939 – 45. Told through introductory narrative plus a good amount of personal recollections. Last chapter runs through the men of the regiment mentioned and their post-war paths, sadly recalling the many that had passed away by 1990. The title comes from the author's experiences recceing tracks and paths, and the impact that had on him. Author was wounded and sent back to the UK in August 1944, returning after his recovery in late January 1945. He continues the narrative during this absence from the regiment. RoH. Loose tipped in 'Honours and Awards' single sided.

Tracks In Time
Swift, Sydney Fox IWM; NAM
No imprint; No imprint; 1992; ISBN None; 32pp/6 x bw SI; s/b; Indexed N; Glossary N; Appendices N; Bibliography N; 208 x 146 (8vo); Uncommon
NOTES: A collection of the author's poems in peace and in war. He was a tank commander in Normandy. Privately printed.

Monkey Business
The Memoirs of General Sir Cecil Blacker
Blacker, Gen. Sir Cecil TM; IWM
London; Quiller Press Limited; 1993; ISBN 1 870948 87 4; viii + 232pp/32 x bw PI/1 x bw SIfep/16 x bw SI/3 x bw M; h/b / d/j Red cloth; Indexed Y; Glossary N; Appendices N; Bibliography N; 240 x 160 (8vo)
NOTES: These memoirs, published 30 years after his first set, *Soldier in the Saddle*, q.v., provide an expanded review of the author's military career, albeit with some natural duplication of description. He served in 5RIDG from before the war until late 1941 and provides several descriptions of fellow officers plus a few comments on the regiment's actions in France 1940. In late 1941 he transferred to 23H as OC C Sqn. Generally his recollections are with the eye of a senior officer. Describing 23H's part in Op. Goodwood in Normandy, he provides an impressive and evocative description of the regiment losing most of its tanks and many of its crews. His recollections turn to swift summary for the period September 1944 to the end of the war. 23pp on 5RIDG and 43pp on 23H.

An Other Rank's War 1939 - 1945
An Autobiography in verse
Swift, Sydney Fox NAM
No imprint; Sydney Fox Swift; 1994; ISBN 0 9525010; 12pp/7 x bw SI; p/b paper; Indexed N; Glossary N; Appendices N; Bibliography N; 210 x 147 (8vo); Uncommon
NOTES: Photocopied self-published, comprises two poems recounting the author's memories across 1939-45.

The Story of the Fifth Royal Inniskilling Dragoon Guards
Together With a Short Account of Their Illustrious Parent Regiments. The Fifth Princess Charlotte of Wales's Dragoon Guards and The Sixth Inniskilling Dragoons
Evans, Roger
Doncaster; D. P. & G. Military Publishers; 2001; ISBN None; xiv + 445pp/Illus.; h/b Green cloth; Indexed N; Glossary N; Appendices N; Bibliography N; 215 x 154 (8vo)
NOTES: D. P. & G. facsimile reprint of 1951 first edition. (Not physically inspected.)

Key to Book Entries
Book Title and Sub-title(s)
Author Museum Holdings
Place of Publication; Publisher; Date of Publication; ISBN; Pages/Illustrations; Binding; Indexed; Glossary; Appendices; Bibliography; Size (in mm); Availability
NOTES:

Section III

Royal Armoured Corps: Light Cavalry

The Light Cavalry comprised fifteen regiments which, in the same manner as the Heavy Cavalry, employed several models of tank and armoured car, with two regiments operating some of Hobart's Funnies. Whereas all of the regiments which came under the old designation of Heavy Cavalry transferred to the Royal Armoured Corps upon its formation, two Light Cavalry regiments determinedly held onto the horse until 1940 and 1941 - 1st The Royal Dragoons and The Royal Scots Greys. The Royals converted to armoured cars late 1940 and the RSG converted to light tanks in the spring of 1941. They both officially joined the RAC in April 1941 under Army Order 49, 1941.

With the exception of two, the Light Cavalry regiments all fought or were deployed in North Africa and the Middle East. The majority of these then went on to serve in Italy and, with the impending invasion of France, several were allocated to North West Europe. 7H were stationed in Egypt when war broke out but in February 1942 were sent to the Far East, the only Light Cavalry regiment to fight in Burma. Refer to 'Appendix A - Theatres' for further details of the theatres where each regiment served.

In the same manner as the heavy cavalry regiments, amalgamations have taken place since the 1950s. In 2015 another will take place when The 9th/12th Royal Lancers (Prince of Wales's) and The Queens Royal Lancers are due to form The Royal Lancers. Refer to 'Appendix C - Cavalry and RTR Regimental Titles Post-war' to see when they amalgamated and the titles they adopted.

Royal Armoured Corps: Light Cavalry

1st The Royal Dragoons — ROYALS

Date of mechanization: December 1940
RAC service: 12/04/1941   Post-war.

Regimental publications:
The Eagle. The Regimental Journal of the Royal Dragoons.
2nd Series No. 1 Jan 1928 to No. 40 Feb 1940 (Varies, intended half-yearly)
Suspended 1941 – 1945
The Eagle. The Regimental Journal of the Royal Dragoons.
3rd Series No. 1 Spring 1946 to No. 28 Feb 1969 (Varies, intended half-yearly)
1st Royal Dragoons newsletter
No. 1 Feb 1945 and No. 2 Oct 1945 (Irregular) (no further issues recorded)

A Day's March Nearer Home
Experiences with The Royals, 1939 - 1945
The Earl of Rocksavage, M.C.   IWM
London; John & Edward Bumpus Ltd; 1947; ISBN None; 261pp/1 x bw PIfep/1 x bw Mbds; h/b (d/j - ne) Blue cloth; Indexed Y; Glossary N; Appendices N; Bibliography N; 222 x 144 (8vo); Uncommon
NOTES: Fascinating set of memoirs including real daily detail. Also interesting from the social perspective of a member of the privileged class of the day. Privately printed.

Short History of The Royal Dragoons
No imprint   IWM; NAM
Aldershot; Gale & Polden Ltd; n.d. [c.1954]; ISBN None; 31pp/1 x clr PIfep; s/b; Indexed N; Glossary N; Appendices N; Bibliography N; 183 x 120 (12mo)
NOTES: Pocket précised history for recruits, 3pp on WWII.

The Story of the Royal Dragoons 1938 - 1945
Being the history of the Royal Dragoons in the campaigns of North Africa, the Middle East, Italy and North-West Europe
Pitt Rivers, J. A.   TM; IWM; NAM; PCL
London; William Clowes and Sons Limited; n.d. [c.1956]; ISBN None; xv + 160pp/40 x bw PI/2 x clr Mbds/1 x clr M/6 x bw M; h/b (d/j - ne) Red cloth; Indexed Y; Glossary N; Appendices Y; Bibliography N; 246 x 176 (8vo)
NOTES: Very useful, full of varied detail including the regiment's vehicles and some uniform information. Appendix V summarises the organisation and equipment of the regiment. RoH/Honours/Awards.

Short History of The Royal Dragoons
Not stated   TM; NAM; PCL
No imprint; Charles Grenier & Co Ltd; n.d. [c.1961]; ISBN None; 28pp/No illus.; s/b (card); Indexed N; Glossary N; Appendices N; Bibliography N; 183 x 121 (12mo)
NOTES: Reprint of the 1954 pocket history, brought up to date. 3pp on WWII.

**The Royal Dragoons
(Famous Regiments)**
Hills, R. J. T.; Horrocks, Lt.-Gen. Sir Brian (Ed.) TM; IWM; NAM; PCL
London; Leo Cooper Ltd; 1972; ISBN 0 85052 120 3; vi + 109pp/22 x bw PI/11 x bw SI;
h/b / d/j Red cloth; Indexed N; Glossary N; Appendices N; Bibliography N; 222 x 140
(8vo)
NOTES: Summary history of WWII covered in 15pp.

Reminiscences
Heathcoat-Amory, Roderick
Not stated; Private; 1989; ISBN 0 9515521 0 4; iv + 156pp/1 x Mfrbd/1 x bw PIrbd/34 x
bw PI/1 x bw M; h/b (d/j - ne) Blue cloth; Indexed N; Glossary N; Appendices N;
Bibliography N; 240 x 155 (8vo); Rare
NOTES: In the first half the author recounts episodes from childhood and service in the
Royals stationed in India and Egypt pre-war. Injured in an accident on patrol in Syria, he
returned to the regiment in February 1942 as 2 i/c B Sqn, then in Libya. Later he would
command C Sqn and ended the war as the regiment's 2 i/c. Interesting for commentary
on fellow officers; engaging and informative memoirs.

Swings and Roundabouts
Fielden, Philip IWM
Not stated; Private (T. J. Gillard Print Services - printers); 1991; ISBN 0-9517155-0-X; x +
182pp/10 x clr PI/20 x bw PI/9 x clr SI/5 x bw SI/1 x bw Mbds/3 x bw M; h/b / d/j Red
cloth; Indexed N; Glossary Y; Appendices N; Bibliography N; 240 x 159 (8vo)
NOTES: The author joined up in December 1939 and went to the Horsed Cavalry OCTU.
A year later he joined the Royals in Palestine and commanded 3Tp, C Sqn, still on horses.
After an introduction to his service in Egypt, the narrative follows, in overview diary
form, to October 1943 in Italy when he transferred to 4AB as GSO III (Ops). The bulk of
the book deals with his post-war racing and fishing reminiscences. No WWII photos;
47pp on WWII.

The Story of The Blues and Royals (Royal Horse Guards and 1st Dragoons)
Watson, J. N. P. TM; IWM; NAM; PCL
London; Leo Cooper; 1993; ISBN 085052 238 2; viii + 328pp/1 x bw PIfep/6 x clr PI/121
x bw PI/22 x bw SI/8 x bw M; h/b / d/j Blue cloth; Indexed Y; Glossary N; Appendices N;
Bibliography Y; 234 x 158 (8vo)
NOTES: A history of The Blues and Royals from 1945 on. One chapter on their respective
histories during WWII covered in 9pp. The author's book, *Through Fifteen Reigns*, q.v.,
provides coverage of WWII.

**Through Fifteen Reigns
A Complete History of the Household Cavalry**
Watson, J. N. P. NAM; PCL
Staplehurst; Spellmount Limited; 1997; ISBN 1-873376-70-7; xiv + 192pp/15 x clr PI/20
x clr SI/66 x bw PI/31 x bw SI/43 x bw M; h/b / d/j Red cloth; Indexed Y; Glossary N;
Appendices Y; Bibliography Y; 283 x 225 (4to)
NOTES: The first chapter provides an excellent summary of the evolution of the
Household Cavalry and its constituent regiments. The book traces the history of three
regiments, Life Guards, Royal Horse Guards and Royal Dragoons through a chapter per

ROYAL ARMOURED CORPS: LIGHT CAVALRY 35

monarch; George VI's is 22pp. The last two regiments were amalgamated as The Blues and Royals in 1969. Extremely good summary accounts of the three regiments in WWII.

Horse Guards
White-Spunner, Harvey   TM; RMAS; PCL
London; Macmillan; 2006; ISBN 978-1-4050-5574-1; xiv + 626pp/1 x clr SIfep/20 x clr PI/122 x clr SI/77 x bw PI/33 x bw SI/25 x clr M; h/b / d/j Black cloth; Indexed Y; Glossary N; Appendices N; Bibliography Y; 266 x 200 (4to)
NOTES: Written to provide a history of all four regiments of the Household Cavalry to coincide with the relaunch of their museum in 2007. It spans the years 1600 – 2006, concentrating on the period up to 1939 with WWII covered in 54pp. A few proofing errors have slipped through the editorial net but a very readable brief history which includes several veterans' quotations.

The Royal Scots Greys (2nd Dragoons)   GREYS

Date of mechanization: May 1941
RAC service: 12/04/1941   Post-war.

Regimental publications:
The Eaglet: the journal of The Royal Scots Greys with which is incorporated no other paper in the world.
No. 1 July 1945 to No. 51 6 July 1946 (Weekly bar 2) Replaced by
The Scots Grey: Journal of The Royal Scots Greys
Vol. 1, No. 1 Spring 1947 to Vol. 2, No. 2 New Year 1950 (Half-yearly till 1948 then annual) Replaced by
The Scots Grey and Regimental Association Report
Vol. 3, No. 1 Christmas 1950 to Vol. 3, No. 7 1957 (Annual) Replaced by
The Journal and Association report of The Royal Scots Greys
Vol. 3, No. 8 1958 to Vol. 3, No. 9 1959 (Annual) Suspended 1960
No. 16 Spring 1961 – No. 26 Spring 1971 (Annual)

Second To None
The Royal Scots Greys, 1919 - 1945
Carver, C.B.E., D.S.O., M.C., Lt-Col R. M. P.   TM; IWM; NAM; RMAS; PCL
Glasgow; The Regiment (Messrs. McCorquodale & Co Ltd - printers); n.d. [1954]; ISBN None; xvi + 210pp/1 x bw PIfep/29 x bw PI/1 x bw SI/1 x clr Mbds/20 x clr Mf; h/b / d/j Blue cloth; Indexed N; Glossary N; Appendices Y; Bibliography N; 220 x 140 (8vo); Uncommon
NOTES: A solid regimental history. Occasional recollections from regiment's personnel. First 35pp cover 1919 – 1938. RoH/Honours/Awards.

The History and Traditions of the Royal Scots Greys
Not stated   NAM; PCL
No imprint; No imprint; n.d. [c.1966]; ISBN None; 18pp/4 x bw PI/3 x clr SI/2 x bw SI; s/b (card); Indexed N; Glossary N; Appendices N; Bibliography N; 214 x 140 (8vo); Uncommon
NOTES: Brief pocket history, 3½ pp on WWII.

The Royal Scots Greys
(Famous Regiments)
Blacklock, Michael; Horrocks, Lt.-Gen. Sir Brian (Ed.)   TM; IWM; NAM; RMAS; PCL
London; Leo Cooper Ltd; 1971; ISBN 0 85052 088 6; 126pp/1 x bw PIfep/11 x bw PI/21 x bw SI; h/b / d/j Green cloth; Indexed N; Glossary N; Appendices Y; Bibliography N; 222 x 143 (8vo)
NOTES: Summary of WWII service in 14pp.

Royal Scots Greys
Osprey Men-At-Arms
Grant, Charles   NAM
Reading; Osprey Publishing Ltd; 1972; ISBN 85045 059 4; 40pp/8 x clr SI/7 x bw PI/23 x bw SI; s/b (card); Indexed N; Glossary N; Appendices N; Bibliography N; 248 x 184 (8vo)
NOTES: From the Osprey Men-At-Arms series, No. 1, providing an overview of the regiment. Extremely well illustrated including the series' familiar 8pp colour illustrations. 4pp on WWII. Reprinted several times.

The History and Traditions of The Royal Scots Dragoon Guards (Carabiniers & Greys)
Not stated   TM; IWM; NAM
Aldershot; The Forces Press (Naafi); n.d. [c.1972]; ISBN None; 29pp/4 x clr SI covers/2 x clr PI/9 x bw PI/15 x bw SI; s/b (card); Indexed N; Glossary N; Appendices N; Bibliography N; 228 x 152 (8vo); Uncommon
NOTES: Brief booklet history of RSDG formed from amalgamation of 3Carbs and RSG. 5pp on WWII, summary history of each regiment.

The History and Traditions of the Royal Scots Dragoon Guards
Not stated   PCL
Yeovil; Edwin Snell (Printers); n.d. [c.1978]; ISBN None; 28pp/2 x clr SI/9 x bw PI/15 x bw SI; s/b (card); Indexed N; Glossary N; Appendices N; Bibliography N; 209 x 147(8vo); Uncommon
NOTES: Reprint of pocket regimental guide.

The History and Traditions of the Royal Scots Dragoon Guards
Not stated   NAM
Yeovil; Edwin Snell (Printers); n.d. [c.1986]; ISBN None; 36pp/2 x clr PI/6 x clr SI/13 x bw PI; s/b (card); Indexed N; Glossary N; Appendices N; Bibliography N; 209 x 147(8vo); Uncommon
NOTES: Reprint of pocket regimental guide. This edition is updated to 1985.

In the Finest Tradition
The Royal Scots Dragoon Guards (Carabiniers & Greys) Its History and Treasures
Wood, Stephen   TM; IWM; NAM; RMAS; PCL
Edinburgh; Mainstream Publishing Company (Edinburgh) Ltd; 1988; ISBN 1 85158 174 X; 160pp/1 x bw SIfep/14 x clr PI/80 x bw PI/26 x bw SI; h/b / d/j Blue cloth; Indexed Y; Glossary N; Appendices N; Bibliography Y; 252 x 193 (4to)
NOTES: The regiments' (3DG & RSG) histories are told through the association with their regimental possessions.

The History and Traditions of the Royal Scots Dragoon Guards
Not stated NAM
Yeovil; Edwin Snell (Printers); 1995; ISBN None; 40pp/4 x clr Pl/4 x clr Sl/12 x bw Pl/10 x bw SI; s/b (card); Indexed N; Glossary N; Appendices N; Bibliography N; 209 x 147(8vo); Uncommon
NOTES: Reprint of pocket regimental guide. This edition updated with 4pp insert covering 1985-1995.

Swifter than Eagles
War memoirs of a young officer 1939-45
Sprot, M.C., Lt-Col Aidan IWM
Bishop Auckland; The Pentland Press Ltd; 1998; ISBN 1-85821-567-6; xvi + 187pp/12 x bw Pl/1 x bw Sl/1 x bw Mbds; h/b / d/j Blue cloth; Indexed N; Glossary N; Appendices Y; Bibliography N; 216 x 150 (8vo)
NOTES: The author signed up at the outbreak of the war and was called up July 1940. He was commissioned into RSG January 1941 but did not join the regiment until 31 August 1941. The Appendix lists officers mentioned in the text with their final rank and positions held. Extremely detailed account, written fresh in 1947 although not published for 50 years. Very much officer oriented.

Second To None
The Royal Scots Greys 1919 - 1945
Carver, Lt-Col R. M. P.
Doncaster; D. P. & G. Military Publishers; 1998; ISBN 1-903972-05-1; xvi + 210pp/Illus.; h/b Blue cloth; Indexed N; Glossary N; Appendices Y; Bibliography N; 215 x 154 (8vo)
NOTES: D. P. & G. facsimile reprint of 1954 first edition. (Not physically inspected.)

My Father's Son
The Memoirs of Major The Earl Haig OBE, DL, ARSA
Major The Earl Haig OBE, DL, ARSA IWM; NAM
Barnsley; Leo Cooper; 2000; ISBN 0 85052 708 2; xiv + 194pp/32 x bw Pl/21 x bw Sl/1 x Mbds; h/b / d/j Black cloth; Indexed Y; Glossary N; Appendices N; Bibliography N; 240 x 160 (8vo)
NOTES: The author served with the RSG from the start of the war until captured whilst on secondment as LO to 22AB, in July 1942. His recollections provide an interesting view into the life of senior officers from England's ruling classes and also the lead-up to the regiment's mechanization and the enthusiasm with which the news was received. He continues, describing his time as a POW in Italy before being transferred to Colditz. As the son of Field Marshal the Earl Haig and his concomitant social standing, he was held as a member of the 'Prominente' there. 33pp cover his service with the regiment and 50pp his time as a POW.

My Autobiography Murray Walker
Unless I'm Very Much Mistaken
Walker, Murray TM
London; CollinsWillow; 2002; ISBN 0 00 712696 4; 394pp/42 x clr Pl/45 x bw PI; h/b / d/j Blue cloth; Indexed Y; Glossary N; Appendices Y; Bibliography N; 240 x 147 (8vo)
NOTES: The author joined the RAC in October 1942. He follows his initial and officer

training, and the life lessons they taught him. He attended Sandhurst late 1943/early 1944 and joined the RSG in September 1944 in Holland when he became a troop officer. His military career is covered briefly in 25pp.

My Autobiography Murray Walker
Unless I'm very much mistaken
Walker, Murray
London; CollinsWillow; 2003; ISBN 0 00 712697 2; 490pp/42 x clr Pl/45 x bw Pl; p/b; Indexed Y; Glossary N; Appendices Y; Bibliography N; 176 x 110 (12mo)
NOTES: Reprint of first hardback edition with one extra final chapter.

3rd The King's Own Hussars — 3 H

Date of mechanization: 1936
RAC service: 04/04/1939 Post-war.

Regimental publications:
The 3rd The King's Own Hussars: the journal for all ranks who have ridden behind the silver drums.
Vol. 1, No. 1 1934 – Vol. 2, No. 3 1940 (Annual) Suspended 1941 – 1945
Vol. 2, No. 4 1946 – Vol. 5, No. 4 1958 (Annual)

A Short History of the 3rd The King's Own Hussars 1685 - 1945
Not stated TM; NAM; RMAS
Aldershot; Gale & Polden Ltd; 1947; ISBN None; 46pp/1 x clr PIfep/5 x clr Pl/4 x bw Pl/3 x bw SI; s/b; Indexed N; Glossary N; Appendices N; Bibliography N; 182 x 123 (12mo); Uncommon
NOTES: Pocket regimental history. 9pp on WWII. List of Colonels and Lt-Colonels throughout regiment's history.

Winged Dagger
Adventures on Special Service
Farran, Capt. Roy NAM
London; Collins; 1948; ISBN None; 348pp/1 x bw SIfep/13 x bw M; h/b / d/j Blue cloth; Indexed N; Glossary N; Appendices N; Bibliography N; 206 x 145 (8vo); Uncommon
NOTES: The author sailed to Egypt with 3H late 1940. He was with the detachment that sailed to Crete, was wounded and captured, and taken to a POW hospital in Greece. He went on to escape and return to Egypt late autumn 1941. Once fit he transferred to 7AD as IO, then ADC to Gen. Jock Campbell. In early 1943 he joined the SAS. Evocatively written account, essential reading. 120pp on service with 3H and capture/escape.

Poems: Tales for Grandchildren
Chadwick, M.C., Captain Tom
London; Rose Garland Press; 1949; ISBN None; 79pp/See Notes; h/b Coloured paper; Indexed N; Glossary N; Appendices N; Bibliography N; V Rare
NOTES: Small collection of eight amusing poems by TC written in the Middle East, some on military subjects. Also includes some of his wartime illustrations. 150 copies published. See *Tom Chadwick and the Grosvenor School of Modern Art* for the life of TC. (Not physically inspected.)

ROYAL ARMOURED CORPS: LIGHT CAVALRY   39

Regimental History The Queen's Own Hussars
Not stated   TM; PCL
London; Collins; n.d. [c.1958]; ISBN None; 7pp/No illus.; Self-card; Indexed N; Glossary
N; Appendices N; Bibliography N; 210 x 105 (8vo); Uncommon
NOTES: Double sided fold out card. Précised, date based listing of 3KOH and 7H.

The Queen's Own Hussars
Not stated   TM
London; Malcolm Page Limited; n.d. [c.1963]; ISBN None; 116pp/5 x clr SI/25 x bw
PI/14 x bw SI; s/b; Indexed N; Glossary N; Appendices N; Bibliography N; 215 x 141
(8vo); Uncommon
NOTES: 1960's regimental/recruiting handbook, 3pp on WWII.

The Galloping Third
The Story of the 3rd The King's Own Hussars
Bolitho, Hector   TM; IWM; NAM; RMAS; PCL
London; 3rd Hussars Regimental Association; 1963; ISBN None; xi + 341pp/1 x clr
PIfep/1 x bw PI/7 x bw SI/2 x Mbds/9 x bw M; h/b / d/j Blue cloth; Indexed N; Glossary
N; Appendices N; Bibliography N; 221 x 142 (8vo)
NOTES: Although there is some detail this is more of an over-view account of the
regiment, 58pp on WWII.

The Queen's Own Hussars
Not stated   PCL
London; Malcolm Page Limited; n.d. [c.1965]; ISBN None; 48pp/14 x bw PI/5 x bw SI;
s/b; Indexed N; Glossary N; Appendices N; Bibliography N; 215 x 138 (8vo); Uncommon
NOTES: 1960's regimental/recruiting handbook with brief mention of WWII.

The Queen's Own Hussars
Tercentenary Edition 1685 - 1985
Various   NAM
Warwick; The Queen's Own Hussars; 1985; ISBN 0-9510300 0 0; 96pp/12 x clr SI/18 x
bw PI/1 x bw SI; s/b; Indexed N; Glossary N; Appendices N; Bibliography Y; 220 x 199
(8vo)
NOTES: Collection of small articles by various authors covering both regiments (3H/7H)
over 300 years. 11pp on WWII, Battle Honours.

The Queen's Own Hussars
Tercentenary Edition 1685 - 1985
Various   TM; IWM; RMAS
London; Brassey's Defence Publishers Ltd; 1985; ISBN 0 08 033595 0; 96pp/12 x clr
SI/18 x bw PI/1 x bw SI; s/b; Indexed N; Glossary N; Appendices N; Bibliography Y; 220
x 199 (8vo)
NOTES: Reprint of edition first published by The Queen's Own Hussars.

Regimental History The Queen's Own Hussars
Not stated   PCL
Germany; Printing Section, Ordnance Services Viersen; 1985; ISBN None; 7pp/No illus.;
Folded card; Indexed N; Glossary N; Appendices N; Bibliography N; 210 x 105 (8vo);
Uncommon
NOTES: Double sided fold out card, negligible WWII.

Winged Dagger
Adventures on Special Service
Farran, Roy
London; Arms and Armour Press; 1986; ISBN 0-85368-734-X; 340pp/13 x bw M; h/b / d/j Grey cloth; Indexed N; Glossary N; Appendices N; Bibliography N; 221 x 145 (8vo)
NOTES: Hardback reprint of 1948 first edition with 'Book IV Post-war' omitted, same pagination to that point. Published under Special Forces Library series.

Winged Dagger
Adventures on Special Service
Farran, Roy
London; Grafton Books; 1988; ISBN 0-586-20085-1; 429pp/13 x bw M; p/b; Indexed N; Glossary N; Appendices N; Bibliography N; 177 x 110 (12mo)
NOTES: Paperback reprint of 1986 edition, different pagination. Published under Special Forces Library series.

An Englishman's Peace and War
Boyd, Neil   IWM
Bishop Auckland; The Pentland Press Ltd; 1994; ISBN 1-85821-215-4; xv + 192pp/6 x bw PI/16 x bw SI/1 x bw M; h/b / d/j Black cloth; Indexed N; Glossary N; Appendices N; Bibliography N; 216 x 153 (8vo)
NOTES: First 50pp deal with the early days, the desert and the author's trials in the Dutch East Indies prior to capture. Taken prisoner by the Japanese, he suffered a truly horrific experience. Declared 'fit' he was transported to the Japanese mainland to work there. His camp was at Hiroshima where he witnessed the dropping of the first A-bomb. The narrative is unfortunately a little rambling and can be difficult to read. Pasted errata label on title page.

Winged Dagger
Adventures on Special Service
Farran, Roy   TM
London; Cassell & Co; 1998; ISBN 0-304-35084-2; 340pp/13 x bw M; p/b; Indexed N; Glossary N; Appendices N; Bibliography N; 198 x 129 (8vo)
NOTES: Paperback reprint of 1986 edition. Itself reprinted 1999 and 2002.

3rd The King's Own Hussars 1685 - 1947
Senior, Sgt Anthony J.
No imprint; No imprint; 2001; ISBN None; 237pp/No illus.; h/b Blue cloth; Indexed N; Glossary N; Appendices Y; Bibliography N; 304 x 214 (4to); Uncommon
NOTES: Privately printed reproduced typescript. Has a good amount of useful detailed information on regiment's equipment. Unfortunately the narrative is slightly disjointed in places. The official history is of more use for the overall WWII history. XXVI appendices, including list of Colonels and a list of officers for 1940 and 1943. 42pp on WWII.

Pippin's Progress
A Soldier Artist's War
Memoirs of a Wartime Officer in the 3rd Hussars
Heseltine, Richard   IWM; NAM
Assington; Silver Horse Press; 2001; ISBN 0 9541623 0 7; xv + 268pp/1 x bw PIfep/18 x bw PI/17 x clr SI/28 x bw SI/3 x clr M; s/b; Indexed Y; Glossary Y; Appendices N; Bibliography N; 240 x 174 (8vo)
NOTES: Very engaging set of memoirs. The author joined 3H at the outbreak of war and was one of only two officers to serve throughout the war in the regiment. He used his talent as an artist to sketch whilst with 3H. Illustrated with many of these sketches, some of which now reside in the regiment's museum. His talent also led to his becoming a successful camouflage expert. After taking the camouflage course he re-joined and took command of A Sqn soon after El Alamein. In February 1943 he was involved in a serious train accident (the same as John Henderson Hodges below). He also provides an insight into the regimental domestic life of well-to-do cavalry officers. In Italy he resumed command of A Sqn until 3H left the campaign at the end of 1944.

An account of the wartime experiences of John Henderson Hodges
Hodges, John Henderson   IWM
No imprint; Holywell Press (Printers); 2010; ISBN None; 148pp/16 x bw PI/2 x bw M; s/b; Indexed N; Glossary N; Appendices Y; Bibliography N; 210 x 148 (8vo); Uncommon
NOTES: The author joined the RAC in June 1941 and trained at Sandhurst during 1942. Commissioned into the ERY in August 1942 for just a few weeks in the UK before being sent to Egypt arriving in January 1943. There he was posted to 3H and travelled to Aleppo, Syria where the regiment was retraining. He was involved in a serious train accident (the same as Richard Heseltine above) putting him out of action for the remainder of 1943. Returned to 3H on light duties while he fully recovered, then served with B Sqn through 3H's Italian campaign and was awarded the MC (the citation is reproduced) in June 1944. He continued to serve with 3H until early 1946.

Tom Chadwick and the Grosvenor School of Modern Art
Francis, Julian   TM; IWM
Upper Denby; Fleece Press; 2012; ISBN 978-0-948375-97-2; 125pp/1 x bw SIfep/2 x clr PI/49 x clr SI/26 x bw PI/43 x bw SI; h/b Red cloth & paper; Indexed Y; Glossary N; Appendices N; Bibliography Y; 338 x 342 (Folio); Rare
NOTES: This book describes the career of Tom Chadwick, an artist who produced his work during the 1930s and who was killed at El Alamein in 1942 aged 30. The book is squarely aimed at TC's art but is included because it does have a substantial section on his war career reproducing some of his war service art and extracts from his wartime diary. A fine example of the independent book printers craft. 210 special copies (978-0-948375-97-2) of the book, in a slipcase, contain 16 tipped-in engravings printed from the original wood blocks. Plus 160 standard copies (978-0-948375-96-5) with reproductions of engravings, no slipcase. Printed publication date 2012 but released March 2013. The Tank Museum and the IWM hold standard copies.

4th Queen's Own Hussars   4 H

Date of mechanization: 1936
RAC service: 04/04/1939   Post-war.

Regimental publications:
IV Hussars Journal
No. 1 1923 – No. 28 1957 (Annual). Suspended 1939 – 1945.

An Account of the Operations Fought by the 9th Lancers
With Under Command the 2nd London Irish Rifles Carried in the Kangaroos of "A" Squadron, "B" Squadron, 4th Hussars in Shermans and "E" Battery, 11th (H.A.C.) R.H.A. With Their Self Propelled 25 Pounders, During the 8th Army Offensive of April 1945 Between the Santerno and the Po
Price, D.S.O., M.C., Lt-Col K. J.   TM; IWM
No imprint; No imprint (In the field); 1945; ISBN None; 26pp/3 x clr M; s/b; Indexed N; Glossary N; Appendices N; Bibliography N; 331 x 208 (Folio); V Rare
NOTES: Typescript single sided 'Roneo-style' copy with hand drawn maps. Detailed description of action from 13 April 1945 to 25 April 1945 written by the CO of the time. Very occasional ref to 4H. (IWM & Tank Museum copies are photocopies.)

4th Hussar
The Story of a British Cavalry Regiment
The Story of the 4th Queen's Own Hussars 1685 - 1958
Scott Daniell, David   TM; IWM; NAM; RMAS; PCL
Aldershot; Gale & Polden Ltd; 1959; ISBN None; xv + 416pp/1 x clr PIfep/9 x clr PI/6 x bw PI/15 x bw Mf/15 x bw M; h/b / d/j Blue cloth; Indexed Y; Glossary N; Appendices Y; Bibliography Y; 236 x 145 (8vo); Rare
NOTES: Well written regimental history, evokes the tribulations this regiment went through, being in danger of becoming dormant during the war. 92pp on WWII. Folding maps are on fine tissue paper.

Irish Hussar
A short history of the Queen's Royal Irish Hussars incorporating the stories of the 4th Queen's Own Hussars, 1685-1958, and the 8th King's Royal Irish Hussars, 1693-1958
Strawson, C.B., O.B.E., Maj-Gen. J. M.; Pierson, Brig. H. T.;   TM; NAM
Rhoderick-Jones, Brig. R. J.
London; The Queen's Royal Irish Hussars Association; 1986; ISBN 0 9512389 0 6; x + 234pp/1 x clr PIfep/5 x clr PI/5 x clr SI/86 x bw PI/5 x bw SI/15 x bw M; h/b / d/j Green imitation leather; Indexed Y; Glossary N; Appendices Y; Bibliography Y; 216 x 154 (8vo)
NOTES: Short but informative 17pp on WWII. Good photograph selection.

Loopy
The Autobiography of George Kennard
Kennard, George   TM; IWM; NAM
London; Leo Cooper; 1990; ISBN 0 85052 1750; xii + 148pp/11 x bw PI/1 x bw SI; h/b / d/j Blue cloth; Indexed Y; Glossary N; Appendices Y; Bibliography N; 222 x 141 (8vo)

NOTES: The author joined the Bays as a reserve officer pre-war and after officer training joined the 4H. (He became ADC to Gen. Wavell just before the war started.) He journeyed to Egypt with the regiment in December 1940 and then to Greece in March 1941. Here he was captured by the Germans and his POW account forms the bulk of his WWII reminiscences. 32pp on WWII.

4th Queen's Own Hussars
Regimental War Diary Italian campaign 1944-1945
Wallington, R. S. J.   IWM; RMAS
Not stated; Not stated; 2000; ISBN None; 98pp/No illus.; Comb; Indexed N; Glossary N; Appendices N; Bibliography N; 297 x 210 (4to); Rare
NOTES: The compiler transcribed the War Diaries from the PRO (now National Archives) without correction but adding Troop Leader names where established. Typed copy of the regiment's War Diary for the period May 1944 to June 1946. IWM's copy is rebound.

4th Queen's Own Hussars
Regimental War Diaries September 1939 - April 1944
Wallington, R. S. J.   IWM
Not stated; Not stated; 2003; ISBN None; 87pp/No illus.; Comb; Indexed N; Glossary N; Appendices N; Bibliography N; 297 x 210 (4to); Rare
NOTES: As above but for the earlier period, September 1939 to April 1944. (Some War Diaries are missing.)

Hussars, Horses and History
The Military Memoirs of Major-General John Strawson
Strawson, John   IWM
Barnsley; Pen & Sword Military; 2007; ISBN 978 1 84415 5828; ix + 246pp/40 x bw Pl; h/b / d/j Black cloth; Indexed Y; Glossary N; Appendices N; Bibliography N; 240 x 160 (8vo)
NOTES: The author joined 3rd Tp, C Sqn, 4H at the end of 1942 on Cyprus, commanding the troop until the end of the war. Horse-centric memoirs, the author went on to command the amalgamated regiment, QRIH, in the early 1960s.

7th Queen's Own Hussars	7 H

Date of mechanization: 1936
RAC service: 04/04/1939   Post-war.

Regimental publications:
The Regimental Journal of the Seventh Queen's Own Hussars
No. 1 1945 – No. 8 Oct 1951 (Annual)
Vol. 15 No. 1 Dec 1952 – Vol. 15 No. 7 Nov 1958 (Annual)

The Seventh and Three Enemies
The Story of World War II and the 7th Queen's Own Hussars
Davy, C. B., C. B. E., D. S. O., Brig. G. M. O. TM; IWM; NAM; RMAS; PCL
Cambridge; W Heffer & Sons Ltd; 1952; ISBN None; xiv + 468pp/1 x bw Pfep/43 x bw PI/21 x bw M; h/b / d/j Blue cloth; Indexed Y; Glossary N; Appendices N; Bibliography N; 228 x 161 (8vo)
NOTES: Exceptionally well detailed narrative with plenty of campaign background. RoH.

Regimental History The Queen's Own Hussars
Not stated TM; PCL
London; Collins; n.d. [c.1958]; ISBN None; 7pp/No illus.; Self-card; Indexed N; Glossary N; Appendices N; Bibliography N; 210 x 105 (8vo); Uncommon
NOTES: Double sided fold out card. Précised, date based listing of 3KOH and 7H.

The Queen's Own Hussars
Not stated TM
London; Malcolm Page Limited; n.d. [c.1963]; ISBN None; 116pp/5 x clr SI/25 x bw PI/14 x bw SI; s/b; Indexed N; Glossary N; Appendices N; Bibliography N; 215 x 141 (8vo); Uncommon
NOTES: 1960's regimental/recruiting handbook, 3pp on WWII.

The Queen's Own Hussars
Not stated PCL
London; Malcolm Page Limited; n.d. [c.1965]; ISBN None; 48pp/14 x bw PI/5 x bw SI; s/b; Indexed N; Glossary N; Appendices N; Bibliography N; 215 x 138 (8vo); Uncommon
NOTES: 1960's regimental/recruiting handbook with brief mention of WWII.

The 7th Queen's Own Hussars
(Famous regiments)
Brereton, J. M.; Horrocks, Lt.-Gen. Sir Brian (Ed.) TM; IWM; NAM; RMAS; PCL
London; Leo Cooper; 1975; ISBN 0 85052 147 5; 221pp/12 x bw PI/11 x bw SI; h/b / d/j Blue-grey cloth; Indexed N; Glossary N; Appendices Y; Bibliography N; 222 x 143 (8vo)
NOTES: Summary history of WWII in 36pp.

The Queen's Own Hussars
Tercentenary Edition 1685 - 1985
Various NAM
Warwick; The Queen's Own Hussars; 1985; ISBN 0-9510300 0 0; 96pp/12 x clr SI/18 x bw PI/1 x bw SI; s/b; Indexed N; Glossary N; Appendices N; Bibliography Y; 220 x 199 (8vo)
NOTES: Collection of small articles by various authors covering both regiments (3H/7H) over 300 years. 11pp on WWII, Battle Honours.

The Queen's Own Hussars
Tercentenary Edition 1685 - 1985
Various TM; IWM; RMAS
London; Brassey's Defence Publishers Ltd; 1985; ISBN 0 08 033595 0; 96pp/12 c clr SI/18 x bw PI/1 x bw SI; s/b; Indexed N; Glossary N; Appendices N; Bibliography Y; 220 x 199 (8vo)
NOTES: Reprint of edition first published by The Queen's Own Hussars.

ROYAL ARMOURED CORPS: LIGHT CAVALRY　　　　　　　　　　　　　　45

Regimental History The Queen's Own Hussars
Not stated 　　　　　　　　　　　　　　　　　　　　　　　　　　　PCL
Germany; Printing Section, Ordnance Services Viersen; 1985; ISBN None; 7pp/No illus.; Folded card; Indexed N; Glossary N; Appendices N; Bibliography N; 210 x 105 (8vo); Uncommon
NOTES: Double sided fold out card, negligible WWII.

The Seventh and Three Enemies
The Story of World War II and the 7th Queen's Own Hussars
Davy, C. B., C. B. E., D. S. O., Brig. G. M. O.
Uckfield; Naval & Military Press Ltd; ISBN 978 1781519578; See Notes; s/b
NOTES: Facsimile reprint by NMP of 1952 first edition, available in s/b.

8th King's Royal Irish Hussars　　　　　　　　　　　　　　　　8 H

Date of mechanization:　　　　1936
RAC service:　　　　　　　　　04/04/1939　　　　　　　Post-war.

Regimental publications:
The "Crossbelts" The Journal of the VIII King's Royal Irish Hussars
Vol. 1, No. 2 1928 – Vol. 3, No. 3 1938 (Annual) Suspended 1939 – 1944
Vol. 4, No. 1 1945 – Vol. 6, No. 2 1958 (Annual)
Bagush Bugle – newspaper
Started 1939, no edition info.

Men of Valour
The Third Volume of the History of The VIII King's Royal Irish Hussars 1927 - 1958
Fitzroy, Olivia 　　　　　　　　　　　　　　　TM; IWM; NAM; RMAS; PCL
Liverpool; C. Tinling & Co Ltd; 1961; ISBN None; xix + 375pp/1 x clr PIfep/103 x bw PI/2 x bw SI/2 x bw Mbds/9 x bw Mf/8 x bw M; h/b (d/j - ne) Green cloth; Indexed Y; Glossary N; Appendices Y; Bibliography N; 251 x 184 (4to); V Rare
NOTES: A comprehensive and well written regimental history. Very good selection of photographs. p23 – p232 cover WWII. RoH/Honours/Awards plus a list of officers of 8H 1928 – 1958. Notes on uniform and tanks employed in the appendices. Continues the history to the end of 1958 when the regiment was amalgamated to form the Queen's Royal Irish Hussars.

Irish Hussar
A short history of the Queen's Royal Irish Hussars incorporating the stories of the 4th Queen's Own Hussars, 1685-1958, and the 8th King's Royal Irish Hussars, 1693-1958
Strawson, C.B., O.B.E., Maj-Gen. J. M.; Pierson, Brig. H. T.; 　　　　　TM; NAM
Rhoderick-Jones, Brig. R. J.
London; The Queen's Royal Irish Hussars Association; 1986; ISBN 0 9512389 0 6; x + 234pp/1 x clr PIfep/5 x clr PI/5 x clr SI/86 x bw PI/5 x bw SI/15 x bw M; h/b / d/j Green imitation leather; Indexed Y; Glossary N; Appendices Y; Bibliography Y; 216 x 154 (8vo)
NOTES: Short but informative 17pp on WWII. Good photograph selection.

A Schoolboy's War
Bellamy, Bill
Northampton; L. G. Bellamy; 1990; ISBN 0 9515481 0 7; vii + 185pp/1 x bw SIfep/48 x bw PI/36 x bw SI/14 x bw M; s/b Limp green leatherette; Indexed N; Glossary N; Appendices N; Bibliography N; 249 x 173 (4to); V Rare
NOTES: Bill Bellamy's first self-published memoirs, formally republished as *Troop Leader*, q.v. His memoirs start in brief with him signing up in 1941, the bulk dealing with the NWE campaign. Initially in Normandy, the author commanded A Squadron's echelon but was soon made troop leader of 3 Tp, A Sqn following the loss of several troop leaders in action. He stayed with the troop until April 1945 when he became 2 i/c Recce Troop. An honest account demonstrating the fears and doubts men can have when dealing with combat situations.

From Horses to Chieftains
The True Story of an Original 'Desert Rat'
Napier, Richard   IWM
Arundel; Woodfield Publishing; 1992; ISBN 1 873203 17 9; x + 188pp/1 x bw PIfep/55 x bw PI; h/b Illustrated; Indexed N; Glossary N; Appendices N; Bibliography N; 216 x 154 (8vo); Uncommon
NOTES: The author joined the 8H as a member of the Boy Band in 1934. The first third covers his early years, service in Egypt with the Boy Band and then as a Bandsman. In 1943 he was posted to 13/18H and served with them throughout the NWE campaign, mainly as a gunner in C Sqn. The rear cover copy incorrectly places the author with 8H throughout the war rather than his split service – 8H 1934 – 1943 & 1946 – 1958, 13/18H 1943 – 1946. Extensive detail and a slightly unusual set of memoirs, the author having moved through the band, echelon and then to a fighting troop with another regiment. 99pp on WWII.

From Horses to Chieftains
My life with the 8th Hussars 1935 - 1959
Napier, Richard
Bognor Regis; Woodfield Publishing; 2002; ISBN 1-873203-17-9; 292pp/1 x bw PIfep/29 x bw PI; s/b; Indexed N; Glossary N; Appendices N; Bibliography N; 205 x 140 (8vo)
NOTES: Softback second edition of 1992 first edition, different pagination and smaller photograph selection.

Shan Hackett
The Pursuit of Exactitude
Fullick, Roy   TM
Barnsley; Leo Cooper; 2003; ISBN 0 85052 975 1; xiv + 231pp/31x bw PI/2 x bw SI/4 x bw M; h/b / d/j Red cloth; Indexed Y; Glossary N; Appendices N; Bibliography Y; 240 x 162 (8vo)
NOTES: Shan Hackett served in 8H before the war and up to late 1942. He then took command of the 4th Parachute Brigade which he famously commanded at Arnhem. 24pp on WWII.

Troop Leader
A Tank Commander's Story
Bellamy, Bill TM
Stroud; Sutton Publishing Limited; 2005; ISBN 0-7509-3979-6; x + 214pp/31 x bw PI/16 x bw SI; h/b / d/j Black cloth; Indexed Y; Glossary N; Appendices N; Bibliography N; 240 x 159 (8vo)
NOTES: Formal publication of the author's previously self-published memoirs under the title *A Schoolboy's War*, q.v., editorially updated and different pagination.

Troop Leader
A Tank Commander's Story
Bellamy, Bill
Stroud; Sutton Publishing Limited; 2007; ISBN 978-0-7509-4534-9; xii + 243pp/31 x bw PI/19 x bw SI/9 x bw M; s/b; Indexed Y; Glossary N; Appendices N; Bibliography N; 197 x 126 (12mo)
NOTES: Paperback reprint of 2005 hardback edition with additional maps, different pagination.

Shan Hackett
The Pursuit of Exactitude
Fullick, Roy
Barnsley; Pen & Sword Military; 2009; ISBN 978 184415 896 6; xiv + 231pp/31x bw PI/2 x bw SI/4 x bw M; s/b; Indexed Y; Glossary N; Appendices N; Bibliography Y; 233 x 156 (8vo)
NOTES: Softback reprint of hardback first edition, same pagination.

9th Queen's Royal Lancers — 9 L

Date of mechanization: 1936
RAC service: 04/04/1939 Post-war.

Regimental publications:
The Delhi Spearman: Regimental Journal of The 9th Queen's Royal Lancers
Vol. 1, No. 4 June 1928 – 1939 (Varies) Suspended 1940 – 1946.
No. 1 (new series) 1949 – No. 12 1960 (Varies).

An Account of the Operations Fought by the 9th Lancers
With Under Command the 2nd London Irish Rifles Carried in the Kangaroos of "A" Squadron, "B" Squadron, 4th Hussars in Shermans and "E" Battery, 11th (H.A.C.) R.H.A. With Their Self Propelled 25 Pounders, During the 8th Army Offensive of April 1945 Between the Santerno and the Po
Price, D.S.O., M.C., Lt-Col K. J. TM; IWM
No imprint; No imprint (In the field); 1945; ISBN None; 26pp/3 x clr M; s/b; Indexed N; Glossary N; Appendices N; Bibliography N; 331 x 208 (Folio); V Rare
NOTES: Typescript single sided 'Roneo-style' copy with hand drawn maps. Detailed description of action from 13 April 1945 to 25 April 1945 written by the CO of the time. Very occasional ref to 4H. (IWM & Tank Museum copies are photocopies.)

HQ Squadron
Not stated TM
Trieste; Arti Grafiche Smolars; 1945; ISBN None; 20pp/No illus.; s/b; Indexed N; Glossary N; Appendices N; Bibliography N; 239 x 171 (8vo); V Rare
NOTES: Summary of operations of HQ Sqn. RoH.

A Squadron - See Notes
NOTES: This entry is conjectural based on the assumption that it might exist because HQ, B & C Squadrons all produced their own publication. However, no evidence has come to light to prove it was published.

B Squadron
Not stated TM
Trieste; Arti Grafiche Smolars; 1945; ISBN None; 12pp/No illus.; s/b; Indexed N; Glossary N; Appendices N; Bibliography N; 239 x 171 (8vo); V Rare
NOTES: RoH and two page summary of operations of B Sqn. TM copy is a photocopy which is missing the publication details, these have been interpreted based on the identical format to HQ & C Sqns, examples of which have been viewed.

History of C Squadron 9th Lancers - World War 1939 - 1945
Not stated [See Notes] TM
Trieste; Arti Grafiche Smolars; 1945; ISBN None; 21pp/No illus.; s/b; Indexed N; Glossary N; Appendices N; Bibliography N; 239 x 171 (8vo); V Rare
NOTES: Excellent précised account across the war. Includes a list of squadron members who served between September 1941 and May 1945. RoH/Honours/Awards. Author is Maj. D. E. C. Steel.

A Short history of the 9th Queen's Royal Lancers 1715 - 1949
Hanwell, Maj. W. TM; IWM; NAM; PCL
Aldershot; Gale & Polden Limited; 1949; ISBN None; xiii + 71pp/2 x bw PI/4 x clr SI/4 x bw SI; p/b; Indexed N; Glossary N; Appendices N; Bibliography N; 215 x 139 (8vo)
NOTES: 14pp on WWII, comprehensive summary, one of the better short histories. Honours/Awards. No RoH but casualty numbers listed for each campaign, although these are from an early compilation and therefore incomplete.

The Ninth Queen's Royal Lancers 1936 - 1945
The Story of an Armoured Regiment in Battle
Bright, O.B.E., Joan (Ed.) TM; IWM; NAM; RMAS; PCL
Aldershot; Gale & Polden Ltd; 1951; ISBN None; xxxi + 359pp/1 x bw PIfep/68 x bw PI/1 x clr SI/1 x bw Mfbds/1 x clr Mrbds/19 x bw Mf; h/b / d/j Blue cloth; Indexed Y; Glossary N; Appendices Y; Bibliography N; 252 x 192 (4to); Uncommon
NOTES: Bulk of the history written by Guy Gardiner and Francis Pym, with Joan Bright as editor. The introduction, by a former CO, runs through many of the officers of the regiment, where they came from, contributions, and where they moved to. Highly competent and comprehensive history. RoH/Honours/Awards including citations to ORs. Appendices include Record of Service of Officers, Other Ranks who served list, 'C' Special Service Sqn on Madagascar and 'Explanation of Wireless' in an armoured regiment. Includes red/yellow silk page ribbon. Folding maps are on fine tissue paper.

ROYAL ARMOURED CORPS: LIGHT CAVALRY

A Short history of the 9th/12th Royal Lancers
No imprint TM; NAM; PCL
No imprint; No imprint; n.d. [c.1970]; ISBN None; 8pp/1 x clr SI r.cover; s/b (card); Indexed N; Glossary N; Appendices N; Bibliography N; 120 x 189 (32mo); Uncommon
NOTES: Brief pamphlet history, 1pp on WWII. One printing has a red and yellow thin border around the front cover.

A Short history of the 9th/12th Royal Lancers (Prince of Wales's)
No imprint TM; PCL
Viersen; Printing Section, Ordnance Depot Viersen; 1980; ISBN None; 12pp/1 x clr PI/2 x bw SI; s/b (card); Indexed N; Glossary N; Appendices N; Bibliography N; 210 x 148 (8vo); Uncommon
NOTES: Brief pamphlet history, 2pp on WWII, 500 copies printed. (This pamphlet was reproduced by the Printing Section in 1984 under the title *9th/12th Royal Lancers (Prince of Wales's) A Brief History.*)

Spearmen
The History of the 9th/12th Royal Lancers
Charrington, Richard TM
Not stated; 9th/12th Royal Lancers Charitable Association; 2010; ISBN 978-0-9566572-0-6; 256pp/60 x clr PI/174 x bw PI/80 x clr SI/14 x bw SI/15 x clr M; h/b / d/j Black cloth; Indexed Y; Glossary N; Appendices N; Bibliography Y; 311 x 257 (Folio)
NOTES: Lavishly produced, this book is an excellent presentation of a regimental history. Superbly illustrated and with well detailed narrative.

10th Royal Hussars (Prince of Wales's Own) — 10 H

Date of mechanization: 1936
RAC service: 04/04/1939 Post-war.

Regimental publications:
The X Royal Hussars (Prince of Wales's Own) Gazette
Vol. 8, No. 1 July 1928 – Vol. 18, No. 4 July 1939 (Varies) Suspended 1940 – 1946.
Vol. 19, No. 1 Jan 1946 – Vol. 22, No. 8 Spring 1969 (Varies)

The 10th Royal Hussars in the Second World War 1939 -1945
Compiled by committee, Chairman - Dawnay, D.S.O., Brig. D. TM; IWM; NAM; PCL
Aldershot; Gale & Polden Ltd; 1948; ISBN None; xiii + 212pp/1 x bw PIfep/3 x clr SI/28 x bw PI/4 x bw SI/22 x bw M; h/b Blue cloth; Indexed Y; Glossary N; Appendices Y; Bibliography N; 221 x 142 (8vo)
NOTES: Capable history but missing real regimental detail, has the feel of committee authorship. RoH/Honours/Awards.

10th Royal Hussars
(Famous Regiments)
Brander, Michael; Horrocks, Lt.-Gen. Sir Brian (Ed.) TM; IWM; NAM; RMAS; PCL
London; Leo Cooper Ltd; 1969; ISBN 85052 014 2; 138pp/18 x bw PI/11 x bw SI; h/b / d/j Green cloth; Indexed N; Glossary N; Appendices N; Bibliography N; 221 x 142 (8vo)
NOTES: Summary history, 26pp on WWII. Several WWII era photographs.

Roscoe The Bright Shiner
The Biography of Brigadier Roscoe Harvey DSO
Fitzgeorge-Parker, Tim   IWM; NAM
London; Severn House Publishers Ltd; 1987; ISBN 0-7278-1495-8; viii + 280pp/17 x bw PI; h/b / d/j Black cloth; Indexed N; Glossary N; Appendices N; Bibliography N; 222 x 137 (8vo)
NOTES: The story of C. B. 'Roscoe' Harvey's life, leaning heavily to his love of, and expertise in, horsemanship. 107pp on wartime career. Interesting view of a senior British cavalry officer although superficial as an overall biography. C. B. Harvey joined 10H in the 1920s and was 2 i/c in France in 1940. At the end of 1940 he was promoted to Lt-Col to command 23H but very soon returned to command 10H, later 8AB and commanded 29AB from the winter of 1943 until the end of the war.

The Tenth
10th Royal Hussars (Prince of Wales's Own) 1715 - 1969
Upton, Peter   IWM; NAM; PCL
Not stated; Old Comrades Association 10th Hussars; 1999; ISBN 0 9535854 0 9; vii + 144pp/1 x clr SIfep/8 x clr PI/28 x clr SI/340 x bw PI/10 x bw SI/4 x bw M; h/b / d/j Blue cloth; Indexed N; Glossary N; Appendices N; Bibliography N; 281 x 213 (4to); Uncommon
NOTES: A pictorial history, summary paragraphs on each campaign plus many photographs of the regiment during those campaigns. 22pp on WWII. Privately published.

There's a Soldier at the Gate
Crocker, Vincent A.   TM; IWM; NAM
Crewe; Trafford Publishing; 2000; ISBN 1-4120-2651-2; 255pp/11 x bw PI; p/b; Indexed N; Glossary N; Appendices N; Bibliography N; 196 x 125 (12mo)
NOTES: An interesting memoir because it shows life in the Echelon, rarely receiving the spotlight that the fighting tank crews understandably do. The memoirs follow the author from joining up late 1940 through the war to September 1945. Print on demand book. The libraries each have a 2005 dated edition.

11th Hussars (Prince Albert's Own)   11 H

Date of mechanization: 1928
RAC service: 04/04/1939   Post-war.

Regimental publications:
XI Hussar Journal
Vol. 1, No. 1 Jan 1910 – Vol. 21, No. 1 War Edition July 1943 (Varies)
Suspended 1944.
Vol. 21, No. 2 Victory Number Nov 1945 – Vol. 38, No. 3 1968 (Varies)
Regimental newspapers:
The Square, (A Squadron)
July 1945 to unknown (Fortnightly, 8pp)

ROYAL ARMOURED CORPS: LIGHT CAVALRY 51

D Sqn XIH May '44 - May '45
Not stated [See Notes]
No imprint; No imprint; 1945; ISBN None; 35pp/No illus.; s/b; Indexed N; Glossary N; Appendices Y; Bibliography N; 231 x 162 (8vo); V Rare
NOTES: This is the squadron CO's account in his own words. A first class mass of details, insights, and honest comment for the NWE campaign at squadron level. RoH/Honours/Awards. Produced in Germany immediately post war; printed June 1945. Author is Maj. J. A. N. 'Tony' Crankshaw, M.C.

The Eleventh at War
Being The Story of the 11th Hussars (Prince Albert's Own) through the years 1934 - 1945
Clarke, C.B., C.B.E., Brig. Dudley TM; IWM; NAM; PCL
London; Michael Joseph Ltd; 1952; ISBN None; 504pp/1 x clr SIfep/40 x bw PI/2 x bw SI/1 x clr Mfep/1 x clr Mrep/14 x bw M; h/b / d/j Maroon cloth; Indexed Y; Glossary N; Appendices Y; Bibliography N; 234 x 149 (8vo)
NOTES: First 70pp cover service in Egypt and the build up to the war. Very capable and well detailed, one of the best regimental histories. Handful of quotes from serving members. RoH/Honours/Awards.

11th Hussars (Prince Albert's Own)
'The Cherrypickers'
Not stated TM; NAM
London; Malcolm Page Limited; n.d. [c.1961]; ISBN None; 104pp/1 x clr PI/3 x clr SI/12 x bw PI/12 x bw SI; s/b; Indexed N; Glossary N; Appendices N; Bibliography N; 217 x 140 (8vo); Uncommon
NOTES: Recruiting booklet, 4pp summary of WWII, Battle Honours.

11th Hussars (Prince Albert's Own)
The Cherrypickers
250th Anniversary
Not stated TM; NAM
London; Malcolm Page Limited; n.d. [1966]; ISBN None; 112pp/1 x clr SIfep/34 x bw PI/1 x bw SI; s/b; Indexed N; Glossary N; Appendices N; Bibliography N; 217 x 140 (8vo); Uncommon
NOTES: Recruiting booklet, one paragraph relating to WWII. Battle Honours.

11th Hussars (Prince Albert's Own)
'The Cherrypickers'
Not stated TM
London; Malcolm Page Limited; n.d. [1967]; ISBN None; 36pp/17 x bw PI; s/b; Indexed N; Glossary N; Appendices N; Bibliography N; 216 x 139 (8vo); Uncommon
NOTES: Recruiting booklet, one paragraph relating to WWII. Battle Honours.

The 11th Hussars
(Famous Regiments)
Brett-Smith, Richard; Horrocks, Lt.-Gen. Sir Brian (Ed.)   TM; IWM; NAM; RMAS; PCL
London; Leo Cooper Ltd; 1969; ISBN 85052 015 0; xiv + 325pp/23 x bw Pl/13 x bw SI; s/b; Indexed N; Glossary N; Appendices N; Bibliography N; 215 x 136 (8vo)
NOTES: A useful summary history, a quarter of the book devoted to WWII. Includes detail not in *The Eleventh at War* and a good selection of photographs. 82pp on WWII.

For You the War is Over
A Suffolk Man recounts his prisoner of war experiences
Buckledee, Harry
Sudbury; Don Fraser Print; 1994; ISBN 0 9523295 1 4; iv + 64pp/10 x bw PI/2 x bw M; s/b; Indexed N; Glossary N; Appendices N; Bibliography N; 194 x 148 (12mo); Uncommon
NOTES: The author joined the army in May 1939, later joining 11H, travelling to join them in Egypt in May 1940. He picks up his story from December 1942 when he was captured west of Misurata. Then follows his time as a PoW through to liberation. He also recounts his trials in the Long March, the trek many PoWs made from east to west toward the end of the war. Reprinted 2012.

The Cherrypickers
11th Hussars (Prince Albert's Own) 1715 - 1969.
Upton, Lt-Col P. K.   TM; IWM; NAM; PCL
Not stated; Old Comrades 11th Hussars; 1997; ISBN 0 9530003 0 3; 144pp/5 x clr PI/1 x clr SIfep/23 x clr SI/325 x bw PI/7 x bw SI/2 x bw M; h/b / d/j Red cloth; Indexed N; Glossary N; Appendices N; Bibliography N; 282 x 213 (4to)
NOTES: A small number of pages provide summaries of various periods. An excellent set of photographs cover the regiment throughout the war, many putting faces to the names in the official history. Pictorial history, 29pp on WWII. Privately published.

Berlin or Bust
Wartime life with the 11th Hussars, the first British Regiment to enter Berlin
Osborne, Keith   TM; IWM; RMAS
Chester; Keith Osbourne; 2000; ISBN None; viii + 124pp/29 x bw PI/11 x bw SI; s/b; Indexed Y; Glossary N; Appendices N; Bibliography N; 210 x 148 (8vo)
NOTES: First 20pp deal primarily with the author's Fire Warden service in London early in the war, before being called up in June 1941. Although joining 11H as a subaltern in the summer of 1942 he did not arrive at the regiment until Easter 1943 and then served with them from North Africa to the end of the war. At first assigned to 'B' Echelon, he was later transferred to A Sqn as trainee troop leader to No. 5 Tp. Provides a good insight into actions and routines of an armoured car regiment in NWE.

The Last Colonel
11th Hussars (Prince Albert's Own) 1715-1969
Lawson, John   IWM
Chester; Keith Osbourne; 2004; ISBN None; vi + 98pp/20 x bw PI; s/b; Indexed Y; Glossary N; Appendices Y; Bibliography N; 210 x 148 (8vo)
NOTES: The author joined 11H in 1933 and the first 30pp deal with his experiences in the desert pre-war. In 1940 he became 2 i/c B Sqn after a short time with the Jordan Trans Frontier Force. In June 1941 he took command of A Sqn and during the Tunisian

campaign was attached to General Patton's staff to provide desert and recce experience. Later returned to the regiment as OC B Sqn in September 1944 and in December 1944 became 11H's 2 i/c before transferring to the IoC as their CO from March 1945. Extremely good account including daily details in the desert from personal hygiene to efficacy or otherwise of their armoured cars. RoH.

The Seven Colonels
The story of seven 11th Hussar subalterns who sailed to Egypt in 1934 and later became the Commanding Officers of several Units which all made a significant contribution to the successful outcome of the Second World War in 1939-45
Osborne, Keith
No imprint; No imprint; n.d.; ISBN None; viii + 92pp/12 x bw PI/1 x bw SI/1 x bw M; s/b; Indexed N; Glossary N; Appendices N; Bibliography N; 210 x 148 (8vo)
NOTES: Essentially a retelling of the regiment's history with occasional reference to the officers rather than the story of those personalities. The seven were George Paul (54th Training Regt, RAC), Bertie Bingley (IoC), Trevor Smail (11H), Geoffrey Miller (Sherwood Foresters), Peter Payne Gallwey (DY), Bill Wainman (11H), and John Lawson (IoC).

For You the War is Over
A Suffolk man recounts his prisoner of war experiences
Buckledee, Harry
Not stated; The Boxford Newsletter Group; 2012; ISBN None; iv + 80pp/1 x bw PIfep/16 x bw PI/3 x bw SI; s/b; Indexed N; Glossary N; Appendices N; Bibliography N; 210 x 148 (8vo)
NOTES: Following a TV programme entitled *The Long March to Freedom*, the author updated his 1994 book and the last third of this revised edition is new.

12th Royal Lancers (Prince of Wales's) — 12 L

Date of mechanization: 1928
RAC service: 04/04/1939   Post-war.

Regimental publications:
The Twelfth Royal Lancers Journal
Vol. 1, No. 1 (2nd series) Apr 1927 – Vol. 3, No. 20 Dec 1938 (Varies)
Suspended 1939 – 1944.
Vol. 4, No. 1 June 1945 – Vol. 4, No. 7 Apr 1960. (Varies)

Through Hell to Dunkirk
de la Falaise, Henry   IWM
Harrisburg, Pennsylvania; The Military Service Publishing Company; 1943; ISBN None; 166pp/1 x bw Mbds; h/b / d/j Red cloth; Indexed N; Glossary N; Appendices N; Bibliography N; 209 x 146 (8vo); Uncommon
NOTES: These memoirs are not from a member of 12L but a French liaison officer attached to A Sqn. Extremely engaging and full of day-to-day detail, they cover the period from 10 May 1940 to 1 June 1940 in diary form. Bruce Shand in *Previous Engagement*, q.v., describes this account as 'a very fair description of the actions of the squadron.' A US wartime publication but included because of its uniqueness.

The History of the XII Royal Lancers (Prince of Wales's) Volume II
Stewart, M.C., Capt. P. F. NAM
London; Oxford University Press; 1950; ISBN None; ix + 270pp/1 x clr SIfep/2 x clr SI/3 x bw SI/6 x bw Mf/2 x bw M; h/b Red cloth; Indexed Y; Glossary N; Appendices Y; Bibliography N; 258 x 167 (4to); Rare
NOTES: Published in two parts, the same content as the single volume below. 120pp on WWII.

The History of the XII Royal Lancers (Prince of Wales's)
Stewart, M.C., Capt. P. F. TM; IWM; RMAS; PCL
London; Oxford University Press; 1950; ISBN None; xvi + 516pp/1 x clr SIfep/3 x clr SI/4 x bw SI/16 x bw M; h/b / d/j Red cloth; Indexed Y; Glossary N; Appendices Y; Bibliography N; 226 x 150 (8vo)
NOTES: Standard regimental history, little regimental detail and lacks RoH/Honours/ Awards. Appendix II provides a list of officers of 12L 1715 – 1948. 120pp on WWII.

A Short history of the 9th/12th Royal Lancers
No imprint TM; NAM; PCL
No imprint; No imprint; n.d. [c.1970]; ISBN None; 8pp/1 x clr SI r.cover; s/b (card); Indexed N; Glossary N; Appendices N; Bibliography N; 120 x 189 (32mo); Uncommon
NOTES: Brief pamphlet history, 1pp on WWII. One printing has a red and yellow thin border around the front cover.

A Short history of the 9th/12th Royal Lancers (Prince of Wales's)
No imprint TM; PCL
Viersen; Printing Section, Ordnance Depot Viersen; 1980; ISBN None; 12pp/1 x clr Pl/2 x bw SI; s/b (card); Indexed N; Glossary N; Appendices N; Bibliography N; 210 x 148 (8vo); Uncommon
NOTES: Brief pamphlet history, 2pp on WWII, 500 copies printed. (This pamphlet was reproduced by the Printing Section in 1984 under the title *9th/12th Royal Lancers (Prince of Wales's) A Brief History.*)

Previous Engagements
Shand, Bruce TM; IWM
Salisbury; Michael Russell (Publishing) Ltd; 1990; ISBN 0 85955 169 5; 175pp/3 x bw M; h/b / d/j Blue cloth; Indexed Y; Glossary N; Appendices N; Bibliography N; 222 x 140 (8vo)
NOTES: The author joined 12L in 1937 and was leading a troop in A Sqn at the outbreak of war. In these memoirs, he spends considerable time describing the character of the men serving with him. He served with the regiment in France and NA becoming OC C Sqn in early 1942. The last 20pp deal with his captivity after being wounded in November 1943.

ROYAL ARMOURED CORPS: LIGHT CAVALRY 55

One Young Soldier
The Memoirs of a Cavalryman
Bishop, Tim; Shand, Bruce (Ed.) TM; IWM
Norwich; Michael Russell (Publishing) Ltd; 1993; ISBN 0 85955 193 8; xvii + 158pp/6 x bw PI/2 x bw SI/3 x bw M; h/b / d/j Red cloth; Indexed Y; Glossary N; Appendices N; Bibliography N; 240 x 159 (8vo)
NOTES: These memoirs have been edited posthumously by the author of *Previous Engagements*, q.v., a fellow 12L officer. The edited original work is interspersed with additional commentary. The first third of the book deals with his time in the Life Guards, he joined them as a trooper in the mid-thirties, before attending Sandhurst and joining 12L in 1938. Thereafter the narrative follows his service through France and NA to Tunisia, serving mainly in RHQ. Engaging narrative and interesting comparison between TB's experience in a pre-war cavalry regiment and the natural changes and progression which were brought to a cavalry regiment in war.

Saturday Night Soldier
Siminson, John IWM
London; Janus Publishing Company; 1994; ISBN 1 85756 117 1; 64pp/7 x bw PI/4 x bw SI/1 x bw M; s/b; Indexed N; Glossary N; Appendices N; Bibliography N; 209 x 147 (8vo); Uncommon
NOTES: The author joined the RWY before the war, was transferred to the Fourth Cavalry Training Regiment soon after war broke out and in May 1943 transferred to 12L. Bulk of the book follows his training, the final 17pp dealing with his service with 12L in their 'B' Echelon.

Spearmen
The History of the 9th/12th Royal Lancers
Charrington, Richard TM
Not stated; 9th/12th Royal Lancers Charitable Association; 2010; ISBN 978-0-9566572-0-6; 256pp/60 x clr PI/174 x bw PI/80 x clr SI/14 x bw SI/15 x clr M; h/b / d/j Black cloth; Indexed Y; Glossary N; Appendices N; Bibliography Y; 311 x 257 (Folio)
NOTES: Lavishly produced, this book is an excellent presentation of a regimental history. Superbly illustrated and with well detailed narrative.

13th/18th Royal Hussars (Queen Mary's Own)	13/18 H

Date of mechanization: January 1939
RAC service: 04/04/1939 Post-war.

    Regimental publications:
    The 13th/18th Royal Hussars Journal (The Journal of the "Lillywhites")
    Vol. 1, No. 1 July 1925 – Vol. 6, No. ? July 1939 (Varies) Suspended 1940 – 1944.
    Vol. 7, No. 1 Sept 1945 – Vol. 10, No. 8 Dec 1967 (Varies); became
    The Lillywhite Gazette. The Journal of the 13th/18th Royal Hussars (Q.M.O.)
    No. 1 May 1968 – No. 11 Autumn 1972; became
    The 13th/18th Royal Hussars Journal (The Journal of the "Lillywhites")
    No. 1 April 1973; became
    The 13th/18th Royal Hussars Journal
    Vol. 12, No. 2 April 1974 – Vol. 15, No. 2 Nov 1992 (Annual)

An Exhibition of a Painting - The Assault, Normandy, 6 June 1944
Cundall, Charles B.
London; Walker's Galleries; 1946; ISBN None; See Notes; V Rare
NOTES: Exhibition catalogue, 13th/18th Royal Hussars (Queen Mary's Own) launching their amphibious tanks. (Not physically inspected.)

History of the 13th/18th Royal Hussars (Queen Mary's Own) 1922 – 1947
Miller, C.B., C.B.E., D.S.O., p.s.c., Maj-Gen. Charles H.   TM; IWM; RMAS
London; Chisman, Bradshaw Ltd; 1949; ISBN None; xviii + 227pp/1 x clr SIfep/15 x bw PI/3 x clr SI/1 x bw SI/12 x clr M; h/b Blue cloth; Indexed Y; Glossary N; Appendices Y; Bibliography N; 248 x 167 (8vo)
NOTES: The first two chapters cover the pre-war history. Includes some excellent squadron level detailed maps. Detailed description of landing DD tanks on D-Day plus officers' reports on these landings. Includes a good number of quotes from personnel of the regiment, although officer-centric. Appendices include: Nominal Roll of Colonels, COs, QM Adj., RSMs and Bandmasters 1922 – 1947; several reports made by officers on the DD launches; WEs for 1939/40 and 1944; Honours/Awards with paragraph explanations of these; RoH divided by campaign. Some of the coloured maps have a printer's off-cut tissue insert to protect the pages from the coloured print.

A Brief History of the 13th/18th Royal Hussars (Queen Mary's Own) "The Lilywhites"
Not stated   IWM
No imprint; No imprint; n.d. [c.1951]; ISBN None; 24pp/4 x bw SI; s/b (card); Indexed N; Glossary N; Appendices N; Bibliography N; 184 x 128 (12mo); Uncommon
NOTES: Brief history for regimental members. 6pp précis on WWII service.

A Short History of the 13th/18th Royal Hussars (QMO) "The Lilywhites"
Not stated   PCL
York; Cansfields Printers; n.d. [c.1961]; ISBN None; 6pp/No illus.; Paper; Indexed N; Glossary N; Appendices N; Bibliography N; 244 x 257 (8vo); Uncommon
NOTES: Trifold leaflet, 1pp on D-Day.

A Brief History of the 13th/18th Royal Hussars (Queen Mary's Own) "The Lilywhites"
Not stated   NAM
Andover; The Standard Press (Andover) Ltd; n.d. [c.1968]; ISBN None; 26pp/No illus.; s/b; Indexed N; Glossary N; Appendices N; Bibliography N; 182 x 124 (12mo); Uncommon
NOTES: Useful pocket history, 5pp on WWII.

13th/18th Royal Hussars (Queen Mary's Own)
An Introduction to your Regiment
Not stated   PCL
No imprint; No imprint; 1973; ISBN None; 16pp/No illus.; s/b (card); Indexed N; Glossary N; Appendices N; Bibliography N; 207 x 146 (8vo); Uncommon
NOTES: Brief history for regimental members, 2pp on WWII.

A Brief History of the 13th/18th Royal Hussars (Queen Mary's Own)
Not stated PCL
No imprint; No imprint; n.d. [c.1982]; ISBN None; 18pp/4 x bw SI; s/b; Indexed N; Glossary N; Appendices N; Bibliography N; 208 x 146 (8vo); Uncommon
NOTES: Brief regimental leaflet, 2pp on WWII.

Evacuation Tarbat Peninsula 1943-4
Fallon, Dr, James A. TM
No imprint; No imprint; n.d. [c.1985]; ISBN None; 29pp/2 x clr PI/4 x clr SI/12 x bw PI/3 x clr M; s/b; Indexed N; Glossary N; Appendices N; Bibliography N; 210 x 147 (8vo)
NOTES: A local heritage booklet that tells the story of the area's evacuation for use as DD tank training, 6pp summarise the use of the area by 4/7DG, 13/18H, SY & ERY.

Young Man In A Tank
Hennessey, Patrick
Private; No imprint; 1988; ISBN None; 118pp/9 x bw PI; Comb with acetate covers; Indexed N; Glossary N; Appendices N; Bibliography N; 209 x 148 (8vo); Rare
NOTES: The author joined the RAC in December 1941, starting his training at Bovington Camp. Memoirs start with fairly detailed chapters on the training and move on to the author's experiences in NWE. He joined 13/18H in June 1942 as a trooper in 4th Tp, A Sqn. Very informative set of memoirs, useful to anyone interested in tanks, not just 13/18H. Reproduced typescript. Second edition with a 2pp postscript printed 1994.

The Memoir of Trooper G Treloar B Squadron 13th/18th Royal Hussars (Q.M.O.) in the Second World War
Treloar, G. TM
No imprint; No imprint; n.d. [c.1990s]; ISBN None; 52pp/1 x clr PI/5 x clr SI/12 x bw PI/1 x clr Mf/3 x clr M; Paper; Indexed N; Glossary N; Appendices N; Bibliography N; 210 x 146 (8vo); Rare
NOTES: The author's self-published memoirs concentrating on D-Day to discharge in 1946. In early 1945 he joined the tank crew of Jack Brookes, author of *A Conscript Goes to War*, q.v. RoH.

Light Dragoons
The Origins of a New Regiment
Mallinson, Allan TM; IWM; NAM; RMAS; PCL
London; Leo Cooper; 1993; ISBN 0 85052 368 0; viii + 352pp/7 x clr PI/18 x clr SI/47 x bw PI/6 x bw SI/1 x bw Mbds/22 x bw M; h/b / d/j Blue cloth; Indexed Y; Glossary N; Appendices N; Bibliography Y; 239 x 160 (8vo)
NOTES: Published after the amalgamation of 13/18H and 15/19H in 1992, this book covers the story of all four regiments from the early 18th century to the 'Options for Change' review which led to the amalgamation. A summary history, it draws heavily on the two official histories for WWII. 45pp on WWII.

Young Man In A Tank
Hennessey, Patrick TM; IWM
Private; Private; 1994; ISBN None; 120pp/9 x bw PI; Comb with acetate covers; Indexed N; Glossary N; Appendices N; Bibliography N; 209 x 148 (8vo); Uncommon
NOTES: 2pp postscript in this revised edition of the 1988 original.

The War Diary of Julius Neave
A personal chronical of the events leading up to, during and after the D-Day Normandy landing, during World War II Winter 1942/3 to May 1945
Neave, Julius　　　　　　　　　　　　　　　　　　　　　　　　　　　　　IWM
No imprint; No imprint; 1994; ISBN None; 378pp/1 x clr SI/20 x bw PI/1 x bw M; s/b; Indexed N; Glossary Y; Appendices Y; Bibliography N; 232 x 147 (8vo); V Rare
NOTES: The author was the Adjutant of 13/18H, joining it in 1940. He kept a diary which forms the basis of this book. Following an introduction focusing on preparations for D-Day, the book takes a diary form reproducing entries from the original diary; he has left his opinions as expressed at the time rather than editing them. Fascinating honest views from a senior regimental officer. Appendices include personal commentary of the four COs he served under and an article on the Rhine Crossing. IWM copy is rebound.

A Conscript Goes to War
In A Tank
Brookes, Jack　　　　　　　　　　　　　　　　　　　　　　　　　　　　　TM; IWM
Derby; Tracprez Publications; 1999; ISBN 0-9530782-7-2; 197pp/No illus.; s/b; Indexed N; Glossary N; Appendices N; Bibliography N; 200 x 140 (8vo); Uncommon
NOTES: The author recounts his training as an infantryman, transferring to the RAC for further training and then assignment to 13/18H in 1942. Loquacious and friendly reminiscences of his 13/18H training days; the last third deals with the NWE campaign. In early 1945 he served in the same tank as gunner George Treloar, author of *The Memoir of Trooper G Treloar...*, q.v. (Manuscript title in Tank Museum's library is *A Conscript Goes to War in a Tank Called Charlie*.) IWM copy is rebound.

Chariots of the Lake
The Story of Britain's Secret Weapon during the Second World War. From Fritton Lake to D-Day and Beyond
Jarvis, Robert B.　　　　　　　　　　　　　　　　　　　　　　　　　　　　TM
Lowestoft; The Heritage Workshop Centre; 2003; ISBN 1-904413-04-8; 131pp/5 x clr PI/56 x bw PI/4 x bw SI/1 x bw M; s/b; Indexed Y; Glossary Y; Appendices N; Bibliography Y; 260 x 210 (4to)
NOTES: Tells the story of the DD tank through the Suffolk training area at Fritton Lake and includes information on the DD equipped regiments: 4/7DG, 13/18H, ERY, SRY, and SY contained in 29pp.

Light Dragoons
The Origins of a New Regiment
Mallinson, Allan　　　　　　　　　　　　　　　　　　　　　　　　　　　　PCL
Barnsley; Pen & Sword Military; 2006; ISBN 1 84415 448 3 / 978 1 84415 448 7; xiii + 362pp/23 x clr PI/18 x clr SI/47 x bw PI/6 x bw SI/1 x bw Mbds/22 x bw M; h/b / d/j Black cloth; Indexed Y; Glossary N; Appendices N; Bibliography Y; 239 x 160 (8vo)
NOTES: Revised second edition contains one extra last chapter bringing the story up to date.

ROYAL ARMOURED CORPS: LIGHT CAVALRY 59

Light Dragoons
The Origins of a New Regiment
Mallinson, Allan RMAS
Barnsley; Pen & Sword Military; 2012; ISBN 978 1 84884 880 1; xiii + 362pp/23 x clr PI/18 x clr SI/47 x bw PI/6 x bw SI/1 x bw Mbds/22 x bw M; s/b; Indexed Y; Glossary N; Appendices N; Bibliography Y
NOTES: Softback reprint of 2006 edition. (Not physically inspected.)

14th/20th King's Hussars — 14/20 H

Date of mechanization: August 1938
RAC service: 04/04/1939 Post-war.

Regimental publications:
The Hawk: Regimental Journal of the 14th/20th King's Hussars
Vol. 1, No. 1 Jan 1948 – not established (Annual)

The Chronicles of Hussar
Rutter, S.Q.M.S. H. W.
No imprint; No imprint; n.d. [1940s/50s]; ISBN None; 8pp/No illus.; s/b; Indexed N; Glossary N; Appendices N; Bibliography N; 146 x 211 (24mo); V Rare
NOTES: A curious booklet presented in the form of pseudo-biblical text. It is a humorous summary of the regiment's travels in the Middle East, Italy and Germany.

A Short History of 14th/20th King's Hussars 1715 - 1950
Not stated TM; IWM; NAM; PCL
Aldershot; Gale & Polden Ltd; n.d. [c.1950]; ISBN None; viii + 54pp/3 x bw PI/1 x bw SIfep/4 x clr SI/1 x bw SI/1 x clr Mf; s/b; Indexed N; Glossary N; Appendices Y; Bibliography N; 215 x 139 (8vo)
NOTES: Short history written for recruits. 6pp on WWII.

14th/20th King's Hussars (Armoured Basic Training Unit)
Notes for recruits
Not stated IWM
Aldershot; Gale & Polden Ltd; n.d. [1950s]; ISBN None; 43pp/6 x bw SI/1 x Mf; s/b; Indexed N; Glossary N; Appendices Y; Bibliography N; 133 x 108 (24mo); Uncommon
NOTES: Booklet produced for National Service or volunteer recruits. 2pp on WWII.

Emperors Chambermaids
The Story Of The 14th/20th Kings Hussars
Oatts, D.S.O., Lt-Col L. B. TM; IWM; RMAS; PCL
London; Ward Lock Limited; 1973; ISBN 706310012; 518pp/2 x clr PI/9 x clr SI/2 x bw PI bds/48 x bw PI/32 x bw SI/6 x clr M/1 x bw ; h/b / d/j Blue cloth; Indexed Y; Glossary N; Appendices Y; Bibliography N; 252 x 192 (4to)
NOTES: Although a summary history, it is well scoped and informative. Contains lists of Colonels, COs, Adjs, RSMs, etc. Unfortunately 14/20H do not have a detailed WWII history. 34 pp on WWII.

The Hawks
A Short History of the 14th/20th King's Hussars
Perrett, Bryan NAM; PCL
Chippenham; Picton Publishing (Chippenham) Ltd; 1984; ISBN 0902633 94 5; viii + 151pp/34 x bw Pl/39 x bw SI; h/b / d/j Blue cloth; Indexed N; Glossary N; Appendices Y; Bibliography N; 216 x 150 (8vo)
NOTES: The book draws heavily on *Emperor's Chambermaids*, q.v.; there are, however, extra details that make this a reference worth consulting. Appendices include lists of Colonels, COs, Adjs, etc. 16pp on WWII.

Medicina Italy, 16th April 1945
The Fortieth Anniversary celebrated at The Regimental Reunion of the 14th/20th King's Hussars London 1985 5th May 1985 Inter-Continental Hotel
Talbot, G. A. L. C. (Ed.) NAM
Chester (Printers); Home Headquarters, 14/20 King's Hussars; 1985; ISBN None; 36pp/21 x bw PI/1 x bw SI/1 x bw M; s/b; Indexed N; Glossary N; Appendices N; Bibliography N; 214 x 150 (8vo); Rare
NOTES: Brief but informative account of the regiment's role in the Battle of Medicina, Italy. Includes contributions by members of the regiment at the time.

The Ramnuggur Boys
14th/20th King's Hussars 1715-1992
Pharo-Tomlin, John TM; IWM; NAM; RMAS; PCL
Preston; Museum of the King's Royal Hussars in Lancashire (14th/20th King's Hussars); 2002; ISBN 0 9542772-0-1; 160pp/33 x clr PI/75 x bw PI/66 x clr SI/9 x bw SI/16 x clr M/1 x bw M; h/b / d/j Blue cloth; Indexed Y; Glossary N; Appendices N; Bibliography Y; 212 x 282 (8vo)
NOTES: Liberally illustrated, this summary history covers the regiment's chequered wartime history most capably. RoH. 11pp on WWII.

15th/19th The King's Royal Hussars — 15/19 H

Date of mechanization: 1939
RAC service: 04/04/1939 Post-war.

Regimental publications:
Regimental Journal. XV. XIX. The King's Royal Hussars
Vol. 1, No. 1 Apr 1960 – Vol. 9 Nov 1992 (Annual)

Push On 20
Butler, M.C., Capt. K.F. IWM; NAM
London; No imprint (Holbrook & Son Ltd - printers); n.d. [c.1945]; ISBN None; 79pp/12 x bw PI/2 x clr Mbds/4 x clr M; h/b / d/j Green cloth & polychromatic paper; Indexed N; Glossary N; Appendices N; Bibliography N; 210 x 138 (8vo); V Rare
NOTES: Memoirs of actions through NWE. The author served in the Recce Troop of 11AD's armoured reconnaissance regiment, 15/19H. The title comes from his call sign and the ever-present Recce call.

ROYAL ARMOURED CORPS: LIGHT CAVALRY 61

Campaign Diary 15th/19th The King's Royal Hussars
North West Europe 1944 - 1945
Not stated IWM
No imprint; No imprint; 1946; ISBN None; 30pp/12 x clr M; s/b; Indexed N; Glossary N; Appendices N; Bibliography N; 332 x 204 (Folio); V Rare
NOTES: Privately printed in Palestine for members of the regiment as an aide-memoire whilst the official regimental history was being written. It covers the campaign in NWE. Maps are white on blue 'blueprint' style. Reproduced typescript.

A Short History of Your Regiment XV. XIX The King's Royal Hussars
Not stated TM; IWM
Aldershot; Gale & Polden Ltd; 1946; ISBN None; 66pp/2 x clr SI/2 x bw SI; s/b; Indexed N; Glossary N; Appendices N; Bibliography N; 175 x 115 (12mo)
NOTES: Although published after the war, this history only takes the regiment up to 1924. IWM copy rebound.

The History of 15/19 The King's Royal Hussars 1939 - 1945
Courage, D.S.O., Maj. G. TM; IWM; NAM; RMAS; PCL
Aldershot; Gale & Polden Limited; 1949; ISBN None; xiii + 329pp/1 x bw PIfep/15 x bw PI/2 x clr Mbds/19 x clr Mf; h/b (d/j - ne) Blue cloth; Indexed Y; Glossary N; Appendices Y; Bibliography N; 250 x 158 (4to); Uncommon
NOTES: A copy of the history was given to the next of kin of each 15th/19th Hussar who lost his life during WWII. Written by OC C Sqn. The margins maintain a running calendar against the narrative. Extremely well detailed and useful history covering many facets of an armoured regiment. Appendices include RoH/Honours/Awards, PoW list, list of officers attached to regiment 1939-45, details of tanks employed, and two officers' escape stories from France 1940.

15th/19th The King's Royal Hussars
Armoured Car Regiment of Northumberland and Durham
Not stated
London; Malcolm Page Limited; 1962; ISBN None; 32pp/17 x bw PI/10 x bw SI; s/b; Indexed N; Glossary N; Appendices N; Bibliography N; 213 x 137 (8vo); Uncommon
NOTES: 1960s recruiting booklet. No reference to WWII history.

A Short History of the 15th/19th King's Royal Hussars
Murray, Maj. J. S. F. TM; NAM; PCL
Aldershot; The Forces Press; 1964; ISBN None; viii + 81pp/1 x bw PIfep/6 x bw PI/5 x clr SI/2 x bw SI; s/b; Indexed N; Glossary N; Appendices N; Bibliography N; 226 x 144 (8vo)
NOTES: Informative short history produced for recruits and members of the regiment. 27pp on WWII.

The 15th/19th The King's Royal Hussars
A Pictorial History
Thompson, Ralph TM; IWM; NAM; RMAS; PCL
Huddersfield; Quoin Publishing Limited; 1989; ISBN 1-85563-004-48; 116pp/27 x clr PI/199 x bw PI; h/b / d/j Blue cloth; Indexed N; Glossary N; Appendices N; Bibliography N; 219 x 280 (8vo)
NOTES: Small but interesting selection of WWII photographs, 10pp on WWII.

Light Dragoons
The Origins of a New Regiment
Mallinson, Allan TM; IWM; NAM; RMAS; PCL
London; Leo Cooper; 1993; ISBN 0 85052 368 0; viii + 352pp/7 x clr PI/18 x clr SI/47 x bw PI/6 x bw SI/1 x bw Mbds/22 x bw M; h/b / d/j Blue cloth; Indexed Y; Glossary N; Appendices N; Bibliography Y; 239 x 160 (8vo)
NOTES: Published after the amalgamation of 13/18H and 15/19H in 1992, this book covers the story of all four regiments from the early 18th century to the 'Options for Change' review which led to the amalgamation. A summary history, it draws heavily on the two official histories for WWII. 45pp on WWII.

Light Dragoons
The Origins of a New Regiment
Mallinson, Allan PCL
Barnsley; Pen & Sword Military; 2006; ISBN 1 84415 448 3 / 978 1 84415 448 7; xiii + 362pp/23 x clr PI/18 x clr SI/47 x bw PI/6 x bw SI/1 x bw Mbds/22 x bw M; h/b / d/j Black cloth; Indexed Y; Glossary N; Appendices N; Bibliography Y; 239 x 160 (8vo)
NOTES: Revised second edition contains one extra last chapter bringing the story up to date.

Led Soldiers
The Second World War Diaries of a Royal Hussar
Mayman, Doug
Sandy; Anchorprint Group Ltd; 2007; ISBN - ne; See Notes; s/b; Indexed N; Glossary N; Appendices Y; Bibliography N; Uncommon
NOTES: Reproduces the contents of two diaries the author kept, one covering training and joining 15/19H, the other covering the period in action in the NWE campaign. Recounting much of the humdrum, this diary is valuable for that simple ordinariness. RoH. (This edition not physically inspected.)

Led Soldiers
The Second World War Diaries of a Royal Hussar
Mayman, Doug TM
Sandy; Authors On Line Ltd; 2008; ISBN 978-07552-0428-1; xiv + 248pp/47 x bw PI/2 x bw SI/8 x bw M; s/b; Indexed N; Glossary N; Appendices Y; Bibliography N; 234 x 156 (8vo)
NOTES: Reprint of 2007 first edition.

Light Dragoons
The Origins of a New Regiment
Mallinson, Allan RMAS
Barnsley; Pen & Sword Military; 2012; ISBN 978 1 84884 880 1; xiii + 362pp/23 x clr PI/18 x clr SI/47 x bw PI/6 x bw SI/1 x bw Mbds/22 x bw M; s/b; Indexed Y; Glossary N; Appendices N; Bibliography Y
NOTES: Softback reprint of 2006 edition. (Not physically inspected.)

ROYAL ARMOURED CORPS: LIGHT CAVALRY

16th/5th Lancers	16/5 L

Date of mechanization: January 1940
RAC service: 04/04/1939   Post-war.

Regimental publications:
The Scarlet and Green Journal
No. 1 1926 – No. 14 1939 (Annual) Suspended 1940 – 1945.
Vol. 4, No. 1 1946 – Vol. 11 1992 (Annual)

16th/5th The Queen's Royal Lancers
Regimental handbook
Not stated
London; Malcolm Page Limited; 1962; ISBN None; 60pp/19 x bw PI/18 x bw SI; s/b; Indexed N; Glossary N; Appendices N; Bibliography N; 212 x 137 (8vo); Uncommon
NOTES: 1960s recruiting booklet. No reference to WWII history.

History of 16th/5th The Queen's Royal Lancers 1925 - 1961
Barclay, C.B.E., D.S.O., Brig. C. N.   TM; IWM; RMAS; PCL
Aldershot; Gale & Polden Ltd; 1963; ISBN None; xii + 235pp/1 x clr SIfep/1 x clr SI/15 x bw PI/2 x bw Mf/6 x bw M; h/b / d/j Red cloth; Indexed Y; Glossary N; Appendices Y; Bibliography N; 285 x 224 (4to); Rare
NOTES: Well detailed, fairly standard regimental history, 107pp on WWII. Appendices include lists of Colonels, COs, Adjs, QMs, RSMs and Bandmasters 1925-1961, RoH. Folding maps printed on fine tissue paper.

16th/5th The Queen's Royal Lancers
(Famous Regiments)
Lunt, James; Horrocks, Lt.-Gen. Sir Brian (Ed.)   TM; IWM; NAM; RMAS; PCL
London; Leo Cooper Ltd; 1973; ISBN 0 85052 135 1; 82pp/11 x bw PI/12 x bw SI; h/b / d/j Red cloth; Indexed N; Glossary N; Appendices Y; Bibliography N; 222 x 143 (8vo)
NOTES: Summary history of WWII in 7pp.

The Scarlet Lancers
The Story of 16th/5th The Queen's Royal Lancers 1689-1992
Lunt, James   TM; IWM; NAM; RMAS; PCL
London; Leo Cooper; 1993; ISBN 0 85052 321 4; 278pp/16 x clr PI/72 x bw PI/39 x bw SI/5 x bw M; h/b / d/j Green cloth; Indexed Y; Glossary N; Appendices Y; Bibliography N; 240 x 162 (8vo)
NOTES: Published upon the amalgamation of 16/5L with 17/21L this book looks at selected events to view their histories. For the WWII period 13pp provide an overview of the regiment's actions.

17th/21st Lancers   17/21 L

Date of mechanization: 1938
RAC service: 04/04/1939   Post-war.

Regimental publications:
The White Lancer and The Vedette: the Regimental Journal of the 17th/21st Lancers
Vol. 13, No. 1 Jan 1925 – Vol. 27, No. 1 Apr 1939 (Varies) Suspended 1940 – 1945.
Vol. 29 1946 – 1992 (Varies)

Death Or Glory
A Short History of the 17th/21st Lancers
Tamplin, Maj. R. L. C.   TM; IWM; NAM; RMAS; PCL
No imprint; No imprint; 1959; ISBN None; xvi + 92pp/1 x clr SI/1 x clr SIfep/10 x bw PI/4 x bw SI/; s/b; Indexed N; Glossary N; Appendices N; Bibliography N; 248 x 184 (8vo); Uncommon
NOTES: Summary history which concentrates on the Battle Honours to describe the story. Produced for serving members of the regiment and as a bridge to the official WWII history yet to be published. Published April 1959 in place of the usual issue of the regimental journal. Lists Colonels, COs, Adjs, QMs, etc.

A History of the 17th/21st Lancers 1922 - 1959
ffrench Blake, D.S.O., Lt-Col R. L. V.   TM; IWM; NAM; PCL
London; Macmillan & Co Ltd; 1962; ISBN None; xv + 284pp/8 x bw PI/1 x bw SI/2 x bw Mbds/10 x bw M; h/b / d/j Blue cloth; Indexed Y; Glossary N; Appendices Y; Bibliography N; 254 x 177 (4to)
NOTES: Provides useful background narrative to the development of British armoured forces and their tactics. Appendices include list of officers commissioned into the 17/21L between 1922 and 1959. RoH. 157pp on WWII.

The 17th/21st Lancers
(Famous Regiments)
ffrench Blake, R. L. V.; Horrocks, Lt.-Gen. Sir Brian (Ed.)   TM; IWM; NAM; RMAS
London; Hamish Hamilton Ltd; 1968; ISBN None; 173pp/14 x bw PI/18 x bw SI/6 x bw M; h/b / d/j Blue cloth; Indexed N; Glossary N; Appendices Y; Bibliography N; 222 x 142 (8vo)
NOTES: Essentially a condensed version of the author's main history, above. Battle Honours. 38pp on WWII.

The 17th/21st Lancers
A Short History of the 17th/21st Lancers
Not stated   NAM
Viersen, Germany; 15 Comp Ord Dep (Printers); 1975; ISBN None; 6pp/3 x bw SI; s/b (card); Indexed N; Glossary N; Appendices N; Bibliography N; 203 x 166 (8vo); Rare
NOTES: Very short history, three paragraphs on WWII. 500 copies printed.

ROYAL ARMOURED CORPS: LIGHT CAVALRY

The 17th/21st Lancers 1759 – 1993
ffrench Blake, R. L. V. TM; NAM; PCL
London; Leo Cooper; 1993; ISBN 0 85052 272 2; 139pp/3 x bw Pl/13 x bw Sl/6 x bw M; h/b / d/j Blue boards; Indexed Y; Glossary N; Appendices Y; Bibliography N; 222 x 141 (8vo)
NOTES: Republished and revised edition of 1968 Famous Regiments series upon the amalgamation of 16/5QRL and 17/21L with an extra chapter to bring it up to date.

Over the next hill....
War Story 1939-1945
Is the Journal of a Junior Officer, Whose Military Career Was, in the Main, Involved in Reconnaissance & is in No Way a Treatise on the Tactics or Strategy of World War II
Stiebel, H. A. J. TM; IWM; NAM
No imprint; H. A. J. Stiebel; 1996; ISBN None; 91pp/1 x clr PIfep/2 x clr PI/7 x bw PI; Comb; Indexed N; Glossary N; Appendices N; Bibliography N; 297 x 210 (4to); V Rare
NOTES: Published by the author essentially for his children, one copy each has been given to The Tank Museum, NAM, IWM and the QRL Museum, Grantham plus five copies to fellow members of C Sqn, 17/21L. The author joined the regiment in April 1944, taking over command of C Squadron's Recce Troop. In April 1945 he was placed in command of 1st Tp, C Sqn. Well written account with good detail, including vehicles employed.

Key to Book Entries
Book Title and Sub-title(s)
Author Museum Holdings
Place of Publication; Publisher; Date of Publication; ISBN; Pages/Illustrations; Binding; Indexed; Glossary; Appendices; Bibliography; Size (in mm); Availability
NOTES:

Section IV

Royal Armoured Corps: War-raised Cavalry

Despite already having twenty regiments in existence, the cavalry were included in the war-time expansion of Britain's armoured forces. The War Office knew they needed regiments for the duration of the war which could be disbanded at the end of hostilities without the potential hue and cry that disbanding re-raised regiments might invoke.

Three new regiments were created in December 1940 - 22nd Dragoons, 23rd Hussars and 24th Lancers and another three were raised in January 1941 - 25th Dragoons, 26th Hussars, and 27th Lancers. Known as war-raised cavalry, within two years of the war's end all had been officially removed from the Army List.

Of the six regiments, 26H was the only one not to see action, being disbanded relatively early in October 1943. The remaining five served thus:

    22D - landed on D-Day equipped with Crabs
    23H - fought in NWE from mid-June 1944. In December 1944, 23H
    was one of the few regiments to start training on the new Comet
    tank, eventually going into action with them in March 1945
    24L – landed in the second wave on D-Day, disbanded at the end of
    July 1944
    25D - served in Burma equipped with Lee/Grant tanks, seeing action
    for the first time in January 1944
    27L - sailed to Egypt in 1943 where they were equipped with
    armoured cars from 1HCR before moving to Italy for the remainder
    of the war.

Each regiment was formed from a cadre supplied by an existing cavalry regiment. The list below shows their heritage:

Regiment	Cadre	Regiment	Cadre
22nd Dragoons	4/7DG and 5DG	25th Dragoons	3DG
23rd Hussars	10H and 15/19H	26th Hussars	14/20H
24th Lancers	9L and 17/21L	27th Lancers	12L

Royal Armoured Corps: War-raised Cavalry

For Hostilities Only
Seaman, Peter   TM; IWM; NAM
Not stated; Peter Seaman; 2010; ISBN 978-0-9524261-1-0; xi + 173pp/138 x clr PI/59 x bw PI/1 x bw SI; s/b; Indexed N; Glossary N; Appendices Y; Bibliography Y; 295 x 208 (4to)
NOTES: A superb reference book on the insignia of the war-raised cavalry regiments. Included here because it also incorporates a summary history of each regiment with highly useful information. Covers 22D, 23H, 24L, 25D, 26H & 27L.

22nd Dragoons   22 D

RAC service:*   01/12/1940   30/11/1945
* Equates to date raised and disbanded.

    Regimental publications:
    Crews Front
    Two issues published late 1942.

XXII Dragoons 1760 - 1945
The Story of a Regiment
Birt, Raymond   TM; IWM; NAM; RMAS; PCL
Aldershot; Gale & Polden Limited; 1950; ISBN None; xxix +349pp/1 x clr SIfep/81 x bw PI/16 x bw SI/5 x bw Mf/10 x bw M; h/b / d/j Green cloth; Indexed Y; Glossary N; Appendices Y; Bibliography N; 222 x 145 (8vo); Rare
NOTES: Engaging and evocative narrative, the first half of which provides an excellent account of how a regiment is raised and trained. The second half covers the regiment's actions in NWE. The author was the regiment's signals officer. RoH.

Will The Real Ian Carmichael...
An Autobiography
Carmichael, Ian
London; Macmillan London Limited; 1979; ISBN 0 333 25476 7; 400pp/1 x bw PIfep/93 x bw PI/3 x bw SI; h/b / d/j Blue cloth; Indexed Y; Glossary N; Appendices N; Bibliography N; 239 x 161 (8vo)
NOTES: Interesting and informative section (98pp) about an officer of a war-raised cavalry regiment. The author was commissioned into the regiment March 1941 and progressed through various appointments until made Brigade Liaison Officer early 1943, a role he maintained to the end of the war.

Will The Real Ian Carmichael...
An Autobiography
Carmichael, Ian
London; Book Club Associates; 1979; ISBN None; 400pp/1 x bw PIfep/93 x bw PI/3 x bw SI; h/b / d/j Green cloth; Indexed Y; Glossary N; Appendices N; Bibliography N; 239 x 161 (8vo)
NOTES: BCA reprint of first edition.

Will The Real Ian Carmichael...
An Autobiography
Carmichael, Ian
London; Futura Publications Limited; 1980; ISBN 0 7088 1860 9; 444pp/14 x bw Pl; p/b; Indexed Y; Glossary N; Appendices N; Bibliography N; 177 x 109 (12mo)
NOTES: Paperback reprint of hardback first edition, different pagination.

Achtung Minen!
The Making of a Flail Tank Troop Commander
Hammerton, Ian C. TM; IWM; NAM
Lewes; The Book Guild Limited; 1991; ISBN 0 86332 533 5; 176pp/39 x bw Pl/1 x bw SI/6 x bw M; h/b / d/j Blue cloth; Indexed N; Glossary N; Appendices N; Bibliography N; 223 x 138 (8vo); Uncommon
NOTES: First third deals with the author's training in 42 & 43 RTR before being commissioned through Sandhurst. He joined 22D as troop leader of 1st Tp, B Sqn, a position he held to the end of the war. Although generally taking a light-hearted tone, occasional gritty detail belies that. Has a very good selection of personal photographs of individual crew and crew groups plus personnel listing for 1st Tp, B Sqn.

Achtung Minen!
The Making of a Flail Tank Troop Commander
Hammerton, Ian C. TM
Not stated; I. C. Hammerton; 2000; ISBN 0-9538978-0-X; 169pp/71 x bw Pl/3 x bw SI/6 x bw M; s/b; Indexed N; Glossary N; Appendices N; Bibliography N; 210 x 145 (8vo)
NOTES: Softback reprint of 1991 first edition, different pagination.

23rd Hussars   23 H

RAC service:*   01/12/1940   21/06/1946
* Equates to date raised and disbanded.

Regimental publications:
The Triangle: 'A' Squadron, 23rd Hussars Magazine
Vol. 1 No. 1 Aug 1945 To Vol. 1 No. 5 Dec 1945 (Unknown) Replaced by
The Turret: 23rd Hussars
Issues not established.

'A' Squadron 23rd Hussars War Diary June 1944 - May 1945
Not stated TM; PCL
No imprint; No imprint; 1945; ISBN None; 36pp/6 x bw Pl/5 x bw M; s/b; Indexed N; Glossary Y; Appendices Y; Bibliography N; 244 x 182 (8vo); V Rare
NOTES: Written in diary format covering 11 June 1944 to 11 May 1945. RoH/Awards. TM's photocopy missing glossary and covers, PCL's copy rebound.

B Squadron 23rd Hussars
No imprint TM
No imprint; No imprint; 1945; ISBN None; 32pp/1 x bw PI/16 x bw SI; s/b / d/j; Indexed N; Glossary N; Appendices N; Bibliography N; 210 x 147 (8vo); V Rare
NOTES: A potted history of the squadron complete with many humorous cartoons illustrating the text. Published for ex-members just prior to disbandment. Includes a full address list of squadron members together with next-of-kin for those killed. This booklet came with a coloured paper 'dust-jacket' which is sometimes missing; printed in Germany. RoH.

C Squadron 23rd Hussars - See Notes
NOTES: This entry is conjectural based on the assumption that it might exist because A and B Squadrons produced their own publication. However, no evidence has come to light to prove it was published.

The Story of the Twenty-Third Hussars 1940 - 1946
Written by members of the Regiment TM; IWM; NAM; RMAS; PCL
No imprint [Germany]; No imprint; 1946; ISBN None; 277pp/53 x bw PI/1 x clr Mfbds/11 x clr Mf; h/b / d/j Green leather; Indexed N; Glossary N; Appendices Y; Bibliography N; 213 x 160 (8vo); Uncommon
NOTES: The first 30pp deal swiftly with the raising and training of the regiment leaving the remaining 230pp to cover the regiment in NWE. Despite being prepared by five authors the narrative is clear and informative. Full of detail, naming ORs and officers and describing many small actions. 3000 copies published. Tipped in delivery cover note apologising for the need to charge rather than giving ex-members a free copy. With a Moroccan grain leather binding, plenty of photographic illustrations and some colourful naïve-style maps, no surprise the 15,000 Mark budget went up to 24,000 Marks! RoH.

Soldier in the Saddle
Modern Men of Action
"Monkey" Blacker IWM
London; Burke Publishing Co Ltd; 1963; ISBN None; 191pp/28 x bw PI; h/b / d/j Red cloth; Indexed N; Glossary N; Appendices N; Bibliography N; 201 x 133 (8vo)
NOTES: Horses dominate the memoirs of this author, who was both a cavalryman and a horseman. He joined 5RIDG in 1936 serving in France, 1940, as Adjutant. A year later he was C Sqn commander in the newly formed 23H and shortly after landing in France in 1944 he was promoted to 2 i/c. His memoirs display a genial tone until he recounts 23H's part in Operation Goodwood, July 1944, where the regiment suffered heavy casualties. (This battle is expanded upon in his later book *Monkey Business*, q.v.) Indeed his military recollections end abruptly after the Goodwood pages with no reference to the rest of the NWE campaign; he went on to command 23H after the war. 48pp on WWII.

23rd. Hussars Twenty Fifth Re-union
Not stated
Northwood; R. H. Warmsley; 1970; ISBN None; 14pp/28 x bw PI; s/b; Indexed N; Glossary N; Appendices N; Bibliography N; 294 x 208 (4to); Rare
NOTES: Commemorative publication for the OCA's re-union of October 1970. Has a one page Regimental History with the bulk comprising personal photographs.

Monkey Business
The Memoirs of General Sir Cecil Blacker
Blacker, Gen. Sir Cecil TM
London; Quiller Press Limited; 1993; ISBN 1 870948 87 4; viii + 232pp/32 x bw Pl/1 x bw SIfep/16 x bw SI/3 x bw M; h/b / d/j Red cloth; Indexed Y; Glossary N; Appendices N; Bibliography N; 240 x 160 (8vo)
NOTES: These memoirs, published 30 years after his first set, *Soldier in the Saddle*, q.v., provide an expanded review of the author's military career, albeit with some natural duplication of description. He served in 5RIDG from before the war until late 1941 and provides several descriptions of fellow officers plus a few comments on the regiment's actions in France 1940. In late 1941 he transferred to 23H as OC C Sqn. Generally his recollections are with the eye of a senior officer. Describing 23H's part in Op. Goodwood in Normandy, he provides an impressive and evocative description of the regiment losing most of its tanks and many of its crews. His recollections turn to swift summary for the period September 1944 to the end of the war. 23pp on 5RIDG and 43pp on 23H.

The Battle
A Tank officer Remembers
Bishop, M.C., Geoffrey S. C. TM; IWM; NAM
Brighton; Fotodirect (Printers) Ltd; n.d.; ISBN None; 91pp/1 x bw Pl; h/b Green cloth; Indexed N; Glossary N; Appendices N; Bibliography N; 228 x 144 (8vo); Uncommon
NOTES: These memoirs start from 14 June 1944 and in diary form run through to 7 August 1944. The author was a troop leader in B & C Sqns. Written in a halting staccato fashion which imparts a sense of urgency and importance to some of the actions described. One of the few sets of memoirs which evoke a time and a place.

24th Lancers — 24 L

RAC service:*   01/12/1940   01/08/1944
* Equates to date raised and disbanded.

Regimental publications:
Lancer Life
No. 1 3 July 1944 to unknown but by disbandment.

None Had Lances
Story of the 24th Lancers
Willis, Leonard TM; IWM; NAM; RMAS; PCL
Old Coulsdon; 24th Lancers OCA; 1986; ISBN 0 9510718 0 7; xix + 245pp/40 x bw Pl/1 x bw SI/8 x bw M; h/b / d/j Blue cloth; Indexed Y; Glossary Y; Appendices N; Bibliography Y; 217 x 155 (8vo)
NOTES: The author has woven into the story reminiscences from a great many 24th Lancers, including many social stories during formation/training. First quarter of the book deals with training the regiment and the remainder covers the period in NWE to disbandment. Four chapters are reproduced brief diaries from men of the regiment: a troop leader, the Padre and the Medical Officer. The last chapter reproduces the citations for awards to 24L including those ex-24L serving with other regiments. RoH.

ROYAL ARMOURED CORPS: WAR-RAISED CAVALRY

Dad's War
A Tank Commander in Europe 1944-45
With the XXIV Lancers and Sherwood Rangers Yeomanry
Cropper, Andy   TM; IWM; NAM
Thurlstone; Anmas Publications; 1994; ISBN 0 95242222 0 4; 108pp/28 x bw Pl; s/b;
Indexed N; Glossary N; Appendices N; Bibliography Y; 210 x 147 (8vo); Rare
NOTES: Written by his son, this book tells of John Cropper's service with 24L from May 1944 to disbandment and then with the SRY. His service with the SRY is covered in the last two-thirds of the book. The narrative is interspersed with his quotations. Provides an insight into some of the minutiae of troop/squadron life; details such as wearing headphones over one ear to be aware of outside sounds. Includes a good selection of private photographs. 500 copies printed.

A Dalesman's War
Morland, Carole
Kirkby Stephen; Hayloft Publishing Ltd; 2010; ISBN 1 904524 78 8; 58pp/17 x bw Pl; s/b; Indexed N; Glossary N; Appendices N; Bibliography N; 210 x 148 (8vo)
NOTES: The author's father joined 24L mid-war as a tank driver. She recounts some early life and his time in Normandy before being transferred to 1RTR upon 24L's disbandment. Not long afterwards he was severely burnt. The final chapters describe his long struggle - two years - before being fully discharged from hospital. The book takes a social commentary stance more than that of pure historical record.

25th Dragoons   25 D

RAC service:*   07/01/1941   08/1947
* Equates to date raised and disbanded.

Regimental publications:
Journal of the 25th Dragoons
July 1946 to unknown.
The Bully-tin
Produced erratically in the field in 1943, started again July 1944, weekly for some months. (Gestetner printing process)

Memories of Youth and War
Into Burma
A personal account of the 25th Dragoons August 1943 to June 1944
Grounds, Tom   NAM
No imprint; Tom Grounds; 1988; ISBN None; 281pp/36 x bw Pl/4 x bw SI/10 x bw M; s/b Comb; Indexed N; Glossary N; Appendices Y; Bibliography N; 297 x 210 (4to); V Rare
NOTES: Privately published, the author has used his many letters home as the basis and added material for the narrative. A detailed account formally published as *Some Letters From Burma* in 1994, q.v.

Some Letters From Burma
The Story of the 25th Dragoons at War
Grounds, Tom TM; IWM; NAM
Tunbridge Wells; Parapress Ltd; 1994; ISBN 1-898594-11-2; xix + 265pp/25 x bw PI/3 x bw SI/6 x bw M; h/b / d/j Red cloth; Indexed Y; Glossary Y; Appendices Y; Bibliography Y; 222 x 144 (8vo)
NOTES: Formal publication of author's previous work, *Memories of Youth and War*, q.v. He reproduces some of his contemporary letters together with a good number of quotations to recount his and the 25D story, starting in August 1943 through to June 1944; he served in B Sqn. The narrative is heavily weighted toward the overall picture rather than the regiment's day-to-day operations. RoH/Honours/Awards. Reprinted in 2006.

Some Letters From Burma
The Story of the 25th Dragoons at War
Grounds, Tom
Tunbridge Wells; Parapress Ltd; 2006; ISBN 978-1898594-81-9; xix + 265pp/25 x bw PI/3 x bw SI/6 x bw M; s/b; Indexed Y; Glossary Y; Appendices Y; Bibliography Y; 215 x 136 (8vo)
NOTES: Softback reprint of 1994 edition, same pagination.

26th Hussars — 26 H

RAC service:*   07/01/1941   10/1943
* Equates to date raised and disbanded.

No publications established.

27th Lancers — 27 L

RAC service:*   07/01/1941   09/1945
* Equates to date raised and disbanded.

No publications established.

Key to Book Entries
Book Title and Sub-title(s)
Author Museum Holdings
Place of Publication; Publisher; Date of Publication; ISBN; Pages/Illustrations; Binding; Indexed; Glossary; Appendices; Bibliography; Size (in mm); Availability
NOTES:

Section V

Royal Armoured Corps: Royal Tank Regiment

The Royal Armoured Corps was created in April 1939. The Cavalry and Royal Tank Corps regiments were incorporated into this new body and, to avoid a corps within a corps, the RTC was retitled Royal Tank Regiment. All but four of the RTR's 24 regiments were in existence prior to the outbreak of WWII; 9RTR to 12RTR were raised during wartime.

The Royal Tank Regiment can trace its heritage back to the First World War and the first tanks of the Tank Corps. Its experience and prestige ensured that it formed many cadres as the basis for new regiments, both before and during the Second World War, and in addition it loaned personnel to newly formed units to assist with their training.

A note on the idiosyncratic regimental nomenclature of the Royal Tank Regiment - before and during the war RTC/RTR units were titled as battalions, e.g. 4th Battalion, Royal Tank Corps. This continued when the RTC became the RTR, e.g. 4th Bn, RTR. Despite the battalion nomenclature, they were routinely referred to as regiments and frequently used the unit title abbreviation of RTR. To clarify this title anomaly the War Office issued an instruction in March 1946, retrospectively applied to September 1945, that all RTR battalions be redesignated regiments. Henceforth they would be referred to as 4th Royal Tank Regiment, etc.

No books have been found for either 10RTR or 12RTR. In the case of 10RTR this is almost certainly due to the fact that it served briefly in the UK before being renamed 7RTR in the spring of 1943. This was in order to resurrect 7RTR which had been destroyed in the siege of Tobruk, June 1942.

12RTR served in Tunisia and Italy, leaving the lack of any story an enigma.

As part of the Army's latest restructuring known as Army 2020, 1RTR and 2RTR have merged to form a single regiment – The Royal Tank Regiment. It held its first parade on 2 August 2014.

This event will undoubtedly feature prominently in the next installment of the regiment's history. To coincide with the 100th Anniversary of the Battle of Cambrai, Charles Messenger is writing a new account, *The Tanks Volume IV, 1976 - 2017* (Kenneth Macksey's *The Tanks, The History of The Royal Tank Regiment, 1945-1975*, is regarded as Volume III.), bringing the regiment's story up-to-date. This is scheduled for publication in 2017.

Royal Armoured Corps: Royal Tank Regiment

Regimental publications:
The Tank Corps Training Centre Journal
Vol. 1, No. 1 Apr 1919 (Monthly); became
The Tank Corps Journal
Vol. 1, No. 2 May 1919 to Vol. 4, No. 55 Nov 1923 (Monthly); became
The Royal Tank Corps Journal
Vol. V, No. 56 Dec 1923 to Vol. XVIII, No. 209 Sept 1936; upon creation of The Tank became
The Royal Tank Corps Journal
Vol. 1, No. 1 Jan 1936 to Vol. 10 1946 (Half yearly)
The Tank. Journal of the Royal Tank Regiment
Vol. XVIII, No. 210 Oct 1936 to present (Monthly to Vol. 57, No. 672 Apr 1975, then Quarterly to Vol. 91, No. 790 Dec 2009, then 3 per year to Vol. 92, No. 796 Winter 2011 and 2 per year from Summer 2012)

The Tanks
The History of the Royal Tank Regiment and its predecessors
Heavy Branch Machine-Gun Corps, Tanks Corps and Royal Tank Corps 1914 - 1945
Volume One 1914 -1939
Liddell Hart, Capt. B. H.   TM; IWM; NAM; RMAS; PCL
London; Cassell & Company Ltd; 1959; ISBN None; xix + 462pp/35 x bw PI/13 x bw SI/3 x bw Mf/5 x bw M; h/b / d/j Black cloth; Indexed Y; Glossary N; Appendices N; Bibliography N; 222 x 148 (8vo)
NOTES: Although covering a period outside the scope of this book, Volume 1 does have one chapter on tank development which covers several of the models in service in the first campaigns of WWII.

The Tanks
The History of the Royal Tank Regiment and its predecessors
Heavy Branch Machine-Gun Corps, Tanks Corps and Royal Tank Corps 1914 - 1945
Volume Two 1939 - 1945
Liddell Hart, Capt. B. H.   TM; IWM; NAM; RMAS; PCL
London; Cassell & Company Ltd; 1959; ISBN None; xiv + 555pp/57 x bw PI/23 x bw SI/17 x bw Mf/27 x bw M; h/b / d/j Black cloth; Indexed Y; Glossary N; Appendices N; Bibliography N; 222 x 148 (8vo)
NOTES: A vast history although sadly there are some errors and omissions (e.g. 10RTR's renaming to 7RTR is not mentioned in the narrative at all, confuses 21ATB/25ATB's constituent regiments.) Essential reading but 'handle with care'.

To The Green Fields Beyond
A Short History of the Royal Tank Regiment
Macksey, Kenneth   TM; IWM; NAM; PCL
London; Regimental Headquarters, Royal Tank Regiment; 1965; ISBN None; 92pp + xvi/1 x bw SIfep/11 x bw PI/3 x bw SI/3 x bw M; s/b; Indexed N; Glossary N; Appendices Y; Bibliography N; 182 x 163 (12mo)

NOTES: Overview history of the RTR with some natural replication from Liddell Hart's *The Tanks*. One appendix includes VC citations. 37pp on WWII. Reprinted in 1976.

The Royal Tank Regiment
50th Anniversary Souvenir 1917-1967
Not stated [See Notes]　　　　　　　　　　　　　　　　　　TM; IWM; NAM; PCL
London; The Royal Tank Regiment Publications Ltd; 1967; ISBN None; 132pp/3 x clr PIfep/30 x bw PI/40 x bw SI; s/b; Indexed N; Glossary N; Appendices N; Bibliography N; 247 x 187 (8vo)
NOTES: A special anniversary edition of *The Tank* to commemorate the 50th Anniversary of Cambrai. Broad-brush overview in 12pp. Includes citations for regiment's two VC winners. Author is Lt-Col R. N. Wilson.

The Royal Tank Regiment
(Famous Regiments)
Chadwick, Kenneth; Horrocks, Lt.-Gen. Sir Brian (Ed.)　　　TM; IWM; NAM; RMAS; PCL
London; Leo Cooper Ltd; 1970; ISBN 085052 020 7; vii + 158pp/24 x bw PI/17 x bw SI; h/b / d/j Red cloth; Indexed N; Glossary N; Appendices N; Bibliography N; 222 x 144 (8vo)
NOTES: Well composed summary of the RTR regiments during WWII - 50pp.

To The Green Fields Beyond
A Short History of the Royal Tank Regiment
Macksey, Kenneth
London; Regimental Headquarters, Royal Tank Regiment; 1976; ISBN None; 92pp + xvi/1 x clr SIfep/11 x bw PI/3 x bw SI/3 x bw M; s/b; Indexed N; Glossary N; Appendices Y; Bibliography N; 208 x 149 (8vo)
NOTES: Second edition, reprint of the 1965 original, same pagination.

The Tanks
The History of The Royal Tank Regiment, 1945-1975
Macksey, Maj. K.　　　　　　　　　　　　　　　　　TM; IWM; NAM; RMAS; PCL
London; Arms and Armour Press; 1979; ISBN 0-85368-293-3; 304pp/36 x bw PI/8 x bw M; h/b / d/j Black cloth; Indexed Y; Glossary N; Appendices Y; Bibliography Y; 222 x 143 (8vo)
NOTES: Although this book covers the post-war period, it does have a few pages on the run-down of RTR regiments immediately after the war and also rounds off the list of RTR general history books.

The Royal Tank Regiment
A Pictorial History 1916-1987
Forty, George　　　　　　　　　　　　　　　　　　TM; IWM; NAM; RMAS; PCL
Tunbridge Wells; Spellmount Ltd; 1988; ISBN 0-87052-569-7; 256pp/12 x clr PI/11 x clr SI/310 x bw PI/21 x bw SI/2x bw PIfeps/7 x bw M; h/b / d/j Red cloth; Indexed Y; Glossary N; Appendices N; Bibliography Y; 287 x 205 (4to)
NOTES: An overview history with selected engagements being given greater detail. Expansive and useful photographic selection, updated and reprinted 2001. 80pp on WWII.

The Royal Tank Regiment
A Pictorial History 1916-2001
Forty, Lt-Col George TM; NAM; PCL
Tiverton; Halsgrove; 2001; ISBN 1 84114 124 0; 272pp/369 x bw Pl/27 x bw Sl/5 x bw M; h/b / d/j Black cloth; Indexed Y; Glossary N; Appendices N; Bibliography Y; 303 x 215 (4to)
NOTES: Reprint of 1988 edition with amended text and photographic selection (minus the colour section) and brought up to date. 74pp on WWII.

1st Bn, Royal Tank Regiment	1 R Tks

RAC service: 04/04/1939 Post-war.

Regimental publications:
The Circle – 1945/46, became:
Red Lanyard: Magazine of The 1st Royal Tank Regiment
Vol. 2, No. 2* May 1946 to Vol. 6, No. 4 Spring 1949 (Irregular)
*The anomalous numbering is a result of *The Circle* being given the status of volume one after it was converted to the *Red Lanyard*.

Handbook of the First Royal Tank Regiment
Preface by Maxwell, Lt-Col J. P.
Omagh; Strule Press; 1954; ISBN None; See Notes; Rare
NOTES: Pocket history for serving members. (Not physically inspected.)

Handbook of the 1st Royal Tank Regiment
Not stated [See Notes] TM; NAM
No imprint; No imprint (Hendon Printing Works Ltd); 1955; ISBN None; 26pp/2 x Mf; s/b (card); Indexed N; Glossary N; Appendices Y; Bibliography N; 189 x 126 (12mo); Rare
NOTES: Pocket history for serving members, 9pp on WWII. (NAM acknowledges author as J. A. Selway.)

The First
Handbook of the First Royal Tank Regiment
Maxwell, Lt-Col J. P. & Newton, Sgt M.
Omagh; The Strule Press; 1974; ISBN None; 52pp/10 x bw Pl/4 x bw Sl/4 x bw Mf; s/b; Indexed N; Glossary N; Appendices N; Bibliography N; 185 x 127 (12mo); Uncommon
NOTES: Although brief, this little booklet is crammed with useful information on the regiment's wartime history; 11pp on WWII. Includes a list of COs and RSMs 1934 – 1974. Honours/Awards. Notes on dress and a useful bibliography.

The 8.15 to War
Memoirs of a Desert Rat
El Alamein, Wadi Halfa, Tunis, Salerno, Garigliano, Normandy and Holland
Roach, Peter TM; IWM
London; Leo Cooper; 1982; ISBN 0 436 41700 6; 184pp/1 x bw Mbds; h/b / d/j Blue cloth; Indexed N; Glossary N; Appendices N; Bibliography N; 222 x 142 (8vo)

NOTES: The author started the war as a merchant seaman, transferring to the RAC in the summer of 1941. He joined 1RTR mid-1942 in time to take part in the battle of El Alamein. Serving in RHQ has allowed the author to write more about mood and life than fighting equipment and combat action, giving these memoirs a subtly different aspect. The author was wounded twice, late 1944 and spring 1945, both times returning to his regiment.

Better than Riches
Pile, Frederick TM; IWM; NAM
Bishop Auckland; The Pentland Press Ltd; 1992; ISBN 1 85821 005 4; xiii + 107pp/29 x bw Pl/5 x bw SI; h/b / d/j Black cloth; Indexed N; Glossary N; Appendices N; Bibliography N; 216 x 153 (8vo)
NOTES: The author was a squadron commander in Normandy. Commissioned into the RTC in 1935, he had various postings, including a time with 6RTC in pre-war Egypt and a brief spell with 2ERY in 1940. Interesting recollection of meeting with a member of the Tank Board in January 1945 to put across his views that British tanks could not engage German tanks on an equal basis. Includes five interesting sketches showing the deployment of a squadron of tanks in NWE under various scenarios. 30pp on WWII.

A Desert Rat in Holburn Street
McGregor, Duncan
Buchan; Ardo Publishing Company; 1994; ISBN 9518464 42; 140pp/25 x bw Pl/2 x bw SI; h/b Black leatherette; Indexed N; Glossary N; Appendices N; Bibliography N; 215 x 150 (8vo); Uncommon
NOTES: The author volunteered at the start of the war, was called up in August 1940 and in January 1941 was shipped to Egypt as part of the reinforcements for 1RTR. He conveys the fear and draining confusion of being in battle and brings an honesty in communicating his feelings of not being able to carry on. He was later downgraded from front line service after a time in NWE and was admitted to hospital for psychiatric treatment. 66pp on WWII.

An Ordinary 'Knight in Armour'
Knight, R. G. TM
No imprint; No imprint; 1996; ISBN None; 109pp/26 x bw Pl/3 x bw SI; s/b; Indexed N; Glossary N; Appendices N; Bibliography N; 297 x 210 (4to); Rare
NOTES: The author was called up in the spring of 1942, joining 1RGH early 1943. He left the RGH mid-1944 and transferred to 1RTR as a reinforcement in September 1944. He served through to the BAOR.

The First
A Handbook of the History and Customs of the 1st Royal Tank Regiment
No imprint
No imprint; No imprint; 1998; ISBN None; 40pp/No illus.; s/b; Indexed N; Glossary N; Appendices N; Bibliography N; 210 x 150 (8vo)
NOTES: Very brief regimental history with passing reference to 4, 7 and 8RTR which, by this time, had been merged into 1RTR. One chapter lists the citations for VC/GC winners.

Leakey's Luck
A Tank Commander with Nine Lives
Leakey, Rea with Forty, George   TM; IWM
Stroud; Sutton Publishing Limited; 1999; ISBN 0 7509 1731 5; x + 158pp/2 x SI bds/1 x bw PIfep/31 x bw PI/7 x bw M; h/b / d/j Black cloth; Indexed Y; Glossary N; Appendices Y; Bibliography Y; 240 x 160 (8vo)
NOTES: The author was commissioned into the RTC in 1936 and served in several RTR regiments, 4RTC (pre-war), 1RTR (1938-1941), 3RTR (1943), 44RTR (1943/44), 7RTR (1944) and 5RTR (1945), commanding the latter two in NWE at the end of the war. He provides an excellent insight into the life of an officer in Egypt just before and early in the war. War suits some people; Rea Leakey recounts many a military adventure, no surprise therefore, that the end papers reproduce a strip from *The Victor* comic of 1969 showing his feats at Tobruk. One claim to fame was as co-inventor of the sun-compass.

Leakey's Luck
A Tank Commander with Nine Lives
Leakey, Rea; Forty, George (Ed.)
Stroud; Sutton Publishing Limited; 2002; ISBN 0 7509 3195 7; x + 230pp/31 x bw PI; p/b; Indexed Y; Glossary N; Appendices Y; Bibliography Y; 198 x 127 (8vo)
NOTES: Paperback reprint of 1999 first edition, different pagination.

Battles With Panzers
Monty's Tank Battalions 1 RTR & 2 RTR at War
Delaforce, Patrick   TM; IWM; NAM
Stroud; Sutton Publishing Limited; 2003; ISBN 0-7509-3244-9; vii + 248pp/77 x bw PI/3 x bw SI/27 x bw M; h/b / d/j Black cloth; Indexed Y; Glossary N; Appendices Y; Bibliography Y; 240 x 159 (8vo)
NOTES: A history of 1 & 2RTR, both regiments receive a WWI and inter-war summary. Borrows from *Leakey's Luck* for early 1RTR anecdotes and *Seconds Out* for 2RTR history. Incorporates a good quantity of contemporary quotes. Excellent reference for the names and positions held of members of 1RTR, particularly through NWE.
1RTR RoH/Honours/Awards.

...And Then The Music Stopped Playing
Ward, Ken   TM; IWM
Felixstowe; Braiswick at By Design; 2006; ISBN 978-1-898030-11-9; 201pp/39 x bw PI/1 x bw SI; s/b; Indexed N; Glossary N; Appendices N; Bibliography N; 214 x 140 (8vo)
NOTES: With his Jewish parents still in Nazi Germany, the author was evacuated to the UK in September 1939 aged 16. The first half deals with growing up in Nazi Germany, coming to England and volunteering for the armed forces. 73pp cover his experiences as the wireless operator in a Firefly in 7 Tp, A Sqn, 1RTR through NWE.

Memories Are Made of This
Hayter, Peter   IWM
Edgworth; Peter Hayter; 2006; ISBN 0-7223-3817-1 / 978-0-7223-3817-9; 132pp/21 x clr SI/15 x bw PI/3 x bw SI; h/b / d/j Brown cloth; Indexed N; Glossary N; Appendices N; Bibliography N; 219 x 140 (8vo); Uncommon
NOTES: The author joined QOYD in 1938, sailing to Palestine with them in 1940. He left for officer training in India and, after commissioning, was posted to 1RTR mid-1941. He

was captured June 1942. 36pp on life as a POW in Italy and in Germany from late 1943. The illustrations include several coloured sketches by POWs in Italy.

Battles With Panzers
Monty's Tank Battalions 1 RTR & 2 RTR at War
Delaforce, Patrick
Stroud; Amberley Publishing Plc; 2010; ISBN 978-1-84868-818-6; 285pp/1 x bw PIfep/95 x bw PI/3 x bw SI/28 x bw M; s/b; Indexed Y; Glossary N; Appendices Y; Bibliography Y; 234 x 156 (8vo)
NOTES: Softback reprint of 2003 first edition.

A Dalesman's War
Morland, Carole
Kirkby Stephen; Hayloft Publishing Ltd; 2010; ISBN 1 904524 78 8; 58pp/17 x bw PI; s/b; Indexed N; Glossary N; Appendices N; Bibliography N; 210 x 148 (8vo)
NOTES: The author's father joined 24L mid-war as a tank driver. She recounts some early life and his time in Normandy before being transferred to 1RTR upon 24L's disbandment. Not long afterwards he was severely burnt. The final chapters describe his long struggle - two years - before being fully discharged from hospital. The book takes a social commentary stance more than that of pure historical record.

2nd Bn, Royal Tank Regiment — 2 R Tks

RAC service: 04/04/1939   Post-war.

Seconds Out!
A History of the 2nd Royal Tank Regiment
Volume One The First Round
Chadwick, 14483488, Sgt K.   TM; IWM; PCL
No imprint; No imprint; n.d. [c.1969]; ISBN None; 180pp/4 x bw PI/4 x bw SI/1 x bw M; s/b; Indexed N; Glossary N; Appendices N; Bibliography N; 247 x 158 (8vo); Rare
NOTES: Vol. 1 covers WWI and the inter-war years. This draft edition of the history was circulated to the RTR Association branches in early 1969, physically smaller than the official run printed later. The copies are numbered, highest seen = 94. Official publication was due to be in late 1970 with a run of 1000 copies, as yet the detail has not been verified. Reproduced typescript. Vol. 2 starts on p181. IWM copies bound together.

Seconds Out!
A History of the 2nd Royal Tank Regiment
Volume Two The Second Round
Chadwick, 14483488, Sgt K.   IWM; PCL
No imprint; No imprint; n.d. [c.1969]; ISBN None; 276pp/7 x bw PI/4 x bw M; s/b; Indexed N; Glossary N; Appendices N; Bibliography N; 247 x 158 (8vo); Rare
NOTES: A fairly comprehensive history of 2RTR during WWII and beyond; coverage ends in 1961. Includes an interesting chapter on the supply issues facing 'B' Echelon in Burma. Awards, two award citations reproduced. Vol. 2 starts on p181. PCL copy has been rebound. IWM copies bound together.

Seconds Out!
A History of the 2nd Royal Tank Regiment
Volume One The First Round
Chadwick, 14483488, Sgt K. TM; RMAS
No imprint; No imprint; n.d. [c.1970]; ISBN None; 130pp/5 x bw PI/1 x bw M; s/b;
Indexed N; Glossary N; Appendices N; Bibliography N; 296 x 207 (4to); Rare
NOTES: Same content and reproduced typescript as the earlier draft edition but produced to A4 size. Vol. 2 starts on p131.

Seconds Out!
A History of the 2nd Royal Tank Regiment
Volume Two The Second Round
Chadwick, 14483488, Sgt K. TM; RMAS
No imprint; No imprint; n.d. [c.1970]; ISBN None; 305pp/7 x bw PI/4 x bw M; s/b;
Indexed N; Glossary N; Appendices N; Bibliography N; 296 x 207 (4to); Rare
NOTES: Same content and reproduced typescript as the earlier draft edition but produced to A4 size. Vol. 2 starts on p131.

Battlefields of Life
Goddard, Fred TM; IWM
Lewes; The Book Guild Ltd; 1999; ISBN 1 85776 426 9; xv + 187pp/40 x bw PI; h/b / d/j
Green cloth; Indexed N; Glossary N; Appendices N; Bibliography N; 223 x 139 (8vo)
NOTES: The author describes his childhood and first jobs before signing up for the RTC late 1938 aged 21. He tells of his time in action in France in 1940 and then in NA in 1940/41 before being wounded and captured in June 1941. He describes in graphic detail the trauma of being a wounded POW going through the transit process from German capture to Italian hospitalisation. In the last chapters the author recounts normal civilian life up to the end of the 1990s describing how being an invalided war veteran impacts on normal life. 89pp on WWII.

Battles With Panzers
Monty's Tank Battalions 1 RTR & 2 RTR at War
Delaforce, Patrick TM; IWM; NAM
Stroud; Sutton Publishing Limited; 2003; ISBN 0-7509-3244-9; vii + 248pp/77 x bw PI/3 x bw SI/27 x bw M; h/b / d/j Black cloth; Indexed Y; Glossary N; Appendices Y; Bibliography Y; 240 x 159 (8vo)
NOTES: A history of 1 & 2RTR, both regiments receive a WWI and inter-war summary. Borrows from *Leakey's Luck* for early 1RTR anecdotes and *Seconds Out* for 2RTR history. Incorporates a good quantity of contemporary quotes. Excellent reference for the names and positions held of members of 1RTR, particularly through NWE.
1RTR RoH/Honours/Awards.

Battles With Panzers
Monty's Tank Battalions 1 RTR & 2 RTR at War
Delaforce, Patrick
Stroud; Amberley Publishing Plc; 2010; ISBN 978-1-84868-818-6; 285pp/1 x bw PIfep/95 x bw PI/3 x bw SI/28 x bw M; s/b; Indexed Y; Glossary N; Appendices Y; Bibliography Y; 234 x 156 (8vo)
NOTES: Softback reprint of 2003 first edition.

3rd Bn, Royal Tank Regiment — 3 R Tks

RAC service: 04/04/1939 Post-war.

Brazen Chariots
A graphic first-hand account of tank warfare in the Western Desert. November - December 1941.
Crisp, Robert   TM; NAM
London; Frederick Muller Ltd; 1959; ISBN None; 223pp/1 x clr Mfbds; h/b / d/j Blue cloth; Indexed N; Glossary N; Appendices N; Bibliography N; 201 x 137 (8vo); Uncommon
NOTES: Crisp wrote two classic war books. This, his first, tells of his actions in North Africa during Operation Crusader, November 1941, concluding with the author receiving a major head wound and being evacuated. Reprinted three times 1959; also published within several various multi-title books. (*The Gods Were Neutral* is the second book, q.v.)

3rd Royal Tank Regiment
Not stated
None stated; None stated; n.d. [c.1959]; ISBN None; 9pp/2 x bw Pl; s/b; Indexed N; Glossary N; Appendices N; Bibliography N; 194 x 150 (12mo); Uncommon
NOTES: Booklet produced upon the merger of 3RTR & 6RTR to form 3RTR. Four paragraphs cover WWII history.

The Gods Were Neutral
Crisp, Robert   TM
London; Frederick Muller Ltd; 1960; ISBN None; 221pp/16 x bw Pl/2 x bw Mbds; h/b / d/j Blue cloth; Indexed N; Glossary N; Appendices N; Bibliography N; 203 x 133 (8vo); Uncommon
NOTES: Crisp wrote two classic war books. This, his second, tells of his actions in the ill-fated Greek campaign, 1941. One of the most detailed accounts of tanks in action and deservedly a classic. (*Brazen Chariots* is the first book, q.v.)

Warriors for the Working Day
Elstob, Peter
London; Jonathan Cape; 1960; ISBN None; 351pp/No illus.; h/b / d/j Red cloth; Indexed N; Glossary N; Appendices N; Bibliography N; 193 x 128 (12mo); Rare
NOTES: This well regarded novel follows a crew just before D-Day right through to the end of the war in Europe and uses the author's experiences in NWE in 3RTR as the basis – hence its inclusion in this bibliography. The main character is loosely based on the author's own tank commander, Fred 'Buck' Kite, three times MM winner. As a novel it recommends itself due to the author's ability to convey more of the innermost thoughts and fears of tank crewmen. In reality the author served in 4 Tp A Sqn and moved to 1 Tp after his tank was knocked out in Operation Goodwood.

Warriors for the Working Day
Elstob, Peter   NAM
London; The Companion Book Club; 1960; ISBN None; 319pp/No illus.; h/b / d/j Brown cloth; Indexed N; Glossary N; Appendices N; Bibliography N; 190 x 128 (12mo)
NOTES: Hardback reprint of 1960 first edition, different pagination.

Brazen Chariots
An account of tank warfare in the Western Desert, November - December 1941
Crisp, Robert
London; Corgi Books (Transworld Publishers Ltd.); 1960; ISBN None; 284pp/1 x bw M; p/b; Indexed N; Glossary N; Appendices N; Bibliography N; 161 x 108 (16mo); Uncommon
NOTES: Paperback reprint of first edition, different pagination.

Warriors for the Working Day
Elstob, Peter
London; The New English Library Ltd. (Four Square Books); 1962; ISBN None; See Notes; p/b; Indexed N; Glossary N; Appendices N; Bibliography N; Uncommon
NOTES: Paperback reprint of first edition, various reprints itself. (Not physically inspected.)

Brazen Chariots
An account of tank warfare in the Western Desert, November - December 1941
Crisp, Robert
London; Corgi Books (Transworld Publishers Ltd.); 1966; ISBN None; 172pp/1 x bw M; p/b; Indexed N; Glossary N; Appendices N; Bibliography N; 180 x 110 (12mo)
NOTES: Reprint of 1960 paperback edition, different pagination.

Call To Arms
Pyman, G.B.E., K.C.B., D.S.O., M.A., Gen. Sir Harold   TM; IWM; NAM
London; Leo Cooper Ltd; 1971; ISBN 0 85052 063 0; ix + 140pp/25 x bw PI/ 2 x bw SI/4 x bw M; h/b / d/j Brown cloth; Indexed N; Glossary N; Appendices N; Bibliography N; 223 x 144 (8vo)
NOTES: Although these memoirs provide little information of 3RTR (20pp as CO of the regiment), they do provide an insight into a senior commander's attitudes and this author passes interesting comments on senior officers including Montgomery and Rommel.

Warriors for the Working Day
Elstob, Peter
Morley; The Emfield Press (A Morley Book); 1973; ISBN 0 7057 0015 1; 351pp/No illus.; h/b / d/j Orange cloth; Indexed N; Glossary N; Appendices N; Bibliography N; 213 x 134 (8vo); Uncommon
NOTES: Reprint of 1960 first edition, different pagination, with new introduction by the author commenting on the veracity of his story following observations received after the original publication.

Warriors for the Working Day
Elstob, Peter
London; Corgi Books; 1974; ISBN 0 552 09524 9; 318pp/No illus.; p/b; Indexed N; Glossary N; Appendices N; Bibliography N; 178 x 110 (12mo)
NOTES: Paperback reprint of 1960 first edition, different pagination.

The Gods Were Neutral
A Story of the Greek Campaign 1941
Crisp, Robert IWM
London; White Lion Publishers Limited; 1975; ISBN 7274 0032 0; 221pp/16 x bw PI/2 x bw Mbds; h/b / d/j Blue cloth; Indexed N; Glossary N; Appendices N; Bibliography N; 204 x 134 (8vo); Uncommon
NOTES: Hardback reprint of 1960 first edition, same pagination.

From the Desert to the Baltic
Roberts, C.B., D.S.O., M.C., Maj-Gen. Pip TM; IWM
London; William Kimber & Co. Limited; 1987; ISBN 0-7183-0639-2; 256pp/30 x bw PI/15 x bw M; h/b / d/j Red cloth; Indexed Y; Glossary Y; Appendices Y; Bibliography N; 240 x 160 (8vo)
NOTES: The author describes his brief time as CO of 3RTR in the thick of the fighting in May 1942; 30pp. He was wounded in June 1942 and after hospitalisation returned to 3RTR very briefly in July, before being appointed temporary CO of 22AB. Commands included: 3RTR Jan - Jul 1942; 22AB Jul 1942 - Jan 1943; 26AB Mar 1943 - May 1943; 30AB Aug – Oct 1943; 11AD Dec 1943 - end of war.

Panzer Bait
With the 3rd Royal Tank Regiment 1940 - 1944
Moore, William TM; IWM; NAM; RMAS; PCL
London; Leo Cooper; 1991; ISBN 0 85052 3281; x + 205pp/15 x bw PI/9 x bw M; h/b / d/j Red cloth; Indexed Y; Glossary N; Appendices N; Bibliography Y; 240 x 160 (8vo)
NOTES: More a campaign history than a regimental one, it follows 3RTR through France, Greece, North Africa and NWE with contributions from three 3RTR members, Bill Close, Fred 'Buck' Kite and Geordie Reay.

All Valiant Dust
An Irishman Abroad
Ross, Peter IWM; NAM
Dublin; The Lilliput Press Ltd; 1992; ISBN 0 946640 89 0; xiv + 166pp/No illus.; h/b / d/j Black cloth; Indexed N; Glossary N; Appendices N; Bibliography N; 223 x 143 (8vo)
NOTES: After a brief introduction to his early life, the author starts his wartime memoirs with his arrival in Egypt in August 1942. After a short period in Cairo he was posted to the Recce Troop of A Squadron, 3RTR. Wounded at El Alamein, he spent a short spell in hospital and convalescence before returning to 3RTR, having been decorated. Wounded again in Tunisia he returned to 3RTR for a time as Liaison Officer and then OC Recce Troop. When 3RTR returned to the UK in 1943 he transferred to XXX Corps staff and at the end of 1944 transferred to RAC OCTU at Sandhurst to become an instructor there. His first book was *To the Stars...*, q.v., a short history of RAC OCTU.

The Battle of El Alamein And Beyond
Morris, G. A. IWM; NAM
Lewes; The Book Guild Ltd; 1993; ISBN 0 86332 626 9; 191pp/31 x bw PI/11 x bw SI/9 x bw M; h/b / d/j Blue cloth; Indexed N; Glossary N; Appendices N; Bibliography N; 222 x 139 (8vo)

NOTES: The author joined the TA Engineers pre-war. He was commissioned into the RTR October 1940, joined 3RTR early 1942 and fought through to August 1944 when wounded. A rather disjointed set of recollections, WWII covered in the first half of the book.

Accidental Journey
A Cambridge Internee's Memoir of World War II
Lynton, Mark IWM
New York; The Overlook Press; 1995; ISBN 0-87951-577-5; viii + 267pp/No illus.; h/b / d/j Brown cloth/orange paper; Indexed N; Glossary N; Appendices N; Bibliography N; 235 x 154 (8vo)
NOTES: The author was born Max Loewenstein in Germany but moved to England in 1936 to attend Cambridge University. Soon after the outbreak of war he was interned and in mid-1940 transferred to Canada. Returning to England early 1941, he volunteered to join the Pioneer Corps as an 'alien', changing his name to Mark Lynton in 1942 and in the spring of 1943 he joined the RAC. In April 1944 he joined A Sqn, 3RTR. Includes an interesting story about being shown secret German night vision equipment in May 1945. 86pp on service in tanks.

A View From the Turret
A History of the 3rd Royal Tank Regiment in the Second World War
Close, M.C., Major Bill TM; IWM; PCL
Bredon; Dell & Bredon; 1998; ISBN 0-9533359-0-9; xviii + 167pp/18 x bw PI/1 x bw M; h/b / d/j Black cloth; Indexed N; Glossary N; Appendices N; Bibliography N; 224 x 142 (8vo)
NOTES: The author started the war as a sergeant in 3RTR and fought in France, Greece and North Africa, where he was commissioned. By early 1943 in Tunisia he had taken command of A Sqn, commanding it almost to the end of the campaign in NWE. He took over B Sqn February 1945 after returning from a bout of malaria. Wounded several times, including once seriously, he was one of that select band to serve with the regiment throughout the war. Reprinted 2013 under the title *Tank Commander, From the Fall of France to the Defeat of Germany, The Memoirs of Bill Close*, q.v.

Leakey's Luck
A Tank Commander with Nine Lives
Leakey, Rea with Forty, George TM; IWM
Stroud; Sutton Publishing Limited; 1999; ISBN 0 7509 1731 5; x + 158pp/2 x SI bds/1 x bw PIfep/24 x bw PI/7 x bw M; h/b / d/j Black cloth; Indexed Y; Glossary N; Appendices Y; Bibliography Y; 240 x 160 (8vo)
NOTES: The author was commissioned into the RTC in 1936 and served in several RTR regiments, 4RTC (pre-war), 1RTR (1938-1941), 3RTR (1943), 44RTR (1943/44), 7RTR (1944) and 5RTR (1945), commanding the latter two in NWE at the end of the war. He provides an excellent insight into the life of an officer in Egypt just before and early in the war. War suits some people; Rea Leakey recounts many a military adventure, no surprise therefore, that the end papers reproduce a strip from *The Victor* comic of 1969 showing his feats at Tobruk. One claim to fame was as co-inventor of the sun-compass.

ROYAL ARMOURED CORPS: ROYAL TANK REGIMENT

Taming the Panzers
Monty's Tank Battalions 3rd RTR at War
Delaforce, Patrick TM; IWM; RMAS; PCL
Stroud; Sutton Publishing Limited; 2000; ISBN 0 7509 2550 7; vi + 218pp/43 x bw Pl/2 x bw Sl/19 x bw M; h/b / d/j Green cloth; Indexed Y; Glossary N; Appendices Y; Bibliography Y; 240 x 160 (8vo)
NOTES: Focusing on the men, the author tells the story of 3RTR during WWII in great personal detail.

Leakey's Luck
A Tank Commander with Nine Lives
Leakey, Rea; Forty, George (Ed.)
Stroud; Sutton Publishing Limited; 2002; ISBN 0 7509 3195 7; x + 230pp/31 x bw Pl; p/b; Indexed Y; Glossary N; Appendices Y; Bibliography Y; 198 x 127 (8vo)
NOTES: Paperback reprint of 1999 first edition, different pagination.

A View From the Turret
A History of the 3rd Royal Tank Regiment in the Second World War
Close, M.C., Major Bill
Tewkesbury; Dell & Bredon; 2002; ISBN 0-9533359-1-7; xviii + 167pp/18 x bw Pl/1 x bw M; s/b; Indexed N; Glossary N; Appendices N; Bibliography N; 216 x 137 (8vo)
NOTES: Softback reprint of 1998 first edition, same pagination.

Time's Long Shadows
Lewis, Iolo IWM; NAM
No imprint; No imprint (PBF Press Limited - printer); n.d. [c.2002]; ISBN None; viii + 192pp/29 x clr Pl/35 x bw Pl; s/b; Indexed N; Glossary N; Appendices N; Bibliography N; 210 x 148 (8vo); Rare
NOTES: Comprises 58pp of memoirs, 100pp of the author's poems (each with a narrative explanation) plus 34pp of photographs. The author served in B Sqn, 1RGH from 1942 although an injury during training left him temporarily downgraded for front line duties. In July 1944 he was transferred to 3RTR, serving through NWE until wounded for a second time in April 1945.

The Sharp End
A Personal Account of Life in a Tank Unit in the Second World War
Langdon, M.C., Maj. John TM
Private; Private (Printondemand-worldwide, Peterborough - printers); 2003; ISBN 978-0-9566406-0-4; 175pp/3 x clr Pl/23 x bw Pl/1 x bw M; h/b / d/j Pictorial illustration; Indexed N; Glossary Y; Appendices N; Bibliography Y; 239 x 160 (8vo); Uncommon
NOTES: The author was commissioned into 7th Bn The Buffs, which converted to 141 RAC. He then served briefly in 111 RAC and 2RGH before joining 3RTR at his own request in July 1943. He served in NWE on which the book concentrates.

Taming the Panzers
Monty's Tank Battalions 3rd RTR at War
Delaforce, Patrick
Stroud; Sutton Publishing Limited; 2003; ISBN 0 7509 3197 3; viii + 264pp/30 x bw PI/2 x bw SI/18 x bw M; p/b; Indexed Y; Glossary N; Appendices Y; Bibliography Y; 196 x 126 (12mo)
NOTES: Softback reprint of 2000 first edition, different pagination.

A Tankie's Travels
World War II experiences of a former member of the Royal Tank Regiment
Watt, Jock
Bognor Regis; Woodfield Publishing; 2006; See Notes; Indexed N; Glossary N; Appendices N; Bibliography N
NOTES: The author joined 3RTC in 1937 and was the CO's staff car driver in France in 1940. Once back in England he transferred to a tank troop in A Sqn, serving in Greece as a tank commander. He provides great detail of his escape from Greece to NA via Crete. Commissioned early 1943, he returned to fight with the regiment in Tunisia. However, suffering from jaundice he did not follow the regiment to Normandy, being tasked with setting up a gunnery course once he had recovered. He took this over to Europe and commanded it to the end of the war. Provides an excellent insight into why men fight despite the common sense urge to get away. (This edition not physically inspected.)

A Tankie's Travels
World War II experiences of a former member of the Royal Tank Regiment
Watt, Jock TM
Bognor Regis; Woodfield Publishing; 2007; ISBN 1-84683-021-4; iv + 205pp/1 x bw PIfep/16 x bw PI/5 x bw M; p/b; Indexed N; Glossary N; Appendices N; Bibliography N; 205 x 139 (8vo)
NOTES: Softback, third edition, reprint of 2006 first edition.

Taming the Panzers
Monty's Tank Battalions 3rd RTR at War
Delaforce, Patrick
Stroud; Amberley Publishing; 2010; ISBN 978-1-84868-820-9; 255pp/1 x bw PIfep/54 x bw PI/4 x bw SI/19 x bw M; s/b; Indexed Y; Glossary N; Appendices Y; Bibliography Y; 235 x 156 (8vo)
NOTES: Softback reprint of first edition but with increased selection of photographs.

Tank Commander
From the Fall of France to the Defeat of Germany
The Memoirs of Bill Close
Close, Bill TM
Barnsley; Pen & Sword Military; 2013; ISBN 978 1 78159 187 1; x + 164pp/21 x bw PI/1 x bw M; h/b / d/j Black cloth; Indexed N; Glossary N; Appendices N; Bibliography N; 240 x 159 (8vo)
NOTES: Reprint of *A View From the Turret*, q.v., different pagination.

ROYAL ARMOURED CORPS: ROYAL TANK REGIMENT

4th Bn, Royal Tank Regiment — 4 R Tks

RAC service: 04/04/1939   Post-war.*
* The regiment was destroyed at Tobruk June 1942 and placed into suspended animation. In March1945, it was resurrected by disbanding and renaming 144 RAC to 4RTR.

Regimental publications:
The Blue Flash. The Weekly Newspaper of the 4th Royal Tank Regt.
No. 1 March 1945 - n/e, at least to No. 44, 14/09/1946 (Weekly)

Blue Flash
The Story of an Armoured Regiment
Jolly, Alan   TM; IWM; NAM; RMAS; PCL
London; The Solicitors' Law Stationery Society Limited; 1952; ISBN None; xi + 168pp/1 x bw PIfep/11 x bw PI/2 x bw Mf/11 x bw M; h/b / d/j Blue cloth; Indexed Y; Glossary N; Appendices Y; Bibliography N; 233 x 161 (8vo); Rare
NOTES: Essentially a history of 144RAC but with 15pp at the end on 4RTR, following the renaming of 144RAC to 4RTR. Written by one of the regiment's COs. Gale & Polden were to publish originally if 600 copies could be sold. A print run of 600 was deemed too expensive and the book was printed by SLSS Ltd based on the actual orders required and various donations. RoH/Honours/Awards. Came with a loose coloured map *The Campaign in Europe*, 565mm x 265mm.

The Fourth Royal Tank Regiment
A Short History
Not stated
Germany; Aug. Linnemann; 1959; ISBN None; See Notes; V Rare
NOTES: Not physically inspected.

Customs of the 4th Royal Tank Regiment
Not stated [See Notes]
Seremban, Malaysia; Regiment; 1965; ISBN None; 12pp/No illus.; s/b (card); Indexed N; Glossary N; Appendices N; Bibliography N; 233 x 182 (8vo); Rare
NOTES: First edition of the Customs set of booklets. Reproduced typescript potted history for the regiment. Revised and re-published 1967. Author is Capt. N. H. Cocking.

Customs of the 4th Royal Tank Regiment
Not stated [See Notes]
Herford; Regiment; 1967; ISBN None; 20pp/No illus.; s/b (card); Indexed N; Glossary N; Appendices N; Bibliography N; 200 x 162 (8vo); Rare
NOTES: Revised first edition, reproduced typescript. Author is Capt. N. H. Cocking.

The Fourth
A Compendium of the history, properties and customs of The 4th Royal Tank Regiment (Second Edition)
Not stated [See Notes]
Not stated; Regiment; 1970; ISBN None; 44pp/No illus.; s/b (card); Indexed N; Glossary N; Appendices N; Bibliography Y; 222 x 181 (8vo); Uncommon

NOTES: Second edition, reproduced typescript, brought up to date and expanded to include VC citations, 1pp plus chronology on WWII. Author is Capt. M. O. H. Carver.

The Chinese Eye
A Short History of the 4th Royal Tank Regiment
Not stated TM
No imprint; No imprint; n.d. [c.1970]; ISBN None; 66pp/No illus.; s/b (card); Indexed N; Glossary N; Appendices N; Bibliography N; 297 x 210 (4to); V Rare
NOTES: Reproduced typescript. 15pp on WWII.

The Fourth
A Compendium of the History and Customs of The 4th Royal Tank Regiment
Not stated [See Notes]
Not stated; Regiment; 1972; ISBN None; See Notes; Indexed N; Glossary N; Appendices N; Bibliography Y; Rare
NOTES: Third edition, essentially the same content brought up to date. Author is Lt-Col L. A. W. New. (Not physically inspected.)

A Historical Record of the Fourth Royal Tank Regiment
Not stated
No imprint; No imprint; n.d. [c.1975]; ISBN None; 4pp/1 x bw SI; s/b (card); Indexed N; Glossary N; Appendices N; Bibliography N; 209 x 148 (8vo); Rare
NOTES: Simple chronological listing of the regiment's history from 1916 to 1975.

The Fourth
A Compendium of the History and Customs of The 4th Royal Tank Regiment
Not stated [See Notes]
Not stated; Regiment; 1978; ISBN None; See Notes; Indexed N; Glossary N; Appendices N; Bibliography Y; Rare
NOTES: Fourth edition, essentially the same content brought up to date. Author/Editor are Capt. M. N. E. Speller/Lt-Col N. H. Cocking. (Not physically inspected.)

From Battered Victory to Final Triumph
Not stated
Munster; Regiment; 1980; ISBN None; 16pp/No illus.; s/b (card); Indexed N; Glossary N; Appendices N; Bibliography N; 206 x 146 (8vo); Rare
NOTES: Published for the regiment on the fortieth anniversary of 4 & 7RTR's actions at Arras, France. Two chapters on their actions at Arras, 1940 and the crossing of the Rhine, 1945.

The Fourth
A Compendium of the History and Customs of The 4th Royal Tank Regiment (Fifth Edition)
Not stated [See Notes] TM
Not stated; Regiment; 1983; ISBN None; 30pp/No illus.; s/b; Indexed N; Glossary N; Appendices N; Bibliography Y; 209 x 148 (8vo); Rare
NOTES: Fifth edition, essentially the same content brought up to date. 1pp plus chronology on WWII, list of COs and RSMs for 4 & 7RTR. Author/Editor are Capt. M. G. V. Stephenson/Lt-Col P. J. Sanders.

ROYAL ARMOURED CORPS: ROYAL TANK REGIMENT 89

One Man's Desert
The Story of Capt. Phillip Gardner VC, MC
Woods, Rex   TM
London; William Kimber & Co. Limited; 1986; ISBN 0-7183-0612-0; 208pp/30 x bw PI/2 x bw SI/9 x bw M; h/b / d/j Brown cloth; Indexed Y; Glossary N; Appendices N; Bibliography N; 239 x 155 (8vo)
NOTES: This book tells of the wartime experiences of RTR VC winner P. .J 'Pip' Gardner. PJG joined the TA pre-war and signed up with the WD in September 1939. After a brief foray with the Commandos he was posted back to the RAC and in April 1941 to A Sqn, 4RTR. Includes many quotes from PJG's letters home. Capt. P. J. Gardner, MC won the VC 23 November 1941 for his actions during the breakout from Tobruk. The citation is reproduced, as is his own letter home describing the action. Early 1942 PJG transferred to 32ATB's staff and was taken prisoner in July 1942. The second half of the book deals with his captivity under the Italians and an adventurous four month escape attempt. After re-capture he spent the remainder of the war in captivity in Germany.

Voyage to the Desert
An Account of the Voyage of 4 Royal Tank Regiment & 4 NZ Fd Arty Regiment in HMT City of London from Liverpool to Suez in the winter of 1940-41
Vaux, Peter   TM
Fleet; Vaux Publications; 1999; ISBN None; 32pp/5 x bw SI/1 x bw M; s/b; Indexed N; Glossary N; Appendices N; Bibliography N; 210 x 150 (8vo); Uncommon
NOTES: Privately printed for the benefit of service charities, the author recounts his experiences of the journey from Liverpool to Port Tewfik, interrupted by an encounter with the German cruiser Admiral Hipper. Reprinted 2002 - identical except for rear cover dropping map for blurb. Reprint includes addendum slip for p23 tipped in.

5th Bn, Royal Tank Regiment	5 R Tks

RAC service: 04/04/1939   Post-war.

Regimental publications:
VeRiToR. The Fortnightly Review of The Fifth Royal Tank Regiment
Vol. 1, No. 1 15 Mar 1946 to Vol. 3, No. 2 Nov 1947 (Fortnightly)
(No. 1 did not have a formal title, announcing instead that the title would be chosen from suggestions. *VeRiToR* being adopted from No. 2. The artwork for every cover is different.)

Prisoner From Alamein
Stone, Brian   TM; IWM; NAM; RMAS
London; H. F. & G. Witherby; 1944; ISBN None; 189pp/1 x bw PIfep/2 x bw PI/1 x bw Mfbds; h/b / d/j Red cloth; Indexed N; Glossary N; Appendices N; Bibliography N; 181 x 127 (12mo)
NOTES: The author served in 5RTR in the Middle East where he was badly wounded, losing a leg. The account is full of well observed comment and graphically describes being wounded, being saved by a German medical team and his subsequent life as a wounded POW under the Italians.

Wardrop of the Fifth
The Diary of Sgt J. R. Wardrop (Jake) of 5th Royal Tank Regiment Nov 1940 - Jan 1944
Wardrop, Jake; Garnett, Jack (Ed.) TM; IWM
No imprint; No imprint (See Notes); 1968; ISBN None; iv + 98pp/7 x bw PI/1 x bw Mf; s/b; Indexed N; Glossary N; Appendices N; Bibliography N; 197 x 134 (12mo); Uncommon
NOTES: Prompted by the disbandment of 5RTR due in 1969. 1000 copies were printed by the Publications Wing RAC Centre - 700 went to 5RTR, 100 to the OCA and 100 to the Tank Museum for sale by donation. Although prepared in 1962, it did not see publication until 1968. (Note: the 2009 Amberley edition includes a missing part of the diary.) Written by the editor from diary notes kept by Jake Wardrop, from October 1940 through to January 1944 in Italy. Jake Wardrop continued to fight in NWE until his death in Germany just weeks before the end of the war. He commanded a Firefly in C Sqn and in April 1945 was killed in action. Reproduced typescript, the original of which is with the Tank Museum. IWM copy is missing the title page and end folding map; due to the title page missing, it is incorrectly dated and titled (as *Red and Blue*) in their listing. The title page is prone to becoming detached due to the simple glue binding employed.

Track Fax
Drew, Brig. Dinham TM
No imprint; No imprint; n.d. [c.1980s]; ISBN None; 36pp/1 x bw SI; s/b; Indexed N; Glossary N; Appendices N; Bibliography N; 162 x 123 (16mo); V Rare
NOTES: Written as a supplement to Liddel Hart's RTR History, the author attempts to clarify the actions of 5RTR in WWII vs. that written by Liddell Hart.

Tanks Across the Desert
The War Diary of Jake Wardrop
Wardrop, Jake; Forty, George (Ed.) TM; IWM
London; William Kimber & Co. Limited; 1981; ISBN 0-7183-0288-5; 222pp/1 x bw PIfep/87 x bw PI/1 x bw SI/1 x bw M; h/b / d/j Brown cloth; Indexed Y; Glossary N; Appendices Y; Bibliography Y; 239 x 158 (8vo)
NOTES: This is a reproduction of the 1968 publication of Jake Wardrop's diary, now with an editor's additional narrative providing a context to the events experienced by JW. There is also an introduction providing a background on JW's early life. Contains a larger photographic selection than the reprinted version by Sutton 2003. (Note: the 2009 Amberley edition, q.v., includes a missing part of the diary.)

Tank Soldier
The Fight to Liberate Europe 1944
Smith, Norman TM; IWM; NAM
Lewes; The Book Guild Limited; 1989; ISBN 0 86332 370 7; 215pp/31 x bw PI/21 x bw SI/6 x bw M; h/b / d/j Blue leatherette; Indexed N; Glossary N; Appendices N; Bibliography N; 218 x 133 (8vo); Uncommon
NOTES: The author was an operator/loader in a B Sqn Cromwell tank and landed with the regiment in Normandy on 7 June 1944. He joined the RAC in January 1943 and was posted to 5RIDG upon completion of training. In January 1944 he was posted to 5RTR. Full of observations on the daily life that faced a tank crew in action together with

comment on higher command. The author of *Press On Regardless*, q.v., was the author's tank commander from late 1944.

Leakey's Luck
A Tank Commander with Nine Lives
Leakey, Rea with Forty, George TM; IWM
Stroud; Sutton Publishing Limited; 1999; ISBN 0 7509 1731 5; x + 158pp/2 x SI bds/1 x bw PIfep/24 x bw PI/7 x bw M; h/b / d/j Black cloth; Indexed Y; Glossary N; Appendices Y; Bibliography Y; 240 x 160 (8vo)
NOTES: The author was commissioned into the RTC in 1936 and served in several RTR regiments, 4RTC (pre-war), 1RTR (1938-1941), 3RTR (1943), 44RTR (1943/44), 7RTR (1944) and 5RTR (1945), commanding the latter two in NWE at the end of the war. He provides an excellent insight into the life of an officer in Egypt just before and early in the war. War suits some people; Rea Leakey recounts many a military adventure, no surprise therefore, that the end papers reproduce a strip from *The Victor* comic of 1969 showing his feats at Tobruk. One claim to fame was as co-inventor of the sun-compass.

Leakey's Luck
A Tank Commander with Nine Lives
Leakey, Rea; Forty, George (Ed.)
Stroud; Sutton Publishing Limited; 2002; ISBN 0 7509 3195 7; x + 230pp/31 x bw PI; p/b; Indexed Y; Glossary N; Appendices Y; Bibliography Y; 198 x 127 (8vo)
NOTES: Paperback reprint of 1999 first edition, different pagination.

Tanks Across the Desert
The War Diary of Jake Wardrop
Wardrop, Jake; Forty, George (Ed.) TM
Stroud; Sutton Publishing Limited; 2003; ISBN 0-7509-3253-8; xvi + 160pp/31 x bw PI; h/b / d/j Black cloth; Indexed Y; Glossary N; Appendices Y; Bibliography Y; 240 x 159 (8vo)
NOTES: Reprinted version of Kimber's 1981 edition with a smaller photographic selection. (Note: the 2009 Amberley edition, q.v., includes a missing part of the diary.)

Press On Regardless
The Story of the Fifth Royal Tank Regiment in World War Two
Wilson, Edward TM; IWM; RMAS; PCL
Staplehurst; Spellmount Limited; 2003; ISBN 1-86227-217-4; xviii + 526pp/15 x bw PI/1 x bw SI/8 x bw M; h/b / d/j Blue cloth; Indexed Y; Glossary N; Appendices Y; Bibliography Y; 240 x 162 (8vo)
NOTES: The author served in the Canadian Army from 1941, transferring to the British Army and 5RTR in 1944. A comprehensive and respected history, extremely detailed with very useful references to the tanks employed by the regiment. Each chapter concludes with a few paragraphs covering aspects of the period from the German side. The author was the tank commander of Norman Smith, author of *Tank Soldier*, q.v.

The Long Drive
Normandy to Hamburg 1944 - 1945
An Illustrated Journey
Huett, Denis
No imprint; No imprint; 2004; ISBN None; 161pp/8 x clr PI/157 x bw PI/1 x bw SI/1 x clr M/1 x bw M; Comb; Indexed N; Glossary N; Appendices N; Bibliography N; 210 x 297 (8vo); Uncommon
NOTES: The author used a liberated German camera to photograph his journey through NWE 1944/45 and has profusely illustrated this self-published book with these photographs. They are accompanied by explanatory text and a narrative of his journey. He joined C Sqn in January 1944 as a gunner/operator and served in NWE in a Sherman Firefly.

Jake Wardrop's Diary
A Tank Regiment Sergeant's Story
Forty, George   IWM
Stroud; Amberley Publishing Plc; 2009; ISBN 978 1 84868 580 2; 249pp/62 x bw PI/10 x bw M; s/b; Indexed N; Glossary N; Appendices Y; Bibliography Y; 246 x 172 (8vo)
NOTES: Following the family discovery of Jake Wardrop's diaries covering the period from January 1944 to the end of 1944, the author has published this updated account reproducing those diary entries. This 'second' diary has a different pace and vividly conveys the thoughts of a battle hardened, war weary sergeant tank commander. Sadly there is no diary from 1945, probably lost during shipping home.

The Tank War
The Men, the Machines and the Long Road to Victory
Urban, Mark   TM; RMAS; PCL
London; Little, Brown; 2013; ISBN 978-1-4087-0363-2; xv + 415pp/40 x bw PI/2 x bw Mfep/14 x bw M; h/b / d/j Brown cloth; Indexed Y; Glossary N; Appendices N; Bibliography Y; 240 x 160 (8vo)
NOTES: The author's aim was to write about a typical regiment that went through the whole war. For this he chose 5RTR. Using many veterans' interviews, this is a highly detailed and valuable addition to the works relating to the regiment. Good selection of veteran supplied photos.

The Tank War
The Men, the Machines and the Long Road to Victory
Urban, Mark
London; Little, Brown; 2013; ISBN 978-1-4087-0364-9; xv + 415pp/40 x bw PI/2 x bw Mfep/14 x bw M; p/b; Indexed Y; Glossary N; Appendices N; Bibliography Y
NOTES: Paperback reprint of hardback first edition, same pagination. (Not physically inspected.)

The Tank War
The British Band of Brothers - One Tank Regiment's World War II
Urban, Mark
London; Abacus; 2014; ISBN 978-0-349-00014-5; xv + 415pp/40 x bw PI/2 x bw Mfep/14 x bw M; p/b; Indexed Y; Glossary N; Appendices N; Bibliography Y
NOTES: Paperback reprint of 2013 hardback first edition, same pagination. (Not physically inspected.)

6th Bn, Royal Tank Regiment — 6 R Tks

RAC service: 04/04/1939 Post-war.

The Lost Years
Miller, J. F. (Peter) — TM
No imprint; No imprint; n.d.; ISBN None; 111pp/1 x clr PI/15 x clr SI/4 x bw PI/4 x bw SI/3 x clr M; h/b Green cloth; Indexed N; Glossary N; Appendices N; Bibliography N; Rare
NOTES: The author sailed to Egypt with 6RTR in mid-1941 and was captured 21 November 1941. The bulk of the book deals with the author's thoughts as a POW of the Italians and then the Germans.

7th Bn, Royal Tank Regiment — 7 R Tks

RAC service: 04/04/1939 Post-war.*
* 7RTR was destroyed at Tobruk in June 1942. Reconstituted 1 April 1943 by renaming 10RTR.

"A" Squadron Diary
7th Royal Tank Regiment
Not stated [See Notes] — TM; IWM; NAM; PCL
Krefeld, Germany; Scherpe; 1946; ISBN None; 72pp/10 x bw PI/1 x bw PIf/1 x bw SI/1 x bw M; h/b Buff paper; Indexed N; Glossary N; Appendices Y; Bibliography N; 215 x 156 (8vo); V Rare
NOTES: The first chapter provides the background to 7RTR forming from the renaming of 10RTR in 1943. (7RTR had been destroyed at Tobruk in 1942.) The book is written by several authors, the squadron CO plus some of his officers, and forms a detailed chronological account of the squadron's actions from the journey to Normandy to the end of the war in NWE. Appendices include RoH and list of squadron members with their full addresses. Fold out squadron photograph from May 1944. Copies at PCL and IWM have been rebound. Authors are Maj. R. A. Joscelyne; Capt. R. A. Pearson; Capt. G. L. Davey & Lt F. C. Wallerstein.

A Brief History of the 7th Royal Tank Regiment
November 1916 - November 1948
Not stated — TM
No imprint; No imprint (F. J. Parsons Ltd, London - printers); 1948; ISBN None; 8pp/No illus.; s/b; Indexed N; Glossary N; Appendices N; Bibliography N; 247 x 186 (8vo); Rare
NOTES: A summary of the regiment's history starting from WWI, 6pp on WWII.

Dan, Dan, The 'I' Tank Man
Williams, R. W. S. TM; IWM; NAM
Ilfracombe; Williams, R. W. S.; 1991; ISBN 0 7223 2569-X; 127pp/11 x bw PI/3 x bw M; s/b; Indexed N; Glossary N; Appendices N; Bibliography N; 211 x 136 (8vo)
NOTES: The author joined 7RTR in August 1938 (D Sqn) and served in France in 1940 as a driver, escaping back to England from Dunkirk. He later journeyed to Egypt with the regiment and the bulk of the book describes his experiences with D Sqn during the first siege of Tobruk. The book concludes with the destruction of 7RTR and the author's capture after the second siege of Tobruk. Pasted in Erratum on title page.

Never a Dull Moment!
Dolby, Eddie TM
No imprint; No imprint; n.d. [c.1994]; ISBN None; 174pp/107 x bw PI/1 x bw SI/3 x bw M; s/b; Indexed N; Glossary N; Appendices Y; Bibliography N; 207 x 147 (8vo)
NOTES: The author volunteered for service at the outbreak of war. A brief overview of the author's time with 7RTR plus introductory comment on 107 RAC before he transferred to 7RTR in December 1943. Served in NWE as the Recce Troop Officer and in 1945 as Regimental Liaison Officer. Bulk of book deals with his post-war career. 51pp on WWII.

Leakey's Luck
A Tank Commander with Nine Lives
Leakey, Rea with Forty, George IWM
Stroud; Sutton Publishing Limited; 1999; ISBN 0 7509 1731 5; x + 158pp/2 x SI bds/1 x bw PIfep/24 x bw PI/7 x bw M; h/b / d/j Black cloth; Indexed Y; Glossary N; Appendices Y; Bibliography Y; 240 x 160 (8vo)
NOTES: The author was commissioned into the RTC in 1936 and served in several RTR regiments, 4RTC (pre-war), 1RTR (1938-1941), 3RTR (1943), 44RTR (1943/44), 7RTR (1944) and 5RTR (1945), commanding the latter two in NWE at the end of the war. He provides an excellent insight into the life of an officer in Egypt just before and early in the war. War suits some people; Rea Leakey recounts many a military adventure, no surprise therefore, that the end papers reproduce a strip from *The Victor* comic of 1969 showing his feats at Tobruk. One claim to fame was as co-inventor of the sun-compass.

Leakey's Luck
A Tank Commander with Nine Lives
Leakey, Rea; Forty, George (Ed.)
Stroud; Sutton Publishing Limited; 2002; ISBN 0 7509 3195 7; x + 230pp/31 x bw PI; p/b; Indexed Y; Glossary N; Appendices Y; Bibliography Y; 198 x 127 (8vo)
NOTES: Paperback reprint of 1999 first edition, different pagination.

8th Bn, Royal Tank Regiment — 8 R Tks

RAC service: 04/04/1939 Post-war.

Brief History of the 8th Royal Tank Regiment
Not stated TM
No imprint; No imprint; 1956; ISBN None; 8pp/No illus.; s/b (card); Indexed N; Glossary N; Appendices N; Bibliography N; 125 x 103 (32mo); Rare
NOTES: Very brief and pocket sized history.

Armoured Odyssey
8th Royal Tank Regiment in The Western Desert 1941-42, Palestine, Syria, Egypt, 1943-44, Italy, 1944-45
Hamilton, M.C., Stuart TM; IWM; RMAS; PCL
London; Tom Donovan Publishing Ltd; 1995; ISBN 1-871085-30-6; xiii + 161pp/43 x bw PI/10 x bw M; h/b / d/j Brown cloth; Indexed Y; Glossary N; Appendices N; Bibliography N; 241 x 160 (8vo)
NOTES: The author left 5RTR to go to officer training in January 1940. He was posted to 8RTR, B Sqn, and travelled to Egypt with them in mid-1941. He became the squadron's Recce Officer, and later OC, and was in charge of B Sqn when it was re-equipped with Crocodiles in February 1945. A classic graphic narrative, demonstrating how physically pushed men were. RoH/Awards.

Hilda's Boys
The Story of the 8th Royal Tank Regiment
Gudgin, Peter
No imprint; No imprint; 1999; ISBN None; xiv + 223pp + 76pp of maps and photographs/Index of 32pp/1 x clr PI/119 x bw PI/8 x bw M; s/b; Indexed Y; Glossary N; Appendices Y; Bibliography Y; 297 x 210 (8vo); Rare
NOTES: Using the War Diaries, veteran interviews and quotations from Stuart Hamilton's book, see above, this is an extensive history of the regiment from WWI to the merger with 5RTR in 1960. Provides serving officer lists at various stages throughout the war. Appendices include RoH/Honours/Awards, lists of officers serving with the regiment plus an Infantry Tank Regiment basic WE. 90pp on WWII. The 32pp index is bound separately.

9th Bn, Royal Tank Regiment — 9 R Tks

RAC service: 27/11/1940 Post-war.

Regimental publications:
9th Bn Royal Tank Regiment Newsletter
November 1944, January and March 1945 – total of three published, not numbered.

9th Battalion Royal Tank Regiment June 1944 - May 1945
Not stated TM
No imprint (Germany); No imprint (Printing & Stationery Services BAOR); 1945; ISBN None; 17pp/No illus.; s/b; Indexed N; Glossary N; Appendices N; Bibliography N; 175 x 139 (12mo); V Rare
NOTES: Memorial service booklet published for the service on 17 June 1945 with a three page operations summary. Incorporates RoH from 1944 memorial, Honours/Awards. 1000 copies printed.

Before I Forget
Young, Robert IWM
Oxford; Robert Young; 1990; ISBN None; 290pp/No illus.; s/b; Indexed Y; Glossary N; Appendices Y; Bibliography N; 197 x 130 (12mo); Uncommon
NOTES: The author served as an officer in 8th Bn Essex Regiment, transferring to 153 RAC upon the 8th's conversion. He was OC 2 Tp, B Sqn and when 153 RAC was disbanded the author transferred to 9RTR (taking command of 12 Tp, C Sqn), rather than to the common destination of 107 RAC or 147 RAC. 64pp on his time in tanks. Forthright and occasionally indignant recollections of his wartime experiences. IWM copy rebound.

One Day at a Time
A Diary of the Second World War
6th June 1944 - 17th April 1945
Greenwood, Richard Trevor; Greenwood, Barry (Ed.) TM
No imprint; No imprint; 1994; ISBN None; 138pp/6 x bw Pl/1 x bw SI; Comb; Indexed N; Glossary Y; Appendices N; Bibliography N; 297 x 210 (4to); V Rare
NOTES: First published in 1988 for family only, this second, privately printed (approx. 80 copies), public edition has been edited by the author's son and includes several photographs found after the first edition. The author served as a sergeant tank commander in C Sqn throughout the NWE campaign and the diary covers, almost uninterrupted, 6 June 1944 – 17 April 1945. This is a verbatim transcription of the diary, edited only to correct spelling errors and add occasional additional editorial comment. By reproducing verbatim, the staccato nature of the diary reveals the vital nature of his experiences. Edited and reprinted 2012 as *D-Day To Victory, The Diaries of a British Tank Commander*, q.v.

Tank Tracks
9th Battalion Royal Tank Regiment at War 1940-45
Beale, Peter TM; IWM; NAM; PCL
Stroud; Alan Sutton Publishing Ltd; 1995; ISBN 0-7509-0880-7; xiv + 238pp/59 x bw Pl/27 x bw M; h/b / d/j Black cloth; Indexed Y; Glossary Y; Appendices Y; Bibliography Y; 254 x 177 (4to)
NOTES: Highly detailed wartime history of the regiment using many contributions from ex-9RTR members. The narrative is divided into an overview, entries from the War Diary, then personal recollections, providing a highly readable division of the phases and operations in which the regiment took part. Extensive appendices including a detailed casualty list. RoH/Honours/Awards.

ROYAL ARMOURED CORPS: ROYAL TANK REGIMENT

Tank Tracks
9th Battalion Royal Tank Regiment at War 1940-45
Beale, Peter
Stroud; Buddings Books (Alan Sutton Publishing Ltd); 1997; ISBN 1-84015-003-3; xiv + 238pp/59 x bw PI/27 x bw M; h/b / d/j Illustrated as d/j; Indexed Y; Glossary Y; Appendices Y; Bibliography Y; 248 x 174 (8vo)
NOTES: Hardback reprint of 1995 first edition, same pagination.

Tank Tracks
9th Battalion Royal Tank Regiment at War 1940-45
Beale, Peter
Stroud; Alan Sutton Publishing Ltd; 1997; ISBN 0-7509-1519-6; xiv + 238pp/59 x bw PI/27 x bw M; s/b; Indexed Y; Glossary Y; Appendices Y; Bibliography Y; 244 x 172 (8vo)
NOTES: Softback reprint of 1995 first edition, same pagination.

D-Day To Victory
The Diaries of a British Tank Commander
Greenwood, Sgt. Trevor; Partington, S.V. (Ed.) IWM
London; Simon & Schuster UK Ltd; 2012; ISBN 978-1-47111-422-9; v + 407pp/27 x bw PI/1 x bw SI/9 x bw M; h/b / d/j; Indexed Y; Glossary Y; Appendices N; Bibliography N; 222 x 140 (8vo)
NOTES: *One Day At a Time*, Sgt Greenwood's diary, was privately published in 1994. This third edition, formally published in association with the IWM, reproduces the same diary content with minor tidying to expand some abbreviations and update previous transcription assumptions. In addition there is a 30pp summary of 9RTR's role in NWE written by John Delaney of the IWM. Expanded selection of photographs.

D-Day To Victory
The Diaries of a British Tank Commander
Greenwood, Sgt. Trevor; Partington, S.V. (Ed.) RMAS
London; Simon & Schuster UK Ltd; 2012; ISBN 978-1-47111-068-9; v + 407pp/27 x bw PI/1 x bw SI/9 x bw M; p/b; Indexed Y; Glossary Y; Appendices N; Bibliography N; 198 x 130 (8vo)
NOTES: Paperback reprint of 2012 edition, same pagination.

10th Bn, Royal Tank Regiment — 10 R Tks

RAC service: 11/1940 01/04/1943*
* 1 April 1943 10RTR renamed 7RTR which was reconstituted following its destruction at Tobruk in June 1942.

No publications established – see section foreword.

11th Bn, Royal Tank Regiment — 11 R Tks

RAC service: 01/01/1941 Post-war.

11th Royal Tank Regiment
Regimental History
Howard Jones, Maj. S (Ed.); Andrews, Capt. K. S. & Barlett, Capt. W. J. C. (Contr.) TM
No imprint; No imprint; n.d. [c.1940s]; ISBN None; 44pp/3 x bw Mf/3 x bw M; s/b;
Indexed N; Glossary N; Appendices Y; Bibliography N; 329 x 202 (8vo); Rare
NOTES: Reproduced typescript - covers the regiment's formation, CDL training, conversion to Buffalos and placing into suspended animation.

The Wartime Adventures of B Squadron 'Corpse'
Wilson, Maurice TM; IWM; NAM
Tunbridge Wells; Parapress Ltd; 1997; ISBN 1-898594-30-9; vi + 138pp/12 x bw PI/1 x
bw SI; s/b; Indexed N; Glossary N; Appendices N; Bibliography N; 215 x 135 (8vo)
NOTES: The author joined 11RTR in January 1941. His memoirs cover the remainder of the war and take the approach of an intellectual vs. the obtuseness of the army, together with several historical asides relating to the locations of the regiment.

A Wartime Voyage To Egypt
From the wartime diary of Monty Rossiter Sergeant - 11 Battalion Royal Tank Regiment
Rossiter, Keith TM
No imprint; No imprint; 2009; ISBN None; 36pp/1 x clr PI/2 x bw PI; s/b; Indexed N;
Glossary N; Appendices N; Bibliography N; 210 x 147 (8vo); Uncommon
NOTES: The author has transcribed his late father's diary covering July 1942 to December 1942, the voyage to and arrival in Egypt.

12th Bn, Royal Tank Regiment — 12 R Tks

RAC service: 12/1940 Post-war.

No publications established – see section foreword.

Key to Book Entries
Book Title and Sub-title(s)
Author Museum Holdings
Place of Publication; Publisher; Date of Publication; ISBN; Pages/Illustrations; Binding;
Indexed; Glossary; Appendices; Bibliography; Size (in mm); Availability
NOTES:

Section VI

Royal Armoured Corps: Reconnaissance Corps

With changes to the role of the mechanized cavalry reconnaissance regiments, most had joined the RAC, and with experience from the British Expeditionary Force, the War Office looked at how to fulfil the needs of infantry division reconnaissance.

The result was the creation of the Reconnaissance Corps, officially raised on 14th January 1941. Battalions were formed over the coming months and the first to see action was the 50th Bn, Reconnaissance Corps at the battle of Knightsbridge in 1942. Over the course of four years the Corps would see action in nearly all theatres, from North Africa and Europe to Singapore and Burma.

The progression toward an armoured role, rather than one of infantry support, was given emphasis in 1942. Officially introduced in the summer, the Recce Corps' nomenclature changed from battalion/company/etc., to regiment/squadron/etc.

The Recce Corps was incorporated into the Royal Armoured Corps on 1st January 1944. A measure of the regard and standing it had achieved in that short period is demonstrated by the fact that it retained its corps designation, rather than being absorbed as the Reconnaissance Regiment, one option proposed at the time. Apart from the adoption of the black beret from early 1944 it also retained its dress distinctions; some regiments took as long as a year to change their khaki berets for black ones.

GHQ Liaison Regiment (Phantom), formerly having no true parent organisation apart from the War Office, had been transferred into the Recce Corps just prior to the Corps' incorporation into the RAC.

After the war, the need to reduce the army and the perception that reconnaissance was integral to the RAC, meant that a specific corps was no longer needed. The Corps was disbanded on 1st August 1946.

(The 2nd Derbyshire Yeomanry was an honorary regiment of the Recce Corps and books listed for it can be found in 'Section VIII – TA Yeomanry'.)

Royal Armoured Corps: Reconnaissance Corps

Corps publications:
The Reconnaissance Journal. Official Organ of the Comrade's Association.
Vol. 1, No. 1 June-August 1944 to Vol. 6, No. 2 Summer 1950 plus Memorial Number Summer 1950 (Quarterly).
Vol. 6, No. 2 was a supplement to the Memorial Number and was a simple copied typescript of 12pp.
The Reconnaissance Weekly [Training Centre's weekly newspaper]
Vol. 1, No. 1 to unknown (at least late 1945) (Weekly)

The Reconnaissance Job
Not stated   TM
No imprint; Reconnaissance Corps Training Centre; n.d. [c.1945]; ISBN None; 8pp/No illus.; s/b (card); Indexed N; Glossary N; Appendices N; Bibliography N; 184 x 121 (12mo); V Rare
NOTES: A booklet produced for Recce Corps recruits providing them with a concise history of the Corps to date.

This Band Of Brothers
A History of the Reconnaissance Corps of the British Army
Taylor, Jeremy   TM; NAM
Bristol; The White Swan Press Ltd; 1947; ISBN None; 271pp/24 x bw Pl/9 x bw M; p/b; Indexed Y; Glossary N; Appendices Y; Bibliography N; 180 x 124 (12mo); Rare
NOTES: The author served in the Recce Corps and his narrative imbues a sense of immediacy to events that took place decades ago. A highly competent, expansive work. The book follows the progress of the war through the theatres starting with the Corps' first action in NA by 50R. All the regiments that fought are featured thus. Appendices include organisation of a Recce regiment, brief service overview of each regiment with lists of COs, ORs' awards and ORs' RoH, plus awards and RoH for all officers. Paperback 'subscription' edition. (Reference may be seen to *"41" The History of the Reconnaissance Corps*, which was the working title of this official history.)

This Band Of Brothers
A History of the Reconnaissance Corps of the British Army
Taylor, Jeremy   TM; IWM; PCL
Bristol; The White Swan Press Ltd; 1947; ISBN None; 271pp/24 x bw Pl/9 x bw M; h/b / d/j Black cloth; Indexed Y; Glossary N; Appendices Y; Bibliography N; 185 x 129 (12mo); V Rare
NOTES: Cloth bound hardback 'public' edition, same pagination, published after the paperback had been sent to subscribers. Dust-jacket is extremely rare.

Toller Reports
Taylor, Jeremy   IWM
Bristol; The White Swan Press Ltd; 1947; ISBN None; 95pp/18 x bw SI; h/b Brown cloth/cream paper; Indexed N; Glossary N; Appendices N; Bibliography N; 251 x 186 (4to); V Rare
NOTES: Advertised for sale in the Summer 1947 Recce Journal as 'a collection of the well

known series of humorous articles on Army life which appeared in *Punch* during the war.' Life in the Recce Corps forms the background for most of the articles.

Before 41
An enquiry into the origins of the Reconnaissance Corps
McEwen Charlish, M. IWM; RMAS
No imprint; M. McEwen Charlish; 1990; ISBN None; iv + 31pp/No illus.; Comb; Indexed N; Glossary N; Appendices Y; Bibliography Y; 297 x 210 (4to); Uncommon
NOTES: The author served in 43R and looks here at the pre-history of the Recce Corps through reference to National Archive documents. The title is a play on before 1941 when the Corps was raised and a pun on the Recce Corps' Unit Serial Number of '41'. One chapter looks at how the Corps' distinctive badge came about.

Only the Enemy In Front
(Every other beggar behind...) The Recce Corps at War 1940 - 1946
Doherty, Richard TM; IWM; NAM; PCL
London; BCA / Tom Donovan Publishing; 1994; ISBN 1 871085 18 7; x + 286pp/22 x bw PI/15 x bw M; h/b / d/j Green cloth; Indexed Y; Glossary N; Appendices N; Bibliography N; 240 x 160 (8vo)
NOTES: The comprehensive account of the Recce Corps during WWII. Includes many quotations from veterans and war diaries.

The British Reconnaissance Corps in WWII (Osprey Elite 152)
Doherty, Richard; Chapman, Rob (Illus.); Windrow, Martin (Ed.) TM; RMAS; PCL
Wellingborough; Osprey Publishing Ltd; 2007; ISBN 978 1 84603 122 9; 64pp/52 x bw PI/8 x clr P; s/b; Indexed Y; Glossary N; Appendices N; Bibliography Y; 248 x 184 (8vo)
NOTES: From the Osprey Elite series, no. 152, providing an overview of the Corps. Extremely well illustrated including the series' familiar 8pp colour illustrations.

Only the Enemy In Front
(Every other beggar behind...)
Doherty, Richard
Stroud; Spellmount Publishers; 2008; ISBN 978 1 86227 443 3; x + 310pp/56 x bw PI/4 x bw SI/16 x bw M; s/b; Indexed Y; Glossary N; Appendices Y; Bibliography N; 235 x 155 (8vo)
NOTES: Same narrative content as 1994 first edition but with much expanded photographic selection and appendices including summary service history of each regiment, war establishments and Honours/Awards.

1st Reconnaissance Regiment — 1 RecceRegt

Date raised/disbanded: 08/01/1941   15/05/1946
RAC service: 01/01/1944   Post-war.

For the Duration
The Journal of a Conscript 1941-1946
Nisbett, Gordon   TM; IWM
Bishop Auckland; The Pentland Press Ltd; 1996; ISBN 1 85821 346 0; xii + 175pp/
1 x bw PIfep/1 x bw SI/1 x bw M; h/b / d/j Black cloth; Indexed N; Glossary N;
Appendices N; Bibliography N; 215 x 153 (8vo)
NOTES: The author registered for service in 1940 aged 18, racked with self-doubt about being capable of joining the army. In October 1941 he joined the Recce Corps, initially with 48 Coy. He soon transferred to 1R and trained for service overseas, landing in Tunisia March 1943. Well detailed daily observations and comment through training and in action.

2nd Reconnaissance Regiment — 2 RecceRegt

Date raised/disbanded: 30/04/1941   November 1946
RAC service: 01/01/1944   Post-war.
Converted Bns: The Loyal Regiment (North Lancashire)
                          5th Bn = 18Recce, 6th Bn = 2Recce & 9th Bn = 148RAC

A Short History of The Loyal Regiment (North Lancashire)
Not stated   NAM; PCL
London; Malcolm Page Limited; n.d. [c.1953]; ISBN None; 60pp/1 x bw PIfep/15 x bw PI; s/b; Indexed N; Glossary N; Appendices N; Bibliography N; 217 x 140 (8vo); Uncommon
NOTES: One paragraph conversion reference to each of 5th, 6th and 9th Bns.

The Loyal Regiment (North Lancashire) 1919-1953
Dean, Capt. C. G. T.   IWM; NAM; PCL
Preston; Regimental Headquarters; 1955; ISBN None; xix + 310pp/1 x bw PIfep/23 x bw PI/2 x bw Mbds/9 x bw Mf/9 x bw M; h/b (d/j - ne) Red cloth; Indexed Y; Glossary N; Appendices Y; Bibliography N; 236 x 161 (8vo); Rare
NOTES: Several chapters cover the regiment's armour converted battalions - 2R is well represented with three chapters on its service. Useful index. Reprinted by the regiment with additional material 2003.

A Short History of The Loyal Regiment (North Lancashire)
Not stated   IWM
London; Malcolm Page Limited; n.d. [c.1964]; ISBN None; 36pp/1 x bw PIfep/18 x bw PI; s/b; Indexed N; Glossary N; Appendices N; Bibliography N; 217 x 140 (8vo); Uncommon
NOTES: One paragraph reference to each of 5th, 6th and 9th Bns.

ROYAL ARMOURED CORPS: RECONNAISSANCE CORPS 103

The Loyal Regiment
(Famous Regiments)
Langley, Michael; Horrocks, Lt.-Gen. Sir Brian (Ed.) TM; IWM; PCL
London; Leo Cooper Ltd; 1976; ISBN 0 85052 075 4; 118pp/7 x bw PI/11 x bw SI; h/b /
d/j Blue cloth; Indexed N; Glossary N; Appendices N; Bibliography N; 222 x 140 (8vo)
NOTES: One paragraph reference to 2R.

The Loyal North Lancashire Regiment 1855 - 1970
Images of England series
Bull, Stephen
Stroud; Tempus Publishing Limited; 2002; ISBN 0 7524 2489 0; 128pp/1 x bw PIfep/
200 x bw PI/4 x bw SI; s/b; Indexed N; Glossary N; Appendices N; Bibliography N; 235 x
165 (8vo)
NOTES: Passing narrative reference to 6th Bn converting to the Reconnaissance Corps, no
photographs.

The Loyal Regiment (North Lancashire) 1919-1970
Dean, Capt. C. G. T. (Additional material: Bird, O.B.E., D.L., Col J. A. C. TM
& Maher, M.B.E., Maj. A. J.)
Preston; D. P. & G. Military Publishers; 2003; ISBN 1-903972-31-0; xix + 349pp/1 x bw
PIfep/35 x bw PI/2 x bw Mf/15 x bw M; h/b Red cloth; Indexed Y; Glossary N;
Appendices Y; Bibliography N; 215 x 154 (8vo)
NOTES: In this expanded edition, the era 1955 - 1970 is dealt with from p.299.
RoH/Honours/Awards, RoH discretely lists 2R, 18R & 148 RAC casualties. 26+pp on
Recce/RAC regiments.

3rd Reconnaissance Regiment	3 RecceRegt

Date raised/disbanded: 30/04/1941   October 1946
RAC service: 01/01/1944   Post-war.

    Regimental publication:
    Tally-Ho (Run not established - edition No. 13 was 14/01/45)

History Of 3rd Reconnaissance Regiment (N.F.) in the Invasion and Subsequent
Campaign in North West Europe 1944 - 1945
Not stated TM; IWM
No imprint; No imprint; n.d. [1946]; ISBN None; 64pp/5 x bw PI; s/b; Indexed N;
Glossary N; Appendices Y; Bibliography N; 239 x 159 (8vo); Rare
NOTES: The book starts at D-Day and follows the regiment, in near diary form, through
to Bremen. 3R provided a dozen Contact Detachments for D-Day. These existed for D-
Day and provided wireless links between the assaulting infantry and brigade HQs.
Officer-centric narrative. Appendices include nominal rolls of officers on 6 June 1944
and 5 June 1945 plus two accounts from commanders of two of the Contact
Detachments. *Tempting the Fates* gives 2 i/c Maj. J. K. Warner as the editor of this
history.

The History of the Royal Northumberland Fusiliers
In the Second World War
Barclay, C.B.E., D.S.O., Brig. C. N.   IWM; NAM; RMAS; PCL
London; William Clowes and Sons Limited; 1952; ISBN None; xxii + 241pp/48 x bw PI/1 x bw SIfep/1 x bw SI/14 x bw Mf/5 x bw M; h/b / d/j Red cloth; Indexed Y; Glossary Y; Appendices Y; Bibliography N; 252 x 192 (4to)
NOTES: Unusually for an infantry regiment's history, this one fully acknowledges its armoured offspring. 15pp plus two photographs succinctly cover 3R. RoH/Honours/Awards - no discrete 3R references. 8th Bn = 3R.

The Royal Northumberland Fusiliers
(The 5th Regiment of Foot)
(Famous Regiments)
Peacock, Basil; Horrocks, Lt.-Gen. Sir Brian (Ed.)   TM; IWM; PCL
London; Leo Cooper Ltd; 1970; ISBN 0 85052 028 2; 128pp/21 x bw PI/11 x bw SI/1 x bw M; h/b / d/j Red cloth; Indexed N; Glossary N; Appendices N; Bibliography N; 222 x 140 (8vo)
NOTES: No direct reference to 4th Bn as Recce, one sentence reference to 8th Bn as Recce; battalions not referenced to their numbered Recce regiments. 4th Bn = 50R, 8th Bn = 3R.

Diary of The Reverend George Fox, M.C.
June 16th 1944 - June 6th 1945
Fox, The Rev. Colin (Ed.)   TM; NAM
York; Wilton 65; 1998; ISBN 0 947828 48 6; vii + 73pp/8 x bw PI; s/b; Indexed Y; Glossary Y; Appendices N; Bibliography N; 209 x 148 (8vo); Uncommon
NOTES: At the outbreak of war, George Fox was attached to 5RIDG as their chaplain and served in France with them. Upon his escape back to England he joined what would become 3R. His diary for the last year of the war, whilst serving with 3R in NWE, is reproduced with minimal editing.

Tempting the Fates
A Memoir of Service in the Second World War, Palestine, Korea, Kenya and Aden
Wilson, CBE, MC, DL, MA, FRGS, Major-General Dare
Barnsley; Pen & Sword Military; 2006; ISBN 1 84415 435 1; xv + 240pp/37 x bw PI/2 x bw SI/5 x bw M; h/b / d/j Black cloth; Indexed Y; Glossary N; Appendices N; Bibliography Y; 240 x 162 (8vo)
NOTES: The author briefly introduces his childhood before, at the age of 18, he joins the Royal Northumberland Fusiliers in September 1939 and is posted to the 8th Bn at the end of the year. 8RNF became 3R and the author recounts his on-off relationship with the regiment. Away from 3R from late 1942 to mid-1944 at Battle School, as chief instructor, and at ME Staff College, he returns with the hope of a sqn command. This comes in September 1944 with the command of A Sqn. Provides an interesting view into how a wartime officer's career could proceed. Rather than train and fight, sometimes the vagaries of War Office command meant long periods awaiting front line command. Approximately one-third of the book deals with 3R.

4th Reconnaissance Regiment — 4 RecceRegt

Date raised/disbanded: 01/01/1941 October 1945
RAC service: 01/01/1944 Post-war.

No publications established.

5th Reconnaissance Regiment — 5 RecceRegt

Date raised/disbanded: 30/01/1941 04/02/1946
RAC service: 01/01/1944 Post-war.

Wheeled Odyssey
The Story of the Fifth Reconnaissance Regt., Royal Armoured Corps
Prince, Lt-Col A. R. (Ed.) TM; IWM
No imprint; No imprint; n.d. [1947]; ISBN None; vii + 68pp/7 x bw Pl/2 x bw M; h/b Blue cloth; Indexed N; Glossary N; Appendices Y; Bibliography N; 188 x 122 (12mo); Uncommon
NOTES: The book traces the history of the regiment from its start in 1940 as 3rd Tower Hamlets Rifles, conversion as one of the first five Recce regiments, to Hanover in 1945. The editor was a former adjutant and squadron OC of the regiment. RoH.

15th Reconnaissance Regiment — 15 RecceRegt

Date raised/disbanded: 15/02/1943* 01/04/1946
RAC service: 01/01/1944 Post-war.
* Had previously existed in the form of 15th Independent Recce Squadron. Formed from the amalgamation of 15th, 45th and 54th Independent Recce Sqns

Regimental publication:
Racecourse Rag - produced by B Sqn mid-1943.

The Scottish Lion on Patrol
Being the story of the 15th Scottish Reconnaissance Regiment 1943 - 1946
Kemsley, Capt. W. & Riesco, Capt. M. R. IWM; NAM; RMAS
Bristol; The White Swan Press Ltd; 1950; ISBN None; 235pp/12 x bw Pl/20 x bw M; h/b Green cloth; Indexed N; Glossary N; Appendices Y; Bibliography N; 215 x 140 (8vo); Uncommon
NOTES: The book traces the regiment's history from the independent forerunner squadrons, through training and on to the campaign in NWE. Comprehensive and well detailed coverage of the regiment's action in NWE. RoH. 500 printed.

15th Recce
A Short History of the 15th Scottish Reconnaissance Regiment
Boynton, Sir John
No imprint; Private; n.d. [poss. 1990s]; ISBN None; 48pp/17 x bw Pl/2 x clr M; Comb; Indexed N; Glossary N; Appendices N; Bibliography N; 297 x 210 (4to); Rare

NOTES: Self-produced summary history of the regiment in NWE written by onetime OC of 5 Troop. Photographic illustrations suffer from reproduction process. Includes a list of burial locations for the regiment's casualties. RoH/Honours/Awards.

Ground Level
Reetham, Edwin
No imprint; Private; 1994; ISBN None; 66pp/8 x bw PI/1 x bw M; Comb; Indexed N; Glossary N; Appendices N; Bibliography N; 297 x 210 (4to); Rare
NOTES: The author was called up in January 1943 and after initial training was posted to the newly formed 15R, where he served in 5 Tp, B Sqn. He comments on life in the lead up to landing in France, late June 1944 and goes on to describe many of the recce patrols in Normandy, often ending in an encounter with French farmers, but all with the threat of a German attack. He was wounded in September 1944 and provides more detail than is usual of the process and journey home. A second edition was issued later with notes on the dedication in 1999 of a regimental plaque at All Hallows Church, London. Includes named photograph group, 5 Tp, B Sqn.

The Scottish Lion on Patrol
Being the story of the 15th Scottish Reconnaissance Regiment 1943 - 1946
Kemsley, Capt. W. & Riesco, Capt. M. R., Chamberlain, Tim   TM; PCL
Barnsley; Pen & Sword Military; 2011; ISBN 978184 884 5695; xvi + 400pp/33 x clr PI/5 x clr SI/124 x bw PI/2 x bw SI/17 x bw M; h/b / d/j Black cloth; Indexed Y; Glossary N; Appendices Y; Bibliography N; 240 x 161 (8vo)
NOTES: An already fine history has been enhanced by 15R Old Comrades Association chairman Tim Chamberlain with the addition of many veterans' quotations, photographs (troop/squadron) and additional material including information on the Old Comrades Association. RoH.

18th Reconnaissance Regiment — 18 ReccoRegt

Date raised/disbanded:	30/04/1941	Into captivity February 1942
RAC service:	n/a	n/a
Converted Bns:	The Loyal Regiment (North Lancashire)	
	5th Bn = 18Recce, 6th Bn = 2Recce & 9th Bn = 148RAC	

A Short History of The Loyal Regiment (North Lancashire)
Not stated   NAM; PCL
London; Malcolm Page Limited; n.d. [c.1953]; ISBN None; 60pp/1 x bw PIfep/15 x bw PI; s/b; Indexed N; Glossary N; Appendices N; Bibliography N; 217 x 140 (8vo); Uncommon
NOTES: One paragraph conversion reference to each of 5th, 6th and 9th Bns.

The Loyal Regiment (North Lancashire) 1919-1953
Dean, Capt. C. G. T.   IWM; NAM; PCL
Preston; Regimental Headquarters; 1955; ISBN None; xix + 310pp/1 x bw PIfep/23 x bw PI/2 x bw Mbds/9 x bw Mf/9 x bw M; h/b (d/j - ne) Red cloth; Indexed Y; Glossary N; Appendices Y; Bibliography N; 236 x 161 (8vo); Rare

NOTES: Several chapters cover the regiment's armour converted battalions - 18R covered in two chapters. Useful index. Reprinted by the regiment with additional material 2003.

A Short History of The Loyal Regiment (North Lancashire)
Not stated   IWM
London; Malcolm Page Limited; n.d. [c.1964]; ISBN None; 36pp/1 x bw PIfep/18 x bw PI; s/b; Indexed N; Glossary N; Appendices N; Bibliography N; 217 x 140 (8vo); Uncommon
NOTES: One paragraph reference to each of 5th, 6th and 9th Bns.

The Loyal Regiment
(Famous Regiments)
Langley, Michael; Horrocks, Lt.-Gen. Sir Brian (Ed.)   TM; IWM; PCL
London; Leo Cooper Ltd; 1976; ISBN 0 85052 075 4; 118pp/7 x bw PI/11 x bw SI; h/b / d/j Blue cloth; Indexed N; Glossary N; Appendices N; Bibliography N; 222 x 140 (8vo)
NOTES: Five paragraph references to 18Recce.

The Flame of Freedom
Corporal RAS Pagani's escape from the Railway of Death
Hamond, Robert   IWM
London; Leo Cooper Ltd; 1988; ISBN 0-85052-2862; 183pp/20 x bw PI/1 x bw SI/2 x bw M; h/b / d/j Blue cloth; Indexed N; Glossary N; Appendices Y; Bibliography Y; 223 x 142 (8vo)
NOTES: The author, himself a POW of the Japanese, recounts the story of 'RAS' Pagani who made the only successful escape from the Burma-Siam Railway. 'RAS' joined the army before the war and after fighting in France in 1940, he volunteered for the Recce Corps joining the ill-fated 18R. He was captured in February 1942 and after a few months working on the railway, he made good his escape. He soon joined forces with a British officer operating a guerrilla force of Karen tribesmen, later commanding a section himself. Recaptured and subjected to horrendous tortures, 'RAS' spent the next 18 months in Rangoon prison before liberation in April 1945 - a story of courage, of cunning and of determination.

From Tweed to Kwai and back
Yule, C.S.M Andrew
Kelso; Royal British Legion Scotland; n.d. [c.1989]; ISBN None; 140pp/1 x bw PIfep/4 x bw PI/3 x bw M; s/b; Indexed N; Glossary N; Appendices N; Bibliography N; 183 x 122 (12mo)
NOTES: An account of the author's travels to Singapore, followed by a sometimes harrowing account as a POW for the rest of the war. Regimental content is very low but an excellent, if at times disturbing, account.

The Loyal North Lancashire Regiment 1855 - 1970
Images of England series
Bull, Stephen
Stroud; Tempus Publishing Limited; 2002; ISBN 0 7524 2489 0; 128pp/1 x bw PIfep/200 x bw PI/4 x bw SI; s/b; Indexed N; Glossary N; Appendices N; Bibliography N; 235 x 165 (8vo)
NOTES: Couple of sentences in the narrative refer to 5th Bn/18R, no photographs.

The Loyal Regiment (North Lancashire) 1919-1970
Dean, Capt. C. G. T. (Additional material: Bird, O.B.E., D.L., Col J. A. C. TM
& Maher, M.B.E., Maj. A. J.)
Preston; D. P. & G. Military Publishers; 2003; ISBN 1-903972-31-0; xix + 349pp/1 x bw
PIfep/35 x bw PI/2 x bw Mf/15 x bw M; h/b Red cloth; Indexed Y; Glossary N;
Appendices Y; Bibliography N; 215 x 154 (8vo)
NOTES: In this expanded edition, the era 1955 - 1970 is dealt with from p.299.
RoH/Honours/Awards, RoH discretely lists 2R, 18R & 148 RAC casualties. 26+pp on
Recce/RAC regiments.

38th Reconnaissance Regiment — 38 RecceRegt

Date raised/disbanded: 10/1943 October 1944 (basis of 80R)
RAC service: 01/01/1944 October 1944

No publications established.

43rd Reconnaissance Regiment* — 43 RecceRegt

* Originally formed as 48th Bn, Recce Corps. 48th Bn was retitled 43rd Bn 14/02/1942.

Date raised/disbanded: 08/01/1942 20/04/1946
RAC service: 01/01/1944 Post-war.
Converted Bns: The Gloucestershire Regiment
 5th Bn = 43R, 6th Bn = 44RTR & 10th Bn = 159RAC

Regimental publication:
Honky Tonk Gazette – HQ Squadron weekly newspaper produced post-war in
Germany. (Run not established)
Spearhead - started after VE Day for C Sqn by squadron OC Lt John Groves. Named
after the cap badge, the paper ran until disbandment. It was resurrected post war
by the regimental OCA. No. 1 July 5 1945 to No. 31 January 1946.

Farewell to Recce
"C" Squadron 43rd Reconnaissance Regiment
Not stated TM
No imprint; No imprint; 1946; ISBN None; 9pp/1 x bw SI; p/b paper; Indexed N;
Glossary N; Appendices N; Bibliography N; 240 x 158 (8vo); V Rare
NOTES: A commemorative pamphlet for serving members with a summary of the
squadron's travels and RoH/Honours/Awards.

Record of a Reconnaissance Regiment
A History of the 43rd Reconnaissance Regiment (The Gloucestershire Regiment) 1939 - 1945
Scott, Anthony; Packer, Cole & Groves J.; TM; IWM; NAM; RMAS; PCL
Taylor, Jeremy (Ed.)
Bristol; The White Swan Press; n.d. [1950]; ISBN None; 252pp/22 x bw PI/31 x bw M/1 x bw SI; h/b / d/j Green cloth; Indexed N; Glossary N; Appendices Y; Bibliography N; 216 x 143 (8vo); Uncommon
NOTES: The history starts with the 5th Bn Gloucestershire Regiment in France in 1940, then to late spring 1941 when the battalion first heard it was to become a reconnaissance regiment. The bulk of the book provides a well written and detailed account of service in NWE with frequent reference to named personnel in the actions described. One chapter provides information on how a Recce Regiment worked – organisation, wireless, tactics, etc. Appendices include early history of 5th Bn, an article from *Autocar* on the regiment in the Reichswald and two articles on the spirit of the regiment and the sinking of the Derrycunihy. RoH (both 5th Bn and 43R)/Honours/Awards. In the Glosters' tradition, the book's boards show a Recce badge on the front and the Glosters' back-badge on the rear board.

Cap of Honour
The Story of The Gloucestershire Regiment (28th/61st Foot) 1694 - 1950
Daniell, David Scott IWM; NAM; PCL
London; George G. Harrap & Co Ltd; 1951; ISBN None; 344pp/1 x clr SIfep/3 x clr SI/8 x bw PI/31 x bw SI/2 x bw M; h/b / d/j Blue cloth; Indexed Y; Glossary N; Appendices Y; Bibliography N; 222 x 145 (8vo)
NOTES: One paragraph reference to 43R. One of the appendices provides an index to the entries for each battalion, including those converted to RTR, Recce and RAC regiments. Reprinted 1953 and revised 1975 and 2005.

Cap of Honour
The Story of The Gloucestershire Regiment (28th/61st Foot) 1694 - 1950
Daniell, David Scott RMAS; PCL
London; George G. Harrap & Co Ltd; 1953; ISBN None; 344pp/1 x clr SIfep/3 x clr SI/8 x bw PI/31 x bw SI/2 x bw M; h/b / d/j Blue cloth; Indexed Y; Glossary N; Appendices Y; Bibliography N; 222 x 145 (8vo)
NOTES: One paragraph reference to 43R. Reprint of 1951 original.

The Slashers
A New Short History of The Gloucestershire Regiment
Not stated IWM; PCL
Gloucester; John Jennings (Printers) Ltd; 1965; ISBN None; 59pp/1 x clr SIfep/2 x bw PI/11x bw SI; s/b; Indexed N; Glossary N; Appendices Y; Bibliography N; 215 x 138 (8vo); Rare
NOTES: One paragraph reference to 43R.

Cap of Honour
The Story of The Gloucestershire Regiment (28th/61st Foot) 1694 - 1975
Daniell, David Scott IWM
London; White Lion Publishers Ltd; 1975; ISBN None; 410pp/1 x clr PIfep/4 x clr PI/4 x bw PI/23 x bw SI/2 x bw M; h/b / d/j Yellow cloth; Indexed Y; Glossary N; Appendices Y; Bibliography N; 222 x 144 (8vo)
NOTES: New, second edition with additional material (non-Recce) covering the period to 1975 including the Korean war. Pasted in Errata slip, flyleaf.

Able Four has Casualties
Sylvester, Fred, in collaboration with Koolwyk, Jos van TM; NAM
No imprint; Private; n.d.; ISBN None; 39pp/9 x bw PI/1 x bw SI/4 x bw M; s/b; Indexed N; Glossary N; Appendices Y; Bibliography Y; 210 x 147 (8vo); Uncommon
NOTES: The author served in 3 Tp, A Sqn. He recounts the actions of one patrol in October 1944 around the Dutch town of Dreumel. Photocopied self-published booklet, illustrations suffer from reproduction process.

A Territorial Army Chaplain In Peace and War
A country cleric in khaki 1938-61
Gethyn-Jones M.B.E., T.D., M.A., F.S.A., Canon J. Eric IWM
East Wittering; Gooday Publishers; 1988; ISBN 1-870568-20-6; vi/213pp/43 x bw PI/ 9 x bw sketch illus.; h/b / d/j Black cloth; Indexed N; Glossary Y; Appendices N; Bibliography N; 222 x 142 (8vo); Uncommon
NOTES: The author became chaplain to 5th Bn, Glosters in 1938. After a brief introduction on his joining the regiment, the book starts with the move to France and the German invasion. He then traces the regiment's moves around the UK, transformation into a recce regiment and its combat service in NWE to February 1945, all with his personal recollections surrounding events. The last portion of the book deals with his time at 21 Army Group and his post-war duties with the TA.

Never Feared a Foe of Any Kind
The Glosters, 1694 - 1991
Not stated
Gloucester; John Jennings (Printers) Ltd; 1991; ISBN None; 73pp/1 x clr PI/2 x bw PI/7 x clr SI/5 x bw SI/1 x bw M; s/b; Indexed N; Glossary N; Appendices Y; Bibliography N; 210 x 148 (8vo)
NOTES: One paragraph reference to 43R.

Never Feared a Foe of Any Kind
The Glosters, 1694 - 1994
Not stated
Gloucester; John Jennings (Printers) Ltd; 1994; ISBN 978 0 9560391 0 1; See Notes; s/b; Indexed N; Glossary N; Appendices Y; Bibliography N
NOTES: Updated reprint of 1991 first edition. (Not physically inspected.)

The Sinking of the SS Derrycunihy T72/MTS
Not stated   NAM
No imprint; Private; n.d. [c.1995]; ISBN None; 16pp/2 x bw PI/1 x bw M; s/b; Indexed N; Glossary N; Appendices N; Bibliography Y; 210 x 147 (8vo); Uncommon
NOTES: Brief but detailed recollection of the fate of A Sqn on-board the Derrycunihy, 24 June 1944. Photocopied self-published booklet, author is Frederick Philip Sylvester.

The Sinking of the Derrycunihy 24 June 1944
Sylvester, Frederick Philip   TM; IWM; NAM
No imprint; No imprint; 1999; ISBN None; 28pp/1 x bw PI/1 x bw SI/1 x bw M; s/b; Indexed N; Glossary N; Appendices N; Bibliography Y; 210 x 147 (8vo); Uncommon
NOTES: Second edition. Photocopied dot-matrix print.

It Had To Be Done
The Raising of the memorial to Ray Hadwin and Reg. Stopher
Sylvester, Fred   NAM
No imprint; Private (Fred Sylvester); 1999; ISBN None; 14pp/1 x clr PIfep; s/b (card); Indexed N; Glossary N; Appendices N; Bibliography N; 206 x 147 (8vo); V Rare
NOTES: Deals mainly with the process of raising the memorial in Holland. There are some notes as background to the deaths of these two soldiers which the author describes more fully in his book, *Able Four Has Casualties*, q.v.

Cap of Honour
The 300 Years of The Gloucestershire Regiment
Daniell, David Scott   PCL
Stroud; Sutton Publishing Limited; 2005; ISBN 0-7509-4172-3; xvi + 446pp/2 x clr PI/14 x clr SI/21 x bw PI/36 x bw SI/2 x bw M; h/b / d/j Black cloth; Indexed Y; Glossary N; Appendices Y; Bibliography Y; 240 x 158 (8vo)
NOTES: Third revised edition, covers to 1994, minor editing to first edition content.

44th Reconnaissance Regiment   44 RecceRegt

Date raised/disbanded: 08/01/1941   November 1945
RAC service: 01/01/1944   Post-war.

No publications established. For an informative brief history of 44R, refer to *The Reconnaissance Journal*, Vol. 3 No. 3 and Vol. 3 No.4.

45th Reconnaissance Regiment — 45 RecceRegt

Date raised/disbanded: 22/01/1941 October 1944
RAC service: 01/01/1944 October 1944 (Disbanded*)
*16/09/43 converted to Chindits as 45 and 54 Columns.

To Be A Chindit
Sharpe, Phil IWM; NAM
Lewes; The Book Guild Ltd; 1995; ISBN 0 86332 981 0; 273pp/40 x bw Pl/8 x bw SI/5 x bw M; h/b / d/j Blue cloth; Indexed N; Glossary N; Appendices Y; Bibliography N; 222 x 139 (8vo)
NOTES: The author was a corporal in the Signal Troop of the newly formed regiment and starts his memoirs with the regiment sailing for the Far East. Highly detailed daily observations - life in camp in India, wireless operations, washing, etc. Mid-point of the book sees 45R reformed as guerrilla columns. Thereafter, the author deals with his time as a signaller in the Chindits in 45 Column. Appendices include brief overview of use of radio call-signs. 113pp on 45R. Reprinted in 1995.

46th Reconnaissance Regiment — 46 RecceRegt

Date raised/disbanded: 11/07/1941 01/01/1946
RAC service: 01/01/1944 Post-war.

Name, Rank and Number
Calvey, Robert W. IWM
Lewes; The Book Guild Ltd; 1998; ISBN 1 85776 207 X; 112pp/2 x bw SI; h/b / d/j Black cloth; Indexed N; Glossary N; Appendices N; Bibliography N; 222 x 139 (8vo); Uncommon
NOTES: The author starts his memoirs with the landing at Salerno and his almost immediate capture. The book continues with his captivity in Italy and Germany.

49th Reconnaissance Regiment — 49 RecceRegt

Date raised/disbanded: 05/09/1942 April 1946
RAC service: 01/01/1944 Post-war.

49 (West Riding) Reconnaissance Regiment Royal Armoured Corps Summary of Operations June 1944 to May 1945
Not stated TM
Neuenkirchen; Wilh. Kroscky; 1945; ISBN None; 24pp/2 x clr Mf; s/b; Indexed N; Glossary N; Appendices N; Bibliography N; 207 x 146 (8vo); Rare
NOTES: A summary, in near diary form, of the regiment's operations in NWE. Published May 1945.

49 (West Riding) Reconnaissance Regiment Roll of Honour
Not stated TM
Hüsten; Wilh. Kroscky; 1945; ISBN None; 15pp/No illus.; s/b; Indexed N; Glossary N; Appendices N; Bibliography N; 207 x 146 (8vo); Rare
NOTES: A list of killed in action, wounded in action and decorations covering the NWE campaign. Published August 1945.

Recce Patrol
Nairn, John TM
Padbury, Western Australia; North Stirling Press (Western Australia); 1989; ISBN 0 9597527 6 5; 290pp/No illus.; s/b; Indexed N; Glossary N; Appendices N; Bibliography N; 212 x 132 (8vo)
NOTES: The author served in B Squadron and recounts the three years of his war; he replaces real names with fictitious ones. He describes himself as 'a non-conformist and a rebel' and these memoirs show a side of life and attitude not usually presented in memoirs, illustrating many of the dodges some soldiers performed. First half deals with training and leave in the UK, the second with the invasion of NWE to March 1945.

A Polar Bear Reflects - Joe Hoadley
Not stated
No imprint; No imprint [St John's History Society]; 2013; ISBN None; 334pp/1 x bw PIfep/fully illustrated; s/b; Indexed N; Glossary N; Appendices N; Bibliography N; 204 x 145 (8vo); Rare
NOTES: Written by The St John's School History Club, this book looks at the life of Joe Hoadley. JH was called up late 1942 and joined 49R in the summer of 1943 where he started in C Sqn's anti-tank troop. He was captured in Belgium at the end of September 1944, not long after he had transferred to 1 Tp, B Sqn. 50pp on WWII and concludes with a 66pp look at Joe's life as a veteran.

50th Reconnaissance Regiment | 50 RecceRegt

Date raised/disbanded: 30/04/1941   10/03/1943
RAC service: n/a   n/a

The Royal Northumberland Fusiliers
(The 5th Regiment of Foot)
(Famous Regiments)
Peacock, Basil; Horrocks, Lt.-Gen. Sir Brian (Ed.) TM; IWM; PCL
London; Leo Cooper Ltd; 1970; ISBN 0 85052 028 2; 128pp/21 x bw PI/11 x bw SI/1 x bw M; h/b / d/j Red cloth; Indexed N; Glossary N; Appendices N; Bibliography N; 222 x 140 (8vo)
NOTES: No direct reference to 4th Bn as Recce, one sentence reference to 8th Bn as Recce; battalions not referenced to their numbered Recce regiments. 4th Bn = 50R, 8th Bn = 3R.

51st Reconnaissance Regiment — 51 RecceRegt

Date raised/disbanded: 08/01/1941 23/03/1943*
RAC service: n/a n/a
*The regiment was destroyed during the Gazala battle of June 1942 and not re-formed; March 1943 officially re-designated 14th Bn, Highland Light Infantry.

A Brief History of the 51st (H) Reconnaissance Regiment (1941-1943) and its involvement in the Desert Campaign.
Meek, Leslie A. TM; IWM
No imprint; Private; 1991; ISBN None; 56pp/2 x bw Pl/5 x bw M; s/b; Indexed N; Glossary N; Appendices N; Bibliography N; 201 x 145 (8vo); Uncommon
NOTES: This booklet, written for the veterans, starts with an introduction to the regiment and its creation and then, in diary form, follows it in North Africa to disbandment. The author served as a troop leader in 11Tp, B Sqn. RoH.

52nd Reconnaissance Regiment — 52 RecceRegt

Date raised/disbanded: 08/01/1941 31/03/1946
RAC service: 01/01/1944 Post-war.

Regimental publication:
The Atom Tribune – produced weekly by HQ Squadron. The final '20th Edition' was published at the time of disbandment in March 1946.

The Echelon Episodes!
Covering the Period from Weybridge to Bremen
Stephenson, Lt J. R. & McQueen Sgt TM
Germany; Regiment; 1945 [October]; ISBN None; ii + 37pp/6 x bw SI; See Notes; Indexed N; Glossary N; Appendices N; Bibliography N; 192 x 135 (12mo); V Rare
NOTES: A commemorative set of recollections for members of 'A' Echelon, 52R, with a list of personnel, covering their time in NWE. TM's copy is a photocopy, the height and width are approximate, only copies seen.

Time Spent
Or The History Of The 52nd (Lowland) Divisional Reconnaissance Regiment R.A.C. January, 1941 - October, 1945
Whitfield, Maj. T. D. W. IWM
Hamilton; The Hamilton Advertiser Limited; n.d. [1946 March]; ISBN None; 84pp/2 x bw M/1 x clr Mf; h/b Green cloth; Indexed N; Glossary N; Appendices N; Bibliography N; 222 x 144 (8vo); Rare
NOTES: The book provides extensive detail of the regiment's time in the UK, from formation to sailing for France in 1944. The second half takes up the story from the landing in September 1944 and continues in the same detailed and informative fashion. The author was 2 i/c of the regiment. RoH/Honours/Awards.

Time Spent
Or The History Of The 52nd (Lowland) Divisional Reconnaissance Regiment R.A.C. January, 1941 - October, 1945
Whitfield, Maj. T. D. W. TM; IWM; NAM
Hamilton; The Hamilton Advertiser Limited; 1946 [June]; ISBN None; 84pp/2 x bw M/1 x clr Mf; h/b Green cloth; Indexed N; Glossary N; Appendices N; Bibliography N; 222 x 144 (8vo); V Rare
NOTES: Reprinted due to demand with corrections and minor additions. Second edition preface by 'J.C.S.D.' - Jamie Stormonth-Darling, OC B Sqn and post war CO.

Memories of the 52nd (Lowland) Reconnaissance Regiment
de Rusett, Alan IWM
No imprint; No imprint; n.d. [c.1950]; ISBN None; 8pp/No illus.; p/b paper; Indexed N; Glossary N; Appendices N; Bibliography N; 183 x 125 (12mo); V Rare
NOTES: Very brief set of summary recollections of the author's service in 52Recce. He served as HQ Squadron's Signal Troop commander.

Shankey's Ponies
Rose, John TM
No imprint; No imprint; 1988; ISBN None; 127pp/1 x bw PIfep/45 x bw PI/5 x bw SI/1 x bw M; Comb; Indexed N; Glossary N; Appendices N; Bibliography N; 297 x 210 (4to); Uncommon
NOTES: Compiled from the author's wartime diary. He comments that this is the 'second edition' published with the encouragement of his daughter. After a short prologue the narrative starts in August 1944 and follows through to the end of the war. Photocopied self-published, the photographs are of average quality as a result.

Two Weddings and a War
Batchellor, F. H. Dr TM; IWM
No imprint; No imprint (C. V. N. Print - printers); n.d. [mid 1990s]; ISBN 0 9527001 07; 142pp/28 x bw PI/4 x bw SI/5 x bw M; s/b; Indexed N; Glossary N; Appendices N; Bibliography N; 203 x 140 (8vo); Uncommon
NOTES: The author qualified as a doctor early in the war and recounts those early days in the first chapters. He was called up in June 1942, joined the RAMC and in December joined 52R as RMO. These memoirs are more a running history of the campaign with occasional references to 52R and there is actually very little on the role of RMO or any medical references. TM's copy is a photocopy.

The Fighting Fifty-Second Recce
The 52nd (Lowland) Divisional Reconnaissance Regiment RAC in north-west Europe September 1944 - March 1946
Shilleto, Carl TM; IWM; PCL
York; Eskdale Publishing; 2001; ISBN 0-9538677-1-4; 192pp/1 x bw PIfep/1 x bw SIfep/42 x bw PI/6 x bw M; h/b / d/j Black cloth; Indexed Y; Glossary Y; Appendices Y; Bibliography Y; 240 x 160 (8vo)
NOTES: The author's grandfather, Bernard Shilleto, served in A Squadron, 52R and this history starts with the regiment sailing for France. Includes many veterans' quotations. RoH includes cemetery locations. Honours/Awards. Appendices include a list of casualties and a reproduction of the farewell letter from ex-CO Lt-Col Hankey.

53rd Reconnaissance Regiment — 53 RecceRegt

Date raised/disbanded: 01/01/1941   01/05/1946
RAC service: 01/01/1944   Post-war.

Regimental publication:
Recce Rag - weekly from October 1941 to 2 February 1946. During the campaign in Normandy it became daily. Issue one comprised ten typewritten copies.

Welsh Spearhead
A History of the 53rd Reconnaissance Regiment 1941 - 1946
Not stated [See Notes]   TM; IWM; NAM
Solingen-Ohligs; Wilhelm Müller jr KG; 1946; ISBN None; 192pp/21 x bw Pl/16 x bw SI/6 x bw M/1 x clr Mf; h/b Red or Blue cloth; Indexed N; Glossary N; Appendices Y; Bibliography N; 212 x 149 (8vo); Rare
NOTES: Highly detailed history, the author (from the Preface, PMC = Maj. P. M. Cowburn) held the posts of Adjutant, OC B Sqn, and post-war CO. Full of uniform and vehicle details, the birth and early history of the regiment is covered in several short introductory chapters. The bulk of the book deals with its service in NWE. RoH. Issued free to all ex-members. (Seen bound in red and in blue – distinction undetermined.)

54th Reconnaissance Regiment — 54 RecceRegt

Date raised/disbanded: 15/07/1941   01/01/1942
RAC service: n/a   n/a

No publications established. For an informative brief history of 54R, refer to *The Reconnaissance Journal*, Vol. 4 No. 1.

56th Reconnaissance Regiment — 56 RecceRegt

Date raised/disbanded: 08/01/1941   October 1945
RAC service: 01/01/1944   Post-war.

Regimental publication:
Tally-Ho Gazette - No. 1 to unknown. (No.2 published 12/02/1943. Double sided single sheet)

Short History of 56th Reconnaissance Regiment, R.A.C. with the compliments of the Intelligence Section
Not stated
No imprint; No imprint; 1945; ISBN None; See Notes; V Rare
NOTES: Précised but very informative summary history; awards/casualty numbers. Original not inspected, re-typed 5pp A4 viewed.

The Regimental History of the 56th Reconnaissance Regiment 1941 - 1945 North Africa, Sicily, Egypt, Austria
Newton, E.T. (John)   TM; IWM
No imprint; Private; 1988; ISBN None; 55pp/16 x bw M; Stapled A5; Indexed N; Glossary N; Appendices N; Bibliography N; 210 x 148 (8vo); Uncommon
NOTES: Although a short history, it is packed with information and general asides commenting on the day. Photocopied self-published.

A British Soldier Remembers
The World War II Reminiscences of Ronald Arthur Tee
Tee, Ronald A. & Dowsett, Ken C.
Ontario; Epic Press; 2001; ISBN 1-55306-277-9; 199pp/19 x bw PI/13 x bw SI/8 x bw M; s/b; Indexed N; Glossary N; Appendices Y; Bibliography Y; 204 x 133 (8vo)
NOTES: After a brief recount of his childhood, the author begins his army career with his call up in December 1939. After a year in the infantry, he volunteered for the Recce Corps, joining 56R, C Sqn, 16 Tp. Landing with the regiment in NA, his memoirs take the form of entitled one page or less vignettes prefaced by an editorial setting the scene. Very good front line anecdotes, little regimental. The final third of the book contains messages from visitors to his web site. Unfortunately, the web site that inspired the book is no longer operational.

59th Reconnaissance Regiment		59 RecceRegt
Date raised/disbanded:	07/07/1941	21/08/1944
RAC service:	01/01/1944	21/08/1944 (Disbanded)

No publications established.

61st Reconnaissance Regiment		61 RecceRegt
Date raised/disbanded:	14/09/1941	February 1945
RAC service:	01/01/1944	February 1945 (Disbanded)

Beaten Paths Are Safest
From D-Day to the Ardennes. Memories of the 61st Reconnaissance Regiment 50th (TT) Northumbrian Division
Howard, Roy   TM; IWM; RMAS
Studley; Brewin Books Ltd; 2004; ISBN 1 85858 256 3; xii 164pp/53 x bw PI/1 x bw SI/1 x bw M/; s/b; Indexed N; Glossary N; Appendices N; Bibliography N; 242 x 170 (8vo)
NOTES: Produced by the son of 61R veteran Roy Howard, this is mostly an amalgam of his father's collection on the subject rather than a description of the service of 61R. RoH.

80th (Holding & Training) Reconnaissance Regiment	80 RecceRegt

Date raised/disbanded: 01/1943 October 1944*
RAC service: 01/01/1944 October 1944
* Re-named 38th (Holding and Training) Reconnaissance Regiment.

No publications established.

161st Reconnaissance Regiment	161 RecceRegt

Date raised/disbanded: 12/10/1943 11/03/1946
RAC service: 01/01/1944 Post-war.
Converted Bns: The Green Howards (Alexandra, Princess of Wales's Own Yorkshire Regt)
12th Bn = 161 RAC, then became 161R.

Regimental publication:
Title unconfirmed - produced in 1946 to at least October.
Associated regimental publication:
The Green Howards Gazette: a monthly chronicle of The Princess of Wales's Own (Yorkshire Regiment)
Vol. 5, No. 49 Apr 1897 to not established (at least 1976) (Monthly)

The Story Of The Green Howards 1939-1945
Synge, Capt. W. A. T.   IWM; NAM; RMAS; PCL
Richmond; The Green Howards; 1952; ISBN None; xxviii + 428pp/22 x bw Pl/15 x clr Mf; h/b (d/j - ne) Green cloth; Indexed Y; Glossary N; Appendices Y; Bibliography N; 222 x 148 (8vo); Uncommon
NOTES: Sadly, the relevant references to the 12th Bn contain factual errors. Two paragraphs, one incorrectly stating that the 12th converted to 161R, not 161 RAC, in July 1942 and one paragraph implying the replacement squadron for 43R was due to fighting casualties rather than the shipwreck.

The Green Howards
(Famous Regiments)
Powell, Geoffrey   TM; IWM; RMAS
London; Hamish Hamilton Ltd; 1968; ISBN None; 144pp/13 x bw Pl/19 x bw SI; h/b / d/j Blue cloth; Indexed N; Glossary N; Appendices N; Bibliography Y; 221 x 142 (8vo)
NOTES: No reference to 12th Bn.

The Green Howards
(Famous Regiments)
Powell, Geoffrey   IWM; RMAS
London; Leo Cooper (Martin Secker & Warburg); 1983; ISBN 0-436-37910-4; 150pp/15 x bw Pl/19 x bw SI; s/b; Indexed N; Glossary N; Appendices N; Bibliography Y; 221 x 142 (8vo)
NOTES: No reference to 12th Bn. Updated edition with one extra chapter covering 1968 - 1982.

ROYAL ARMOURED CORPS: RECONNAISSANCE CORPS

The History Of The Green Howards
Three Hundred Years of Service
Powell, Geoffrey IWM; NAM; RMAS
London; Arms and Armour Press; 1992; ISBN 1-85409-149-2; 287pp/3 x bw PIfep/5 x clr PI/28 x clr SI/92 x bw PI/9 x bw SI/14 x bw M; h/b / d/j Green cloth; Indexed Y; Glossary Y; Appendices Y; Bibliography Y; 241 x 161 (8vo)
NOTES: One tabular reference to 161R.

It's The Same Brush...
A History of the 12th Battalion Green Howards and its Successors The 161st Regiment Royal Armoured Corps (Green Howards) and The 161st Reconnaissance Regiment Royal Armoured Corps
Sylvester, Fred (Vic) NAM
No imprint; Private self-published; 1997; ISBN None; 150pp/8 x bw PI/8 x bw SI; s/b; Indexed N; Glossary N; Appendices Y; Bibliography Y; 297 x 210 (4to); Rare
NOTES: The author joined 161 RAC early in 1943 and was one of the men detailed to join 43R in 1944. He recounts the history of 161 RAC/R, units which never fought as regiments but which supplied one squadron wholesale to replace 43R's losses in the Derrycunihy sinking of June 1944. Full of regimental detail, especially uniform and vehicle notes. Appendices include officer lists for 12th Bn GH and 161 RAC and relevant notes extracted from the *Green Howards Gazette*. 30pp on 161 RAC, 60pp on 161R. Reproduced dot-matrix format.

The History Of The Green Howards
Three Hundred Years of Service
Powell, Geoffrey and Powell, John NAM; RMAS; PCL
Barnsley; Leo Cooper; 2002; ISBN 085052 857 7; 316pp/2 x bw PIfep/5 x clr PI/28 x clr SI/82 x bw PI/7 x bw SI/15 x bw M; h/b / d/j Green cloth; Indexed Y; Glossary N; Appendices Y; Bibliography Y; 240 x 160 (8vo)
NOTES: Revised and enlarged reprint of 1992 edition. One tabular reference to 161R.

The Green Howards
A History In Photographs 1855 - 2006
Chapman, M.B.E., M.A., Maj. Roger IWM
Scarborough; The Green Howards Regimental Museum in association with Great Northern Publishing; 2006; ISBN 095401412 / 9780954014124; 392pp/1 x bw PIfep/1048 x bw PI; h/b / d/j Black cloth; Indexed N; Glossary N; Appendices Y; Bibliography Y; 240 x 160 (8vo)
NOTES: No narrative mention of 161R, 1 x photograph of officers of 161RAC in 1942 incorrectly titled as 161R.

1st Airborne Reconnaissance Squadron	[1 Abn Recce Sqn]

Date raised/disbanded: 01/1941   01/08/1946 (Disbanded)
RAC service: 01/01/1944   Post-war.

By Air To Battle
The Official Account of the British Airborne Divisions
Not stated   TM; IWM; NAM; PCL
London; His Majesty's Stationery Office; 1945; ISBN None; 144pp/7 x bw M; s/b;
Indexed Y; Glossary N; Appendices N; Bibliography N; 225 x 144 (8vo)
NOTES: Few passing references to 1 Abn Recce Sqn.

Remember Arnhem
The Story of the 1st Airborne Reconnaissance Squadron at Arnhem
Fairley, John   IWM; RMAS
Aldershot; Pegasus Journal; 1978; ISBN 0 9506096 0 9; xvi + 235pp/29 x bw Pl/11 x bw
M; h/b / d/j Red cloth; Indexed Y; Glossary N; Appendices N; Bibliography Y; 250 x 185
(4to); Uncommon
NOTES: Exceptionally detailed book that presages works from the 1990s and 2000s and
the ever increasing fashion for detail. An essential reference work.

Remember Arnhem
The Story of the 1st Airborne Reconnaissance Squadron at Arnhem
Fairley, John   TM
Aldershot; Pegasus Journal; 1978; ISBN 0 9506096 1 7; xvi + 235pp/29 x bw Pl/11 x bw
M; s/b; Indexed Y; Glossary N; Appendices N; Bibliography Y; 240 x 178 (8vo);
Uncommon
NOTES: Softback reprint, same pagination.

Remember Arnhem
The Story of the 1st Airborne Reconnaissance Squadron at Arnhem
Fairley, John
Glasgow; Peaton Press; 1979; ISBN 0 9515509 0 X; xvi + 235pp/30 x bw Pl/11 x bw M;
s/b; Indexed Y; Glossary N; Appendices N; Bibliography Y; Uncommon
NOTES: Softback reprint. (Not physically inspected.)

Remember Arnhem
The Story of the 1st Airborne Reconnaissance Squadron at Arnhem
Fairley, John   NAM; PCL
Glasgow; Peaton Press; 1990; ISBN 0 9515509 0 X; xvi + 235pp/30 x bw Pl/11 x bw M;
s/b; Indexed Y; Glossary N; Appendices N; Bibliography Y; 242 x 181 (8vo); Uncommon
NOTES: Second edition with new preface, same pagination but slightly different photo
selection.

Traitor of Arnhem
Samm, Allan A. IWM
London; Minerva Press; 1996; ISBN 1 86106 175 7; xi + 162pp/12 x bw Pl; s/b; Indexed N; Glossary N; Appendices N; Bibliography N; 210 x 150 (8vo); Uncommon
NOTES: The author joined a Young Soldiers Battalion and recounts his training days with them before volunteering for the new airborne troops. He was accepted for 1ARS and served in HQ Troop. As one of the Squadron's despatch riders (DRs) he describes some of his actions in Italy late 1943. The final half deals with the Arnhem operation. In graphic and uncomplicated terms, he describes his house to house fighting, being trapped in the Oosterbeek 'Cauldron' and his escape across the Rhine in the evacuation. Second impression also published in 1996.

By Air To Battle
The Official Account of the British Airborne Divisions
Not stated
Smalldale; MLRS Books; 2004; ISBN 1-904951-08-2; See Notes
NOTES: Facsimile reprint by MLRS Books of 1945 first edition.

Airborne Armour
Tetrarch, Locust, Hamilcar and the 6th Airborne Armoured Reconnaissance Regiment 1938 - 50.
Flint, Keith TM; IWM; PCL
Solihull; Helion & Company Limited; 2004; ISBN 1 874622 37 X; vi/223pp/30 x bw PI/4 x bw SI/7 x bw M; h/b / d/j Red cloth; Indexed N; Glossary N; Appendices N; Bibliography Y; 236 x 152 (8vo)
NOTES: Although only brief mention of 1ARS, does include highly pertinent 4pp on formation and equipment of the squadron.

Airborne Armour
Tetrarch, Locust, Hamilcar and the 6th Airborne Armoured Reconnaissance Regiment 1938 - 50.
Flint, Keith PCL
Solihull; Helion & Company Limited; 2010; ISBN 978-1-906033-80-4; vi/223pp/30 x bw PI/4 x bw SI/7 x bw M; s/b; Indexed N; Glossary N; Appendices N; Bibliography Y; 230 x 146 (8vo)
NOTES: Reprint of 2004 first edition, same pagination.

6th Airborne Armoured Reconnaissance Regiment* [6 Abn RecceRegt]

*24/06/42 Airborne Light Tank Sqn, RAC raised from disbanded 'C' Special Service Sqn, RAC. Mid-1943 Airborne Light Tank Sqn, RAC transferred to 6th Airborne Division. 14/01/1944 Airborne Armoured Recce Regt, RAC raised from disbanded Airborne Light Tank Squadron, RAC. 01/04/1944 unit designation changed to 6th Airborne Armoured Reconnaissance Regiment, RAC.

Date raised/disbanded: 14/01/1944   01/02/1946 (Disbanded)
RAC service: 14/01/1944   Post-war.

By Air To Battle
The Official Account of the British Airborne Divisions
Not stated TM; IWM; NAM; PCL
London; His Majesty's Stationery Office; 1945; ISBN None; 144pp/7 x bw M; s/b;
Indexed Y; Glossary N; Appendices N; Bibliography N; 225 x 144 (8vo)
NOTES: Passing reference to 6AARR.

Go To It!
The Illustrated History of The 6th Airborne Division
Harclerode, Peter IWM; RMAS; PCL
London; Bloomsbury Publishing Limited; 1990; ISBN 0-7475-0808-9; 192pp/3 x bw
PIfep/248 x bw PI/1 x bw SI/1 x bw M; h/b / d/j Black cloth; Indexed N; Glossary N;
Appendices N; Bibliography Y; 280 x 222 (4to)
NOTES: Comprehensive history of 6th Airborne Division and all its constituent parts.
6AARR's history is told in distinct sections throughout the book totalling approximately
2pp plus occasional sentences within the story of other divisional elements. Includes five
photographs relating to 6AARR. *Airborne Armour*, q.v., provides a better history of the
unit's formation.

Go To It!
The Illustrated History of The 6th Airborne Division
Harclerode, Peter
London; Caxton Editions; 2000; ISBN 1 84067 136 X; 192pp/3 x bw PIfep/248 x bw PI/1
x bw SI/1 x bw M; h/b / d/j Illustrated as d/j; Indexed N; Glossary N; Appendices N;
Bibliography Y; 280 x 222 (4to)
NOTES: Reprint of 1990 first edition, same pagination.

By Air To Battle
The Official Account of the British Airborne Divisions
Not stated
Smalldale; MLRS Books; 2004; ISBN 1-904951-08-2; See Notes
NOTES: Facsimile reprint by MLRS Books of 1945 first edition.

Airborne Armour
Tetrarch, Locust, Hamilcar and the 6th Airborne Armoured Reconnaissance
Regiment 1938 - 50
Flint, Keith TM; IWM; PCL
Solihull; Helion & Company Limited; 2004; ISBN 1 874622 37 X; vi/223pp/30 x bw PI/
4 x bw SI/7 x bw M; h/b / d/j Red cloth; Indexed N; Glossary N; Appendices N;
Bibliography Y; 236 x 152 (8vo)
NOTES: The author first reviews the tanks and gliders to be used by airborne armour. He
then traces the history of 6AARR from its early days as 'C' Special Service Squadron
through to the second and last ever use of airborne armour in the crossing of the Rhine
in 1945. Extremely well researched and presented definitive account of 6AARR. Contains
many veterans' quotations.

Airborne Armour
Tetrarch, Locust, Hamilcar and the 6th Airborne Armoured Reconnaissance Regiment 1938 - 50
Flint, Keith PCL
Solihull; Helion & Company Limited; 2010; ISBN 978-1-906033-80-4; vi/223pp/30 x bw PI/4 x bw SI/7 x bw M; s/b; Indexed N; Glossary N; Appendices N; Bibliography Y; 230 x 146 (8vo)
NOTES: Reprint of 2004 first edition, same pagination.

GHQ Liaison Regiment (Phantom)* [Phantom]

* The regiment formed under the title GHQ Reconnaissance Unit.

Date raised/disbanded:	07/1940	01/05/1947
RAC service:	01/01/1944	Post-war.

Regimental publication:
The Bray - 'A' Sqn (No.1 GHQ) magazine.
Phantasia - No. 3 GHQ Liaison magazine.

Confession of Faith
Baker, Peter IWM
London; The Falcon Press; 1946; ISBN None; 233pp/No illus.; h/b / d/j Red cloth; Indexed N; Glossary N; Appendices N; Bibliography N; 220 x 144 (8vo); Uncommon
NOTES: The author received his commission through the Royal Artillery early in the war. In October 1941 he was posted to Military Intelligence from where he transferred to Phantom mid-1942, joining E Sqn. In a quarter of the book he recounts his experiences in Italy with operational detail and commentary on some military and political events impacting on the campaign. After Italy he left Phantom for Military Intelligence where he commanded a unit in NWE until his capture late 1944. Expanded and republished in 1955 as *My Testament*, q.v.

The Enemy Within
A Personal Impression of the Invasion of Normandy 1944
Watney, John
London; Hodder and Stoughton, Limited; 1946; ISBN None; 254pp/No illus.; h/b / d/j Brown cloth; Indexed N; Glossary N; Appendices N; Bibliography N; 203 x 140 (8vo)
NOTES: The author served with Phantom from 1942 to 1944. Written in novel style but all the characters and events are true; some characters' and place names have been altered. The first third describes the build-up and crossing to France for D-Day. The story then follows the Normandy campaign until the author is wounded and evacuated mid-July 1944. Provides a genuine insight into the workings of Phantom on D-Day and thereafter. Reprinted in year of publication.

There Is A Spirit in Europe . . .
A Memoir of Frank Thompson
Thompson, T. J. and Thompson, E. P.
London; Victor Gollancz Ltd; 1947; ISBN None; 191pp/8 x bw Pl/1 x bw M; h/b / d/j
Green cloth; Indexed N; Glossary N; Appendices N; Bibliography N; 203 x 137 (8vo);
Uncommon
NOTES: Written by Frank Thompson's mother and younger brother, this book contains some of his poetry but mostly extracts from his diary and letters. The bulk is taken up with FT's commentary on the Soviet Union (he was a Communist Party member) whilst the Phantom commentary is reserved for the invasion of Sicily. Final third of the book deals with his SOE training and deployment into Bulgaria where he was executed in June 1944. See *A Very English Hero* for a modern biography on FT.

There Is A Spirit in Europe . . .
A Memoir of Frank Thompson
Thompson, T. J. and Thompson, E. P.
London; Victor Gollancz Ltd; 1948; ISBN None; 191pp/8 x bw Pl/1 x bw M; h/b / d/j
Green cloth; Indexed N; Glossary N; Appendices N; Bibliography N; 203 x 137 (8vo);
Uncommon
NOTES: Second edition, has an updated account of FT's death following investigations. (Not physically inspected.)

Phantom Was There
Hills, R. J. T. TM; IWM; NAM
London; Edward Arnold & Co; 1951; ISBN None; 344pp/9 x bw M; h/b / d/j Black cloth; Indexed N; Glossary N; Appendices N; Bibliography N; 220 x 144 (8vo); Uncommon
NOTES: The author served in Phantom, firstly as QM in 1940 and later as OC L Sqn when it was raised. He retells the story of the regiment with a particular verve of the era. Comprehensive and highly detailed considering how soon after the war and with limited public documents.

My Testament
Baker, M.C., Capt. Peter IWM
London; John Calder (Publishers) Ltd; 1955; ISBN None; 288pp/9 x bw Pl/; h/b / d/j
Red cloth; Indexed N; Glossary N; Appendices N; Bibliography N; 220 x 144 (8vo);
Uncommon
NOTES: The author joined Phantom in 1941 and served in 'E' Sqn in Italy and later in NWE. He was captured in late 1944 in Holland, 66pp dealing with his time as a POW. An expanded version of his 1946 book, *Confession of Faith*, q.v.

Army Phantom Signal Regiment (Princess Louise's Kensington Regiment) T.A. 1859 - 1959
Not stated NAM
No imprint; No imprint; n.d. [1959]; ISBN None; 16pp/2 x clr SI/3 x bw SI; s/b (card); Indexed N; Glossary N; Appendices N; Bibliography N; 220 x 142 (8vo); Uncommon
NOTES: Short commemorative booklet published upon the regiment's 100th anniversary. Despite the inference from the title, the regiment's Phantom association is only post-war, from 1947.

Tribal Feeling
Astor, Michael   IWM
London; John Murray; 1963; ISBN None; xi + 224pp/9 x bw Pl/1 x bw SI; h/b / d/j Green cloth; Indexed Y; Glossary N; Appendices N; Bibliography N; 222 x 142 (8vo)
NOTES: Within this self and family memoir is one chapter on the author's wartime experiences. He joined the post-Dunkirk Phantom and served as a squadron 2 i/c in Normandy. The narrative is sparse on Phantom per se, being recollections of surrounding events. 24pp on WWII.

Tribal Feeling
Astor, Michael
London; Readers Union; 1964; ISBN None; xi + 224pp/9 x bw Pl/1 x bw SI; h/b / d/j Red cloth; Indexed Y; Glossary N; Appendices N; Bibliography N; 202 x 130 (8vo)
NOTES: Reprint of 1963 first edition, same pagination.

Anything But A Soldier
Hislop, John   IWM
London; Michael Joseph Ltd; 1965; ISBN None; 189pp/1 x bw PIfep/42 x bw Pl/1 x bw SI; h/b / d/j Red cloth; Indexed Y; Glossary N; Appendices N; Bibliography N; 235 x 158 (8vo); Uncommon
NOTES: The author's second set of memoirs; the first described this jockey and racing journalist's life up to war. He started in the Royal Artillery serving in France in 1940, transferring to Phantom in March 1941 and serving under David Niven in A Sqn. He lived his life around horses and suffered a serious leg injury during an off-duty racing event, leading to him being invalided out of the army. He regained his fitness and rejoined Phantom in March 1943, being posted to F Sqn. In early 1944 he was part of a team selected to provide the SAS with a Phantom patrol. Interesting commentary on Phantom/SAS interoperability. Recounts the dangerous and exhilarating attachment of his Phantom patrol to the SAS for Operation Loyton – parachuted into the Vosges mountains. Personal recollections of fellow officers, all interspersed with comment on horses and horse racing.

The Moon's A Balloon
Reminiscences by David Niven
Niven, David
London; Hamish Hamilton Ltd; 1971; ISBN 0 241 02062 X; See Notes; h/b / d/j (cloth - ne); Indexed Y; Glossary N; Appendices N; Bibliography N; Uncommon
NOTES: Short but informative section on time in Phantom. 49pp on WWII, 18pp on Phantom. (Not physically inspected.)

The Moon's A Balloon
Reminiscences by David Niven
Niven, David   IWM
London; Coronet Books; 1972; ISBN 0 340 15817 4; 336pp/20 x bw Pl; p/b; Indexed Y; Glossary N; Appendices N; Bibliography N; 178 x 110 (12mo)
NOTES: First paperback edition, multiple reprints.

Last On The List
Reid, M.B.E., M.C., D.L., Miles   IWM; NAM
London; Leo Cooper Ltd; 1974; ISBN 0 85052 159 9; xii + 228pp/5 x bw Pl/2 x bw M;
h/b / d/j Black cloth; Indexed Y; Glossary N; Appendices Y; Bibliography N; 222 x 144
(8vo)
NOTES: The author joined Phantom at its inception and commanded 'A' Sqn in Greece.
The last 27pp deal with the author's life as a POW.

Last On The List
Reid, M.B.E., M.C., D.L., Miles
London; New English Library Limited; 1975; ISBN 450 02411 3; 207pp/2 x bw M; p/b;
Indexed N; Glossary N; Appendices Y; Bibliography N; 174 x 102 (12mo)
NOTES: Paperback reprint of 1974 first edition, different pagination.

In the Office of Constable
An Autobiography
Mark, Sir Robert
London; William Collins Sons & Co Ltd; 1978; ISBN 0 00 216032 3; 320pp/26 x bw Pl;
h/b / d/j Black cloth; Indexed Y; Glossary N; Appendices N; Bibliography N; 235 x 153
(8vo)
NOTES: Recollections from the former Commissioner of the Metropolitan Police. He
joined up in August 1942 and trained at Sandhurst before being posted to an armoured
regiment. Very quickly he transferred to Phantom and in July 1944 he moved to
Normandy and served with Phantom HQ liaising with US forces. 12pp on WWII.

In the Office of Constable
Mark, Sir Robert
London; Fontana; 1979; ISBN 0 00 635783 0; 343pp/13 x bw Pl; p/b; Indexed Y;
Glossary N; Appendices N; Bibliography N; 175 x 105 (12mo)
NOTES: Paperback reprint of 1978 first edition. Different pagination.

Phantom
Warner, Philip   IWM; RMAS
London; William Kimber & Co. Limited; 1982; ISBN 0-7183-0458-6; 218pp/22 x bw Pl/6
x bw M; h/b / d/j Brown cloth; Indexed Y; Glossary N; Appendices Y; Bibliography Y; 240
x 154 (8vo)
NOTES: In the first half the author tells the sometimes complicated story of Phantom
from birth to the end of the war. In the second half are several personal accounts, from
chapter length to a few paragraphs.

"George" 1940 - 1946
A Collection of Letters from George Stammer to His Sister
Stammer, Olive Wood (Ed.)   IWM
No imprint; No imprint (Carmichael & Co. Ltd. - printers); 1986; ISBN None; 80pp/9 x
bw Pl; s/b; Indexed N; Glossary N; Appendices N; Bibliography N; 212 x 148 (8vo);
Uncommon
NOTES: Reproduction of letters from January 1940 to December 1945. From February
1940 he writes from HQ Sqn where he served throughout the war. Although extremely

little on Phantom, an interesting look at an ordinary sergeant writing ordinary domestic letters to his sister in wartime.

Time To Explain
Mayhew, Christopher   IWM
London; Hutchinson Ltd; 1987; ISBN 0 09 168440 4; vi + 226pp/17 x bw Pl/1 x bw SI; h/b / d/j Red cloth; Indexed Y; Glossary N; Appendices N; Bibliography N; 222 x 144 (8vo)
NOTES: After serving with the Surrey Yeomanry in France 1940, the author returned to the UK and joined the SOE. Through connections there he transferred to Phantom and joined J Sqn. He took part in the invasion of Sicily after which he moved to Special Forces for the invasion of Europe. 42pp on WWII, 6pp on Phantom service.

Tricks of Memory
An Autobiography
Worsthorne, Peregrine
London; Weidenfeld & Nicolson; 1993; ISBN 0 297 81186 X; ix + 290pp/29 x bw Pl/6 x bw SI; h/b / d/j Red cloth; Indexed Y; Glossary N; Appendices Y; Bibliography N; 240 x 161 (8vo)
NOTES: The author joined the Ox & Bucks in 1941. After an unusual mid-war term at Oxford University, brought about following a training injury, he transferred to B Sqn, Phantom. He arrived at the squadron late 1944 in Holland. His wartime years are covered in 25pp, Phantom briefly in 11pp.

The Moon's A Balloon
Niven, David
London; Penguin Books Ltd; 1994; ISBN 0-14-023924-3; 336pp/20 x bw Pl; p/b; Indexed Y; Glossary N; Appendices N; Bibliography N; 180 x 111 (12mo)
NOTES: Penguin reprint of Coronet paperback, itself reprinted 2005.

Life As a Wireless Operator With "Phantom" - 1943 - 1945
Littlewood, Pete
Caversham; P E T Littlewood; 1994; ISBN 0 9529774 0 0; 30pp + 16pp illus./21 x bw Pl; Acetate/Card; Indexed N; Glossary N; Appendices N; Bibliography N; 297 x 210 (4to); V Rare
NOTES: The memoirs comprise a mixture of commentary on domestic army life and operations with Phantom in NWE. The author also provides a background description of Phantom's 'J' Service which provided higher command with unit reports before those reports got back through the usual channels. He served with the 'J' Service in NWE. Reproduced typescript.

Always and Always
The Wartime Letters of Hugh and Margaret Williams
Williams, Hugh, Williams, Margaret; Dunn, Kate (Ed.) IWM
London; John Murray (Publishers) Ltd; 1995; ISBN 0-7195-5472-1; x + 276pp/18 x bw Pl/2 x bw SI; h/b / d/j Red cloth; Indexed Y; Glossary N; Appendices N; Bibliography N; 240 x 160 (8vo)
NOTES: Hugh Williams (HW) was commissioned into the 8th Devons in 1940 but reprised his acting career starring in several mid-war films. He re-joined the army at the end of 1942 and Phantom soon after. The book reproduces their letters between October 1939 and December 1945. In February 1943 HW sailed to NA with K Sqn where he was Intelligence Officer. Modest amount of Phantom related information within the letters, although comments on everyday army concerns provide additional interest.

When the Grass Stops Growing
A War Memoir by Carol Mather
Mather, M.C., Carol IWM
Barnsley; Leo Cooper; 1997; ISBN 0 85052 576 4; xii + 323pp/25 x bw Pl/1 x bw Mbds/1 x bw M; h/b / d/j Red cloth; Indexed Y; Glossary N; Appendices N; Bibliography N; 240 x 160 (8vo)
NOTES: The author was commissioned into the Welsh Guards at the beginning of the war but soon joined the embryonic Commandos. In August 1941 he transferred to Phantom in Cairo after his special Commando unit was disbanded. The recollections focus more on campaign events than Phantom with occasional reference to H Squadron's activities. He left in the spring of 1942 to join the SAS and the bulk of the book deals with his service there and later with Montgomery's HQ as a liaison officer. Reprinted in same format 1999 with errata on verso of p323 - none refer to Phantom contents.

Phantom At War
The British Army's Secret Intelligence and Communication Regiment of World War Two
Parlour, Andy & Sue RMAS
Bristol; Cerberus Publishing Limited; 2003; ISBN 1 84145 118 5; xii + 340pp/67 x bw Pl/2 x bw SI; h/b / d/j Black cloth; Indexed Y; Glossary N; Appendices Y; Bibliography Y; 240 x 163 (8vo); Uncommon
NOTES: The authors provide further focus on the history of Phantom with this, the third overall history of the regiment. Perhaps because two histories already existed, in this book a substantial part is given over to elaborating on the strategic situations and general events surrounding Phantom's activities. Contains a good selection of photographs and includes several accounts by Phantom veterans plus the final chapters reproduce recollections from officers and men.

Phantom
Warner, Philip NAM
Barnsley; Pen & Sword Military; 2005; ISBN 1 84415 218 9; 218pp/22 x bw Pl/6 x bw M; h/b / d/j Black cloth; Indexed Y; Glossary N; Appendices Y; Bibliography Y; 240 x 160 (8vo)
NOTES: Reprint of 1982 first edition, same pagination, small change in photo selection.

A Very English Hero
The Making of Frank Thompson
Conradi, Peter J.
London; Bloomsbury Publishing Plc; 2012; ISBN 978 1 4088 0243 4; xi + 419pp/68 x bw PI/2 x bw SI/2 x bw M; h/b / d/j Brown cloth; Indexed Y; Glossary N; Appendices Y; Bibliography Y; 240 x 159 (8vo)
NOTES: War throws complicated characters such as Frank Thompson to the fore. An intellectual idealist and Communist Party member, he actively sought postings where he thought he could make a difference. Called up in October 1939 to the Royal Artillery, commissioned in March 1940 and transferred to Phantom's Intelligence Section in July 1940. He sailed with H Sqn in early 1941 headed for Greece which fell before they arrived. After taking part in the Sicily invasion with H Sqn, FT transferred to SOE in September 1943. Whilst serving in Bulgaria he was executed in June 1944. 210pp on WWII, 113pp on Phantom.

A Very English Hero
The Making of Frank Thompson
Conradi, Peter J.
London; Bloomsbury Publishing Plc; 2013; ISBN 978 1 4088 3092 5; xi + 419pp/68 x bw PI/2 x bw SI/2 x bw M; p/b; Indexed Y; Glossary N; Appendices Y; Bibliography Y; 197 x 128 (12mo)
NOTES: Paperback reprint of hardback first edition, same pagination.

Note on Colonial Regiments.
Colonial regiments are outside the remit of this work. There are two such reconnaissance regiments - 81st (West African) and 82nd (West African) Reconnaissance Regiments. Readers interested in them will find both well referenced in *The History of the Royal West African Frontier Force* by Col A. Haywood. 81(WA)R has brief, unnamed, reference in *Jungle Commando, The Story of the West African Expeditionary Force's First Campaign in Burma*, published November 1944, and some information in Vol. 2, No.4 of the *Reconnaissance Journal*. Additionally, a couple of paragraphs on both regiments appear in the appendix to *This Band of Brothers*, q.v.

Key to Book Entries
Book Title and Sub-title(s)
Author   Museum Holdings
Place of Publication; Publisher; Date of Publication; ISBN; Pages/Illustrations; Binding; Indexed; Glossary; Appendices; Bibliography; Size (in mm); Availability
NOTES:

Section VII

Royal Armoured Corps: Supplementary Reserve

The North Irish Horse (NIH) held a unique position within the RAC. It was the senior regiment of the reserve forces and the sole active regiment within the Supplementary Reserve branch of the RAC during WWII.

Prior to the war, it was listed in the Army List under Cavalry – Militia but in September 1939 the NIH was transferred from the Cavalry of the Line to the RAC's new branch, the Supplementary Reserve; this placed them in senior precedence to the Yeomanry regiments of the RAC.

The regiment was thus formed as a light armoured regiment and, after training in Northern Ireland and on the mainland, it went on to serve in North Africa and then Italy.

See also 'Appendix A – Theatres' regarding the anomalous seniority of the regiment when brigaded in 21st Tank Brigade in 1944.

Royal Armoured Corps: Supplementary Reserve

North Irish Horse — NIH

Date of mechanization: 11/09/1939
RAC service: 11/09/1939   Post-war.

Regimental journal/magazine:
None established.

The North Irish Horse Battle Report
North Africa & Italy 1943 - 1945
Not stated   TM; IWM; NAM
Belfast; W & G Baird Ltd; 1946; ISBN None; 108pp/1 x clr Mfrbd*; h/b Green cloth; Indexed N; Glossary N; Appendices N; Bibliography N; 221 x 139 (8vo); Rare
NOTES: Text is very dry, appearing to slightly embellish War Diary information. It does, however, provide excellent information on the men of the regiment in the form of four complete listings at significant points during the Italian Campaign. RoH/Honours/Awards. *The folding map is of a significant size, approx. 575mm square.

To The Green Fields Beyond
Hunt, Donald F.   NAM
Durham; The Pentland Press Ltd; 1993; ISBN 185821 030 5; 228pp/218pp/23 x bw Pl; h/b / d/j Green cloth; Indexed N; Glossary N; Appendices N; Bibliography N; 216 x 151 (8vo); Uncommon
NOTES: Within this autobiography the author recounts his wartime experiences with the NIH. He joined up in late 1941 and was commissioned into the regiment in the spring of 1943. He joined the regiment in Algeria after the NA campaign and took over 5 Tp, A Sqn. He recounts leading the troop in Italy with some good practical detail. Seriously wounded in September 1944, he was invalided out of the army as a result. 70pp on WWII, 40pp on NIH service.

North Irish Horse
Hitler Line Battle 23rd May 1944 50th Anniversary
Not stated [See Notes]   TM; IWM
No imprint; No imprint; n.d. [1994]; ISBN None; 10pp/1 x bw Mf; s/b; Indexed N; Glossary N; Appendices N; Bibliography N; 209 x 147 (8vo); Rare
NOTES: Commemorative booklet with background to the action of 23rd May 1944. RoH for that day. Author is Lt-Col R. J. Griffith.

Fighting for Freedom and for Fun
Pope, M.C., Maj. Michael   TM
London; Tiger & Tyger Limited; 1999; ISBN 1 902914 01 5; iv + 95pp/36 x bw Pl/2 x bw SI/1 x bw M; s/b; Indexed Y; Glossary N; Appendices Y; Bibliography N; 215 x 137 (8vo)
NOTES: The author was commissioned into the NIH and sailed to NA with them, commanding 4 Tp, B Sqn. He was promoted to Adjutant after the NA campaign and then became 2 i/c B Sqn in Italy, ending the war again as Adjutant. Potted commentary on selected experiences. 40pp on WWII.

The North Irish Horse Battle Report
North Africa & Italy 1943 - 1945
Not stated PCL
Uckfield; Naval & Military Press Ltd; ISBN 978 1843425236; See Notes; Indexed N; Glossary N; Appendices N; Bibliography N; 215 x 136 (8vo)
NOTES: Facsimile reprint by NMP of 1946 first edition, available in s/b and h/b.

The North Irish Horse
A Hundred Years of Service
Doherty, Richard TM; IWM
Staplehurst; Spellmount Limited; 2002; ISBN 1-86227-190-9; xi + 276pp/24 x bw Pl/4 x bw M; h/b / d/j Green cloth; Indexed Y; Glossary N; Appendices Y; Bibliography Y; 240 x 159 (8vo)
NOTES: A full wartime history with many personal accounts, WWII occupies the bulk of the book. RoH/Honours/Awards.

Key to Book Entries
Book Title and Sub-title(s)
Author Museum Holdings
Place of Publication; Publisher; Date of Publication; ISBN; Pages/Illustrations; Binding; Indexed; Glossary; Appendices; Bibliography; Size (in mm); Availability
NOTES:

Section VIII

Royal Armoured Corps: TA - Yeomanry

Regiments of the Yeomanry (the Territorial Army cavalry) were amongst the very early adopters of armour. After World War One the Yeomanry was restructured, resulting in different roles from that of traditional horsed cavalry. The senior regiments retained that cavalry role whilst many others became artillery and one or two became signals or infantry. Eight regiments were reduced in size and between 1920 and 1922 converted to armoured car companies of the Tank Corps - forming 19th to 26th Armoured Car Companies.

These eight companies therefore became part of the Royal Armoured Corps upon its creation in April 1939. The doubling of the Territorial Army in early 1939 created an additional seven armoured Yeomanry regiments and by mid-1941 the last horsed cavalry Yeomanry regiments had joined the RAC; the Yorkshire Dragoons (Queen's Own) did not finally relinquish their horses until February 1942.

Those regiments which joined the RAC during 1941 were The Royal Wiltshire Yeomanry, The Warwickshire Yeomanry, The Yorkshire Hussars, Sherwood Rangers, and The Staffordshire Yeomanry – all in April. The Cheshire Yeomanry, Yorkshire Dragoons, and The North Somerset Yeomanry joined in September.

With the complicated expansion and balancing of Britain's armed forces during the early part of WWII, some regiments were part of the RAC for just a few months and some never saw a tank before reconverting to a different role. The Yorkshire Dragoons had perhaps the most nebulous relationship with the tank. Transferred to the RAC in September 1941 they were intended to convert to an armoured regiment. A lack of tanks, however, meant that they were then allocated to operate as a dummy tank unit, which they did during the middle of 1942. The continuing lack of tanks meant that they never adopted their intended armoured role and in September that year they converted to an infantry motor battalion. The regiment's transformational woes did not end there and in December 1942 the War Office decided it should become an infantry battalion, the 9th Battalion K.O.Y.L.I. (Yorkshire Dragoons).

The 2nd Derbyshire Yeomanry held an unusual position within the RAC by virtue of being an honorary member of the Reconnaissance Corps; the Recce Corps Journal features articles and notes on the regiment throughout its publication. Indeed, The White Swan Press, which published the Recce Journal, also published 2DY's official history in 1949. The link was enhanced through their commanding officer, Lt-Col Walter P Serracold. He had been Chief Instructor at the Reconnaissance Training Centre, before taking command of 2DY in Normandy until late 1945.

Royal Armoured Corps: TA - Yeomanry

The Yeomanry
A Short History
Mileham, P. J. R. TM; IWM; NAM
Edinburgh; Yeomanry Association; 1983; ISBN None; 28pp/24 x bw PI/1 x bw SIfep/17 x bw SI; s/b; Indexed N; Glossary N; Appendices N; Bibliography N; 211 x 146 (8vo)
NOTES: A precursor to the author's later works, this booklet looks at the regiments with a few paragraphs on each campaign. 5pp on WWII.

Armoured Yeomanry 1939 - 45
Bellis, M. A. TM
Not stated; M. A. Bellis; 1985; ISBN None; 27pp/No illus.; Paper; Indexed Y; Glossary N; Appendices Y; Bibliography Y; 297 x 210 (4to); Rare
NOTES: Précis of each regiment's RAC service.

The Yeomanry Regiments
A Pictorial History
Mileham, P. J. R. IWM; NAM; RMAS
Tunbridge Wells; Spellmount Ltd Publishers; 1985; ISBN 0-946771-96-0; 128pp/11 x clr SI/91 x bw PI/89 x bw SI; h/b / d/j Brown cloth; Indexed Y; Glossary N; Appendices N; Bibliography Y; 252 x 192 (4to)
NOTES: Overview of WWII campaigns with a good photo selection in 14pp; the second half of the book provides a very brief summary of each regiment.

The Yeomanry Regiments
200 Years of Tradition
Mileham, P. J. R. NAM
Edinburgh; Canongate Academic; 1994; ISBN 1 898410 36 4; 128pp/11 x clr SI/91 x bw PI/89 x bw SI; h/b / d/j Black cloth; Indexed Y; Glossary N; Appendices N; Bibliography Y; 253 x 194 (4to)
NOTES: Second edition of book above, published on 200th Anniversary of the Yeomanry, with some errors corrected and narrative brought up to date; identical pagination.

Year of the Yeomanry 1794 - 1994
Not stated TM; NAM
Winchester; Army Museums Ogilby Trust; 1994; ISBN 0 9515714 8 6; 108pp/1 x bw PIfep/17 x clr PI/ 2 x clr SI/119 x bw PI/61 x bw SI; s/b; Indexed N; Glossary N; Appendices N; Bibliography Y; 297 x 209 (4to)
NOTES: A précised history of each yeomanry regiment across the 200 years, minor references to WWII.

Yeomanry Wars
The History of the Yeomanry, Volunteer and Volunteer Association Cavalry
Athawes, Peter D. TM; IWM; NAM; RMAS
Aberdeen; Scottish Cultural Press; 1994; ISBN 1 898218 02 1; xxi + 262pp/1 x clr SIfep/1 x clr PI/9 x clr SI/37 x bw PI/28 x bw SI/12 x bw M; h/b / d/j Green cloth; Indexed Y; Glossary Y; Appendices Y; Bibliography Y; 303 x 215 (4to)
NOTES: Comprehensive history of the Yeomanry. 11pp chapter on WWII. Appendices include: precedence, succession tables, battle honours, and cap badges, 15 x clr PI cap badge illustrations and 337 x bw PI cap badges illustrations. Errata slip tipped in.

The Yeomanry Regiments
Over 200 Years of Tradition
Mileham, P. J. R. IWM
Staplehurst; Spellmount Limited; 2003; ISBN 1-86227-167-4; 128pp/11 x clr SI/91 x bw PI/89 x bw SI; h/b / d/j Red cloth; Indexed Y; Glossary N; Appendices N; Bibliography Y; 252 x 192 (4to)
NOTES: Third edition with some errors corrected and narrative brought further up to date. Same pagination, minor alteration to '1945 – Present' chapter.

The Royal Wiltshire Yeomanry (Prince of Wales's Own)	R WILTS YEO

Date of mechanization: Spring 1941
RAC service: 12/04/1941 Post-war.

Royal Wilts
The History of the Royal Wiltshire Yeomanry, 1920 - 1945
Pitt, T.D., Lt-Col P. W. TM; IWM; NAM; RMAS
London; Burrup, Mathieson & Co Ltd; 1946; ISBN None; 234pp/58 x bw PI/2 x bw SI/2 x clr Mbds/1 x clr Mf/7 x clr M/1 x bw Mf/14 x bw M; h/b Blue cloth; Indexed N; Glossary N; Appendices Y; Bibliography N; 252 x 191 (4to); Uncommon
NOTES: Regimental history covering the wartime record of the RWY in a conversational style. First half deals with the regiment as horsed yeomanry, the second as a tank regiment. Appendices include lists of personnel upon embodiment, 1939, and Palestine 1940; RoH/Honours/Awards. Reprinted by Naval & Military Press 2012.

Under Any Sky
Being some letters of a Subaltern on Active Service overseas, 1942-1944
Not stated IWM
Ditchling; Private (Ditchling Press - printers); 1956; ISBN None; 172pp/1 x bw PIfep/3 x bw PI/1 x bw SI; h/b Coloured paper; Indexed N; Glossary N; Appendices N; Bibliography N; 222 x 143 (8vo); Rare
NOTES: Reproduced letters of Lt David F Gilliatt from April 1942 to July 1944. He joined 2RGH July 1942 serving in H and G Sqns as a troop leader. When 2RGH was disbanded he went with G Sqn to the RWY. Views of a young subaltern in North Africa and from May 1944, until his death* in August, in Italy. (* see p182 in Platt's RWY, q.v., history for the circumstances.)

The Royal Wiltshire Yeomanry (Prince of Wales's Own) 1907 – 1967
Platt, D.S.O., O.B.E., Brig. John R. I. TM; IWM; NAM; RMAS; PCL
London; Garnstone Press Limited; 1972; ISBN 0 85511 200 X; 272pp/2 x clr SIfep/51 x bw Pl/1 x bw SI/7 x bw M; h/b / d/j Green cloth; Indexed N; Glossary N; Appendices Y; Bibliography N; 222 x 143 (8vo)
NOTES: Overall history of the regiment complementary to Pitt's; lacking an index. Appendices include: list of officers 1908 – 1967, honorary colonels, COs, Adjutants and Quartermasters, etc., RoH/Honours/Awards, AFVs used. 119pp on WWII.

A History of the Royal Wiltshire Yeomanry
Platt, D.S.O., O.B.E., Brig. J. R. I. NAM
No imprint; Thamesdown Borough Council; n.d. [c.1980s]; ISBN None; 19pp/6 x bw PI; s/b (card); Indexed N; Glossary N; Appendices N; Bibliography N; 297 x 210 (4to); Uncommon
NOTES: Published following the establishment of the RWY Museum. 5pp on WWII.

Royal Wilts
The History of the Royal Wiltshire Yeomanry, 1920 - 1945
Pitt, T.D., Lt-Col P. W.
Uckfield; Naval & Military Press Ltd; ISBN 978 1781519646; See Notes; s/b; Indexed N; Glossary N; Appendices Y; Bibliography N
NOTES: Facsimile reprint by NMP of 1946 first edition, available in s/b.

The Warwickshire Yeomanry — WARWICK YEO

Date of mechanization: April 1941
RAC service: 12/04/1941 Post-war.

Regimental publications:
The Warwickshire Yeomanry Journal
Vol. 1 No. 1 Jan 1955 to Vol. 1 No. 5 Nov 1956 (Irregular)

The Warwickshire Yeomanry
No imprint NAM
Warwick; Phillips Design and Print Ltd (Printers); n.d. [1957]; ISBN None; 20pp/16 x bw PI/1 x bw SI; p/b (card); Indexed N; Glossary N; Appendices N; Bibliography N; 268 x 209 (4to); Uncommon
NOTES: Published upon the amalgamation of the regiment into the The Queen's Own Warwickshire and Worcestershire Yeomanry in 1957. Competent précis of role in WWII; 5pp on WWII.

Yeoman Yeoman
The Warwickshire Yeomanry 1920 - 1956
Baker, Paul TM; IWM
Birmingham; The Queen's Own Warwickshire and Worcestershire Yeomanry Regimental Association; 1971; ISBN 9501971 0 6; vii + 123pp/1 x bw PIfep/32 x bw P/2 x clr Mbds/2 x clr M/3 x bw M; h/b / d/j Blue cloth; Indexed N; Glossary Y; Appendices Y; Bibliography N; 225 x 151 (8vo)
NOTES: First third deals with the regiment as horsed yeomanry and then motorized infantry prior to its conversion to tanks. Occasional quotes from veterans. The remainder covers NA, battle of El Alamein and Italy to the war's end. Produced under an author-editorship by Paul Baker who served in C Sqn until severely wounded in June 1944. RoH/Honours/Awards, list of wounded and POWs.

The Yorkshire Hussars (Alexandra, Princess of Wales's Own)	YORKS H

Date of mechanization: April 1941
RAC service: 12/04/1941 Post-war.

Regimental publications:
The Yorkshire Hussars Magazine
Vol. 1 No. 1 July 1927 to Vol. 11 No. 46 Oct 1938 (Quarterly)

No publications established.

The Nottinghamshire (Sherwood Rangers) Yeomanry	NOTTS YEO

Date of mechanization: April 1941
RAC service: 12/04/1941 Post-war.

Regimental publications:
The Sherwood Rangers Yeomanry Regimental Association Magazine
No 1 1965 to No 2 1966 (Annual)
Sherwood Siren (in the field)
Issue dates unknown.

Alamein to Zem Zem
Douglas, Keith
London; Editions Poetry London; 1946; ISBN None; 141pp + xiv/1 x clr SIfep/3 x clr SI/11 x bw SI; h/b / d/j Red cloth/grey paper; Indexed N; Glossary N; Appendices N; Bibliography N; 228 x 175 (8vo); Rare
NOTES: The author left Oxford College in 1940 and sailed to the ME in August 1941. Posted to divisional staff on camouflage training, he took the unusual step of leaving without permission to re-join his regiment to get to the fight. He joined them at the end of 1942, mid-El Alamein and the narrative starts with the lead-up to that battle. Essential reading - few memoirs achieve the same level of visceral description. Illustrations by the

author. (KD gave some sketches to Stanley Christopherson, his squadron commander and later CO in Normandy; three from 1943 are reproduced in SC's diary, *An Englishman at War*, q.v.) Contains 16 poems by the author not reproduced in later printings.

The Collected Poems of Keith Douglas
Douglas, Keith; Waller, John & Fraser, G. S. (Eds.)
London; Editions Poetry London; 1951; ISBN None; xiv + 151pp/1 x bw PIfep/3 x bw PI/1 x bw SI; h/b / d/j Red cloth; Indexed N; Glossary N; Appendices N; Bibliography N; 226 x 144 (8vo); Rare
NOTES: Collection of the author's poems collated as closely as possible to the final versions he left after his death. Published in reverse chronological order.

Sherwood Rangers
The Story of the Nottinghamshire Sherwood Rangers Yeomanry in the Second World War
Lindsay, T. M.   TM; IWM; NAM; RMAS; PCL
London; Burrup, Mathieson & Co Ltd; 1952; ISBN None; 182pp/65 x bw PI/2 x clr Mbds/1 x clr M/4 x bw M; h/b / d/j Green cloth; Indexed N; Glossary N; Appendices N; Bibliography N; 250 x 190 (4to); Uncommon
NOTES: This history, written by a serving officer, traces the regiment from horsed yeomanry to motorized infantry to an armoured regiment that would land on D-Day. The narrative is interwoven with veteran's quotations and conveys both the strategic scene and the face of battle. RoH/Honours/Awards/list of citations.

A Short History of the Sherwood Rangers Yeomanry 1794 - 1953
Not stated   TM; IWM
Worksop; Sissons & Son Ltd; n.d. [c.1953]; ISBN None; 48pp/1 x bw PIfep/4 x bw M; s/b; Indexed N; Glossary N; Appendices N; Bibliography N; 216 x 141 (8vo); Uncommon
NOTES: Summary history for the regiment, 11pp on WWII based on T M Lindsay, q.v. above.

Selected Poems
Keith Douglas
Douglas, Keith; Hughes, Ted (Ed.)   IWM
London; Faber and Faber Limited; 1964; ISBN None; 63pp/No illus.; h/b / d/j Red cloth; Indexed N; Glossary N; Appendices N; Bibliography N; 206 x 135 (8vo); Uncommon
NOTES: A collection of 40 of the author's poems with an introduction by Ted Hughes. Presented in editorial rather than chronological order.

Alamein to Zem Zem
Douglas, Keith; Waller, John; Fraser, G. S. & Hall, J. C. (Eds.)   TM
London; Faber and Faber Limited; 1966; ISBN None; 152pp/1 x bw PIfep/11 x bw SI; h/b / d/j Blue cloth; Indexed N; Glossary N; Appendices N; Bibliography N; 222 x 144 (8vo); Uncommon
NOTES: Minor changes from first edition and colour illustrations and poem selection not reproduced; introduction by Lawrence Durrell.

Keith Douglas
Collected Poems
Douglas, Keith; Waller, John; Fraser, G. S. & Hall, J. C. (Eds.)   NAM
London; Faber and Faber Limited; 1966; ISBN None; 164pp/1 x bw PIfep/1 x bw PI/5 x bw SI; h/b / d/j Green cloth; Indexed Y; Glossary N; Appendices N; Bibliography N; 222 x 143 (8vo)
NOTES: Based on the EPL edition of 1951, the poems are presented here in chronological rather than reverse order. One new poem is added, one revised and some minor revisions to the narrative. This edition also includes some of the author's illustrations. The middle section of the book contains his wartime poems.

Alamein to Zem Zem
Douglas, Keith; Waller, John; Fraser, G. S. & Hall, J. C. (Eds.)
Harmondsworth; Penguin Books Ltd; 1969; ISBN None; 167pp/11 x bw SI; p/b; Indexed N; Glossary N; Appendices N; Bibliography N; 180 x 110 (12mo)
NOTES: Paperback reprint of 1966 edition with some corrections and excludes Lawrence Durrell introduction, different pagination.

Keith Douglas 1920 - 1944
A Biography
Graham, Desmond   IWM
Oxford; Oxford University Press; 1974; ISBN 0 19 211716 5; xiii + 295pp/1 x bw PIfep/43 x bw PI/27 x bw SI/1 x bw M; h/b / d/j Black cloth; Indexed Y; Glossary N; Appendices N; Bibliography Y; 240 x 162 (8vo)
NOTES: Formal biography, first half deals with his childhood up to Oxford University. Second half deals with his wartime career, some of his letters and his body of poetry with critique. (Note: the book *Selected Poems*, John Bale & Staples, 1943, is not listed because it is pre-SRY content.)

Keith Douglas
Complete Poems
Douglas, Keith; Graham, Desmond (Ed.)
Oxford; Oxford University Press; 1978; ISBN 0-19-211876-5; xiv + 145pp/No illus.; h/b / d/j Black cloth; Indexed Y; Glossary N; Appendices N; Bibliography N; 240 x 157 (8vo); Uncommon
NOTES: More expanded listing of the author's poems than in EPL edition; from 1934 to 1944 in chronological order.

Keith Douglas
Complete Poems
Douglas, Keith; Graham, Desmond (Ed.)
Oxford; Oxford University Press; 1979; ISBN 0-19-211876-5; xiv + 145pp/No illus.; h/b / d/j Black cloth; Indexed Y; Glossary N; Appendices N; Bibliography N; 240 x 157 (8vo); Uncommon
NOTES: Reprint of 1978 hardback edition, same pagination.

Alamein to Zem Zem
Douglas, Keith; Graham, Desmond (Ed.) IWM
Oxford; Oxford University Press; 1979; ISBN 0 19 281267 X; 156pp/1 x bw PIfep/11 x bw SI; p/b; Indexed N; Glossary N; Appendices N; Bibliography N; 196 x 129 (12mo)
NOTES: Paperback reprint of 1966 edition with new mini-biographical introduction by Desmond Graham; different pagination.

Keith Douglas The Complete Poems
Douglas, Keith; Graham, Desmond (Ed.)
Oxford; Oxford University Press; 1987; ISBN 0-19-281964-X ; xxvii + 145pp/See Notes; p/b; Indexed Y; Glossary N; Appendices N; Bibliography N; Uncommon
NOTES: Second edition. New introduction by Ted Hughes. (Not physically inspected.)

Keith Douglas 1920 - 1944
A Biography
Graham, Desmond
Oxford; Oxford University Press; 1988; ISBN 0-19-282114-8; xvii + 295pp/1 x bw PIfep/43 x bw PI/27 x bw SI/1 x bw M; p/b; Indexed Y; Glossary N; Appendices N; Bibliography Y; 196 x 128 (12mo)
NOTES: Paperback reprint of 1974 first edition with minor corrections plus minor updates based on new information. New paperback foreword, body of same pagination as first edition.

Keith Douglas
A Study
Scammell, William IWM
London; Faber and Faber Limited; 1988; ISBN 0-571-14500-9; xiv + 226pp/No illus.; p/b; Indexed Y; Glossary N; Appendices N; Bibliography Y; 198 x 123 (8vo)
NOTES: This book is a critical study of KD's poetry and starts with a 10pp summary of his wartime career. In addition there is a 30pp literary review of *Alamein to Zem Zem*.

Keith Douglas The Complete Poems
Douglas, Keith; Graham, Desmond (Ed.)
Oxford; Oxford University Press; 1990; See Notes
NOTES: Reprint of 1987 second edition. (Not physically inspected.)

The Man Who Worked On Sundays
The personal War Diary June 2nd 1944 to May 17th 1945 of Revd. Leslie Skinner RAChD. Chaplain, 8th (Independent) Armoured Brigade attached The Sherwood Rangers Yeomanry Regiment.
Skinner, RAChD., Rvd Leslie IWM; NAM
Not stated; Not stated; n.d. [c.1991]; ISBN None; 164pp/7 x bw PI/4 x bw SI/2 x bw M; s/b; Indexed N; Glossary Y; Appendices N; Bibliography N; 206 x 147 (8vo); Uncommon
NOTES: After becoming an army chaplain in the summer of 1941, the author initially served in NA. In March 1944 he became the senior chaplain of 8AB and was attached to SRY for the NWE campaign. This is a reproduction of the diary he kept from 2 June 1944 to 17 May 1945. He adds notes throughout to explain or expand on certain entries. Fascinating insight into the rarely revealed work of the front line army chaplain and full

of detail pertinent to the casualties of the regiment. Includes a sketch map of the location of Keith Douglas' battlefield burial site. See also the companion volume *Sherwood Rangers Casualty Book 1944 – 1945*.

Alamein to Zem Zem
Douglas, Keith
London; Faber and Faber Ltd; 1992; ISBN 0-571-16264-9; xvi + 152pp/1 x bwPIfep/11 x bw SI; p/b; Indexed N; Glossary N; Appendices N; Bibliography N; 196 x 125 (12mo)
NOTES: Paperback reprint of 1966 edition, same narrative pagination as 1966 but introduction same as 1979 OUP edition.

El Alamein
A Tank Soldier's Story
Reddish, Arthur   TM; IWM; NAM
Wanganui, New Zealand; Arthur Reddish; n.d. [c.1992]; ISBN 0-473-01644-3; 96pp/1 x bw PIfep/27 x bw PI/5 x bw M; s/b; Indexed N; Glossary N; Appendices Y; Bibliography Y; 240 x 170 (8vo); Uncommon
NOTES: The author joined the SRY in July 1942 and in this, his first volume, his research of the strategic picture is interspersed with personal recollections of El Alamein where he served as a Sherman tank lap-gunner. See also *Normandy 1944 From the Hull of a Sherman* and *Sherwood Rangers Yeomanry The Final Advance*.

Sherwood Rangers
The Story of the Nottinghamshire Sherwood Rangers Yeomanry in the Second World War
Lindsay, T. M.
York; Wilton 65; 1992; See Notes; h/b Green cloth; Indexed N; Glossary N; Appendices N; Bibliography N; Rare
NOTES: Facsimile reprint of 1952 first edition with amendments. 250 copies printed. (Not physically inspected.)

Dad's War
A Tank Commander in Europe 1944-45
With the XXIV Lancers and Sherwood Rangers Yeomanry
Cropper, Andy   TM; IWM
Thurlstone; Anmas Publications; 1994; ISBN 0 95242222 0 4; 108pp/28 x bw PI; s/b; Indexed N; Glossary N; Appendices N; Bibliography Y; 210 x 147 (8vo); Rare
NOTES: Written by his son, this book tells of John Cropper's service with 24L from May 1944 to disbandment and then with the SRY. His service with the SRY is covered in the last two-thirds of the book. The narrative is interspersed with his quotations. Provides an insight into some of the minutiae of troop/squadron life; details such as wearing headphones over one ear to be aware of outside sounds. Includes a good selection of private photographs. 500 copies printed.

A Trooper's Desert War
Foster, Philip TM; IWM; NAM
York; Wilton 65; 1994; ISBN 0 947828 37 0; 160pp/1 x bw PIfep/35 x bw PI/3 x bw M; s/b; Indexed Y; Glossary N; Appendices N; Bibliography N; 206 x 147 (8vo); Uncommon
NOTES: The author joined the RAC in the summer of 1941; nearly 18 months later he was in the desert with C Sqn, SRY. With extensive and interesting detail, he starts with the journey to Egypt. During the battle of El Alamein he was posted to B Echelon, to the fitters, and afterwards to a B Sqn Sherman as wireless operator. His memoirs end poignantly with the final chapter describing his tank being hit on D-Day and him being medically downgraded to non-combatant as a result of his wounds.

Keith Douglas The Complete Poems
Douglas, Keith; Graham, Desmond (Ed.)
Oxford; Oxford University Press; 1995; See Notes
NOTES: Reissue of 1987 second edition. (Not physically inspected.)

Normandy 1944 From the Hull of a Sherman
Limited Edition
Reddish, Arthur TM
Wanganui, New Zealand; Battlefield Associates / Ken Ewing Publications; 1995; ISBN 0-473-03268-6; 104pp/1 x bw PIfep/45 x bw PI/8 x bw M; s/b; Indexed N; Glossary N; Appendices Y; Bibliography Y; 240 x 170 (8vo); Uncommon
NOTES: Interesting recollections of life in a Sherman tank in Normandy. See also *El Alamein, A Tank Soldier's Story* and *Sherwood Rangers Yeomanry The Final Advance*.

The Man Who Worked On Sundays
The personal War Diary June 2nd 1944 to May 17th 1945 of Revd. Leslie Skinner RAChD. Chaplain, 8th (Independent) Armoured Brigade attached The Sherwood Rangers Yeomanry Regiment.
Skinner, RAChD., Rvd Leslie TM
Epsom; Revd. Leslie Skinner; 1996; ISBN 0 9527774 0 1; 164pp/7 x bw PI/4 x bw SI/2 x bw M; s/b; Indexed N; Glossary Y; Appendices N; Bibliography N; 206 x 147 (8vo); Uncommon
NOTES: Although stated as the first edition, this is a reprint of the c.1991 edition, same pagination.

Sherwood Rangers Casualty Book 1944 - 1945
The Personal Notebook of Revd. Leslie Skinner RAChD
Skinner, RAChD., Rvd Leslie TM; NAM
Epsom; Revd. Leslie Skinner RAChD; 1996; ISBN 0 9527774 1 X; 191pp/16 x bw PI; s/b; Indexed Y; Glossary N; Appendices N; Bibliography N; 206 x 146 (8vo); Uncommon
NOTES: Reproduces facsimiles of the author's hand written notes, and occasional sketch maps, listing the regiment's casualties. At the end of the book is a list of wounded and killed together with the location of their graves. Separate is a list of war cemeteries and the SRY soldiers buried there. Companion volume to *The Man Who Worked On Sundays*, q.v.

Sherwood Rangers Yeomanry The Final Advance. Trials and Transgressions, A Trooper's War Memoirs
Reddish, Arthur TM
York; Wilton 65; 1997; ISBN 0 947828 49 4; 90pp/1 x bw PIfep/33 x bw PI/1 x bw M; s/b; Indexed N; Glossary N; Appendices N; Bibliography N; 210 x 147 (8vo); Uncommon
NOTES: Published posthumously, this book completes the author's war from August 1944 through to emigration to New Zealand in 1949. See also *El Alamein, A Tank Soldier's Story* and *Normandy 1944 From the Hull of a Sherman*.

Keith Douglas The Complete Poems
Douglas, Keith; Graham, Desmond (Ed.)
Oxford; Oxford University Press; 1998; ISBN 0-19-288087-X; xxxvi + 164pp/No illus.; p/b; Indexed Y; Glossary N; Appendices N; Bibliography N; 196 x 130 (12mo)
NOTES: Third edition. Revised text and new preface, revisions to 19 poems.

Mareth, March 1943 Break through at the Tebaga Gap With N.Z. Corps 8th Armoured Brigade
Ewing, Ken & Leppard, Ernie IWM
York; Wilton 65; 1999; ISBN 0 947828 79 6; 65pp/9 x clr PI/1 x clr SI/13 x bw PI/2 x clr M/2 x bw M; Comb; Indexed Y; Glossary N; Appendices N; Bibliography N; 297 x 210 (4to); Uncommon
NOTES: An account of a single action, Tebaga Gap, using original sources and memoirs. Both authors served in SRY, K. Ewing at the time of the action.

Keith Douglas The Letters
Douglas, Keith; Graham, Desmond (Ed.)
Manchester; Carcanet Press Limited; 2000; ISBN 1 85754 477 3; xxv + 369pp/No illus.; p/b; Indexed Y; Glossary N; Appendices N; Bibliography N; 216 x 136 (8vo)
NOTES: A collection of poet Keith Douglas's letters written between 1925 and 1944.

Keith Douglas Complete Poems
Douglas, Keith; Graham, Desmond (Ed.)
London; Faber and Faber Limited; 2000; ISBN 978-0-571-27671-4; xxxvi + 164pp/No illus.; p/b; Indexed Y; Glossary N; Appendices N; Bibliography N; 198 x 130 (8vo)
NOTES: Reprint of 1998 third revised edition.

Sherwood Rangers
The Story of the Nottinghamshire Sherwood Rangers Yeomanry in the Second World War
Lindsay, T. M.
York; Wilton 65; 2001; ISBN 0 947828 86 0; 182pp/65 x bw PI/5 x bw M; h/b Green cloth; Indexed N; Glossary N; Appendices N; Bibliography N; 250 x 178 (4to)
NOTES: Facsimile reprint of 1992 amended reprint.

By Tank Into Normandy
A Memoir of the Campaign in North-West Europe from D-Day to VE Day
Hills, M.C., Stuart TM; IWM; NAM
London; Cassell & Co; 2002; ISBN 0-304-36216-6; 255pp/24 x bw Pl/8 x bw M; h/b / d/j
Grey cloth; Indexed Y; Glossary N; Appendices N; Bibliography Y; 240 x 162 (8vo)
NOTES: The author was a troop leader in C Sqn and later commanded the Recce Troop. He took part in the NWE campaign from the D-Day landings to the victory in Europe. Remarkably he was the only troop leader of the regiment not to be killed or wounded during the campaign. After setting the scene for D-Day, he recounts his childhood and military training. He then turns to the landings and produces one of the most readable and informative accounts of tank combat. Full of operational detail, comment on combat, uniforms, meals, etc. See also his driver's memoirs, *Normandy 1944 From the Hull of a Sherman* by Arthur Reddish.

By Tank Into Normandy
A Memoir of the Campaign in North-West Europe from D-Day to VE Day
Hills, M.C., Stuart
London; Cassell Military Paperbacks; 2003; ISBN 0-304-36640-4; 255pp/24 x bw Pl/8 x bw M; p/b; Indexed Y; Glossary N; Appendices N; Bibliography Y; 198 x 128 (8vo)
NOTES: Paperback reprint of 2002 first edition. (Publisher sometimes listed as Phoenix but this is not referenced in the book. Cassell and Phoenix are part of the Orion Publishing Group.)

Chariots of the Lake
The Story of Britain's Secret Weapon during the Second World War. From Fritton Lake to D-Day and Beyond
Jarvis, Robert B. TM
Lowestoft; The Heritage Workshop Centre; 2003; ISBN 1-904413-04-8; 131pp/5 x clr Pl/56 x bw Pl/4 x bw Sl/1 x bw M; s/b; Indexed Y; Glossary Y; Appendices N; Bibliography Y; 260 x 210 (4to)
NOTES: Tells the story of the DD tank through the Suffolk training area at Fritton Lake and includes information on the DD equipped regiments: 4/7DG, 13/18H, ERY, SRY, and SY contained in 29pp.

It Is Bliss Here
Letters Home 1939 - 1945
Hildyard, Myles TM; IWM
London; Bloomsbury Publishing Plc; 2005; ISBN 9780747578024; 323pp/24 x bw PI; h/b / d/j Black cloth; Indexed N; Glossary N; Appendices N; Bibliography N; 240 x 158 (8vo)
NOTES: These memoirs comprise the author's letters written to his parents and a brother, covering the period of the war. He served as IO from late 1940 and moved to Crete in 1941 where he was captured but escaped and returned to the regiment in November. In May 1942 he transferred to divisional staff returning to the SRY as Adjutant in December 1942. In the summer of 1943 he left the regiment for the remainder of the war, serving as IO with 7AD HQ. References to the regiment are occasional amongst the letters home which reveal everyday content on foods, scenery,

books read, etc.; some detail from the period in Tunisia, 1943. See also *Sherwood Rangers* by Lindsay for a chapter on the author's Cretan experience.

It Is Bliss Here
Letters Home 1939 - 1945
Hildyard, Myles
London; Bloomsbury Publishing Plc; 2006; ISBN 9780747581208; 335pp/24 x bw Pl/2 x bw M; p/b; Indexed Y; Glossary N; Appendices N; Bibliography N; 197 x 128 (12mo)
NOTES: Paperback reprint of first edition, same pagination but with the addition of an index.

Keith Douglas
Poems selected by Ted Hughes
Douglas, Keith
London; Faber and Faber Limited; 2006; ISBN 978-0-571-23038-9; xii + 49pp/No illus.; p/b; Indexed N; Glossary N; Appendices N; Bibliography N; 196 x 119 (12mo)
NOTES: Reprint of Ted Hughes' selection published in 1964 but with editorial changes made in *The Complete Poems* of 1978. From the Poet-to-Poet series.

Alamein to Zem Zem
Douglas, Keith
London; Faber and Faber Ltd; 2008; ISBN 978-0-571-24194-1; 167pp/11 x bw SI; p/b; Indexed N; Glossary N; Appendices N; Bibliography N; 216 x 134 (8vo)
NOTES: Paperback reprint of 1966 edition excluding Lawrence Durrell introduction, different pagination. Reprinted 2014 with new preface by Richard Skinner.

Keith Douglas, 1920 - 1944
A Biography
Graham, Desmond
London; Faber and Faber Ltd; 2009; ISBN 978-0-571-25415-6; xvii + 295pp/1 x bw Plfep/45 x bw Pl/23 x bw SI/1 x bw M; p/b; Indexed Y; Glossary N; Appendices N; Bibliography Y; 198 x 125 (8vo)
NOTES: Reprint of 1974 first edition with new paperback preface.

An Englishman At War
The Wartime Diaries of Stanley Christopherson DSO, MC, TD
1939-45
Christopherson, DSO, MC, TD, Stanley; Holland, James (Ed.)
London; Bantam Press; 2014; ISBN 978 0593068373; 552pp/1 x clr Pl/100 x bw Pl/3 x bw SI/2 x clr Mbds/1 x bw M; h/b / d/j Blue cloth; Indexed Y; Glossary Y; Appendices Y; Bibliography N; 240 x 156 (8vo)
NOTES: Stanley Christopherson had a remarkable war. He joined the SRY in October 1939 as a subaltern in 3 Tp, C Sqn, and ended the war as the regiment's commanding officer, hardly ever absent in six years. His diary starts in January 1940 with the regiment sailing for Palestine and runs through, in considerable detail, to the end of the campaign in North Africa. The entries are almost daily from 1940 to 1943 and, upon returning to the UK, carry on in continuous narrative. The diary is interspersed with editorial comment, expanding on certain events or observations. The three sketch

illustrations are by fellow officer Keith Douglas, given to SC by the poet. SC's diaries shadow the transformation of the British Army from its ill-equipped, peacetime territorial days to a professional, well-equipped army, honed through years of experience; a particularly instructive set of memoirs.

An Englishman At War
The Wartime Diaries of Stanley Christopherson DSO, MC, TD
1939-45
Christopherson, DSO, MC, TD, Stanley; Holland, James (Ed.)
London; Corgi Books (Transworld Publishers Ltd.); 2015; ISBN 978 0552165655; 416pp/Illus.; p/b
NOTES: Paperback reprint of 2014 first edition, scheduled for publication in 2015.

The Staffordshire Yeomanry (Queen's Own Royal Regiment)	STAFFS YEO

Date of mechanization: June 1941
RAC service: 12/04/1941   Post-war.

The Staffordshire Yeomanry (Q.O.R.R.)
In the First and Second World Wars 1914 - 1918 and 1939 - 1945
Kemp, R.N. (Retd), Lt-Cmdr P. K.   TM; IWM; NAM; RMAS; PCL
Aldershot; Gale & Polden Ltd; 1950; ISBN None; xii + 168pp/1 x bw PIfep/19 x bw PI/1 x bw SI/1 x clr M/17 x bw M; h/b Blue cloth; Indexed N; Glossary N; Appendices Y; Bibliography N; 221 x 144 (8vo)
NOTES: Covers both WWI and WWII, each in approximately half the book. Well detailed narrative of actions. RoH includes service number and theatre. RoH/Honours/Awards.

The Story of the Staffordshire Yeomanry (Queen's Own Royal Regt)
The Regiment; 1952; ISBN None; 6pp/See Notes; Rare
NOTES: Not physically inspected.

Evacuation Tarbat Peninsula 1943-4
Fallon, Dr, James A.   TM
No imprint; No imprint; n.d. [c.1985]; ISBN None; 29pp/2 x clr PI/4 x clr SI/12 x bw PI/3 x clr M; s/b; Indexed N; Glossary N; Appendices N; Bibliography N; 210 x 147 (8vo)
NOTES: A local heritage booklet that tells the story of the area's evacuation for use as DD tank training, 6pp summarise the use of the area by 4/7DG, 13/18H, SY & ERY.

Queen's Own Royal Regiment
The Staffordshire Yeomanry. An account of the operations of the Regiment during World War II 1939 - 1945
Underhill, Maj. D. F.   TM; IWM
Stafford; Staffordshire Libraries, Arts and Archives; 1994; ISBN 0-903363-58-5; 43pp/8 x bw PI/1 x Mf; s/b; Indexed N; Glossary Y; Appendices N; Bibliography N; 289 x 203 (4to)

NOTES: Short but informative narrative originally written in 1945/46. The author served in the regiment and he used the regiment's war diary and serving personnel to record its activities. Fifty years on this record was put into print by the regimental museum. Reprinted in 2000, q.v., excluding the folding map.

Silver Spoon
Spencer-Nairn, M. A.
Bishop Auckland; The Pentland Press Ltd; 1996; ISBN 1-85821-343-6; vii + 210pp/20 x bw Pl; h/b / d/j Black cloth; Indexed N; Glossary N; Appendices N; Bibliography N; 215 x 152 (8vo); Uncommon
NOTES: In this autobiography the author describes some wartime memories in 21pp, 14pp for 2FFY and 7pp for SY. He was OC C Sqn in 2FFY from the outset of war until February 1944, when he transferred to the SY as OC A Sqn.

Queen's Own Royal Regiment
The Staffordshire Yeomanry. An account of the operations of the Regiment during World War II 1939 - 1945
Underhill, Maj. D. F.
Stafford; Staffordshire Yeomanry Museum; 2000; ISBN 0-903363-58-5; 43pp/8 x bw Pl; s/b; Indexed N; Glossary Y; Appendices N; Bibliography N; 293 x 208 (4to)
NOTES: Reprint of 1994 edition but without the folded map at the rear.

Chariots of the Lake
The Story of Britain's Secret Weapon during the Second World War. From Fritton Lake to D-Day and Beyond
Jarvis, Robert B. TM
Lowestoft; The Heritage Workshop Centre; 2003; ISBN 1-904413-04-8; 131pp/5 x clr Pl/56 x bw Pl/4 x bw Sl/1 x bw M; s/b; Indexed Y; Glossary Y; Appendices N; Bibliography Y; 260 x 210 (4to)
NOTES: Tells the story of the DD tank through the Suffolk training area at Fritton Lake and includes information on the DD equipped regiments: 4/7DG, 13/18H, ERY, SRY, and SY contained in 29pp.

The Staffordshire Yeomanry (Queen's Own Royal Regiment)
German, David, and Coogan, Chris TM
Leek; Churnet Valley Books; 2006; ISBN 978-1-904546-7; 128pp/193 x bw Pl/17 x bw Sl/1 x bw M; s/b; Indexed N; Glossary N; Appendices N; Bibliography N; 244 x 169 (8vo)
NOTES: An illustrated history covering 1794 - 1967. 30pp and 49 bw photographs of WWII.

The Cheshire (Earl of Chester's) Yeomanry — CHESHIRE YEO

Date of mechanization: n/a
RAC service: 26/09/1941   16/03/1943*
* 28 February 1942 became 5th Line of Communication Signal (Cheshire Yeomanry) but not until 16 March 1943 was it officially transferred to Royal Corps of Signals.

The Cheshire (Earl of Chester's) Yeomanry 1898 - 1967
The last regiment to fight on horses
Verdin, O.B.E., T.D., Lt-Col Sir Richard   IWM; NAM
Not stated; Not stated (Willmer Brothers Limited – printers); 1971; ISBN None; xviii + 666pp/3 x clr SIfep/66 x bw PI/1 x bw SI/10 x bw M; h/b / d/j Blue & white cloth; Indexed Y; Glossary N; Appendices Y; Bibliography N; 234 x 159 (8vo)
NOTES: Although there is no narrative directly covering the regiment's transfer to the RAC, the author provides a very good chronicle describing the see-saw instructions to horsed yeomanry regiments due for mechanization in Palestine during 1940 and 1941.

The Yorkshire Dragoons (Queen's Own) — YORK DGNS

Date of mechanization: n/a
RAC service: 26/09/1941   19/12/1942*
* September 1942 converted to a motor battalion and December 1942 transferred to infantry as 9th Bn, KOYLI (Yorkshire Dragoons).

Francis Hugh Peter Courtenay Wood
Born 5 October 1916. Died in action in the Battle of Alamein 26 October 1942
Prescot, H. K. (Ed.)   IWM
Oxford; University Press, Oxford; 1951; ISBN None; vi + 147pp/1 x bw PIfep/9 x bw PI; h/b (d/j - ne) Red cloth; Indexed N; Glossary N; Appendices N; Bibliography N; 224 x 149 (8vo); Uncommon
NOTES: Peter Wood served in the regiment from the start of the war until his death at El Alamein. Comprises narrative interspersed with letters to and from Peter Wood plus a selection of his prose, verse and miscellaneous articles. No reference to the time the regiment spent as a dummy tank unit.

A Short Record of The Queen's Own Yorkshire Dragoons 1794 - 1954
Not stated [See Notes]   IWM; NAM
Aldershot; Gale & Polden Ltd; n.d. [1954]; ISBN None; 31pp/1 x bw SIfep; s/b; Indexed N; Glossary N; Appendices Y; Bibliography N; 183 x 120 (12mo); Uncommon
NOTES: Pocket record of the regiment, 8pp on WWII, one oblique paragraph on duties as a dummy armoured regiment; no mention of transfer to RAC. Authors are Col C. J. Hirst and Maj. J. R. P. Warde-Aldam 1794 – 1920s and Col Hanwell 1920s to 1954.

The Doncaster Yeomanry
Southern Regiment West Riding Yeomanry Corps. First West York Yeomanry Cavalry, Queen's Own Yorkshire Dragoons.
Manby, T. G. NAM
Doncaster; Doncaster Arts & Museum Society; 1972; ISBN None; 39pp/1 x bw SIfep/12 x bw PI; s/b; Indexed N; Glossary N; Appendices N; Bibliography Y; 224 x 141 (8vo)
NOTES: Written when the Yorkshire Yeomanry was reduced to cadre strength. One informative page on the regiment in WWII.

No Secret So Close
The Biography of Bruce Hobbs MC
Fitzgeorge-Parker, Tim IWM
London; Pelham Books Ltd; 1984; ISBN 0 7207 1552 1; x + 182pp/36 x bw PI; h/b / d/j Black cloth; Indexed Y; Glossary N; Appendices N; Bibliography N; 239 x 160 (8vo)
NOTES: Bruce Hobbs was a famous jockey prior to the war and joined the NSY at the outbreak of war. In mid-1940 he was commissioned into the QOYD, at that time in Palestine. He was invalided out of the army in late 1944 due to a pre-existing horse-racing injury. Interesting brief commentary on OQYD operating dummy tanks. 36pp concern BH's wartime experiences, the book being primarily concerned with his career with horses.

Memories Are Made of This
Hayter, Peter IWM
Edgworth; Peter Hayter; 2006; ISBN 0-7223-3817-1 / 978-0-7223-3817-9; 132pp/21 x clr SI/15 x bw PI/3 x bw SI; h/b / d/j Brown cloth; Indexed N; Glossary N; Appendices N; Bibliography N; 219 x 140 (8vo)
NOTES: The author joined QOYD in 1938, sailing to Palestine with them in 1940. He left for officer training in India and, after commissioning, was posted to 1RTR mid-1941. He was captured June 1942. 36pp on life as a POW in Italy and in Germany, from late 1943. The illustrations include several coloured sketches by POWs in Italy.

The North Somerset Yeomanry	N SOMERSET YEO

Date of mechanization: n/a
RAC service: 26/09/1941   16/03/1943*
* July 1942 became 4th Air Formation Signals (North Somerset Yeomanry) but not until 16 March 1943 was it officially transferred to Royal Corps of Signals.

No publications established.

1st Derbyshire Yeomanry   1 DERBY YEO

Date of mechanization: 1921
RAC service: 04/04/1939   Post-war.

Regimental publications:
The Rose and Crown. The Magazine of the 1st Derbyshire Yeomanry
Aug 1946 to unknown.(Monthly)

1st Derbyshire Yeomanry
Scrapbook 1939 - 1947
Not stated   TM; IWM; PCL
Derby; Bemrose & Sons Ltd; n.d. [c.1948]; ISBN None; xii + 183pp/1 x bw PIfep/219 x bw PI/2 x bw SI/1 x clr Mf/2 x clr M/1 x bw M; h/b Blue cloth; Indexed N; Glossary N; Appendices N; Bibliography N; 278 x 208 (4to); Uncommon
NOTES: This history adopts a unique approach. Many ex-members of the regiment have provided mini-chapter recollections presented chronologically, all supplemented by a large selection of period unofficial photographs. Provides an excellent view of the spirit of the regiment. Detail on vehicles, uniforms, etc. is somewhat sparse. Includes a full personnel list for 10 November 1942 - as sailed for North Africa. RoH/Honours/Awards. RoH includes service number, rank, date and theatre.

Khaki Parish
Our War - Our Love 1940 - 1946
Cook, Helen & Bill   IWM
Worthing; Churchman Publishing Limited; 1988; ISBN 1 85093 097 X; 356pp/36 x bw PI/2 x bw Mbds/1 x bw M; h/b / d/j Green cloth; Indexed N; Glossary N; Appendices Y; Bibliography N; 223 x 143 (8vo)
NOTES: The distillation of 6,000 letters written between the chaplain attached to 1DY from 6AD and his wife during the period of the war. Narrative explanations and background run throughout.

Khaki Parish
Our War - Our Love 1940 - 1946
Cook, Helen & Bill
London; Hodder and Stoughton Limited; 1989; ISBN 0 340 51061 7; 356pp/36 x bw PI/2 x bw M; p/b; Indexed N; Glossary N; Appendices Y; Bibliography N; 178 x 110 (12mo)
NOTES: Paperback reprint of 1988 first edition, same pagination.

2nd Derbyshire Yeomanry	2 DERBY YEO

Date of mechanization: 01/07/1939 (Raised)
RAC service: 01/07/1939   Post-war.

Regimental publications:
Yeoman: News Journal of the 2nd Derbyshire Yeomanry
Vol. 1 No. 1 14 Oct 1945 to Vol. 1 No. 9 (Souvenir Number) 22 Feb 1946 (Bi-monthly)

The Second Derbyshire Yeomanry
A Short History of the Regiment
Not stated   IWM
No imprint; No imprint; 1945; ISBN None; 41pp/No illus.; Folder; Indexed N; Glossary N; Appendices Y; Bibliography N; 343 x 214 (Folio); V Rare
NOTES: Typewritten notes and appendices, perhaps written and collated as the basis for a published history. RoH/Honours/Awards. Possibly a one-off as held at IWM.

The Second Derbyshire Yeomanry
An account of the Regiment during the World War 1939 -45
Jones, M.B.E., Capt. A. J.   TM; IWM; NAM
Bristol; The White Swan Press Ltd; 1949; ISBN None; 134pp/1 x bw PIfep/5 x bw PI/5 x bw M; h/b (d/j - ne) Blue cloth; Indexed N; Glossary N; Appendices Y; Bibliography N; 215 x 142 (8vo); Rare
NOTES: After a few pages of introduction covering the early days, this history starts with the move to the Middle East; just under half the book deals with the campaign in NWE. Well detailed narrative of the regiment's actions. RoH/Honours/Awards. A copy was given to the next of kin of those killed in service.

The Mad Recce
Knappett, Frank   IWM; RMAS
Braunton; Merlin Books Ltd; 1984; ISBN 0 86303 123-4; 133pp/27 x bw PI; s/b; Indexed N; Glossary N; Appendices N; Bibliography N; 210 x 146 (8vo)
NOTES: The author was called up at the end of 1940 and starts his memoirs with basic training. He joined 2DY in July 1941, being posted to 3 Tp, C Sqn, at that time operating Guy armoured cars. He provides a highly detailed and varied narrative. A rich source of regimental detail and life in the desert and in NWE.

The Seven Colonels
The story of seven 11th Hussar subalterns who sailed to Egypt in 1934 and later became the Commanding Officers of several Units which all made a significant contribution to the successful outcome of the Second World War in 1939-45
Osborne, Keith
No imprint; No imprint; No imprint; ISBN None; viii + 92pp/12 x bw PI/1 x bw SI/1 x bw M; s/b; Indexed N; Glossary N; Appendices N; Bibliography N; 210 x 148 (8vo)
NOTES: Essentially a retelling of 11H's history with occasional reference to the officers rather than the story of those personalities. The seven were George Paul (54th Training Regt, RAC), Bertie Bingley (IoC), Trevor Smail (11H), Geoffrey Miller (Sherwood Foresters), Peter Payne Gallwey (DY), Bill Wainman (11H), and John Lawson (IoC).

Royal Gloucestershire Hussars — RGH

Regimental publications:
Journal of The Royal Gloucestershire Hussars
No. 1 1964 to No. 2 1966 (Irregular)

Royal Gloucestershire Hussars
Coronation Year
Not stated — IWM
No imprint (Edgware); No imprint (Maurice Linton Publications - W. G. & F. Musgrave, Ltd - printers); 1953; ISBN None; 48pp/13 x bw PI/1 x bw SI; s/b; Indexed N; Glossary N; Appendices N; Bibliography N; 217 x 137 (8vo); Uncommon
NOTES: Recruitment booklet with 2pp and four photographs on WWII service. Of the 48pp, 32pp are devoted to advertisers. No imprint but publishers information established from advertisement.

The Royal Gloucestershire Hussars
Clifford, Rollo — IWM; NAM; RMAS; PCL
Stroud; Alan Sutton Publishing Ltd; 1991; ISBN 0 86299 982 0; 192pp/1 x bw PIfep/325 x bw PI/1 x bw SIfep/1 x bw SI/4 x bw M; h/b / d/j Black cloth; Indexed N; Glossary N; Appendices N; Bibliography N; 254 x 176 (4to)
NOTES: A pictorial history covering the late 1800s to 1990. 24pp on WWII predominantly of 2RGH.

1795 - 1995 A Short History of the Royal Gloucestershire Hussars
Bicentenary Year
Morgan, Paul; McMahon, Capt. T.; Bird, S/Sgt D. — TM
No imprint; No imprint (Jonah Graphics - printers); 1995; ISBN None; 16pp/No illus.; s/b (card); Indexed N; Glossary N; Appendices N; Bibliography Y; 206 x 146 (8vo); Uncommon
NOTES: Concise history.

1st Royal Gloucestershire Hussars — 1 RGH

Date of mechanization: 1922
RAC service: 04/04/1939   Post-war.

Time's Long Shadows
Lewis, Iolo — IWM; NAM
No imprint; No imprint (PBF Press Limited - printer); n.d. [c.2002]; ISBN None; viii + 192pp/29 x clr PI/35 x bw PI; s/b; Indexed N; Glossary N; Appendices N; Bibliography N; 210 x 148 (8vo); Rare
NOTES: Comprises 58pp of memoirs, 100pp of the author's poems (each with a narrative explanation) plus 34pp of photographs. The author served in B Sqn, 1RGH from 1942 although an injury during training left him temporarily downgraded for front line duties. In July 1944 he was transferred to 3RTR, serving through NWE until wounded for a second time in April 1945.

2nd Royal Gloucestershire Hussars	2 RGH

Date of mechanization: 24/08/1939 (Raised)
RAC service: 24/08/1939   15/01/1943 (Disbanded)

Second Royal Gloucestershire Hussars
Libya - Egypt 1941 - 1942
Pitman, Maj. Stuart   TM; IWM; NAM; RMAS
London; The Saint Catherine Press Ltd; 1950; ISBN None; xix + 96pp/1 x bw PIfep/26 x bw PI/4 x clr Mf/1 x bw Mf; h/b Grey cloth & blue paper; Indexed N; Glossary N; Appendices N; Bibliography N; 221 x 140 (8vo)
NOTES: The author served in the regiment and starts the history from their arrival in Egypt in October 1941. Highly creditable and well detailed account of this regiment's short life, although information regarding its formation is sparse. RoH/Honours/Awards plus Wounded/POW.

Under Any Sky
Being some letters of a Subaltern on Active Service overseas, 1942-1944
Not stated   IWM
Ditchling; Private (Ditchling Press - printers); 1956; ISBN None; 172pp/1 x bw PIfep/3 x bw PI/1 x bw SI; h/b Coloured paper; Indexed N; Glossary N; Appendices N; Bibliography N; 222 x 143 (8vo); Rare
NOTES: Reproduced letters of Lt David F Gilliatt from April 1942 to July 1944. He joined 2RGH July 1942 serving in H and G Sqns as a troop leader. When 2RGH was disbanded he went with G Sqn to the RWY. Views of a young subaltern in North Africa and from May 1944, until his death* in August, in Italy. (* see p182 in Platt's RWY, q.v., history for the circumstances.)

When We Were Young
A collection of memories from old comrades of the 2nd Royal Gloucestershire Hussars
Dallas, Ron   IWM
Not stated; BJT Print Services Limited; n.d. [c.1990]; ISBN None; vi + 150pp/10 x bw PI; s/b; Indexed N; Glossary N; Appendices N; Bibliography N; 205 x 147 (8vo); Uncommon
NOTES: A collection of short reminiscences set down by over 20 veterans of the regiment. Some run into their service post disbandment or as POWs.

Second Royal Gloucestershire Hussars
Libya - Egypt 1941 - 1942
Pitman, Maj. Stuart
Uckfield; Naval & Military Press Ltd; ISBN 978 1845749927; See Notes; s/b; Indexed N; Glossary N; Appendices N; Bibliography N
NOTES: Facsimile reprint by NMP of 1950 first edition, available in s/b.

The Forgotten Regiment
The Full Story of The 2nd Royal Gloucestershire Hussars Libya - Egypt 1941/1942
Burton, Brian
Oakleigh South, Australia; Brian Burton Books; 2008; ISBN 978-0-9806068-0-5; xxvi + 351pp/3 x clr SI/51 x bw PI/22 x bw SI/2 x clr Mf/5 x clr M/6 x bw M; s/b; Indexed N; Glossary Y; Appendices N; Bibliography Y; 250 x 175 (4to); V Rare
NOTES: The author served in F Sqn and took part in the desert battles until severely wounded at Alam Halfa in August 1942. This is a personal study of the strategic events during which the regiment fought several tough battles in 1941/42 before being disbanded. RoH/Honours/Awards. Only 50 copies placed on sale in the UK.

Rogue Male
Death and Seduction in World War II with Mister Major Geoff
Gordon-Creed, Geoffrey; Field, Roger
London; Coronet; 2011; ISBN 978 1 444 70633 8; xi + 370pp/28 x bw PI/2 x bw SI/2 x bw M; h/b / d/j Black cloth; Indexed Y; Glossary N; Appendices Y; Bibliography Y; 240 x 162 (8vo)
NOTES: The author sets down the memoirs of Geoffrey Gordon-Creed (GCC) amongst his own narrative. GCC was of that rare type to whom war is practically a calling. He started the war in the 5th (Ski Regiment) Bn, Scots Guards. After their disbandment he joined the RAC and trained during 1940. He joined H Sqn, 2RGH at the end of 1940 and sailed with them to Egypt a year later. His memoirs show a man at the heart of the battle and one who thrived in that environment. With 2RGH spent as a fighting force, GCC left to join the SAS and later the SOE. The appendix reproduces the War Diary from November 1941 to December 1942. 46pp on 2RGH.

Rogue Male
Sabotage and Seduction Behind German Lines with Geoffrey Gordon-Creed DSO, MC
Gordon-Creed, Geoffrey; Field, Roger
London; Coronet; 2012; ISBN 978 1 444 70635 2; xi + 370pp/28 x bw PI/2 x bw SI/2 x bw M; p/b; Indexed Y; Glossary N; Appendices Y; Bibliography Y; 197 x 128 (12mo)
NOTES: Paperback reprint, same pagination.

Lothians & Border Horse Yeomanry	LOTHIANS

Sabres to Scout Cars
An Illustrated History of The Lothians and Border Horse
Gardiner, Andrew S.   IWM; NAM
Not stated; Private; n.d. [1985]; ISBN 09510882 0 3; 48pp/5 x clr SI/10 x bw PI/1 x bw SI; s/b; Indexed N; Glossary N; Appendices N; Bibliography N; 210 x 150 (8vo)
NOTES: Brief but excellent summary of the two regiments with particularly useful information on uniforms, 9pp on WWII.

1st Lothians & Border Yeomanry* | 1 LOTHIANS

* The regiment's title was officially 1st Lothians & Border Horse Yeomanry but the unofficial title was used throughout the war.

Date of mechanization: 1922
RAC service: 04/04/1939 Post-war.

A Short Account of the 1st Lothians & Border Yeomanry in the campaigns of 1940 and 1944-45
Woolward, W. A. TM; IWM
Edinburgh; The Lothians & Border Regimental Association; n.d. [1946]; ISBN None; 108pp/1 x bw PIfep/3 x bw M; s/b; Indexed N; Glossary N; Appendices Y; Bibliography N; 214 x 138 (8vo); Rare
NOTES: First quarter deals with the campaign in France 1940 and subsequent reforming of the regiment in England; the remainder covers its actions in NWE from July 1944 to VE Day. Comprehensive following of regiment's route, sparse on its equipment. Appendices include an outline WE for a flail regiment. RoH/Honours/Awards.

Soldier On
An Autobiography by Colonel Sir Mike Ansell
Ansell, Col Sir Mike TM; IWM; NAM
London; Peter Davies Ltd; 1973; ISBN None; xi +180pp/38 x bw PI/1 x bw SI; h/b / d/j Green cloth; Indexed Y; Glossary N; Appendices N; Bibliography N; 238 x 156 (8vo)
NOTES: The author's autobiography revolves around his love of horses and family history with the army. He was serving in 5RIDG when war broke out and moved to France with them where he was given command of 1LBY in March 1940. After being severely wounded (he was blinded) just as the regiment was making its breakout, he was taken POW and remained so until his repatriation in October 1943. 44pp on WWII with 16pp on 1LBY.

A Chaplain's Diary 1939 - 1940
Rankin, Eric IWM
No imprint; Private (R. & R. Clark Ltd - printers); 1978; ISBN None; 122pp/3 x bw SI; s/b; Indexed N; Glossary N; Appendices N; Bibliography N; 213 x 137 (8vo); Uncommon
NOTES: The author served as chaplain to 1LBY in France in 1940 where he was captured. He remained a POW in Germany for the remainder of the war.

2nd Lothians & Border Horse* | 2 LOTHIANS

* The regiment's title was officially 2nd Lothians & Border Horse Yeomanry but the unofficial title was used throughout the war.

Date of mechanization: May 1939 (Raised)
RAC service: May 1939 Post-war.

Driver Advance!
Being a short account of the 2nd Lothians & Border Horse 1939 -1946
Antonio, D. G. TM; IWM
Edinburgh; Lothians & Border Regimental Association; 1947; ISBN None; 119pp/1 x bw
PIfep/1 x bw SI; s/b; Indexed N; Glossary Y; Appendices Y; Bibliography N; 215 x 139
(8vo); Rare
NOTES: A couple of pages introduce the regiment's early days. Part I is a reprint of
articles which appeared in *Blackwood's Magazine* in 1945, taking the perspective of a
crew member, rather than a strict history of the Tunisian campaign. Part II follows with
a conventional narrative history of the regiment based on War Diaries covering Italy
1943 – 1946. Appendices include a sketch WE; RoH split by campaigns.
RoH/Honours/Awards.

Mull of Kintyre to Moosburg
Memories of Peace and War: 1914-1945
Young, Lachlan B. IWM
Perth; Perth and Kinross District Libraries; 1994; ISBN 0 905452 15 1; 206pp/17 x bw
PI/3 x bw M; s/b; Indexed Y; Glossary N; Appendices N; Bibliography N; 234 x 155 (8vo)
NOTES: The author was called up at the end of 1940 and quickly moved into officer
training in 1941. He was posted to B Sqn, 2LBH at the very end of 1941. He sailed to NA
with the regiment and was captured with his crew in February 1943; he remained a
POW until May 1945. Having studied psychology he provides an interesting description
of some of the behaviours and effects of being a POW. 64pp on WWII.

Cassino to the River Po Italy 1944-45
A personal account of the life and action in a tank troop.
Martin, Lt G. W. TM; IWM
Chesterfield; G. W. Martin; 1999; ISBN 0 953512 0 7; 122pp/1 x clr PIfep/1 x clr
PIrep/61 x bw PI/2 x bw SI/2 x bw M; s/b; Indexed N; Glossary N; Appendices N;
Bibliography N; 228 x 179 (8vo); Uncommon
NOTES: The author joined 2LBH as a junior officer mid-1943 in NA, before they moved
to Italy. His memoirs cover his experiences in Italy from May 1944 to May 1945 in fine
detail. Commentary on a wide range of issues and experiences that a junior officer and
troop leader encounters, all with the backdrop of fighting in Italy.

A Princes Street Lancer 1936 - 1946
Simpson, Gordon R.
Port of Menteith; Gordon R. Simpson; 2004; ISBN None; 75pp/See Notes; Rare
NOTES: The author was a squadron commander in the regiment and in July 1944 was
promoted to command it. (Not physically inspected.)

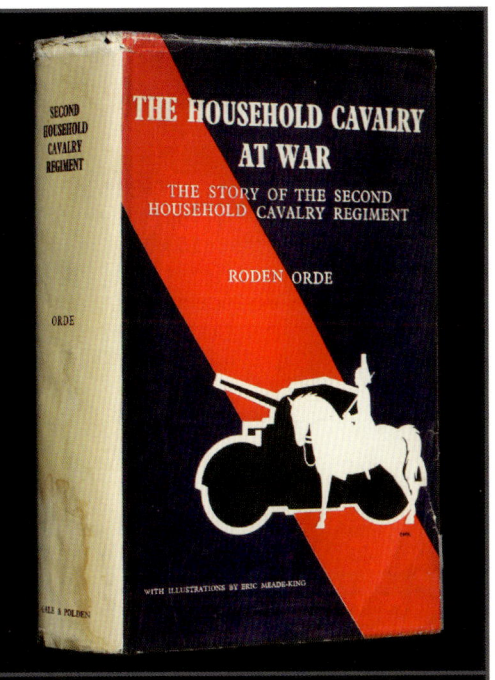

1. The Household Cavalry at War. Second Household Cavalry Regiment
Orde, R.

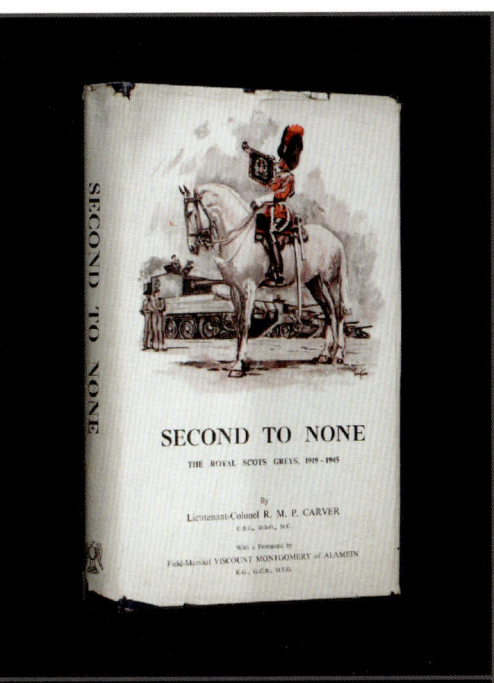

2. Second To None, The Royal Scots Greys, 1919 - 45
Carver, C.B.E., D.S.O., M.C., Lt-Col R. M. P.

3. "Push On 20" [15/19 H]
Butler, M.C., Capt. K .F.

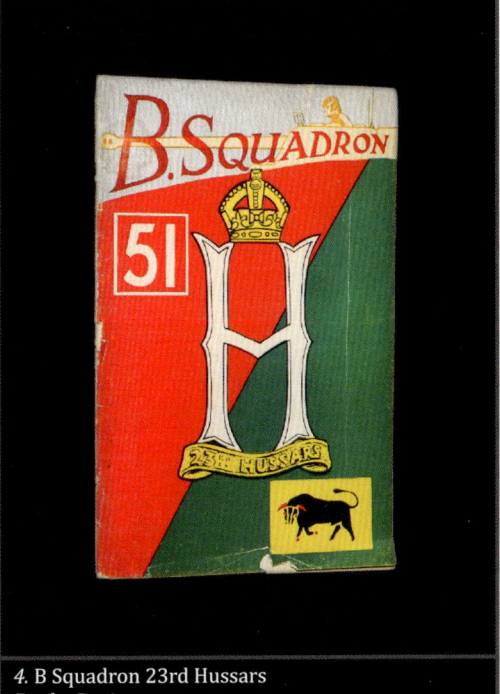

4. B Squadron 23rd Hussars
By the Regiment

5. The Story of the Twenty-Third Hussars 1940 -1946 - with dust-jacket

6. The Story of the Twenty-Third Hussars 1940 -1946 - showing leather binding

7. Seconds Out! A History of the 2nd Royal Tank Regiment [Draft edition]   *Chadwick, Sgt K.*

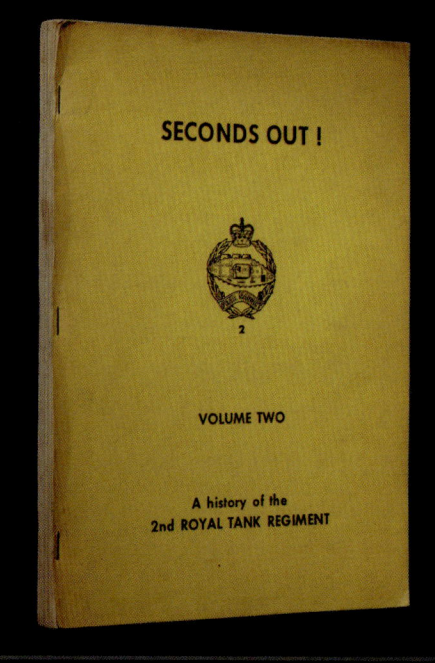

8. Seconds Out! A History of the 2nd Royal Tank Regiment ‡ [Official edition]   *Chadwick, Sgt K.*

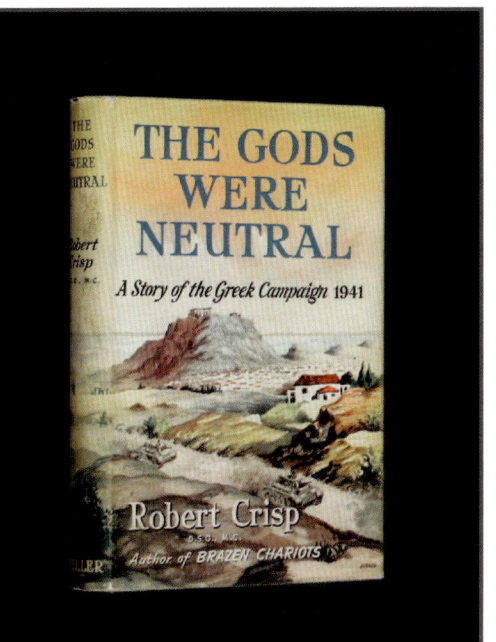

9. The Gods Were Neutral [3RTR]
Crisp, Robert

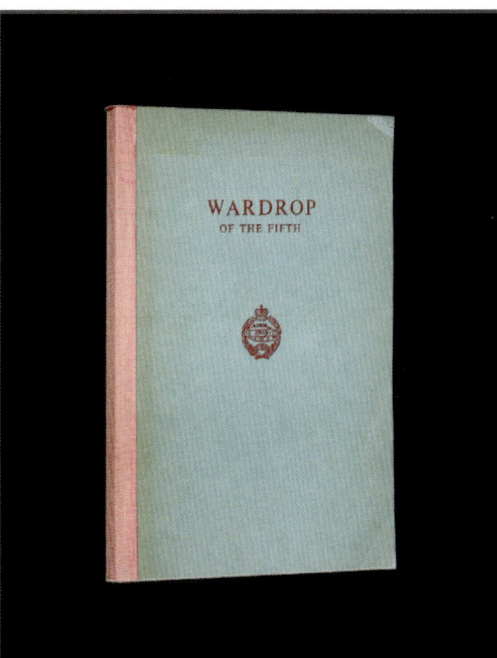

10. Wardrop of the Fifth
Wardrop, Jake; Garnett, Jack (Ed.)

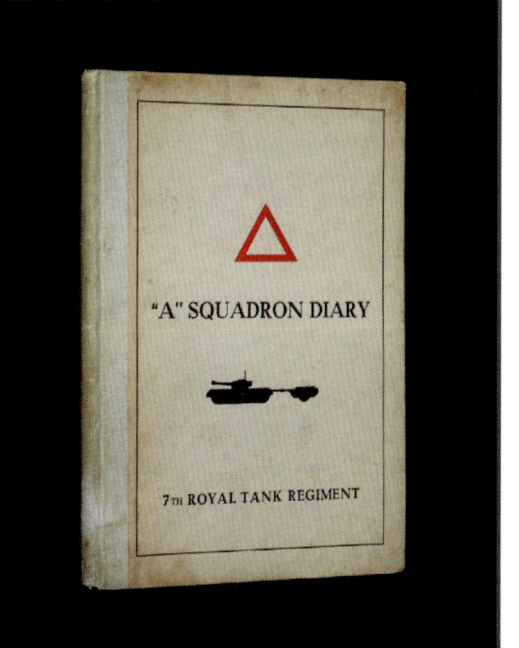

11. "A" Squadron Diary, 7th Royal Tank Regiment
(Joscelyne, Maj. R. A.)

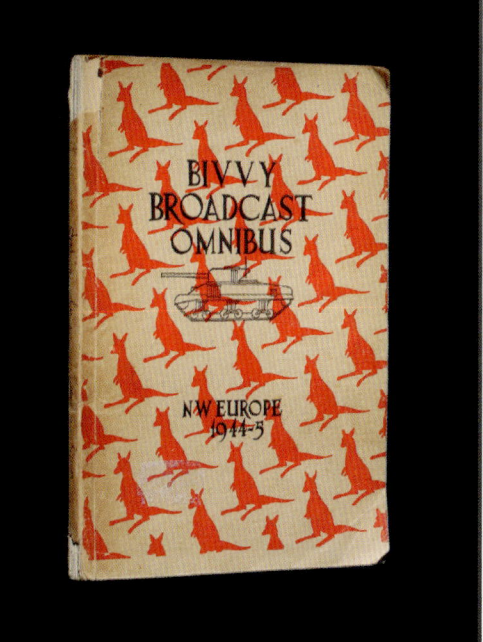

12. Bivvy Broadcast Omnibus NW Europe 1944-5 [49RTR]

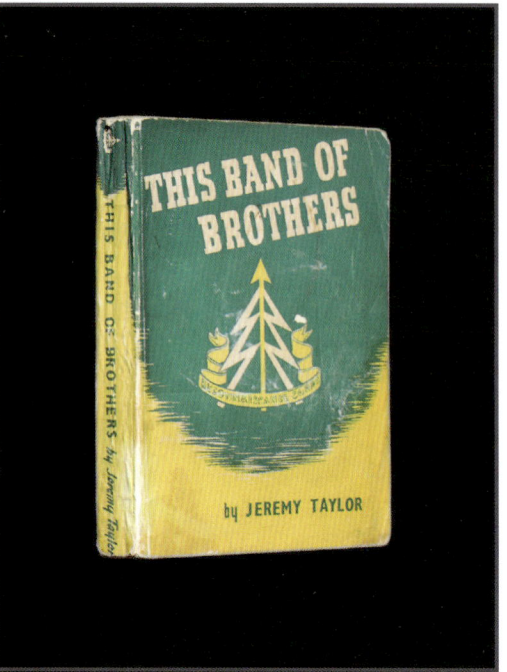

13. This Band of Brothers - paperback
Taylor, Jeremy

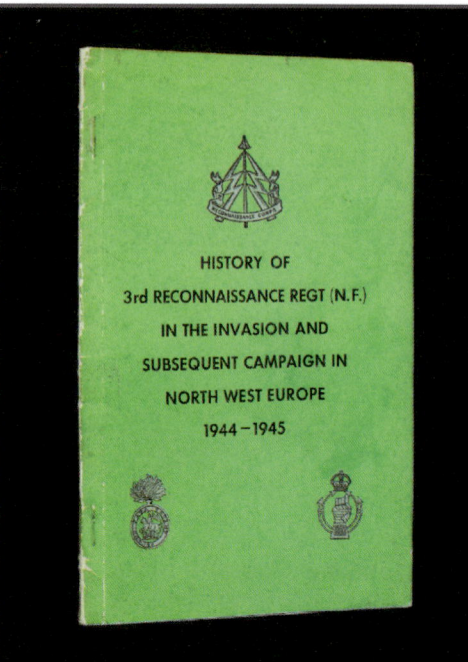

14. History Of 3rd Reconnaissance Regt (N.F.) ...
in North West Europe 1944 - 1945

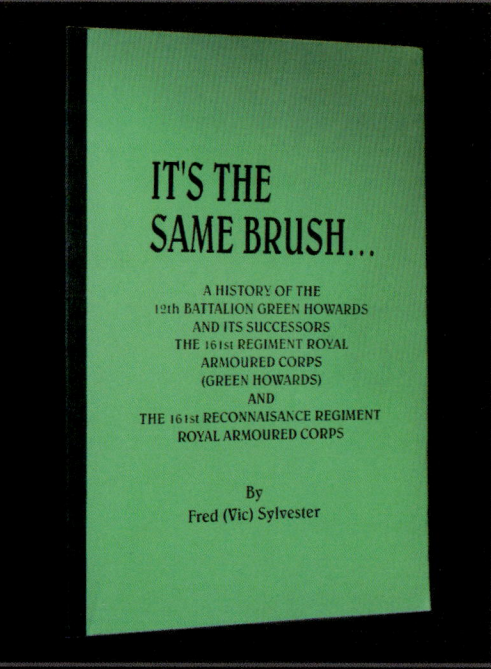

15. It's The Same Brush... A History of 161RAC
and 161 Recce Regt. ‡   *Sylvester, Fred (Vic)*

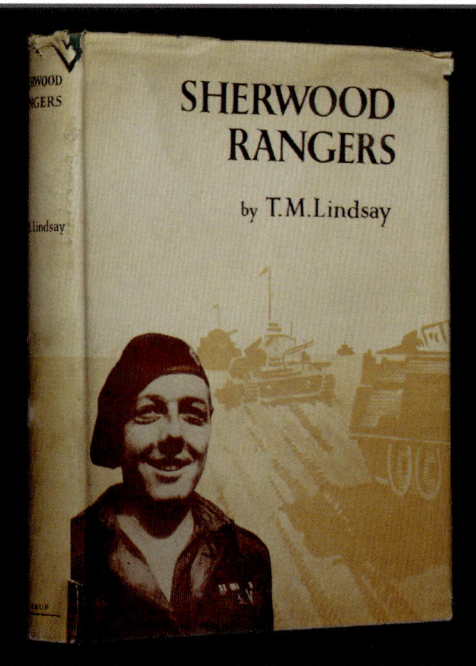

16. Sherwood Rangers
Lindsay, T. M.

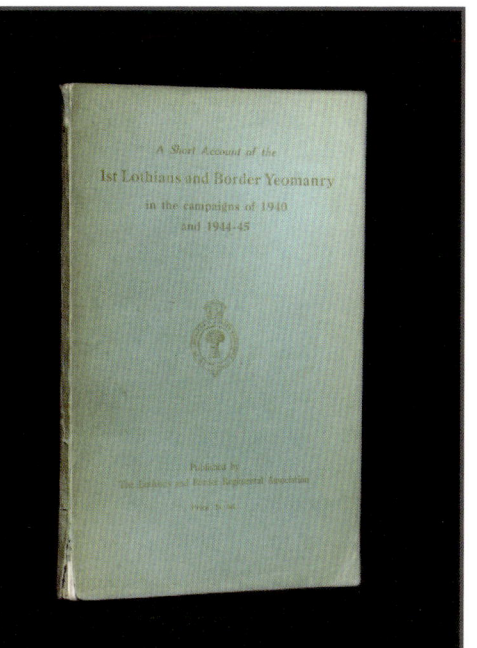

17. A Short Account of the 1st Lothians & Border Yeomanry *Woolward, W. A.*

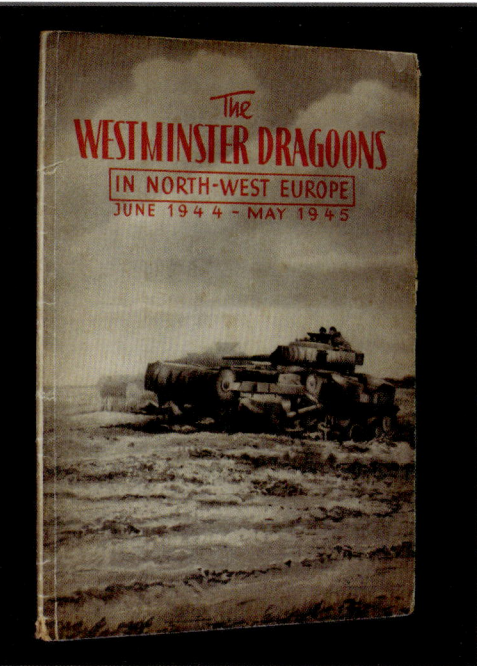

18. The Story of the Westminster Dragoons In North West Europe, June 1944 - May 1945 ‡

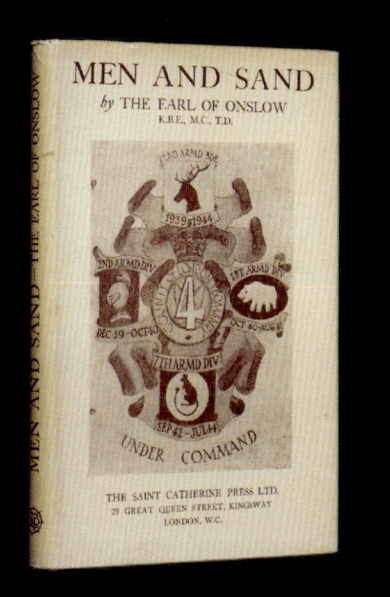

19. Men and Sand [4CLY]
The Earl of Onslow, K.B.E., M.C., T.D.

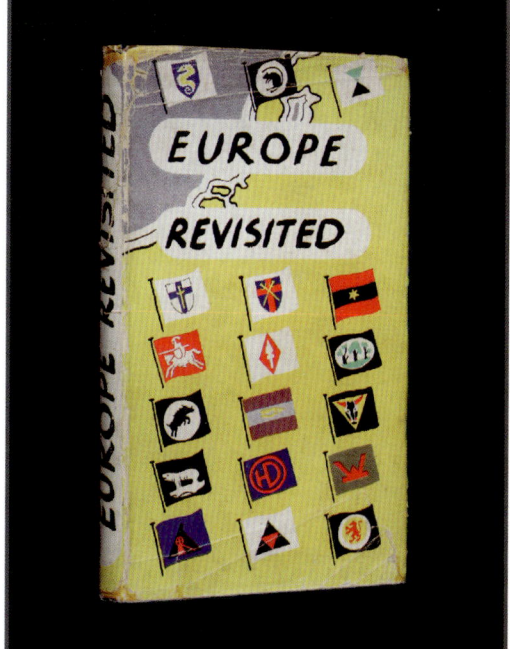

20. Europe Revisited, The East Riding Yeomanry...
Ellison, V. C.

21. "We Were There!" The Story of a Journey Made by C Squadron The Inns Of Court Regiment

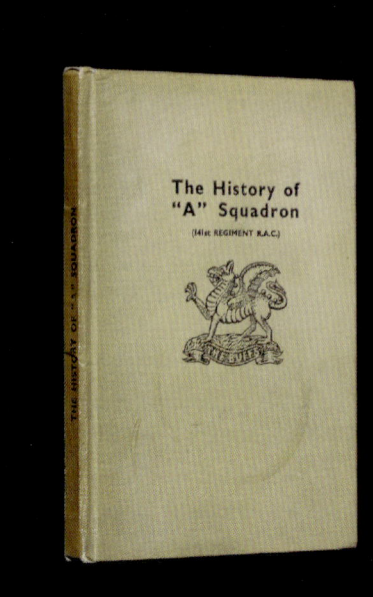

22. The History of "A" Squadron 141st Regiment R.A.C. (The Buffs.)   *(Storrar, Maj. George)*

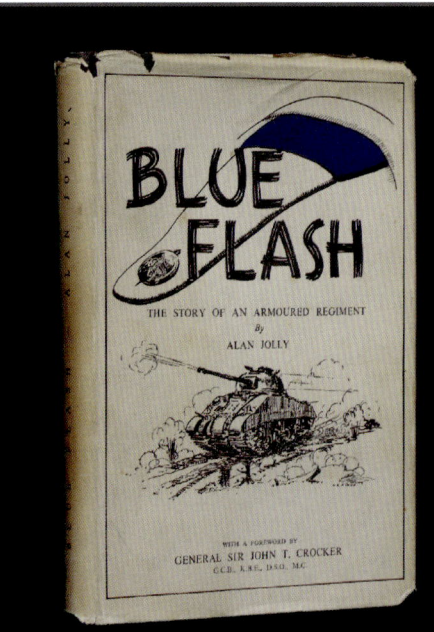

23. Blue Flash. The Story of an Armoured Regiment
Jolly, Alan [144RAC/4RTR]

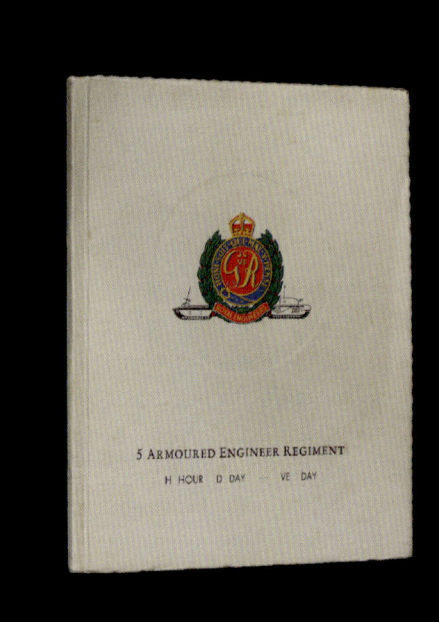

24. 5 Armoured Engineer Regiment, H Hour D Day - VE Day

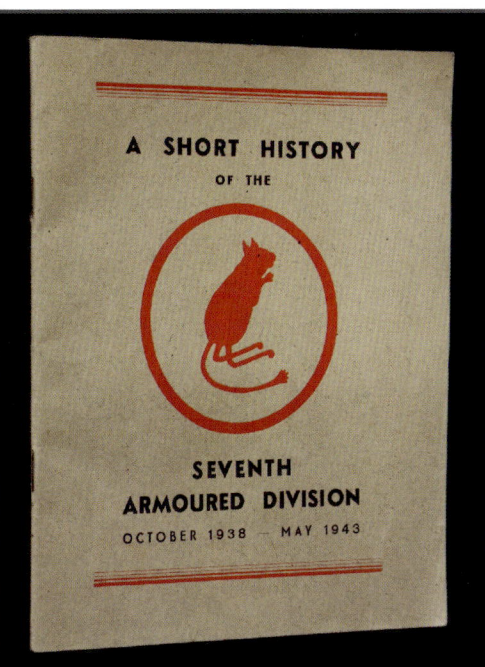

25. A Short History Of The Seventh Armoured Division, 1938 - 1943   *Carver, Lt-Col R. M. P.*

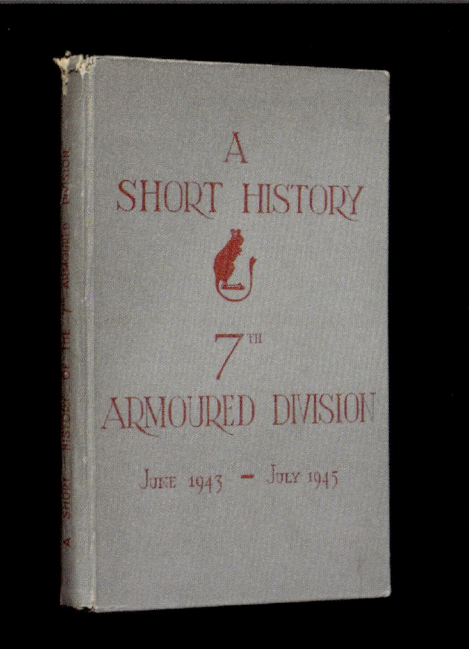

26. A Short History Of The 7th Armoured Division
Lindsay, Capt. M. & Johnston, Capt. M.

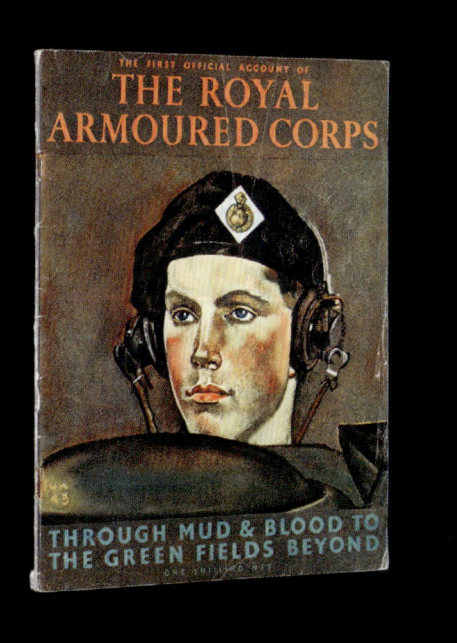

27. The First Official Account of the Royal Armoured Corps - cover   *Owen, Frank & Atkins, H. W.*

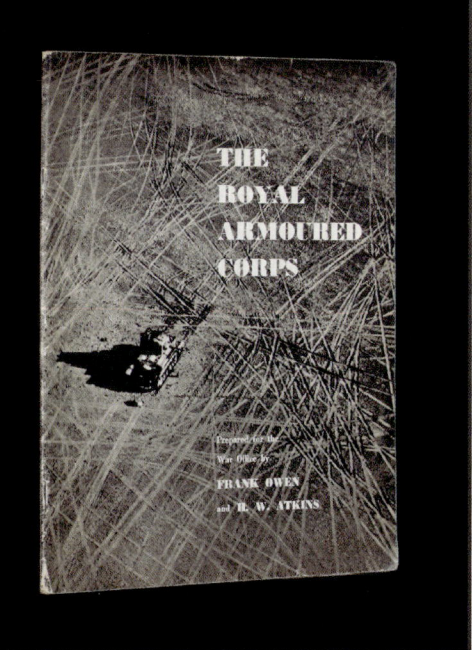

28. The First Official Account of the Royal Armoured Corps - w/o cover   *Owen, Frank & Atkins, H. W.*

29. The Blue Flash. The Weekly Newspaper of the 4th Royal Tank Regt. ‡

30. VeRiToR. The Fortnightly Review of The Fifth Royal Tank Regiment

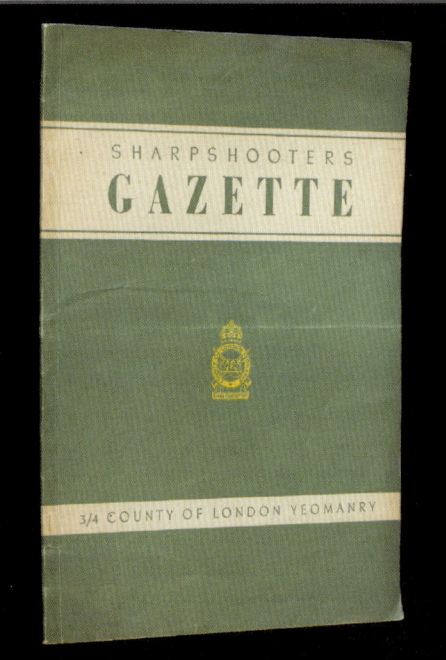

31. Sharpshooter's Gazette. Journal of the 3rd/4th County of London Yeomanry

32. Milestone. News and Views of 141st Regt. RAC (The Buffs) ‡

The Fife & Forfar Yeomanry — FF YEO

The Fife & Forfar Yeomanry 1919 - 1956
Sellar, R. J. B. TM; IWM; NAM; RMAS
Edinburgh; William Blackwood & Sons Limited; 1960; ISBN None; xiii + 289pp/26 x bw Pl/2 x clr Mbds; h/b / d/j Red cloth; Indexed N; Glossary N; Appendices Y; Bibliography N; 222 x 146 (8vo)
NOTES: This history tells the story of the regiments in two discrete parts, 115pp for 1FFY and 124pp for 2FFY. 1FFY is notable as being one of only three regiments equipped with flame throwing Crocodile tanks. Men of all ranks of the regiment are mentioned throughout the narrative. Photographs include many groups - officers, squadrons, etc. Tantalising, rather than thorough, information on equipment. RoH does not differentiate between the first and second line. RoH/Honours/Awards.

1st The Fife & Forfar Yeomanry — 1 FF YEO

Date of mechanization: 1921
RAC service: 04/04/1939   Post-war.

Regimental publications:
The Sporran: 1st Fife and Forfar Yeomanry Quarterly Magazine
No. 1 Christmas 1945 (possibly single issue)
The Red Circle Gazette (produced for 'C' Sqn, 1FFY)
No. 1 16 Oct 1945 to No. 6 16 Mar 1946 (Irregular)

No publications established.

2nd The Fife & Forfar Yeomanry — 2 FF YEO

Date of mechanization: 24/08/1939 (Raised)
RAC service: 24/08/1939   Post-war.

Memoirs
Grimond, Jo IWM
London; William Heineman Limited; 1979; ISBN 434 30600 2; 316pp/35 x bw Pl/1 x bw SI; h/b / d/j Red cloth; Indexed Y; Glossary N; Appendices N; Bibliography N; 240 x 162 (8vo)
NOTES: The author joined 2FFY days before the outbreak of war. In mid-1940 he was sent to train as a Staff Officer. Only 3pp refer to 2FFY, 11pp in total on his wartime experiences. Reprinted 1979.

Silver Spoon
Spencer-Nairn, M. A.
Bishop Auckland; The Pentland Press Ltd; 1996; ISBN 1-85821-343-6; vii + 210pp/20 x bw PI; h/b / d/j Black cloth; Indexed N; Glossary N; Appendices N; Bibliography N; 215 x 152 (8vo); Uncommon
NOTES: In this autobiography the author describes some wartime memories in 21pp, 14pp for 2FFY and 7pp for SY. He was OC C Sqn in 2FFY from the outset of war until February 1944, when he transferred to the SY as OC A Sqn.

2nd County of London Yeomanry (Westminster Dragoons) — W DGNS

Date of mechanization: 1920
RAC service: 16/11/1940* Post-war.
* Previously operated as 102nd Officer Cadet Training Unit (WD)

Regimental publications:
Dragoon: The Journal of the Westminster Dragoons (2CLY)
Vol. 1 No. 1 Spring 1956 to Vol. 1 No. 2 Summer 1956 (Quarterly) Only two issues published, approximately 500 copies each.

The Story of the Westminster Dragoons
In North West Europe from June 6th 1944 - May 8th 1945
Not stated [See Notes] TM; IWM
Germany; Lüneburger Landeszeitung; n.d. [1945]; ISBN None; 53pp/11 x bw PI/9 x bw SI; s/b; Indexed N; Glossary N; Appendices N; Bibliography N; 299 x 219 (4to); Rare
NOTES: One of the swiftest publications brought to print after the end of the war, this was published in June 1945. This concise history, published for members of the regiment, follows its complicated actions as a specialist flail unit from D-Day to VE-Day. Author is Keith S. T. Ravensdale.

A History of the Westminster Dragoons 1901 to 1967
Lawson, Capt. C. C. P. & Huw-Williams, Capt. N. TM; IWM; PCL
No imprint; Private; n.d. [1969]; ISBN None; xiv + 359pp/15 x bw SI/3 x bw M; s/b; Indexed N; Glossary N; Appendices Y; Bibliography N; 251 x 200 (4to); Uncommon
NOTES: A comprehensive history of the regiment with 83pp devoted to WWII. Aimed squarely at members of the regiment, it has plenty of detail although the subscribers' errors letter suggests readers found many a fault. Subscribers received a loose 4pp list of errors and omissions. Includes several veterans' quotations. Reproduced typescript. Appendices include lists of colonels, COs and Adjutants. RoH/Honours/Awards. Reprinted 1987.

A Short History of the Westminster Dragoons 1901 to 1987
Huw-Williams, Capt. N. TM; IWM
No imprint; No imprint; n. d. [c.1987]; ISBN None; 56pp/10 x bw PI/17 x bw SI; s/b; Indexed N; Glossary N; Appendices Y; Bibliography N; 210 x 148 (8vo); Uncommon
NOTES: Heavily précised from the 1901 – 1967 book; 4pp on WWII.

D-Day Remembered
Personal Recollections of Members of the Westminster Dragoons (2nd County of London Yeomanry) Who Landed in Normandy on 6 June 1944
Bullock, Richard (Ed.) TM; IWM; NAM
No imprint; Private; 1997; ISBN None; 74pp/4 x bw PI/1 x bw Mf; s/b (acetate/card); Indexed N; Glossary Y; Appendices N; Bibliography N; 297 x 210 (4to); Uncommon
NOTES: A collection of memories from 19 members of the WD who landed on D-Day. Reproduced word processor type.

A History of the Westminster Dragoons 1901 to 2001
A Diary of 100 years of Yeoman Service
Lawson, Capt. C. C. P. & Huw-Williams, Capt. N. Revised by Sankey, Martin L. H. TM
No imprint; No imprint; n.d. [2001]; ISBN None; ix + 167pp/2 x clr SI/154 x bw PI/4 x bw SI/2 x bw M; s/b; Indexed N; Glossary N; Appendices Y; Bibliography N; 297 x 210 (4to)
NOTES: Honours/Awards. Based on the 1901 - 1967 and 1901 - 1987 histories but fully revised, this edition presents the regiment's history in diary form.

County of London Yeomanry (Sharpshooters) — SHARPSHOOTERS

Regimental publications:
Gazette of the 4th County of London Yeomanry
Vol. 1 No. 1 June 1944 replaced by
Gazette of the 3rd/4th County of London Yeomanry (Sharpshooters)
The volume and issue labelling is confusing because a pattern was not followed. Each edition will be listed for clarity:
No. 2 Vol. 1 June 1945 and Vol. 3 No. 1 November 1945; became
Sharpshooter's Gazette. Journal of the 3rd/4th County of London Yeomanry (Sharpshooters)
Vol. 2 No. 1 April 1946 and Vol. 2 No. 2 September 1946; suspended after disbandment and reinstated after being re-raised as a TA unit in 1947.
Sharpshooter's Gazette. Journal of the 3rd/4th County of London Yeomanry (Sharpshooters)
Vol. 3 No. 1 April 1949 to Vol. 3 No. 4 Oct 1950 (Half-yearly); Vol. 3 No. 5 October 1951; replaced by
Sharpshooters Newsletter
October 1952 – the last publication before the
Sharpshooters Yeomanry Association newsletter started in 1962 which went on to become
The Sharpshooter from 1993.

Standing Orders of the 3rd/4th County of London Yeomanry "Sharpshooters"
Not stated TM; IWM; NAM; PCL
No imprint; No imprint; n.d. [c.1946]; ISBN None; 75pp/No illus.; h/b; Indexed Y; Glossary N; Appendices Y; Bibliography N; 218 x 142 (8vo)
NOTES: Regular set of Standing Orders which include a 12pp brief history of 3/4CLY plus lists of COs 1939-45.

Sharpshooters at War
The 3rd, 4th and the 3rd/4th County of London Yeomanry 1939 - 1945
Graham, Andrew TM; IWM; RMAS; PCL
London; Sharpshooters Regimental Association; 1964; ISBN None; xvii + 252pp/65 x bw PI/1 x bw Mfbd/6 x bw M; h/b / d/j Green cloth; Indexed Y; Glossary N; Appendices Y; Bibliography N; 228 x 147 (8vo)
NOTES: Follows both 3CLY and 4CLY throughout their active service and divides the narrative in a clear and readable manner. History prior to active service is covered in 8pp. Appendices include Battle Honours. RoH/Honours/Awards - the RoH is presented via a photograph of the RoH board; no differentiation between 3 and 4CLY.

The Sharpshooters
3rd County of London Yeomanry 1900 - 1961. Kent and County of London Yeomanry 1961 - 1970
Mollo, Boris TM; IWM; NAM; RMAS
London; Historical Research Unit; 1970; ISBN 92162107 2; 83pp/1 x clr SIfep/2 x clr SI/41 x bw PI/26 x bw SI/2 x Mbds; h/b / d/j Green cloth; Indexed N; Glossary N; Appendices Y; Bibliography Y; 220 x 135 (8vo)
NOTES: Concise history published soon after the creation of The Kent and County of London Yeomanry (Sharpshooters). It provides a well detailed pocket book on 3CLY and 4CLY. 17pp on WWII, appendices include Battle Honours, changes to regimental title, Colonels, COs, and a very useful uniforms and insignia section.

The Sharpshooters 1900 - 1992
Not stated TM
No imprint; No imprint (Cravitz Printing Company Limited - printers); 1992; ISBN None; 20pp/1 x bw PI; s/b; Indexed N; Glossary N; Appendices N; Bibliography Y; 148 x 104 (16mo)
NOTES: The photograph in the central pages is of 3/4CLY's RoH plaque. Pocket history which deals mainly with WWII.

The Sharpshooters 1900 - 2000
Mollo, Boris TM; IWM
Croydon; Kent and Sharpshooters Yeomanry Museum Trust; 2000; ISBN None; 65pp/50 x clr PI/152 x bw PI/3 x bw SI/2 x bw Mbds; s/b; Indexed N; Glossary N; Appendices N; Bibliography Y; 296 x 209 (4to)
NOTES: Essentially the 1900 – 1961 history brought up to date for the 100th Anniversary but with a much expanded photographic selection. 13pp on WWII.

3rd County of London Yeomanry (Sharpshooters) — SHARPSHOOTERS [3 CLY]

Date of mechanization: 1920
RAC service: 04/04/1939   Post-war.

My Longest Day
The factual account of 24 hours in the life of a Tank Troop Leader of the 3rd/4th County of London Yeomanry (Sharpshooters) in the 1939-45 War
Mortimer, Denzil   TM; IWM
No imprint; No imprint; 1984; ISBN None; 32pp/11 x bw PI/7 x bw SI; s/b; Indexed N; Glossary N; Appendices N; Bibliography N; 212 x 150 (8vo); Uncommon
NOTES: The author has set down a very specific set of memories for one day. 4CLY attacked Uedem, Germany in February 1945 and lost several men at this late stage of the war.

4th County of London Yeomanry (Sharpshooters) — SHARPSHOOTERS [4 CLY]

Date of mechanization: 27/09/1939 (Raised)
RAC service: 27/09/1939   31/07/1944*
* Disbanded and merged with 3CLY to form 3/4CLY.

Come to Dust
Maugham, Robin   TM; IWM; NAM
London; Chapman & Hall Ltd; 1945; ISBN None; 191pp/1 x bw PIfep; h/b / d/j Buff cloth; Indexed N; Glossary N; Appendices N; Bibliography N; 191 x 129 (12mo); Uncommon
NOTES: At the outbreak of war the author was a trooper in the IoC and in 1940 was commissioned into 4CLY. He fought as a troop leader during the desert campaigns, becoming IO in 1942 shortly before being badly wounded. He wrote this book whilst recuperating and changed the names of the officers and men of his regiment – they were still fighting. Written in the form of a novel, it is essentially an account of his experience in the desert. Some wonderful vignettes of tank crew and their jobs. It was published to some critical acclaim.

Come to Dust
Maugham, Robin
London; Chapman & Hall Ltd; 1948; ISBN None; 144pp/See Notes; p/b; Indexed N; Glossary N; Appendices N; Bibliography N; Uncommon
NOTES: First paperback edition with subsequent multiple reprints. (Not physically inspected.)

Come to Dust
Maugham, Robin
London; Corgi Books (Transworld Publishers Ltd.); 1957; ISBN None; 192pp/No illus.; p/b; Indexed N; Glossary N; Appendices N; Bibliography N; 161 x 108 (16mo); Uncommon
NOTES: Slightly abridged version of 1945 first edition, different pagination.

Come to Dust
Maugham, Robin   TM
London; Ace Books Limited; 1961; ISBN None; 128pp/No illus.; p/b; Indexed N; Glossary N; Appendices N; Bibliography N; 177 x 113 (12mo); Uncommon
NOTES: Paperback reprint of abridged version, different pagination.

Men and Sand
The Earl of Onslow, K.B.E., M.C., T.D.   IWM; NAM; PCL
London; The Saint Catherine Press Ltd; 1961; ISBN None; xi + 140pp/1 x bw PIfep/18 x bw PI/3 x bw M; h/b / d/j Brown cloth/orange paper; Indexed Y; Glossary N; Appendices N; Bibliography N; 222 x 144 (8vo); Uncommon
NOTES: The author joined 4CLY at its formation as Assistant Adjutant from the LG. Although he went on to command 4CLY mid-1943, in this book he primarily deals with the desert from October 1941 to June 1943. Quantity of mini character sketches of the men under his command. Scant reference to his few months as CO of SRY. The book ends with him taking command of 4CLY and a brief summary of NWE to his capture at Villers Bocage. A few editorial name and date errors thankfully do not detract from the quality of the scenes described. RoH/Honours/Awards/Battle Honours.

Come to Dust
Maugham, Robin
London; The New English Library Ltd.; 1968; ISBN None; 128pp/No illus.; p/b; Indexed N; Glossary N; Appendices N; Bibliography N; 180 x 108 (12mo); Uncommon
NOTES: Re-issue of 1961 Ace Books edition.

Come to Dust
Maugham, Robin
London; W H Allen; 1973; ISBN 0 491 01181 4; 192pp/No illus.; h/b / d/j Blue cloth; Indexed N; Glossary N; Appendices N; Bibliography N; 204 x 131 (8vo); Uncommon
NOTES: Reprint of the abridged version with preface by author.

Before I Forget
Some Recollections of a Sharpshooter 1939 - 1946.
Cawston, Roy   TM; IWM; NAM
Ewell; Chiavari Publishing; 1993; ISBN 0 9520592 0 7; iv + 151pp/50 x bw PI/3 x bw SI/4 x bw M; h/b / d/j Green cloth; Indexed Y; Glossary Y; Appendices Y; Bibliography N; 248 x 174 (8vo)
NOTES: The author joined 3CLY at the beginning of 1939 and transferred to C Sqn, 4CLY upon its formation. He pays particular attention to the early days in the UK, providing an uncommonly detailed view of the time. RC was taken POW in the regiment's first engagement, November 1941, and the bulk of the book recounts his experiences as a

POW in Italy and Germany. Broad detail of the life of a POW, including being on a 400 mile march in early 1945. Erratum slip for p131 tucked in.

A Rat In A Tank
Gell, Harry IWM
London; Minerva Press; 1995; ISBN 1 85863 549 7; 202pp/No illus.; s/b; Indexed N; Glossary N; Appendices N; Bibliography N; 205 x 147 (8vo); Uncommon
NOTES: The author's recollections start with his journey out to the ME in May 1942, whilst serving with 41RTR. They comprise his letters home plus occasional narrative in explanation or more detailed comment on men he served alongside. He details the minutiae of army life, dominated by food, the notes and letters being written at the time or very soon after the event. On the breakup of 41RTR he was transferred to 4CLY in December 1942, remaining with them until the war's end (as 3/4CLY.) In February 1945 his tank was hit and he suffered burns; the letters end at this point.

Memory Diary
A Record of the Desert Campaign from Egypt to Tunisia November 1941 to May 1943 with 4th County of London Yeomanry (Sharpshooters)
Ramsbottom, Harry
Epsom; Chiavari Publishing; 1995; ISBN 0 9520592 1 5; 93pp/3 x bw M; Comb; Indexed Y; Glossary N; Appendices Y; Bibliography N; 297 x 210 (4to); Uncommon
NOTES: The author joined the Signals Corps in November 1939 and was posted to 4 Sqn, Middx. Yeo. (Signals), 22AB in the summer of 1940. He joined 4CLY early 1941 as a signaller where he served in HQ Tank Troop. Although not a member of 4CLY, he served with them in an HQ tank during the war and his memoirs provide some insight into a little described topic, HQ signals. Written and distributed to veterans in the 1980s, published via 4CLY veteran Roy Cawston.

Sharpshooter Snapshots
Fisher, John TM; IWM; NAM
Wells; Portway Publishing; 1996; ISBN 1 901324 00 1; ix + 199pp/16 x bw Pl/8 x bw M; s/b; Indexed N; Glossary Y; Appendices N; Bibliography Y; 207 x 146 (8vo)
NOTES: The author joined up in 1943, and after an introduction to his training and a very brief period with the 15/19H, he joined 1 Tp, A Sqn, 4CLY in early 1944. His memoirs recount various aspects of the NWE campaign and his services as a Cromwell gunner. Full of incidental detail about uniforms, life in tanks and fellow crew. Erratum slip for p15 tucked in.

Carpiquet Bound
A pictorial tribute to 4th County of London Yeomanry (Sharpshooters) 1939 to 1944
Allen, W. D. & Cawston, R. F. H. TM; IWM
Ewell; Chiavari Publishing; 1997; ISBN 0 9520592 6 6; 207pp/295 x bw Pl/8 x bw SI/7 x bw M; h/b Green cloth; Indexed Y; Glossary N; Appendices Y; Bibliography Y; 303 x 215 (4to); Uncommon
NOTES: Superb photo history with detailed text in accompaniment. Includes several quotations from veterans. RoH for 4CLY and 3/4CLY, no differentiation as to rank.

Men and Sand
The Earl of Onslow, K.B.E., M.C., T.D.   TM
York; Wilton 65; 1999; ISBN 0 947828 73 7; xi + 140pp/1 x bw PIfep/18 x bw PI/3 x bw
M; h/b Brown cloth/cream paper; Indexed Y; Glossary N; Appendices N; Bibliography N;
213 x 150 (8vo); Uncommon
NOTES: Hardback facsimile reprint of the 1961 first edition.

Men and Sand
The Earl of Onslow, K.B.E., M.C., T.D.
York; Wilton 65; 1999; ISBN 0 947828 73 7; xi + 140pp/1 x bw PIfep/18 x bw PI/3 x bw
M; s/b; Indexed Y; Glossary N; Appendices N; Bibliography N; 211 x 148 (8vo);
Uncommon
NOTES: Softback facsimile reprint of the 1961 first edition.

A Wandering Yeoman
Dyas, O.B.E., Patrick
Not stated; Not stated (Sovereign Printers); 2001; ISBN None; 40pp/See Notes; s/b; Rare
NOTES: Privately published memoirs. (Not physically inspected.)

Sharpshooter
Memories of Armoured Warfare 1939 - 1945
Cloudsley-Thompson, J. L.
Fleet Hargate; Arcturus Press; 2006; ISBN 978 1 905703 01 2; viii + 150pp/20 x bw PI/3
x bw M; s/b; Indexed N; Glossary N; Appendices Y; Bibliography Y; 210 x 148 (8vo)
NOTES: The author recounts time spent training in 1940 and his posting to Sandhurst
OCTU in January 1941, being commissioned into 4H before transferring to 4CLY in
August 1941. He recollects his experiences in the desert as B Sqn Transport Officer, later
commanding a Crusader tank. He was badly wounded in 1942, returning to the UK at the
end of that year. During 1943 he served as a gunnery instructor at Sandhurst before
'fudging' his fitness test to be graded fit for active service in February 1944 and re-
joining 4CLY. He served in NWE, including the action at Villers-Bocage, until the
amalgamation with 3CLY when he returned to the UK as a gunnery instructor.

Under-gunned with the Sharpshooters
Allen, W. D.   TM
Epsom; Roy Cawston; 2007; ISBN None; 60pp/64 x bw PI/1 x bw SI/2 x bw M; Comb;
Indexed Y; Glossary Y; Appendices N; Bibliography Y; 297 x 210 (4to)
NOTES: The author joined 3CLY in late 1938 and 4CLY upon its formation. He served in
B Sqn and recounts the early days in the UK before moving to Egypt in 1941; he served
as a wireless-operator and later as tank commander. He continued into Italy and then
NWE where he commanded a Cromwell tank. After the amalgamation of 3 and 4CLY , he
became an instructor at RAC camps in Belgium and Holland. The photo selection is taken
from his collaborative work, *Carpiquet Bound*, q.v. TM has a photocopy.

The Northamptonshire Yeomanry — N YEO

The 1st and 2nd Northamptonshire Yeomanry 1939 - 1946
Not stated [See Notes]   TM; IWM; NAM; PCL
Brunswick, Germany; Joh. Heinr. Mayer; 1946; ISBN None; 141pp/24 x bw Pl/14 x bw SI/12 x clr M; h/b Blue cloth; Indexed N; Glossary N; Appendices Y; Bibliography N; 248 x 174 (8vo); Uncommon
NOTES: The book is split into two parts, one per regiment. Both receive a single overview chapter on their UK history before dealing with their service in NWE. Plenty of operational detail with frequent reference to named personnel in 1NY part. 2NY's progress well detailed but few named references. Appendices include list of wounded and POW for both regiments. RoH/Honours/Awards. (Authors - Pt I is Capt. Reginald F. Neville and Pt II is Lt-Col Lord George Scott) Reprinted by Naval & Military Press 2011.

Northamptonshire Yeomanry 1794-1964
Cazenove, H. De L.   TM; IWM; NAM
Northampton; H de L Cazenove; 1966; ISBN None; 19pp/10 x bw Pl/1 x bw SI; h/b Blue cloth; Indexed N; Glossary N; Appendices N; Bibliography N; 218 x 144 (8vo)
NOTES: Pocket history with 6pp on WWII. The author served in 2NY as OC B Sqn early part of the war.

Northamptonshire Yeomanry 1794-1964
Cazenove, H. De L.   PCL
Northampton; H de L Cazenove; 1966; ISBN None; 19pp/10 x bw Pl/1 x bw SI; p/b; Indexed N; Glossary N; Appendices N; Bibliography N; 218 x 140 (8vo)
NOTES: Paperback reprint of hardback first edition, same pagination.

200 Years of Peace and War
A History of the Northamptonshire Yeomanry
Lawrence, Vic & Hill, Peter   IWM; NAM
Not stated; Orman Publishing; 1994; ISBN 09518199 5 X; xiii + 155pp/10 x bw Pl/35 x bw SI/3 x clr M; s/b; Indexed N; Glossary N; Appendices N; Bibliography Y; 252 x 174 (4to)
NOTES: This book includes a reproduction of *The 1st and 2nd Northamptonshire Yeomanry 1939 - 1946* including the maps of Pt II but not those of Pt I. There is an early history summary plus assorted illustrations.

The 1st and 2nd Northamptonshire Yeomanry 1939 - 1946
Not stated
Uckfield; Naval & Military Press Ltd; 2011; ISBN 978 1845749972; See Notes; s/b; Indexed N; Glossary N; Appendices Y; Bibliography N
NOTES: Facsimile reprint by NMP of 1946 first edition, available in s/b.

1st The Northamptonshire Yeomanry — 1 N YEO

Date of mechanization: 1922
RAC service: 04/04/1939   Post-war.

The First Northamptonshire Yeomanry in Northwest Europe
Neville, Capt. R. F.   TM; IWM
Brunswick, Germany; Joh. Heinr. Mayer; 1946; ISBN None; 104pp/21 x bw Pl/14 x bw Sl/8 x clr M; h/b Blue cloth & grey paper; Indexed N; Glossary N; Appendices N; Bibliography N; 245 x 172 (8vo); Uncommon
NOTES: Essentially the same book as Part I of *The 1st and 2nd Northamptonshire Yeomanry 1939 - 1946*, q.v., with minor editorial changes. RoH/Honours/Awards.

Scenes from a One Way Journey
Cooper, Alexander   IWM; NAM
Glossop; Senior Publications; 1982; ISBN 903839 91 1; 72pp/1 x bw Plfep/7 x bw Pl; s/b (card); Indexed N; Glossary N; Appendices N; Bibliography N; 193 x 143 (12mo); Uncommon
NOTES: The author was serving in 9th Bn, Loyal Regiment when it converted to 148 RAC. He served in Normandy with them until they disbanded, then transferred to 1NY, serving through to the end of the war. The book is a collection of his poetry on his military and civilian experiences.

Tank!
40 hours of battle, August 1944
Tout, Ken   TM; IWM
London; Robert Hale Limited; 1985; ISBN 0 7090 2277 8; 208pp/3 x bw M; h/b / d/j Black cloth; Indexed N; Glossary N; Appendices N; Bibliography N; 241 x 159 (8vo)
NOTES: The first of a trio of recollections by this author based on his experiences in C Sqn, 1NY. Here he tells the story of the battle for St Aignan-de-Cramesnil over the 7/8 August 1944. A renowned book providing a highly detailed, intimate and evocative view of a tank crew. Published at the beginning of the resurgence of interest in the Normandy campaign following the 40th anniversary.

Tank!
40 hours of battle, August 1944
Tout, Ken
London; Sphere Books; 1986; ISBN 0 7221 8561 8; xv + 253pp; p/b; Indexed N; Glossary N; Appendices N; Bibliography N; 180 x 112 (12mo)
NOTES: Paperback reprint, itself reprinted 1987. (Not physically inspected.)

Tanks, Advance!
Normandy to the Netherlands, 1944
Tout, Ken   TM; IWM
London; Robert Hale Limited; 1987; ISBN 0-7090-2930-6 ; 215pp/2 x bw M; h/b / d/j Black cloth; Indexed N; Glossary N; Appendices N; Bibliography N; 241 x 159 (8vo)

NOTES: In his second book, the author recollects his experiences from landing in Normandy to returning to the UK, following an injury in the Netherlands in October 1944. During this period he commanded a Stuart, was a gunner on a Sherman, then commanded a Sherman. Not quite as engaging as his first book but does complement it.

Tanks, Advance!
Normandy to the Netherlands, 1944
Tout, Ken
London; Grafton Books; 1989; ISBN 0-586-20321-4; 267pp/No illus.; p/b; Indexed N; Glossary N; Appendices N; Bibliography N; 177 x 111 (12mo)
NOTES: Reprint of first edition, different pagination.

To Hell With Tanks!
Tout, Ken TM; IWM
London; Robert Hale Limited; 1992; ISBN 0 7090 4810 6; 207pp/1 x bw M; h/b / d/j
Black cloth; Indexed N; Glossary N; Appendices N; Bibliography N; 241 x 159 (8vo)
NOTES: This is the third and concluding set of memoirs from Ken Tout. Here he amends the brief to include recollections from others and covers his return to the regiment in Holland through to VE Day; he also drops the diary entry style. After this book, the author went on to write several books about campaigns or aspects of them.

Tank!
40 hours of battle, August 1944
Tout, Ken
London; Robert Hale Limited; 1994; ISBN 0 7090 5583 9; 208pp/See Notes; p/b; Indexed N; Glossary N; Appendices N; Bibliography N; Uncommon
NOTES: Paperback reprint of 1985 first edition. (Not physically inspected.)

Tommy Cooker
Memoirs of a Sherman Tank and its Crew Normandy 1944 - VE Day Holland 1945
Taylor, Les
Private; Les Taylor; 1995; ISBN None; 79pp/1 x bw PIfep/39 x bw PI/6 x bw SI/ x bw M; Strip binder; Indexed N; Glossary N; Appendices N; Bibliography N; 210 x 297 (8vo); Rare
NOTES: Of the home-produced variety, this author's memoirs were published ad hoc: 1st edition 1986, 2nd edition 1993 with illustrations, and 3rd edition 1995 in 'new improved format'; these were available direct from the author. He joined the RAC in July 1942 and served with 1NY from January 1943 to the war's end. He was a driver in a Crusader AA in the AA Troop. After the AA Troop disbanded in August 1944, he transferred to a Sherman in 4 Tp, A Sqn as the lap-gunner. Some very open descriptions of witnessing dead crew inside tanks that had been hit. Les Taylor brought the 1NY vs. Michael Wittman story to light in *After The Battle* magazine No 48, 1985 and some of that article's text is reproduced here.

By Tank
D to VE Days
Tout, Ken
London; Robert Hale Limited; 2007; ISBN 978 0 7090 8148 7; 240pp/No illus.; h/b / d/j (cloth - ne); Indexed N; Glossary N; Appendices N; Bibliography N; 241 x 159 (8vo)
NOTES: *By Tank* is an edited and abridged version of *Tank!*, *Tanks Advance!* and *To Hell With Tanks!*, q.q.v.

By Tank
D to VE Days
Tout, Ken
London; Robert Hale Limited; 2010; ISBN 978 0 7090 9115 8; 240pp/No illus.; p/b; Indexed N; Glossary N; Appendices N; Bibliography N; 233 x 155 (8vo)
NOTES: Paperback reprint of 2007 first edition.

2nd The Northamptonshire Yeomanry — 2 N YEO

Date of mechanization: 27/09/1939 (Raised)
RAC service: 27/09/1939   15/09/1944 (Disbanded)

Sixty-four Days of a Normandy Summer
With a Tank unit After D-Day
Jones, Keith   TM; IWM
London; Robert Hale Limited; 1990; ISBN 0 7090 4240 X; 189pp/13 x bw PI/6 x bw M; h/b / d/j Black cloth; Indexed Y; Glossary Y; Appendices N; Bibliography N; 220 x 144 (8vo)
NOTES: The author was transferred to 2NY from 162RAC when they disbanded in 1943. He served as Regimental Liaison Officer in Normandy for a short period before being promoted and serving in A Sqn HQ as Rear Link. In mid-July he became 2 i/c C Sqn, a position he held until the regiment's disbandment. Interesting view into the higher command aspects of a tank regiment and how an officer can move from role to role within it. The sixty-fourth day saw 2NY disbanded.

East Riding Yeomanry — E RIDING YEO

East Riding Yeomanry (TA)
Not stated   NAM
London; Goddard-Lawrence & Co; n.d. [1950]; ISBN None; 32pp/7 x bw PI; s/b; Indexed N; Glossary N; Appendices N; Bibliography N; 144 x 215 (24mo); Uncommon
NOTES: Post war TA recruiting booklet with a 2pp brief history covering WWII.

ROYAL ARMOURED CORPS: TA - YEOMANRY   169

Yeomanry of the East Riding
Sumner, Ian and Wilson, Roy   TM; IWM; NAM; RMAS; PCL
Beverley; The Hutton Press Ltd; 1993; ISBN 1 872167 47 0; 126pp/8 x clr PI/4 x clr
SI/138 x bw PI/8 x bw SI; s/b; Indexed N; Glossary N; Appendices Y; Bibliography N; 224
x 244 (8vo)
NOTES: A photo history with 3pp of text covering WWII, 1pp of which is on uniforms.
Excellent 15pp photo selection from WWII. Battle Honours. RoH.

The Fighting Tykes
The History of the Yorkshire Regiments in the Second World War
Whiting, Charles and Taylor, Eric   IWM; NAM; PCL
Barnsley; Leo Cooper; 1993; ISBN 0 85052 357 5; xiii + 238pp/59 x bw PI; s/b; Indexed
Y; Glossary N; Appendices N; Bibliography Y; 222 x 140 (8vo)
NOTES: Well composed brief history in 37pp, approximately half on France 1940 and
half on NWE. Draws on *Yeoman Soldier, Prussian Farmer*, and *Europe Revisited*, q.q.v.

Forrard
The Story of the East Riding Yeomanry
Mace, Paul   TM; IWM; NAM; RMAS; PCL
Barnsley; Leo Cooper; 2001; ISBN 0 85052 800 3; xxiv + 232pp/34 x bw PI/9 x bw M;
s/b; Indexed Y; Glossary N; Appendices Y; Bibliography N; 234 x 156 (8vo)
NOTES: The author joined the ERY at the end of 1944 and interviewed and questioned
many veterans of both regiments to produce this comprehensive history. First half of the
book deals with the early history of 1 & 2ERY, the demise of 2ERY after the fall of France,
and the UK history of ERY, as the new lone regiment became known. The second half
deals with its active service in NWE. Full of operational detail and veterans' quotations.
RoH/Honours/Awards. Battle Honours.

The Fighting Tykes
An Informal History of the Yorkshire Regiments in the Second World War
Whiting, Charles and Taylor, Eric
Barnsley; Pen & Sword Military; 2008; ISBN 978 1 84415 6 450; xiii + 238pp/59 x bw PI;
s/b; Indexed Y; Glossary N; Appendices N; Bibliography Y; 234 x 157 (8vo)
NOTES: Softback reprint of 1993 first edition, same pagination.

1st East Riding Yeomanry / East Riding Yeomanry*	1 E RIDING YEO

* After the fall of France, most men from 2ERY were moved to 1ERY and 2ERY's
remaining men transferred to The Green Howards. From the summer of 1940, 1ERY's
title became simply ERY.

Date of mechanization: 1920
RAC service: 04/04/1939   Post-war.

Europe Revisited
The East Riding Yeomanry in the liberation of Europe and the Defeat of Germany
Ellison, V. C. TM; IWM; NAM; PCL
Hull; A Brown & Sons Ltd; n.d. [c.1946]; ISBN None; ix + 101pp/1 x bw PIfep/2 x bw
PIf/26 x bw PI/2 x bw Mf; h/b / d/j Brown cloth; Indexed N; Glossary N; Appendices Y;
Bibliography N; 229 x 143 (8vo); Rare
NOTES: Written by the regiment's 2 i/c, this book deals with ERY's campaign history through NWE. Well detailed with frequent reference to named officers and NCOs. Fold out photographs of officers and NCOs of the regiment, May 1945. RoH/Honours/Awards. According to *Forrard*, q.v., this regimental history was paid for through the sales of gin and spirits 'acquired' at the end of the war from Hamburg and sold to the Officers' and Sergeants' Messes. A free copy was intended to be given to every serving member.

Yeoman Soldier Prussian Farmer
An Autobiography of the war years
Harvey, Richard TM; IWM
Dewsbury; The Stanley Press Ltd; 1981; ISBN None; 154pp/13 x bw PI/10 x bw SI/1 x clr Mbds; h/b / d/j Red cloth; Indexed N; Glossary N; Appendices N; Bibliography N; 209 x 138 (8vo)
NOTES: The author served in 4 Tp, C Sqn as a gunner/operator in a Bren Carrier. Evocatively written, he recounts his time with the regiment in France in 1940 before being taken POW. The bulk of the book is the story of his capture and captivity, almost exclusively working on a Prussian farm. First Limited Edition.

Evacuation Tarbat Peninsula 1943-4
Fallon, Dr, James A. TM
No imprint; No imprint; n.d. [c.1985]; ISBN None; 29pp/2 x clr PI/4 x clr SI/12 x bw PI/3 x clr M; s/b; Indexed N; Glossary N; Appendices N; Bibliography N; 210 x 147 (8vo)
NOTES: A local heritage booklet that tells the story of the area's evacuation for use as DD tank training, 6pp summarise the use of the area by 4/7DG, 13/18H, SY & ERY.

Chariots of the Lake
The Story of Britain's Secret Weapon during the Second World War. From Fritton Lake to D-Day and Beyond
Jarvis, Robert B. TM
Lowestoft; The Heritage Workshop Centre; 2003; ISBN 1-904413-04-8; 131pp/5 x clr PI/56 x bw PI/4 x bw SI/1 x bw M; s/b; Indexed Y; Glossary Y; Appendices N; Bibliography Y; 260 x 210 (4to)
NOTES: Tells the story of the DD tank through the Suffolk training area at Fritton Lake and includes information on the DD equipped regiments: 4/7DG, 13/18H, ERY, SRY, and SY contained in 29pp.

World War 2 and me
The story of a young man's wartime activities, from a brief spell in the Royal Air Force Volunteer Reserve to four years in a Tank Regiment, including battles from D-Day to VE Day in north-west Europe
Davies, Peter TM
Not stated; Peter Davies; 2008; ISBN None; viii + 128pp/40 x bw PI/2 x bw M; s/b; Indexed N; Glossary N; Appendices N; Bibliography N; 234 x 156 (8vo); Uncommon

ROYAL ARMOURED CORPS: TA - YEOMANRY

NOTES: In 1941 the author, aged 17, joined the RAF Volunteer Reserve. He transferred to the RAC in 1942 and joined the ERY. He recounts his memories of service in NWE in a series of single chapter vignettes.

2nd East Riding Yeomanry   2 E RIDING YEO

Date of mechanization: 24/08/1939 (Raised)
RAC service: 24/08/1939   25/06/1940*
* After the fall of France, most men from 2ERY were moved to 1ERY and the remaining men transferred to The Green Howards.

No publications established.

The Inns of Court Regiment   INNS OF COURT

Not strictly classed as Yeomanry until after the war, the Inns of Court are listed in the 1944 Army Lists at the end of the RAC Yeomanry regiments.

Date of mechanization: 01/04/1937
RAC service: 28/02/1941*   Post-war.
* Previously operated as RAC (Inns of Court) Wing of 101 OCTU.

> **Regimental publications:**
> **The Inns of Court Regiment, 'The Devil's Own', Regimental News**
> No. 8 June 1932 to No. 21 Dec 1938 (Varies)
> **Red Devil. Inns of Court Regt.**
> Run not established, editions are undated (Quarterly)
> **Tarfon, the monthly journal of 'A' Squadron, The Inns of Court Regiment**
> Vol. 1, No. 1 July 1945 to Vol. 1, No. 3 Sept 1945 (Monthly)
> **Vanguard. Journal of The Inns of Court and City Yeomanry Association**
> From unknown to current (Annual)

Note: No evidence has been established that 'A' or 'B' Squadrons produced similar souvenir booklets as 'C' and 'D' Squadrons did, q.v. below.

The Inns of Court Regiment
Standing Orders 1938
Not stated   IWM; NAM
London; W W Sprague & Co Ltd; 1938; ISBN None; 58pp/5 x bw Pl; h/b Green cloth; Indexed N; Glossary N; Appendices N; Bibliography N; 198 x 144 (8vo)
NOTES: Although strictly outside the date range of this book, these SOs provide a curious insight into the split world of British cavalry vs. mechanization with war only a year away; the regiment comprised two light tank squadrons plus one cavalry squadron. The photographic illustrations show only cavalry marching order.

The Long Road Home
The Story of D Squadron The Inns of Court Regt. And Their Travels From Normandy to the Danish Frontier
Not stated [See Notes] IWM
No imprint; No imprint; n.d. [c.1945]; ISBN None; 55pp/15 x bw PI; s/b; Indexed N; Glossary N; Appendices N; Bibliography N; 204 x 147 (8vo); Rare
NOTES: Written as a souvenir for the squadron by a serving member. Informative narrative with personnel listings for the landing in Normandy, the re-organisation July 1944, and for the Rhine crossing in 1945. RoH. Honours/Awards. Author is Sgt J. F. O. Laing.

"We Were There!"
The Story of a Journey Made by C Squadron The Inns Of Court Regiment 1941 – 1945
Various IWM
Flensburg; (Emil Schmidt Söhne – printers); n.d. [1946]; ISBN None; 89pp/14 x bw PI/11 x bw SI; s/b; Indexed N; Glossary N; Appendices N; Bibliography N; 208 x 149 (8vo); Rare
NOTES: Souvenir compilation of memories contributed by squadron members. A few chapters provide recollections from the early days with the majority reflecting on the squadron's activities in NWE. RoH/Honours/Awards.

To the Stars...
A Tribute to the Junior Officers of the Royal Armoured Corps
Mabyn Ross, Peter TM; IWM; NAM
Bovington; RAC Publications; n.d. [1946]; ISBN None; 96pp/3 x bw PIfep/19 x bw SI; h/b / d/j Red cloth; Indexed N; Glossary N; Appendices N; Bibliography N; 222 x 142 (8vo); Uncommon
NOTES: The book goes through, in reasonable detail, the training and courses of an RAC officer cadet. It also provides some brief early information on the Inns of Court regiment. Also by author – *All Valiant Dust*, see 3RTR listing.

An Outline of the History of The Inns Of Court Regiment
Not stated
Niebüll, Germany; (Johannes Klink - printer); n.d. [c. 1946]; ISBN None; 11pp/No illus.; s/b (card); Indexed N; Glossary N; Appendices N; Bibliography N; 113 x 93 (32mo); V Rare
NOTES: Pocket summary history of the regiment from 1584 to c. 1946, 1½ pp on WWII. (The London Metropolitan Archives hold a document with a very similar title but which is a set of seven single-sided typed pages, 1pp on WWII.)

Needs Must...
The History of the Inns of Court Regiment 1940 - 1945
Not stated [See Notes] TM; IWM; NAM
London; F Mildner & Sons; 1949; ISBN None; 103pp/1 x bw PIfep/11 x bw PI; h/b Black cloth; Indexed N; Glossary N; Appendices N; Bibliography N; 216 x 144 (8vo); Rare

NOTES: After a single page on the 'Early Days', this history starts with C Sqn landing on D-Day and then follows the regiment across Europe; well composed narrative in a diary form. RoH/Honours/Awards. Author is Capt. A. F. J. Taggart.

Needs Must...Maps I - XI
Not stated IWM
No imprint; No imprint; n.d. [1949]; ISBN None; 103pp/1 x bw PIfep/11 x bw PI; h/b Black cloth; Indexed N; Glossary N; Appendices N; Bibliography N; 214 x 142 (8vo); V Rare
NOTES: No text, comprises 11 original folded colour GSGS maps covering the regiment's route, no annotation. Noted as V Rare although strictly, exceptionally rare.

The Devil's Own
A History of the Inns of Court Regiment
Hatton TD, Major, D. M. TM; IWM; NAM; RMAS; PCL
London; J. A. Allen & Co; 1992; ISBN 0-85131-550-X; xx + 340pp/1 x clr SIfep/3 x clr PI/12 x clr SI/35 x bw PI/1 x bw SI/7 x clr Mf; h/b Green cloth; Indexed Y; Glossary Y; Appendices Y; Bibliography Y; 242 x 162 (8vo)
NOTES: Overall history of the regiment spanning 1584 – 1987 with 58pp covering WWII. One short chapter on formation and UK training. Honours/Awards – listed within the WWII section. Battle Honours. Six appendices including information on Colonels, COs, WE, and dress regulations.

The Seven Colonels
The story of seven 11th Hussar subalterns who sailed to Egypt in 1934 and later became the Commanding Officers of several Units which all made a significant contribution to the successful outcome of the Second World War in 1939-45
Osborne, Keith
No imprint; No imprint; No imprint; ISBN None; viii + 92pp/12 x bw PI/1 x bw SI/1 x bw M; s/b; Indexed N; Glossary N; Appendices N; Bibliography N; 210 x 148 (8vo)
NOTES: Essentially a retelling of 11H's history with occasional reference to the officers rather than the story of those personalities. The seven were George Paul (54th Training Regt, RAC), Bertie Bingley (IoC), Trevor Smail (11H), Geoffrey Miller (Sherwood Foresters), Peter Payne Gallwey (DY), Bill Wainman (11H), and John Lawson (IoC).

Key to Book Entries
Book Title and Sub-title(s)
Author Museum Holdings
Place of Publication; Publisher; Date of Publication; ISBN; Pages/Illustrations; Binding; Indexed; Glossary; Appendices; Bibliography; Size (in mm); Availability
NOTES:

Section IX

Royal Armoured Corps: TA – Royal Tank Regiment

The British Army had started to expand its forces in the years prior to the Second World War. Included in this expansion was the armoured branch and in November 1938, six Territorial Army (TA) infantry battalions were converted to tanks to form new Royal Tank Regiment battalions.* These were 40th to 45th Bn, RTR and existing regular RTR battalions provided cadres.

In May 1939 as part of the overall doubling of TA battalions, these six RTR units raised cadres themselves to form a further six tank battalions, being 46th to 51st Bn, RTR.

* Refer to the introduction of 'Section V' and the note on the RTR's regimental nomenclature.

The table below provides a summary of each TA RTR battalion listing its antecedent infantry battalion and RTR cadre.

RTR Bn	Converted Inf. Bn	Conversion date	RTR Cadre
40RTR	7th Bn The King's (Liverpool Regiment)	1 November 1938	1RTR
41RTR	10th Bn The Manchester Regiment	1 November 1938	3RTR
42RTR	7th Bn (23rd London) The East Surrey Regiment	1 November 1938	8RTR
43RTR	6th Bn The Royal Northumberland Fusiliers	1 November 1938	7RTR
44RTR	6th Bn The Gloucestershire Regiment	1 November 1938	5RTR
45RTR	7th (Leeds Rifles) Bn, The West Yorkshire Regiment (The Prince of Wales's Own)	1 November 1938	6RTR
46RTR	-	May 1939	40RTR
47RTR	-	May 1939	41RTR
48RTR	-	May 1939	42RTR
49RTR	-	May 1939	43RTR
50RTR	-	May 1939	44RTR
51RTR	-	May 1939	45RTR

Royal Armoured Corps: TA - Royal Tank Regiment

Regimental publications:
The Tank Corps Training Centre Journal
Vol. 1, No. 1 Apr 1919 (Monthly); became
The Tank Corps Journal
Vol. 1, No. 2 May 1919 to Vol. 4, No. 55 Nov 1923 (Monthly); became
The Royal Tank Corps Journal
Vol. V, No. 56 Dec 1923 to Vol. XVIII, No. 209 Sept 1936; upon creation of **The Tank** became
The Royal Tank Corps Journal
Vol. 1, No. 1 Jan 1936 to Vol. 10 1946 (Half yearly)
The Tank. Journal of the Royal Tank Regiment
Vol. XVIII, No. 210 Oct 1936 to present (Monthly to Vol. 57, No. 672 Apr 1975, then Quarterly to Vol. 91, No. 790 Dec 2009, then 3 per year to Vol. 92, No. 796 Winter 2011 and 2 per year from Summer 2012)

40th Bn, Royal Tank Regiment — 40 R Tks

RAC service: 04/04/1939 Post-war.

No publications established, but refer to *Armour in Action 1, The Valentine in North Africa* - Section XVI - Miscellaneous.

41st Bn, Royal Tank Regiment — 41 R Tks

RAC service: 04/04/1939 01/01/1944 (Suspended animation)

'B' Squadron 41st Royal Tank Regiment
The Battle of the Minefields October 1942
MacDonald, Maj. N. P. IWM
Not stated; Not stated; n.d. [c.1942]; ISBN None; 27pp/2 x bw Mf; s/b (no covers); Indexed N; Glossary N; Appendices N; Bibliography N; 216 x 165 (8vo); V Rare
NOTES: Written by the OC B Sqn, the booklet documents the squadron's actions in the battle of El Alamein. Reproduced typescript.

A Rat in a Tank
Gell, Harry IWM
London; Minerva Press; 1995; ISBN 1 85863 549 7; 202pp/No illus.; s/b; Indexed N; Glossary N; Appendices N; Bibliography N; 205 x 147 (8vo); Uncommon
NOTES: The author's recollections start with his journey out to the ME in May 1942, whilst serving with 41RTR. They comprise his letters home plus occasional narrative in explanation or more detailed comment on men he served alongside. He details the minutiae of army life, dominated by food, the notes and letters being written at the time or very soon after the event. On the breakup of 41RTR he was transferred to 4CLY in December 1942, remaining with them until the war's end (as 3/4CLY.) In February 1945 his tank was hit and he suffered burns; the letters end at this point.

41st Royal Tank Regiment 1938 to 1943
Notes on the History of the Regiment
Taylor Firth, J. N. TM
No imprint; No imprint; 2001; ISBN None; No pagination/8 x clr SI/50 x bw PI/2 x bw SI/2 x bw M; s/b; Indexed N; Glossary N; Appendices Y; Bibliography N; 297 x 210 (4to)
NOTES: Strictly outside the scope of this book, this is private research deposited with the Tank Museum. Should a reader visit their library, here is a treasure trove of notes and details on the regiment, including reproduction of War Diary entries, crew names, tank names, etc. See also the author's work on 48RTR in the same format.

42nd Bn, Royal Tank Regiment	42 R Tks

RAC service: 04/04/1939 30/10/44 (Suspended animation)
See also *Armour in Action 2, The Matilda* - Section XVI – Miscellaneous.

Regimental publications:
World News
No. 1 June 1944 to No. 137 12 Oct 1944 (Daily)

42nd Royal Tank Regiment 1938 - 1944
Not stated TM; IWM; NAM
London; No imprint; n.d. [c.1951]; ISBN None; 37pp/7 x bw M; s/b; Indexed N; Glossary N; Appendices N; Bibliography N; 250 x 204 (4to); Rare
NOTES: Detailed account of the regiment's actions in NA 1941/42. In 1942 the regiment started training with CDL tanks and trained with them until placed in suspended animation in November 1944. Reproduced typescript.

On Track 1939 - 1953
From El Alamein to Korea
Senior, M.C., Colonel Victor J. IWM
Co. Limerick; Victor Senior; 2001; ISBN None; 208pp/1 x bw PIfep/35 x bw PI/2 x bw SI/7 x bw M; s/b; Indexed N; Glossary N; Appendices N; Bibliography N; 210 x 148 (8vo); Uncommon
NOTES: The author signed up at the outset of the war and was posted to 42RTR, going to the ME with them where he attended OCTU during 1942. Upon being commissioned, he was posted to 50RTR as a troop leader, just before El Alamein. The book comprises articles published by the author in *Tank*, the RTR journal, letters home, plus further material of the author's experiences including the little written about Greek campaign of 1945.

Escape of a Trooper
the wartime memories of Bob Ford
Hall, Roger; Richardson, Sue (Ed.) IWM
Manchester; Roger Hall; 2011; ISBN 978 185216 171 2; 36pp/34 x bw PI/3 x bw M; s/b (card); Indexed N; Glossary N; Appendices N; Bibliography N; 296 x 207 (4to); Rare

NOTES: Published by the author's nephew, BF joined the regiment early 1939 and moved to NA with them in late 1941. He was captured June 1942 and his memoirs focus on his time as a POW and his attempts at escaping whilst in Italy and Austria. Honest descriptions of the conditions and poor health the POWs endured.

43rd Bn, Royal Tank Regiment — 43 R Tks

RAC service: 04/04/1939 Post-war.

Regimental publications:
Pennant. The Monthly Journal of the 43rd Royal Tank Regiment
Vol. 1, No. 1 November 1945 to Vol. 1, No. 4 Aug. 1946, then
Pennant. The Journal of the 43rd Royal Tank Regiment
Vol. 1, No. 5 October 1946 to unknown (last seen Vol. 1, No. 6 April 1947) Irregular

The History of the Royal Northumberland Fusiliers
In the Second World War
Barclay, C.B.E., D.S.O., Brig. C. N. IWM; NAM; RMAS; PCL
London; William Clowes and Sons Limited; 1952; ISBN None; xxii + 241pp/48 x bw PI/1 x bw SIfep/1 x bw SI/14 x bw Mf/5 x bw M; h/b / d/j Red cloth; Indexed Y; Glossary Y; Appendices Y; Bibliography N; 252 x 192 (4to)
NOTES: Unusually for an infantry regiment's history, this one fully acknowledges its armoured offspring. A 4pp chapter summarises the histories of 43RTR and 49RTR. RoH/Honours/Awards - RoH lists 'Tpr' but there is no differentiation by regiment. 6th Bn = 43RTR.

43rd Bn. Royal Tank Regiment
This is a personal account of my service with the Regiment Between April 1945 and October 1947.
Woolley, J. F. TM
Not stated; Private; 1995; ISBN None; 30pp/23 x bw PI; s/b (card); Indexed N; Glossary N; Appendices N; Bibliography N; 219 x 147 (8vo); Uncommon
NOTES: The author was posted to 43RTR in April 1945 and his story continues with the regiment in India as a CDL regiment, although the detail is post war. Rewritten and published 2005.

44th Bn, Royal Tank Regiment — 44 R Tks

RAC service: 04/04/1939 Post-war.
See also *Armour in Action 2, The Matilda* - Section XVI – Miscellaneous.

44th Royal Tank Regiment Territorial Army
Not stated TM
London; Goddard-Lawrence & Co; n.d. [c.1949]; ISBN None; 28pp/5 x bw PI; s/b; Indexed N; Glossary N; Appendices N; Bibliography N; 140 x 216 (24mo); Uncommon
NOTES: A TA recruiting booklet with 7pp on WWII.

A History Of The 44th Royal Tank Regiment in the War Of 1939-45
Brown, M.C., Lt-Col A. G.; Dodwell, K. C. E.; Honniball, F. E.; TM; NAM; RMAS
Hopkinson, C.B., D.S.O., O.B.E., M.C., Maj-Gen G. C.
No imprint; No imprint; n.d. [c.1965]; ISBN None; xi + 214pp/1 x bw PIfep/17 x bw M; h/b Black cloth; Indexed N; Glossary N; Appendices Y; Bibliography N; 222 x 144 (8vo); Rare
NOTES: Reasonably well detailed account of the regiment's history written by ex-members (inc. two COs) covering NA, Sicily, Italy and NWE. Includes one chapter on the function of 'B' Echelon. Unfortunately there is only passing reference to the regiment's use of Scorpion mine clearing tanks at El Alamein. RoH/Honours/Awards. Maps on tissue paper.

Proven Beyond Doubt
Thorogood, George Grant TM; IWM
Solihull; Thorogood Publications; 1995; ISBN 0 9525394 03; xi + 148pp/40 x bw PI/1 x bw M; h/b / d/j Black cloth; Indexed N; Glossary N; Appendices Y; Bibliography Y; 217 x 149 (8vo)
NOTES: The author describes his journey to establish the events surrounding the death of his brother, John, in Holland in September 1944. John Thorogood was killed in action after his tank was knocked out. Interesting reproduction of the letter of condolence from JT's commanding officer to his mother; one example of thousands of such letters written throughout the war. RoH.

Return To Durham
Via Libya, Italy, Germany and France
The Exploits of a Durham 'Desert Rat'
Anderson, Ray TM; IWM
Spennymoor; Ray Anderson; n.d. [c.1997]; ISBN 0 9530865 0 X; 186pp/12 x bw PI/1 x bw M; s/b; Indexed N; Glossary N; Appendices N; Bibliography N; 210 x 150 (8vo); Uncommon
NOTES: The author joined the RAC in 1940 and was posted to C Sqn 44RTR in September 1940. He describes his days of training to become a Driver Mechanic. His first role was as regimental dispatch rider and once in the desert he joined 'A' Echelon. For Operation Crusader he was moved into a fighting troop as a driver, before being captured by the Germans in June 1942. The final two-thirds of the book recount his engaging and poignant POW experiences. He escaped during the German takeover after Italy surrendered and was on the run for a few months before being recaptured by the Germans and sent to Germany. He was liberated in April 1945.

Memoirs of a Trooper, 1942 - 1945
Whitehead, Robert
Leeds; R Whitehead; 1998; See Notes; Rare
NOTES: Not physically inspected.

Leakey's Luck
A Tank Commander with Nine Lives
Leakey, Rea with Forty, George   IWM
Stroud; Sutton Publishing Limited; 1999; ISBN 0 7509 1731 5; x + 158pp/2 x SI bds/1 x bw PIfep/24 x bw PI/7 x bw M; h/b / d/j Black cloth; Indexed Y; Glossary N; Appendices Y; Bibliography Y; 240 x 160 (8vo)
NOTES: The author was commissioned into the RTC in 1936 and served in several RTR regiments, 4RTC (pre-war), 1RTR (1938-1941), 3RTR (1943), 44RTR (1943/44), 7RTR (1944) and 5RTR (1945), commanding the latter two in NWE at the end of the war. He provides an excellent insight into the life of an officer in Egypt just before and early in the war. War suits some people; Rea Leakey recounts many a military adventure, no surprise therefore, that the end papers reproduce a strip from *The Victor* comic of 1969 showing his feats at Tobruk. One claim to fame was as co-inventor of the sun-compass.

Leakey's Luck
A Tank Commander with Nine Lives
Leakey, Rea; Forty, George (Ed.)
Stroud; Sutton Publishing Limited; 2002; ISBN 0 7509 3195 7; x + 230pp/31 x bw PI; p/b; Indexed Y; Glossary N; Appendices Y; Bibliography Y; 198 x 127 (8vo)
NOTES: Paperback reprint of 1999 first edition, different pagination.

45th Bn, Royal Tank Regiment   45 R Tks

RAC service: 04/04/1939   08/03/1943 (Suspended animation)

Standing orders of the 45th (Leeds Rifles) Battalion The Royal Tank Regiment
Tetley, Lt-Col, T.D., J. N.   IWM
Leeds; Regiment (Walter Gardham Ltd - printers); 1940; ISBN None; xii + 131pp/No illus.; h/b Red cloth; Indexed Y; Glossary N; Appendices Y; Bibliography N; 190 x 126 (12mo); Rare
NOTES: Usual regimental Standing Orders.

A Short History 45/51 (Leeds Rifles) Royal Tank Regt. (TA)
Not stated   NAM
Not stated; 1954; ISBN None; 14pp/No illus.; Indexed N; Glossary N; Appendices N; Bibliography N; A4; V Rare
NOTES: Research monograph; that held by NAM is a set of photocopied sheets, not original. 4pp on WWII.

So Much For the Fog of War
The Leeds Rifles at El Alamein
Podmore, M.B.E., T.D., Maj. A. J.   TM
No imprint; Private; 1996; ISBN None; 44pp/1 x bw SI/10 x bw M; s/b (card); Indexed N; Glossary N; Appendices Y; Bibliography N; 297 x 210 (4to); Uncommon
NOTES: This booklet provides a brief background history of the regiment and a highly detailed account of its part in the El Alamein battle.

The 45th (Leeds Rifles) Royal Tank Regiment in the Second World War
Addyman, Ronald   PCL
Leeds; R Addyman; 2006; ISBN 978 09547807 8 4; xxiii + 32pp/4 x clr Pl/13 x bw Pl/5 x clr M; h/b / d/j Red cloth; Indexed Y; Glossary N; Appendices Y; Bibliography Y; 275 x 215 (4to)
NOTES: The book focuses on the battle for El Alamein and references the private account, *A Personal Narrative of El Alamein*, by Maj. Flatow, TD. The second half of the book deals with the strategic actions affecting the battle of El Alamein. Extensive RoH detailing date, army number, relations and war cemetery details. The author prints on demand and incorporates any new material regularly; dates of publication and content, therefore, are for guidance. Example examined was a 2009 reprint.

46th Bn, Royal Tank Regiment*   46 R Tks

* Evidence suggests that the regiment used (Liverpool Welsh) in the title only after the war.

RAC service: 04/04/1939   Post-war.
See also *Armour in Action 1, The Valentine in North Africa* - Section XVI – Miscellaneous.

A Short History of the 46th Liverpool Welsh Royal Tank Regiment
Not stated   TM; IWM
No imprint; No imprint; n.d. [c.1950]; ISBN None; 5pp/No illus.; Gatefold sheet; Indexed N; Glossary N; Appendices N; Bibliography N; 219 x 176 (8vo); Uncommon
NOTES: Very brief but well detailed history of the regiment. Published date surmised from this manuscript held at The Tank Museum.

47th Bn, Royal Tank Regiment   47 R Tks

RAC service: 05/1939   15/01/1943 (Disbanded)

47th Royal Tank Regiment 1938 to 1943
Notes on the History of the Regiment
Taylor Firth, J. N.   TM
No imprint; No imprint; 2000; ISBN None; No pagination/7 x clr Sl/50 x bw Pl/1 x bw Sl/3 x clr Mf/1 x bw Mf/2 x bw M; Comb; Indexed N; Glossary N; Appendices Y; Bibliography N; 297 x 210 (4to)
NOTES: Strictly outside the scope of this book, this is private research deposited with the Tank Museum. Should a reader visit their library, here is a treasure trove of notes and details on the regiment, including reproduction of War Diary entries, crew names, tank names, etc. Revised 2001 and 2002 - edition viewed. RoH. See also the author's work on 41RTR in the same format.

48th Bn, Royal Tank Regiment — 48 R Tks

RAC service: 05/1939 Post-war.

Regimental publications:
The B Line. Magazine of B Squadron 48th Bn. R.T.R.
January 1943 to August 1945 plus September 1945 Souvenir Issue (monthly) – individual covers, generally hand drawn; approximately 120 copies of each edition were printed.

The B Line
Magazine of B Squadron 48th Bn. R.T.R. Souvenir Number
Regiment
Hounslow; Cedar Press, Thomasons Ltd; 1945; ISBN None; 34pp/16 x bw PI/1 x bw SI/3 x bw M; s/b; Indexed N; Glossary N; Appendices N; Bibliography N; 284 x 226 (4to); Rare
NOTES: A special edition of B Squadron's monthly magazine, *The B-Line*, published in the summer of 1945, 'freed from the shackles of censorship,'. Diary style summary of the squadron's history from 1939 to 1945. Last half includes retrospectives, list of squadron personnel and a well reproduced set of troop photographs. RoH/Decorations. The *Souvenir Number* was the only properly printed edition, others were typescript published on a duplicating machine in the field.

Lines From a War
Verses by Soldiers on Active Service
Thomason, G. G. TM
Windsor; G. G. Thomason; 1991; ISBN None; 74pp/26 x bw PI; s/b; Indexed N; Glossary N; Appendices N; Bibliography N; 210 x 145 (8vo); Uncommon
NOTES: A collection of verse printed in different issues of *The B-Line* squadron paper together with pictures of the covers of the majority of issues.

Tanks for the Memory
The Story of the 48th Battalion Royal Tank Regiment
Gudgin, Peter TM
London; 48th Royal Tank Regiment Association; 1993; ISBN 0-9521699-0-8; vi + 199pp/1 x bw PIfep/141 x bw PI/3 x bw SI/9 x bw M; s/b; Indexed Y; Glossary N; Appendices Y; Bibliography Y; 198 x 134 (8vo); Rare
NOTES: One of the very best unit histories, full of personal quotes and action/equipment detail. The author served with 48RTR from late 1942 when he commanded 4th Tp, A Sqn. Includes nominal roll of regiment's members, in the case of C Sqn down to tank crew. RoH/Honours/Awards. Later republished as *With Churchills To War*.

With Churchills to War
48th Battalion RTR at war 1939-45
Gudgin, Peter TM; IWM; RMAS; PCL
Stroud; Sutton Publishing Limited; 1996; ISBN 0-7509-1239-1; xxii + 193pp/144 x bw PI/1 x bw SI/9 x bw M; h/b / d/j Black cloth; Indexed Y; Glossary Y; Appendices Y; Bibliography Y; 250 x 178 (4to)
NOTES: Essentially a reprint of *Tanks for the Memory* with minor editorial updates.

Another War, Another Corporal
A Collection of 40 vignettes of Life in the Royal Tank Regiment 1939 - 1946 with poems by the Author
Cook, Edmund, M.B.E.   TM
No imprint; No imprint; 2007; ISBN None; xv + 199pp/14 x bw Pl; h/b / d/j Red cloth; Indexed N; Glossary Y; Appendices N; Bibliography N; 216 x 150 (8vo)
NOTES: Originally written in 1983, with addenda 1986, it was not until 2007 that the author's son was able to publish his father's book. The author volunteered two months after the start of the war and was posted to 48RTR before the end of 1939. The first role he describes was as regimental despatch rider. He was transferred to a fighting troop in C Sqn and saw action from Tunisia onward in a Churchill tank, later serving as B Sqn OC's wireless operator. The author tackles daily life in the army as opposed to combat action, avoiding harsh realities through the use of humour. These memoirs are a collection of individual short stories and events. RoH.

49th Bn, Royal Tank Regiment / 49th Armoured Personnel Carrier Regiment*	49 R Tks

* Renamed 49th Armoured Personnel Carrier Regiment in October 1944.

RAC service: 05/1939   Post-war.

     Regimental publications:
     Bivvy Broadcast
     05/09/1944 to 22/12/1944 plus Christmas Supplement (Daily)
     Chads Chatter
     Unknown to No. 8 Souvenir Edition 10/12/1945 (Weekly)

Bivvy Broadcast Omnibus NW Europe 1944-5
Not stated   TM
Celle, Germany; Regiment; 1945; ISBN None; 166pp/4 x bw SI; s/b; Indexed N; Glossary N; Appendices N; Bibliography N; 217 x 149 (8vo); Rare
NOTES: This book, published June 1945, is a compilation of reproduced regimental newspapers called *The Bivvy Broadcast* which ran from 05/09/1944 through to 22/12/1944. It ran daily until 23/10/1944 and then irregularly until the final December issue. The masthead was introduced from 16/09/1944 although it has been reproduced in this compilation from issue one. The majority were double side single sheets with the occasional 4pp editions. Each contained humorous tales, poems, quizzes, etc.; they were not used to impart official regimental business. The 8pp Christmas special provides a 2pp summary of the regiment in WWII. RoH/Honours/Awards.

The History of the Royal Northumberland Fusiliers
In the Second World War
Barclay, C.B.E., D.S.O., Brig. C. N.   IWM; NAM; RMAS; PCL
London; William Clowes and Sons Limited; 1952; ISBN None; xxii + 241pp/48 x bw Pl/1 x bw SIfep/1 x bw SI/14 x bw Mf/5 x bw M; h/b / d/j Red cloth; Indexed Y; Glossary Y; Appendices Y; Bibliography N; 252 x 192 (4to)

NOTES: Unusually for an infantry regiment's history, this one fully acknowledges its armoured offspring. A 4pp chapter summarises the histories of 43RTR and 49RTR. RoH/Honours/Awards - RoH lists 'Tpr' but there is no differentiation by regiment. 49RTR raised from cadre of 43RTR, 6th Bn = 43RTR.

49th Unparalled
The Story of the 49th Battalion Royal Tank Regiment Later Designated as an Armoured Personal Carrier Regiment 1939 - 1945
Scull, M.M., L. V. IWM
No imprint; No imprint (Parchment (Oxford) Ltd - printers); 2002; ISBN None; 65pp/27 x bw PI/3 x bw SI/3 x clr M; s/b; Indexed N; Glossary N; Appendices N; Bibliography N; 204 x 144 (8vo); Rare
NOTES: Includes some detailed descriptions of the operation of CDL tanks. Detailed account of the regiment's operations involving the carrying of infantry in its APCs. Photocopy quality illustrations. RoH/Honours/Awards.

49th Unparalled
The Story of the 49th Battalion Royal Tank Regiment Later Designated as an Armoured Personal Carrier Regiment 1939 - 1945
Scull, M.M., L. V. TM; IWM
No imprint; No imprint; 2004; ISBN None; 68pp/27 x bw PI/3 x bw SI/3 x clr M; Comb; Indexed N; Glossary N; Appendices N; Bibliography N; 297 x 210 (4to); Rare
NOTES: Second edition printed, as the author interestingly states, 'in A4 format so much more suited to the veteran's optical capabilities,'.

The Lost Hussar
My life with the armoured units 1938 - 1968
Booth, Tony
Needham Market; Private (Gipping Press Ltd - printers); 2010; ISBN None; 62pp/26 x bw PI; s/b; Indexed N; Glossary N; Appendices N; Bibliography N; 210 x 147 (8vo); Uncommon
NOTES: The author joined 4H before the war and upon war transferred to a training regiment before being posted to 49RTR which became a CDL regiment. 28pp on WWII. New revised edition 2011.

The Lost Hussar
My life with the armoured units 1938 - 1968
Booth, Tony TM
Needham Market; Private (Gipping Press Ltd - printers); 2011; ISBN None; 62pp/26 x bw PI; s/b; Indexed N; Glossary N; Appendices N; Bibliography N; 210 x 147 (8vo); Uncommon
NOTES: New 2011 edition with additional material.

50th Bn, Royal Tank Regiment	50 R Tks

RAC service: 05/1939 Post-war.
See also *Armour in Action 1, The Valentine in North Africa* - Section XVI – Miscellaneous.

50th Royal Tank Regiment
Memories "C" Squadron Men's Mess
Not stated TM
No imprint; No imprint; 1945; ISBN None; 25pp/No illus.; s/b; Indexed N; Glossary N; Appendices N; Bibliography N; 195 x 161 (12mo); V Rare
NOTES: A curious collection of memories of C Squadron's canteen from mid-1943 to the end of the war.

50th Royal Tank Regiment
The Story of a Regiment
50RTR Old Comrades Association TM; IWM; NAM
No imprint; No imprint; n.d. [c.1982]; ISBN None; 44pp/14 x bw M; s/b; Indexed N; Glossary N; Appendices N; Bibliography N; 294 x 204 (4to); Rare
NOTES: Computer print, brief history of the regiment from its inception to disbandment. 150 copies printed for private circulation.

50th Royal Tank Regiment
The Complete History
Hamilton, Stephen D. TM; IWM; RMAS; PCL
Cambridge; The Lutterworth Press; 1996; ISBN 0 7188 2938 7; xii + 292pp/55 x bw PI/10 x bw M; h/b / d/j Black cloth; Indexed Y; Glossary N; Appendices Y; Bibliography Y; 238 x 159 (8vo)
NOTES: Includes a good many personal recollections, with well detailed references to the personnel of the regiment. Same level of coverage applies to the little reported Greek campaign of late 1944/early 1945. Less comprehensive on the regiment's vehicles. Highly detailed RoH with squadron, service number, place of death, relations and war cemetery details. Appendices include RoH/Honours/Awards/list of officers 1939-45, list of personnel wounded or missing in action.

Two Birds and No Stones
It's a short life - fill it!
Morris, Geoffrey
Northwich; Léonie Press; 2000; ISBN 1 901253 17 1; v + 201pp/25 x bw PI/47 x bw SI; s/b; Indexed N; Glossary N; Appendices N; Bibliography N; 206 x 146 (8vo)
NOTES: The author takes a potted, humorous, journey through his life. He served in 7 Tp, B Sqn; his wartime experiences cover 68pp.

On Track 1939 - 1953
From El Alamein to Korea
Senior, M.C., Colonel Victor J. IWM
Co. Limerick; Victor Senior; 2001; ISBN None; 208pp/1 x bw PIfep/35 x bw PI/2 x bw SI/7 x bw M; s/b; Indexed N; Glossary N; Appendices N; Bibliography N; 210 x 148 (8vo); Uncommon

NOTES: The author signed up at the outset of the war and was posted to 42RTR, going to the ME with them where he attended OCTU during 1942. Upon being commissioned, he was posted to 50RTR as a troop leader, just before El Alamein. The book comprises articles published by the author in *Tank*, the RTR journal, letters home, plus further material of the author's experiences including the little written about Greek campaign of 1945.

51st Bn, Royal Tank Regiment — 51 R Tks

RAC service: 05/1939 Post-war.

A Short History of the 51st Battalion Royal Tank Regiment
Not stated TM; IWM
Not stated; Printing & Stationery Services; 1945; ISBN None; 29pp/No illus.; s/b; Indexed N; Glossary N; Appendices N; Bibliography N; 203 x 127 (8vo); Rare
NOTES: Brief but highly informative summary history of the regiment. RoH/Honours/Awards and list of wounded in action, nominal roll of officers who served with the regiment overseas. Published in October 1945, 800 copies printed. The author was one-time OC, A Sqn. This booklet was reprinted in 1970 by Publications Wing, Bovington Camp, discernible by its orange card covers.

A Short History 45/51 (Leeds Rifles) Royal Tank Regt. (TA)
Not stated NAM
Not stated; 1954; ISBN None; 14pp/No illus.; Indexed N; Glossary N; Appendices N; Bibliography N; A4; V Rare
NOTES: Research monograph; that held by NAM is a set of photocopied sheets, not original. 4pp on WWII.

The 51st Royal Tank Regiment
Morley, Tunisia and Italy, 1939 - 1945
Addyman, Ronald TM; PCL
Leeds; R Addyman; 2004; ISBN 978 0 9547807 0 8; viii, 44pp/12 x clr Pl/1 x bw Plfep/24 x bw Pl/1 x bw Sl/7 x clr M; h/b / d/j Red cloth; Indexed Y; Glossary N; Appendices N; Bibliography N; 266 x 210 (4to)
NOTES: Self-published summary account of the regiment, focusing on the Italian campaign. The author prints on demand and incorporates any new material regularly, dates of publication and content, therefore, are for guidance, 2009 edition examined. Third impression in PCL, 2009 edition in TM.

Key to Book Entries
Book Title and Sub-title(s)
Author Museum Holdings
Place of Publication; Publisher; Date of Publication; ISBN; Pages/Illustrations; Binding; Indexed; Glossary; Appendices; Bibliography; Size (in mm); Availability
NOTES:

Section X

Royal Armoured Corps:
TA – Royal Armoured Corps Regiments

The War Office recognised the need to expand the British Army as soon as the war started. The fall of France in June 1940 accelerated that expansion and in July 1940 sixty additional infantry battalions were created. At the same time, the Army desperately needed more armoured regiments and, to some extent, this need was fulfilled by the growth of existing traditional cavalry sources. However, the War Office recognised a shortfall and in late 1941 ordered the conversion of several of the new infantry battalions to armour. In total, thirty-three infantry battalions were transformed to RAC regiments between November 1941 and July 1942. By that stage of the war, losses in infantry units were already starting to be felt, causing many to be reconverted to infantry; some existed in the armoured role for a mere six months and never saw a tank.

As a consequence of the short life of some RAC regiments, or even due to the attitude of the parent infantry regiment, there are many gaps in the list of books recording their histories. Some infantry regiments' histories pay little attention, if any, to their armoured brethren. In some cases this might have been due to understandable inter-branch snobbery but in others simply because the battalion converted to tanks, stayed in the UK, often without tanks, then re-converted to infantry. If all that occurred within the space of just a few months, there was not much of a tale to tell.

Those regiments that saw action generally receive the coverage they deserve; out of the thirty-three, twelve went into action. There are also a few personal memoirs to add to the coverage that these regiments have received.

RAC regiments saw service in all theatres of war with 142 RAC being the first to see action in Tunisia, February 1943. The last regiment into action was 116 RAC, fighting in Burma in August 1945.

There are two regiments involved in a slightly complicated title swap that warrants further explanation. 107 RAC and 151 RAC were both raised from battalions of The King's Own Royal Regiment (Lancaster) - 107 RAC from the 5th Bn and 151 RAC from the 10th Bn. In February 1943, 107 RAC's role was changed and it became a training regiment with the amended title: 107th Training Regiment, RAC (King's Own). This role was relatively short-lived and at the end of 1943 the regiment was disbanded. As 5th Bn was senior to 10th Bn, the decision was taken to disband 151RAC and retitle it to 107 RAC, rather than have 107 RAC disappear from the Army's list. 151 RAC ceased to exist but it took the full title and the traditions of the 5th Battalion from which 107 RAC had been raised; it also absorbed men from the original 107 RAC. 107 RAC, therefore, served between 1941 and 1945 and fought in NWE, whilst 151 RAC existed only during 1942 and 1943.

Royal Armoured Corps: TA - Royal Armoured Corps Regiments

107th Regiment, Royal Armoured Corps (King's Own) — 107 RAC

RAC service: 01/11/1941 Post-war.*
* 107 RAC was disbanded 31/12/43 but as of 01/01/44, 151 RAC assumed the title of 107 RAC.
Converted Bns: The King's Own Royal Regiment (Lancaster)
5th Bn = 107 RAC & 10th Bn = 151 RAC

Regimental publications:
The Lion and the Rose: The King's Own (Royal Lancaster) Regimental Gazette
Vol. 9, No. 1 Jan 1921 to Vol. 47, No. 4 Nov 1959 (Quarterly)

The History of the 107 Regiment Royal Armoured Corps (Kings Own)
June 1940 - February 1946
Not stated TM; IWM; NAM; PCL
Lengerich; Birschof & Klein; n.d. [1946]; ISBN None; 93pp/No illus.; h/b Brown cloth & buff paper; Indexed N; Glossary N; Appendices N; Bibliography N; 208 x 142 (8vo); V Rare
NOTES: Of all the books listed here, this is the least story-like and most official recounting of fact. It summarises the regiment's NWE story in 16pp. The rest of the book consists of a detailed section on actions between 8-28 February 1945 with a 'lessons learnt' summary, plus expansive notes of the citations for honours and awards. Reads more like an official War Office review but is nonetheless interesting and informative. RoH includes service number and squadron. Issued with a small compliments slip from the CO of the regiment. Copy at PCL rebound.

The King's Own
The Story of a Royal Regiment Volume III 1914-1950
Cowper, Col J. M. IWM; NAM; RMAS; PCL
Aldershot; Gale & Polden Ltd; 1957; ISBN None; xv + 527pp/15 x bw PI/1 x bw SI/6 x bw Mf/9 x bw M; h/b (d/j - ne) Blue cloth; Indexed Y; Glossary N; Appendices Y; Bibliography Y; 235 x 161 (8vo)
NOTES: One of the best infantry histories covering those converted to armour. Both regiments receive several entries throughout: 107 RAC approximately 8pp plus one photograph and 151 RAC approximately 1pp. Excellent index. Honours/Awards lists denote battalion of recipient.

Mailed Fist
Foley, John
London; Panther Books Ltd; 1957; ISBN None; 190pp/No illus.; p/b; Indexed N; Glossary N; Appendices N; Bibliography N; 180 x 115 (12mo); Uncommon
NOTES: Well-deserved reputation for a set of memoirs in novel form; as in the author's note, it is a true story with some names changed. The author commanded a troop of Churchills in NWE; full of day-to-day intimate detail, particularly lucid. (The author's similar work, *Death of a Regiment* is pure fiction, hence is not included in this listing.)

The Kings Own Royal Regiment (Lancaster)
Not stated NAM; PCL
Morecambe; The Morecambe Bay Printers Ltd; n.d. [c.1957]; ISBN None; 64pp/1 x bw SIfep/21 x bw PI/8 x bw SI; s/b; Indexed N; Glossary N; Appendices N; Bibliography N; 221 x 141 (8vo); Uncommon
NOTES: 1950's recruiting booklet, one paragraph mentioning 5th Bn conversion to 107 RAC, no mention of 10th Bn.

The King's Own Royal Border Regiment
Not stated NAM
Morecambe; The Morecambe Bay Printers Ltd; n.d. [c.1961]; ISBN None; 104pp/1 x bw PIfep/55 x bw PI/2 x clr SI/8 x bw SI/2 x bw M; s/b; Indexed N; Glossary N; Appendices N; Bibliography N; 220 x 145 (8vo); Uncommon
NOTES: 1960's recruiting booklet, no mention of 5th or 10th Bns.

The King's Own Royal Border Regiment
Not stated NAM
Morecambe; The Morecambe Bay Printers Ltd; 1963; ISBN None; 70pp/1 x bw PIfep/42 x bw PI/2 x clr SI/1 x bw M; s/b; Indexed N; Glossary N; Appendices N; Bibliography N; 220 x 145 (8vo); Uncommon
NOTES: Slightly reduced reprint of the c.1961 recruiting booklet, no mention of 5th or 10th Bns.

Mailed Fist
Foley, John
London; Panther Books Ltd; 1966; ISBN None; 172pp/No illus.; p/b; Indexed N; Glossary N; Appendices N; Bibliography N; 177 x 111 (12mo); Uncommon
NOTES: Reprint of 1957 first edition, different pagination; reprinted 1968.

The King's Own Royal Regiment (Lancaster) (the 4th Regiment of Foot) (Famous Regiments)
Green, Howard; Horrocks, Lt.-Gen. Sir Brian (Ed.) TM; IWM; NAM; RMAS; PCL
London; Leo Cooper Ltd; 1972; ISBN 0 85052 090 8; 143pp/18 x bw PI/14 x bw SI; h/b / d/j Green cloth; Indexed N; Glossary N; Appendices N; Bibliography N; 222 x 140 (8vo)
NOTES: One paragraph reference to 107 RAC.

Mailed Fist
Foley, John
St Albans; Granada Publishing Limited (Mayflower Books Ltd); 1975; ISBN 583 12491 7; 172pp/No illus.; p/b; Indexed N; Glossary N; Appendices N; Bibliography N; 176 x 109 (12mo)
NOTES: Reprint of 1966 edition, same pagination.

The King's Own Royal Border Regiment 1680 – 1980
A short Regimental History written to mark the Regimental Tercentenary on the 13th July 1980
May, Col Ralph IWM; NAM
Not stated; North West Publications Limited; 1980; ISBN None; 46pp/1 x bw PIfep/9 x bw PI/8 x bw SI; s/b; Indexed N; Glossary N; Appendices N; Bibliography N; 238 x 182 (8vo); Uncommon
NOTES: One paragraph reference to conversion of 5th Bn, The King's Own.

The King's Own Royal Border Regiment 1680 - 1984
A Short Regimental History written To mark the 25th Anniversary of the Amalgamation of The King's Own Royal Regiment and The Border Regiment, 1st October 1984
May, Col Ralph IWM; NAM
Not stated; North West Publications (U.K.) Limited; 1984; ISBN None; 20pp/1 x bw PIfep/16 x bw PI/8 x bw SI; s/b; Indexed N; Glossary N; Appendices N; Bibliography N; 297 x 208 (4to); Uncommon
NOTES: Reissue and re-formatted version of 1980 booklet. One paragraph reference to conversion of 5th Bn, The King's Own.

The King's Own Royal Border Regiment
A background to the Regiment including its Customs and Traditions
Not stated NAM
Carlisle; Regimental Headquarters, The King's Own Royal Border Regiment; 1985; ISBN None; 38pp/No illus.; s/b; Indexed N; Glossary N; Appendices N; Bibliography Y; 221 x 159 (8vo); Uncommon
NOTES: 1980s regimental booklet, no mention of armoured regiments.

Lions of England
A pictorial history of the King's Own Royal Regiment (Lancaster), 1680 - 1980
Eastwood, Stuart TM; IWM; NAM; RMAS; PCL
Kettering; Silver Link Publishing Ltd; 1991; ISBN 0-947971-68-8; 192pp/1 x bw PIfep/250 x bw PI/26 x bw SI/1 x bw M; h/b / d/j Black cloth; Indexed Y; Glossary N; Appendices Y; Bibliography Y; 283 x 218 (4to)
NOTES: Each period has an introductory few pages plus the photo selection. 107 and 151 RAC together receive two full paragraphs and 107 RAC has 11 photos.

Tank Twins
East End Brothers-in-Arms 1943 - 1945
Dyson, Stephen W. TM; IWM
London; Leo Cooper in association with the IWM; 1994; ISBN 0 85052 274 9; xv + 207pp/10 x bw PI/1 x bw M; h/b / d/j Red cloth; Indexed Y; Glossary N; Appendices N; Bibliography N; 240 x 160 (8vo)
NOTES: The author tells his wartime story with frequent reference to his twin brother, Tom Dyson, who also served in 107 RAC. They both joined the RAC in December 1942 training on Churchill tanks before being assigned to 151 RAC mid-1943. After a few chapters describing some experiences in the UK, he continues with his story in NWE when 107 RAC landed there in July 1944. A fine set of memoirs from a tank crewman in NWE with some forceful descriptions of wounded comrades.

The History of the 107th Regiment RAC (Kings Own) June 1940 - Feb 1946
Not stated TM
Lancaster; King's Own Royal Regiment Museum; 2003; ISBN 978 1 904448 08 9; 52pp/No illus.; Stapled A4; Indexed N; Glossary N; Appendices Y; Bibliography N; 297 x 210 (4to)
NOTES: Museum's typed reprint of 1946 book, stated as second edition in 2003, reprinted in 2007.

The History of the 107th Regiment RAC (Kings Own) June 1940 - Feb 1946
Not stated
Lancaster; King's Own Royal Regiment Museum; 2007; ISBN 978 1 904448 08 2; 52pp/No illus.; Stapled A4; Indexed N; Glossary N; Appendices Y; Bibliography N; 297 x 210 (4to)
NOTES: Museum's typed reprint of 1946 book; reprint of 2003 edition.

108th Regiment, Royal Armoured Corps (The Lancashire Fusiliers) — 108 RAC

RAC service:	01/11/1941	01/01/1944 (Suspended animation)
Converted Bns:	The Lancashire Fusiliers	
	1st /5th Bn = 108 RAC, 1st /6th = 109 RAC & 9th Bn = 143 RAC	

Regimental publications:
The Gallipoli Gazette, Regimental Journal of XX The Lancashire Fusiliers
1931 to 1968

Handbook of XX The Lancashire Fusiliers
Surtees, C.B., C.B.E., M.C., Maj-Gen G. IWM; PCL
London; Malcolm Page Ltd; 1952; ISBN None; 184pp/1 x clr SI/31 x bw PI/8 x bw SI; s/b; Indexed N; Glossary N; Appendices N; Bibliography Y; 227 x 154 (8vo); Uncommon
NOTES: Regimental recruitment handbook. Single paragraph reference to each of 108/109 and 143 RAC.

A Short History of XX The Lancashire Fusiliers
Surtees, C.B., C.B.E., M.C., Maj-Gen G. IWM; NAM; RMAS
London; Malcolm Page Ltd; 1955; ISBN None; 244pp/2 x clr SI/27 x bw PI/13 x bw SI; s/b; Indexed Y; Glossary N; Appendices N; Bibliography Y; 213 x 137 (8vo); Uncommon
NOTES: Updated edition of the 1952 Handbook. Single paragraph reference to each of 108/109 and 143 RAC.

Regiment of the Line
The Story of XX The Lancashire Fusiliers
Ray, Cyril NAM; RMAS; PCL
London; B. T. Batsford Ltd; 1963; ISBN None; xiii + 194pp/1 x bw SIfep/5 x bw PI/26 x bw SI; h/b / d/j Red cloth; Indexed Y; Glossary N; Appendices N; Bibliography Y; 227 x 154 (8vo)
NOTES: One paragraph reference to RAC regiments.

ROYAL ARMOURED CORPS: TA - ROYAL ARMOURED CORPS REGIMENTS

The Lancashire Fusiliers
(The 20th Regiment of Foot)
(Famous Regiments)
Ray, Cyril; Horrocks, Lt.-Gen. Sir Brian (Ed.)   TM; IWM; RMAS; PCL
London; Leo Cooper Ltd; 1971; ISBN 0 85052 068 1; 135pp/6 x bw PI/19 x bw SI; h/b /
d/j Blue cloth; Indexed N; Glossary N; Appendices N; Bibliography N; 222 x 140 (8vo)
NOTES: Single paragraph reference to the RAC regiments. From the title page -
'Abbreviated from *Regiment of the Line* by Cyril Ray, published by Batsford, 1963.'

The History Of Lancashire Fusiliers 1939 - 1945
Hallam, John   IWM; RMAS; PCL
Stroud; Alan Sutton Publishing Ltd; 1993; ISBN 0-7509-0409-7; viii + 232pp/24 x bw
PI/4 x bw SI/21 x bw M; h/b / d/j Black cloth; Indexed Y; Glossary N; Appendices Y;
Bibliography Y; 255 x 175 (4to)
NOTES: Two paragraphs cover 108/109 and 143 RAC. Honours/Awards.

109th Regiment, Royal Armoured Corps (The Lancashire Fusiliers)	109 RAC

RAC service: 01/11/1941   01/01/1944 (Suspended
                                                animation)
Converted Bns: The Lancashire Fusiliers
                        1st /5th Bn = 108 RAC, 1st /6th = 109 RAC & 9th Bn = 143 RAC

Regimental publications:
The Gallipoli Gazette, Regimental Journal of XX The Lancashire Fusiliers
1931 to 1968

Handbook of XX The Lancashire Fusiliers
Surtees, C.B., C.B.E., M.C., Maj-Gen G.   IWM; PCL
London; Malcolm Page Ltd; 1952; ISBN None; 184pp/1 x clr SI/31 x bw PI/8 x bw SI;
s/b; Indexed N; Glossary N; Appendices N; Bibliography Y; 227 x 154 (8vo); Uncommon
NOTES: Regimental recruitment handbook. Single paragraph reference to each of
108/109 and 143 RAC.

A Short History of XX The Lancashire Fusiliers
Surtees, C.B., C.B.E., M.C., Maj-Gen G.   IWM; NAM; RMAS
London; Malcolm Page Ltd; 1955; ISBN None; 244pp/2 x clr SI/27 x bw PI/13 x bw SI;
s/b; Indexed Y; Glossary N; Appendices N; Bibliography Y; 213 x 137 (8vo); Uncommon
NOTES: Updated edition of the 1952 Handbook. Single paragraph reference to each of
108/109 and 143 RAC.

Regiment of the Line
The Story of XX The Lancashire Fusiliers
Ray, Cyril   NAM; RMAS; PCL
London; B. T. Batsford Ltd; 1963; ISBN None; xiii + 194pp/1 x bw SIfep/5 x bw PI/26 x
bw SI; h/b / d/j Red cloth; Indexed Y; Glossary N; Appendices N; Bibliography Y; 227 x
154 (8vo)
NOTES: One paragraph reference to RAC regiments.

**The Lancashire Fusiliers
(The 20th Regiment of Foot)
(Famous Regiments)**
Ray, Cyril; Horrocks, Lt.-Gen. Sir Brian (Ed.) TM; IWM; RMAS; PCL
London; Leo Cooper Ltd; 1971; ISBN 0 85052 068 1; 135pp/6 x bw PI/19 x bw SI; h/b /
d/j Blue cloth; Indexed N; Glossary N; Appendices N; Bibliography N; 222 x 140 (8vo)
NOTES: Single paragraph reference to the RAC regiments. From the title page -
'Abbreviated from *Regiment of the Line* by Cyril Ray, published by Batsford, 1963.'

The History Of Lancashire Fusiliers 1939 - 1945
Hallam, John IWM; RMAS; PCL
Stroud; Alan Sutton Publishing Ltd; 1993; ISBN 0-7509-0409-7; viii + 232pp/24 x bw
PI/4 x bw SI/21 x bw M; h/b / d/j Black cloth; Indexed Y; Glossary N; Appendices Y;
Bibliography Y; 255 x 175 (4to)
NOTES: Two paragraphs cover 108/109 and 143 RAC. Honours/Awards.

110th Regiment, Royal Armoured Corps (The Border Regiment)	110 RAC

RAC service: 01/11/1941 01/01/1944 (Suspended animation)

Converted Bns: The Border Regiment
5th Bn = 110 RAC

Regimental publications:
The Border magazine: Journal of The Border Regiment
Vol. 1, No. 1 Sept 1947 to Vol. 4, No. 25 Sept 1959 (Half-yearly)

The Story Of The Border Regiment 1939-1945
Shears, Philip J. IWM; RMAS; PCL
London; Nisbet & Co Ltd; 1948; ISBN None; xv + 184pp/8 x bw M; h/b / d/j Green cloth;
Indexed N; Glossary N; Appendices Y; Bibliography N; 220 x 144 (8vo)
NOTES: The 5th Bn's story is contained within 12pp, 2pp of which deal with 110 RAC.
Honours/Awards.

The Border Regiment 1702 - 1952
Not stated IWM; NAM
No imprint; No imprint (F. J. Parsons Ltd - printers); 1952; ISBN None; 28pp/9 x bw PI/9
x clr SI/9 x bw SI; s/b; Indexed N; Glossary N; Appendices N; Bibliography N; 235 x 184
(8vo)
NOTES: One line reference to 5th Bn converting to tanks.

The King's Own Royal Border Regiment
Not stated NAM
Morecambe; The Morecambe Bay Printers Ltd; n.d. [c.1961]; ISBN None; 104pp/1 x bw
PIfep/55 x bw PI/2 x clr SI/8 x bw SI/2 x bw M; s/b; Indexed N; Glossary N; Appendices
N; Bibliography N; 220 x 145 (8vo); Uncommon
NOTES: 1960's recruiting booklet, no reference to 5th Bn/110 RAC.

ROYAL ARMOURED CORPS: TA - ROYAL ARMOURED CORPS REGIMENTS

The King's Own Royal Border Regiment
Not stated NAM
Morecambe; The Morecambe Bay Printers Ltd; 1963; ISBN None; 70pp/1 x bw PIfep/42 x bw PI/2 x clr SI/1 x bw M; s/b; Indexed N; Glossary N; Appendices N; Bibliography N; 220 x 145 (8vo); Uncommon
NOTES: Slightly reduced reprint of the c.1961 recruiting booklet, no reference to 5th Bn/110 RAC.

Tried and Valiant
The History of The Border Regiment 1702 - 1959
Sutherland, Douglas TM; IWM; NAM; RMAS; PCL
London; Leo Cooper Ltd; 1972; ISBN 0 85052 042 8; 239pp/25 x clr SIfep/21 x bw SI/1 x bw Mbds; h/b / d/j Green cloth; Indexed Y; Glossary N; Appendices Y; Bibliography N; 223 x 143 (8vo)
NOTES: Single paragraph derived from *The Story Of The Border Regiment 1939-1945*, q.v.

The King's Own Royal Border Regiment 1680 - 1980
A short Regimental History written to mark the Regimental Tercentenary on the 13th July 1980
May, Col Ralph IWM; NAM
Not stated; North West Publications Limited; 1980; ISBN None; 46pp/1 x bw PIfep/9 x bw PI/8 x bw SI; s/b; Indexed N; Glossary N; Appendices N; Bibliography N; 238 x 182 (8vo)
NOTES: One paragraph reference to conversion of 5th Bn, The Border Regiment.

The King's Own Royal Border Regiment 1680 - 1984
A short Regimental History written to mark the 25th Anniversary of the Amalgamation of The King's Own Royal Regiment and The Border Regiment, 1st October 1984
May, Col Ralph IWM; NAM
Not stated; North West Publications (U.K.) Limited; 1984; ISBN None; 20pp/1 x bw PIfep/16 x bw PI/8 x bw SI; s/b; Indexed N; Glossary N; Appendices N; Bibliography N; 297 x 208 (4to)
NOTES: Reissue and re-formatted version of 1980 booklet. One paragraph reference to conversion of 5th Bn, The Border Regiment.

The King's Own Royal Border Regiment
A background to the Regiment including its Customs and Traditions
Not stated NAM
Carlisle; Regimental Headquarters, The King's Own Royal Border Regiment; 1985; ISBN None; 38pp/No illus.; s/b; Indexed N; Glossary N; Appendices N; Bibliography Y; 221 x 159 (8vo); Uncommon
NOTES: 1980s regimental booklet, no mention of armoured regiments.

111th Regiment, Royal Armoured Corps (Manchester) — 111 RAC

RAC service: 01/11/1941 31/12/1943 (Disbanded)
Converted Bns: The Manchester Regiment
5th Bn = 111 RAC

Regimental publications:
The Manchester Regiment Gazette
Vol. 2, No. 1 Jan 1921 to Vol. 11, No .7 July 1939 (Quarterly) Suspended 1940 – 1944.
Vol. 11, No. 8 Dec 1945 to Vol, 17. No 11 Sept 1958 (Quarterly)

A Short History of the Manchester Regiment (Regular Battalions)
Wylly, C.B., Col H. C. IWM; NAM
Aldershot; Gale & Polden Ltd; 1950; ISBN None; 43pp/No illus.; s/b; Indexed N; Glossary N; Appendices N; Bibliography N; 183 x 120 (12mo)
NOTES: 4th Revised Edition. One paragraph reference to 111 RAC.

Turning Points
In a Life With War
The memoirs of Kenneth Macksey
Macksey, Kenneth TM
Beaminster; Newtown Publications; 1997; ISBN 0 9508536 1 5; 216pp/1 x bw PIfep/12 x bw PI; s/b; Indexed N; Glossary N; Appendices N; Bibliography N; 215 x 136 (8vo); Uncommon
NOTES: In his life story, this prolific military author recounts his war years in 95pp. He signed up in late 1942, being posted to 111 RAC (8pp). He then moved to 144 RAC (8pp) before going to OCTU in 1943. He joined 141 RAC in July 1944 as troop leader of 5 Tp, A Sqn. He was wounded twice in late 1944 and was sent to a Battle Exhaustion Hospital before being medically downgraded. 45pp on 141 RAC service. There is one chapter commenting on the insubordination episode involving William Douglas Home – refer to books by William Douglas Home listed under 141 RAC.

'Difficulties be damned'
The King's Regiment 8th, 63rd, 96th
A History of the City Regiment of Manchester and Liverpool
Mileham, Patrick IWM
Not stated; Fleur de Lys Publishing; 2000; ISBN 0 1873907 10-9; 246pp/12 x clr PI/10 x clr SI/123 x bw PI/20 x bw SI/16 x bw M; h/b / d/j Green cloth; Indexed Y; Glossary N; Appendices Y; Bibliography Y; 304 x 216 (4to)
NOTES: No reference to 111 RAC. 1000 copies published.

112th Regiment, Royal Armoured Corps (Sherwood Foresters) — 112 RAC

RAC service: 01/11/1941 14/10/1944 (Suspended animation)
Converted Bns: The Sherwood Foresters (Nottinghamshire and Derbyshire Regiment)
9th Bn = 112 RAC & 13th Bn = 163 RAC

Regimental publications:
The Sherwood Foresters, Nottinghamshire and Derbyshire Regiment: Regimental Annual
No. 7 1920 to No. 25 1938 (Annual) Suspended 1940 – 1947, replaced by
The Forester: the Regimental Journal of The Sherwood Foresters (Nottinghamshire and Derbyshire Regiment)
Vol. 1, No. 1 Sept 1948 to Vol. 6, No. 9 Jan 1970 (Half-yearly)

A Short History of The Sherwood Foresters (Nottinghamshire and Derbyshire Regiment)
Not stated PCL
Aldershot; Gale & Polden Ltd; 1945; ISBN None; 32pp/No illus.; s/b; Indexed N; Glossary N; Appendices N; Bibliography N; 182 x 120 (12mo); Uncommon
NOTES: Although printed in 1945, this short history ends with WWI rather than WWII.

The History Of The Sherwood Foresters (Nottinghamshire and Derbyshire Regiment) 1919-1957
Barclay, C.B.E., D.S.O., Brig. C. N. IWM; NAM; RMAS; PCL
London; William Clowes and Sons Limited; 1959; ISBN None; xvi + 182pp/1 x clr SIfep/25 x bw PI/4 x bw Mf/10 x bw M; h/b (d/j - ne) Red & green cloth; Indexed Y; Glossary N; Appendices Y; Bibliography N; 247 x 183 (8vo)
NOTES: Two paragraphs each on 112 RAC and 163 RAC. Appendices list COs of the regiments.

The Sherwood Foresters Nottinghamshire and Derbyshire Regiment
A Regiment of the Mercian Brigade
Regimental History and Recruiting Handbook
Not stated
London; Malcolm Page Limited; n.d. [c.1962]; ISBN None; 96pp/14 x bw PI/1 x bw M; s/b; Indexed N; Glossary N; Appendices N; Bibliography N; 215 x 139 (8vo); Uncommon
NOTES: Regimental recruiting handbook, 4pp on WWII, no mention of 112 RAC.

113th Regiment, Royal Armoured Corps — 113 RAC

RAC service: 20/07/1942 26/09/1943 (Suspended animation)
Converted Bns: The West Yorkshire Regiment (The Prince of Wales's Own)
2nd/5th Bn = 113 RAC

Regimental publications:
Ca Ira: the Journal of The West Yorkshire Regiment (The Prince of Wales's Own)
Vol. 1, No. 1 Sept 1924 to Vol. 11, No. 3 Mar 1943 (Quarterly) Suspended 1944 – 46
Vol. 12, No. 1 Mar 1947 to Vol. 17, No. 6 June 1958 (Quarterly)
The West Yorkshire Regiment (The Prince of Wales's Own) Newsletter
No. 1 Jan 1945 to No. 4 July 1946 (Half-yearly) (Mar 1946 title includes 'Ca Ira')

From Pyramid to Pagoda
The Story of the West Yorkshire Regiment (The Prince of Wales's Own) In the War 1939-45 and afterwards
Sandes, D.S.O., M.C., R.E. (Retd), Lt-Col E. W. C. IWM; NAM; RMAS; PCL
London; F. J. Parsons Ltd; n.d. [1952]; ISBN None; xiii + 306pp/1 x clr Plfep/1 x bw
Plfep/10 x bw Mf/17 x bw M; h/b / d/j Red cloth; Indexed Y; Glossary N; Appendices N;
Bibliography N; 288 x 223 (4to); Rare
NOTES: This history is devoted to the 1st and 2nd Battalions but does have one chapter on the non-regular battalions. Two paragraphs on 113 RAC plus occasional sentences elsewhere.

The West Yorkshire Regiment
(The XIVth Regiment of Foot)
(Famous Regiments)
Barker, A. J.; Horrocks, Lt.-Gen. Sir Brian (Ed.) TM; IWM; NAM; RMAS; PCL
London; Leo Cooper Ltd; 1974; ISBN 0 85052 150 5; 80pp/20 x bw PI/5 x bw SI; h/b / d/j Grey cloth; Indexed N; Glossary N; Appendices N; Bibliography N; 222 x 141 (8vo)
NOTES: One sentence reference to 113 RAC.

114th Regiment, Royal Armoured Corps — 114 RAC

RAC service: 20/07/1942 26/09/1943 (Disbanded)
Converted Bns: The Duke of Wellington's Regiment (West Riding)
2nd/6th Bn = 114 RAC, 2nd /7th Bn = 115 RAC, 8th Bn = 145 RAC & 9th Bn = 146 RAC

Regimental publications:
The Iron Duke: The Regimental Magazine of The Duke of Wellington's Regiment (West Riding)
Vol. 1, No. 1 May 1925 to current (Quarterly to 1967, then three per year, now twice per year)

The History Of The Duke Of Wellington's Regiment 1919 - 1952
Barclay, C.B.E., D.S.O., Brig. C. N. TM; IWM; NAM; RMAS; PCL
London; William Clowes and Sons Limited; 1953; ISBN None; xxi + 398pp/1 x clr SIfep/26 x bw PI/1 x bw SI/1 x clr Mf/9 x bw Mf/7 x bw M; h/b / d/j Red cloth; Indexed Y; Glossary Y; Appendices Y; Bibliography N; 254 x 196 (4to)
NOTES: No mention of 114 RAC specifically, 115 RAC mentioned in relation to 2nd Armoured Delivery Squadron which these both formed after being disbanded. Appendices include COs of RAC regiments. 114 RAC = 2pp; 115 RAC = 1pp; 145 RAC = 3 chapters; 146 RAC = 2 chapters. Two photos each of 145 & 146 RAC. RoH by battalion, Honours/Awards.

The Duke Of Wellington's Regiment (West Riding)
Not stated IWM; PCL
London; Malcolm Page Limited; n.d. [c.1956]; ISBN None; 108pp/2 x clr SI/16 x bw PI/1 bw M; s/b; Indexed N; Glossary N; Appendices N; Bibliography N; 215 x 140 (8vo); Uncommon
NOTES: Post Korean War recruiting pamphlet. Passing reference to RAC regiments, including a statement that 2nd/6th Bn and 2nd/7th Bn were infantry only; location of 145 and 146 RAC regiments on maps.

The Duke Of Wellington's Regiment (West Riding)
Not stated IWM; NAM
London; Malcolm Page Limited; n.d. [c.1960]; ISBN None; 96pp/1 x clr SI/17 x bw PI/2 x bw SI/2 x bw M; s/b; Indexed N; Glossary N; Appendices N; Bibliography N; 214 x 138 (8vo); Uncommon
NOTES: Reprint of recruiting booklet.

A Short History of The Duke Of Wellington's Regiment (West Riding)
Savory, M.B.E., Maj. A. C. S.
No imprint; Reuben Holroyd Ltd (Printers); n.d. [c.1987]; ISBN None; 48pp/1 x clr SIfep/1 x clr PI/3 x clr SI/11 x bw SI/2 x bw M; s/b (card); Indexed N; Glossary N; Appendices N; Bibliography N; 208 x 145 (8vo); Uncommon
NOTES: Regimental booklet, no reference to either 114 RAC or 115 RAC.

The History Of The Duke Of Wellington's Regiment (West Riding) 1702 – 1992
Brereton, J. M. and Savory, A. C. S. IWM; NAM
Halifax; The Duke of Wellington's Regiment; 1993; ISBN 0 9521552 0 6; x + 446pp/1 x clr PIfep/1 x clr PI/21 x clr SI/65 x bw PI/33 x bw SI/37 x bw M; h/b / d/j Red cloth; Indexed Y; Glossary N; Appendices Y; Bibliography Y; 252 x 196 (4to)
NOTES: One paragraph reference to 114 & 115 RAC although not named by RAC title.

The Duke Of Wellington's Regiment (West Riding)
1702 - 2002 Fortune Favours The Brave
The Dukes 1702 - 2002
Not stated NAM
Halifax; The Duke of Wellington's Regiment; 2002; ISBN None; 34pp/27 x clr PI/22 x clr SI/91 x bw PI/6 x bw SI/1 x bw M; s/b; Indexed N; Glossary N; Appendices N; Bibliography N; 297 x 210 (4to); Uncommon

NOTES: Tercentenary publication for regiment, no reference to 2nd/6th Bn and 2nd/7th Bn converting to tanks.

The 'Dukes' 1702 - 2006
A concise history and digest of The Duke of Wellington's Regiment (West Riding) with memoirs from the 20th Century
Butterworth, Terry; Flaving, Scott and Harvey, Richard
No imprint; The Duke of Wellington's Regiment Museum and Archive; 2009; ISBN None; 139pp/Fully illustrated; h/b / d/j Red cloth; Indexed N; Glossary N; Appendices N; Bibliography N; 303 x 215 (4to)
NOTES: Updated history published after the amalgamation of The Duke of Wellington's Regiment (West Riding), The Prince of Wales's Own and The Green Howards. Passing reference to the converted battalions.

115th Regiment, Royal Armoured Corps — 115 RAC

RAC service:	20/07/1942	26/09/1943 (Disbanded)
Converted Bns:	The Duke of Wellington's Regiment (West Riding) 2nd/6th Bn = 114 RAC, 2nd /7th Bn = 115 RAC, 8th Bn = 145 RAC & 9th Bn = 146 RAC	

Regimental publications:
The Iron Duke: The Regimental Magazine of The Duke of Wellington's Regiment (West Riding)
Vol. 1, No. 1 May 1925 to current (Quarterly to 1967, then three per year, now twice per year)

The History Of The Duke Of Wellington's Regiment 1919 - 1952
Barclay, C.B.E., D.S.O., Brig. C. N. TM; IWM; NAM; RMAS; PCL
London; William Clowes and Sons Limited; 1953; ISBN None; xxi + 398pp/1 x clr SIfep/26 x bw PI/1 x bw SI/1 x clr Mf/9 x bw Mf/7 x bw M; h/b / d/j Red cloth; Indexed Y; Glossary Y; Appendices Y; Bibliography N; 254 x 196 (4to)
NOTES: No mention of 114 RAC specifically, 115 RAC mentioned in relation to 2nd Armoured Delivery Squadron which these both formed after being disbanded. Appendices include COs of RAC regiments. 114 RAC = 2pp; 115 RAC = 1pp; 145 RAC = 3 chapters; 146 RAC = 2 chapters. Two photos each of 145 & 146 RAC. RoH by battalion, Honours/Awards.

The Duke Of Wellington's Regiment (West Riding)
Not stated IWM; PCL
London; Malcolm Page Limited; n.d. [c.1956]; ISBN None; 108pp/2 x clr SI/16 x bw PI/1 bw M; s/b; Indexed N; Glossary N; Appendices N; Bibliography N; 215 x 140 (8vo); Uncommon
NOTES: Post Korean War recruiting pamphlet. Passing reference to RAC regiments, including a statement that 2nd/6th Bn and 2nd/7th Bn were infantry only; location of 145 and 146 RAC regiments on maps.

The Duke Of Wellington's Regiment (West Riding)
Not stated IWM; NAM
London; Malcolm Page Limited; n.d. [c.1960]; ISBN None; 96pp/1 x clr SI/17 x bw PI/2 x bw SI/2 x bw M; s/b; Indexed N; Glossary N; Appendices N; Bibliography N; 214 x 138 (8vo); Uncommon
NOTES: Reprint of recruiting booklet.

A Short History of The Duke Of Wellington's Regiment (West Riding)
Savory, M.B.E., Maj. A. C. S.
No imprint; Reuben Holroyd Ltd (Printers); n.d. [c.1987]; ISBN None; 48pp/1 x clr SIfep/1 x clr PI/3 x clr SI/11 x bw SI/2 x bw M; s/b (card); Indexed N; Glossary N; Appendices N; Bibliography N; 208 x 145 (8vo); Uncommon
NOTES: Regimental booklet, no reference to either 114 RAC or 115 RAC.

The History Of The Duke Of Wellington's Regiment (West Riding) 1702 - 1992
Brereton, J. M. and Savory, A. C. S. IWM; NAM
Halifax; The Duke of Wellington's Regiment; 1993; ISBN 0 9521552 0 6; x + 446pp/1 x clr PIfep/1 x clr PI/21 x clr SI/65 x bw PI/33 x bw SI/37 x bw M; h/b / d/j Red cloth; Indexed Y; Glossary N; Appendices Y; Bibliography Y; 252 x 196 (4to)
NOTES: One paragraph reference to 114 & 115 RAC although not named by RAC title.

The Duke Of Wellington's Regiment (West Riding)
1702 - 2002 Fortune Favours The Brave
The Dukes 1702 - 2002
Not stated NAM
Halifax; The Duke of Wellington's Regiment; 2002; ISBN None; 34pp/27 x clr PI/22 x clr SI/91 x bw PI/6 x bw SI/1 x bw M; s/b; Indexed N; Glossary N; Appendices N; Bibliography N; 297 x 210 (4to); Uncommon
NOTES: Tercentenary publication for regiment, no reference to 2nd/6th Bn and 2nd/7th Bn converting to tanks.

The 'Dukes' 1702 – 2006
A concise history and digest of The Duke of Wellington's Regiment (West Riding) with memoirs from the 20th Century
Butterworth, Terry; Flaving, Scott and Harvey, Richard
No imprint; The Duke of Wellington's Regiment Museum and Archive; 2009; ISBN None; 139pp/Fully illustrated; h/b / d/j Red cloth; Indexed N; Glossary N; Appendices N; Bibliography N; 303 x 215 (4to)
NOTES: Updated history published after the amalgamation of The Duke of Wellington's Regiment (West Riding), The Prince of Wales's Own and The Green Howards. Passing reference to the converted battalions.

116th Regiment, Royal Armoured Corps (Gordon Highlanders) — 116 RAC

RAC service: 27/07/1942 Post-war.
Converted Bns: The Gordon Highlanders
9th Bn = 116 RAC

Regimental publications:
The Tiger and Sphinx. The Journal of the Gordon Highlanders
(Run not established)

Soldier With The Gordons
The Pride of them All
Not stated PCL
London; Malcolm Page Limited; n.d. [c.1959]; ISBN None; 92pp/21 x bw PI/7 x bw SI; s/b; Indexed N; Glossary N; Appendices N; Bibliography N; 215 x 140 (8vo); Uncommon
NOTES: Two minor references to 116 RAC.

The Life of a Regiment Volume V
The Gordon Highlanders 1919 - 1945
Miles, Wilfrid TM; IWM; RMAS
Aberdeen; The University Press; 1961; ISBN None; xv + 422pp/1 x bw PIfep/11 x bw PI/2 x bw SI/45 x bw M; h/b (d/j – ne) Green cloth; Indexed Y; Glossary N; Appendices N; Bibliography N; 252 x 164 (4to)
NOTES: Brief information on regiment's formation plus 20pp on its period in action in 1945.

The Gordon Highlanders
(Famous Regiments)
Sinclair-Stevenson, Christopher; Horrocks, Lt.-Gen. Sir TM; IWM; RMAS; PCL
Brian (Ed.)
London; Hamish Hamilton Ltd; 1968; ISBN None; 133pp/14 x bw PI/15 x bw SI; h/b / d/j Green cloth; Indexed N; Glossary N; Appendices N; Bibliography N; 222 x 143 (8vo)
NOTES: One paragraph reference to 116 RAC.

The Gordon Highlanders
(Famous Regiments)
Sinclair-Stevenson, Christopher; Horrocks, Lt.-Gen. Sir NAM
Brian (Ed.)
London; Leo Cooper Ltd; 1969; ISBN 85052 021 5; 133pp/14 x bw PI/15 x bw SI; h/b / d/j Green cloth; Indexed N; Glossary N; Appendices N; Bibliography N; 222 x 143 (8vo)
NOTES: Leo Cooper reprint of H. Hamilton 1968 edition.

The Gordon Highlanders
Not stated
Glenrothes; J. B. White Ltd (Printers); n.d. [c.1972]; ISBN None; 13pp/4 x bw PI/2 x bw SI; s/b (card); Indexed N; Glossary N; Appendices N; Bibliography N; 182 x 139 (12mo)
NOTES: Pocket history produced by the regimental museum, one paragraph on 116 RAC.

The Life of a Regiment Volume V
The Gordon Highlanders 1919 - 1945
Miles, Wilfrid
London; Frederick Warne; 1980; See Notes; h/b / d/j Green cloth; Indexed Y; Glossary N; Appendices N; Bibliography N; 252 x 164 (4to)
NOTES: Reprint of 1961 first edition. (Not physically inspected.)

The Gordon Highlanders
A Concise History
Royle, Trevor PCL
Edinburgh; Mainstream Publishing Company (Edinburgh) Ltd; 2007; ISBN 9781845962708; 240pp/1 x clr Pl/9 x clr Sl/8 x bw Pl; h/b / d/j Red cloth; Indexed Y; Glossary N; Appendices Y; Bibliography Y; 222 x 142 (8vo)
NOTES: Two pages with reference to 116 RAC.

141st Regiment, Royal Armoured Corps (The Buffs) — 141 RAC

RAC service: 08/11/1941 Post-war.
Converted Bns: The Buffs (Royal East Kent Regiment)
7th Bn = 141 RAC

Regimental publications:
The Dragon: The Regimental Paper of The Buffs. A Paper For The Buffs and Men of Kent.
No. 250 June 1920 to Vol. 77, No. 735 Feb 1961 (Monthly)
Milestone. News and Views of 141st Regt. RAC (The Buffs)
No. 1 - 10/08/1945 to No. 14 - 09/11/1945 (Weekly)

The History of "A" Squadron 141st Regiment R.A.C. (The Buffs.)
June, 1940 - November, 1945
Not stated [See Notes] TM; IWM; PCL
Cupar; J. & G. Innes, Ltd (Printers); 1946; ISBN None; 85pp/10 x bw Pl; h/b Green cloth; Indexed N; Glossary N; Appendices N; Bibliography N; 202 x 137 (8vo); V Rare
NOTES: Thorough, well detailed history of the squadron's actions through NWE. List of wounded plus RoH/Honours/Awards. Author is Maj. George Storrar who served in A Sqn. Published September 1946.

"Playboys"
Not stated [See Notes] IWM
No imprint; No imprint (J H Davenport & Sons Ltd - printers); n.d. [c.1946]; ISBN None; 137pp/13 x bw Sl/1 x bw Mbds/4 x bw M; h/b Blue cloth; Indexed N; Glossary N; Appendices N; Bibliography N; 226 x 148 (8vo); V Rare
NOTES: Written by the one-time IO of the regiment, this book takes a highly detailed and often carefree look (born of hard experience) at the history of the squadron in NWE. Highly evocative narrative. Some of the maps are detailed to individual tanks. RoH. Author is Capt. H. Bailey who was IO late 1944.

A Short History of The Buffs
Royal East Kent Regiment (3rd Foot)
Formerly designated The Holland Regiment and Prince George of Denmark's Regiment
Foster Hall, M.C., Brigadier E.   IWM; RMAS; PCL
London; The Medici Society Ltd; 1950; ISBN None; viii + 128pp/1 x SIfep/10 x bw SI/4 x bw M; s/b; Indexed N; Glossary N; Appendices Y; Bibliography N; 137 x 108 (8vo); Uncommon
NOTES: Only one page on 141 RAC.

Historical Records of The Buffs Royal East Kent Regiment (3rd Foot) Formerly designated The Holland Regiment and Prince George of Denmark's Regiment 1919 - 1948
Knight, O.B.E., Col C. R. B.   TM; IWM; NAM; RMAS; PCL
London; The Medici Society, Limited; 1951; ISBN None; xxiv + 512pp/1 x bw PIfep/20 x bw PI/1 x bw SI/3 x bw Mbds/9 x bw Mf/7 x bw M; h/b / d/j Blue cloth; Indexed Y; Glossary N; Appendices Y; Bibliography Y; 224 x 148 (8vo)
NOTES: One chapter of 40pp given over to the history of 141 RAC. No comment on the early history and training, but a richly detailed description of the regiment's operations in NWE as a specialist tank regiment operating Crocodiles. Appendices include list of COs. RoH does not differentiate battalion/regiment. Honours/Awards do note battalion/regiment.

Half Term Report
An Autobiography
Douglas Home, William   IWM
London; Longmans, Green & Co; 1954; ISBN None; 209pp/No illus.; h/b / d/j Blue cloth; Indexed N; Glossary N; Appendices N; Bibliography N; 221 x 148 (8vo)
NOTES: The author was an officer serving with the battalion when it was converted to tanks. The period of the war is covered in 68pp, the majority of which sets out his political views and career as a 'political objector' to the war. He refused an order involving the attack on Le Havre, sent a public letter regarding his actions and served a 12-month jail sentence as a consequence. The author's later biography, *Mr Home Pronounced Hume*, q.v., has only a couple of oblique paragraphs referring to his court martial incident. Should be read in conjunction with *Sins of Commission*, q.v. pub. 1985.

Half Term Report
An Autobiography
Douglas Home, William
London; Longmans, Green & Co; 1954; ISBN None; See Notes; p/b; Indexed N; Glossary N; Appendices N; Bibliography N; Uncommon
NOTES: Paperback reprint of 1954 first edition. (Not physically inspected.)

Half Term Report
An Autobiography
Douglas Home, William
London; The Quality Book Club; 1955; ISBN None; 209pp/No illus.; h/b / d/j Red cloth; Indexed N; Glossary N; Appendices N; Bibliography N; 213 x 139 (8vo)
NOTES: Reprint of 1954 first edition, same pagination.

Flame Thrower
Wilson, Andrew IWM
London; William Kimber and Co. Limited; 1956; ISBN None; 202pp/1 x bw PIfep/12 x bw PI/2 x bw Mbds; h/b / d/j Red cloth; Indexed N; Glossary N; Appendices N; Bibliography N; 221 x 148 (8vo); Uncommon
NOTES: The author joined 141 RAC in 1943. His memoirs provide some domestic detail of the regiment prior to sailing to Normandy in June 1944. He arrived in Reserve Squadron and was given command of 14 Troop, C Sqn in July 1944. Wounded in late 1944 and evacuated to the UK, he returned to the same troop in February 1945 to continue fighting to the end of the war in Europe. Unusually written in the third person, the tempo of his story is very well controlled.

The Buffs
Royal East Kent Regiment
Not stated IWM
London; Malcolm Page Ltd; n.d. [1960s]; ISBN None; 32pp/11 x bw PI/2 x bw SI; s/b; Indexed N; Glossary N; Appendices N; Bibliography N; 215 x 140 (8vo); Uncommon
NOTES: 1960s recruiting booklet. One paragraph reference to 141 RAC.

The Story of The Queen's Own Buffs The Royal Kent Regiment
Blaxland, Gregory IWM; NAM
No imprint; No imprint (Gibbs & Sons Ltd - printers); n.d. [c.1963]; ISBN None; 91pp/4 x clr SI/1 x bw SIfep/17 x bw SI/5 x bw M; s/b; Indexed N; Glossary N; Appendices Y; Bibliography N; 215 x 138 (8vo)
NOTES: Concise history published after the amalgamation of the Buffs and the Royal West Kent regiments. One paragraph reference to 141 RAC.

The Buffs
(Royal East Kent Regiment) (The 3rd Regiment of Foot)
(Famous Regiments)
Blaxland, Gregory TM; IWM; NAM; RMAS
London; Leo Cooper Ltd; 1972; ISBN 0 85052 092 4; iv + 127pp/16 x bw PI/12 x bw SI; h/b / d/j Blue cloth; Indexed N; Glossary N; Appendices Y; Bibliography N; 222 x 143 (8vo)
NOTES: One sentence reference to 141 RAC.

Flame Thrower
Wilson, Andrew
London; Corgi Books; 1973; ISBN 0 552 09383 3; 172pp/14 x bw PI; p/b; Indexed N; Glossary N; Appendices N; Bibliography N; 176 x 111 (12mo)
NOTES: Paperback reprint of 1956 first edition, includes one additional photo illustration to 1956 and 1974 editions.

Flame Thrower
Wilson, Andrew NAM
Maidstone; George Mann; 1974; ISBN 0 7041 0042 8; 202pp/7 x bw PI/2 x bw Mbds; h/b / d/j Blue cloth; Indexed N; Glossary N; Appendices N; Bibliography N; 218 x 142 (8vo)
NOTES: Reprint of 1956 first edition, reduced photo selection, same pagination.

Mr Home pronounced Hume
An Autobiography
Douglas Home, William
London; William Collins Sons & Co Ltd; 1979; ISBN 0 00 216076 5; 218pp/21 x bw Pl; h/b / d/j Blue cloth; Indexed Y; Glossary N; Appendices N; Bibliography N; 235 x 152 (8vo)
NOTES: In this full autobiography, the author deals with his wartime service, political principles and court-martial conviction in a more summarised form, 8pp, than in *Half Term Report*, q.v. Should be read in conjunction with *Sins of Commission*, q.v. pub. 1985.

Flame Thrower
Wilson, Andrew   IWM
London; William Kimber and Co. Limited; 1984; ISBN 0-7183-0522-1; xvi + 202pp/1 x bw Plfep/12 x bw Pl/2 x bw Mbds; h/b / d/j Black cloth; Indexed N; Glossary N; Appendices N; Bibliography N; 222 x 143 (8vo)
NOTES: Revised and updated reprint of 1956 first edition (real names replace previously false ones) with new introduction by author for this edition, same main pagination.

Sins of Commission
Douglas Home, William   IWM
Salisbury; Michael Russell (Publishing) Ltd; 1985; ISBN 0 85955 115 6; 96pp/No illus.; h/b / d/j Blue cloth; Indexed N; Glossary N; Appendices N; Bibliography N; 222 x 140 (8vo)
NOTES: In this book the author deals solely with events surrounding his refusal to obey an order in September 1944. Using family letters he wrote between 1939 and 1945, he reproduces several of those with commentary alongside many.

In At The Finish
North West Europe 1944/45
Smith, J. G.   TM; IWM
London; Minerva Press; 1995; ISBN 1 85863 516 0; x + 330pp/13 x bw Pl/13 x bw M; s/b; Indexed N; Glossary N; Appendices Y; Bibliography N; 205 x 143 (8vo); Uncommon
NOTES: An honest, expansive and extremely detailed personal account starting with the author landing in Normandy in July 1944 as a reinforcement. He explains much of the otherwise obscure elements of army life, organisation and thinking within the realm of a trooper. He was assigned to 13 Tp, C Sqn in August 1944 as a wireless operator and fought through to the end of the war.

Turning Points
In a Life With War
The memoirs of Kenneth Macksey
Macksey, Kenneth   TM
Beaminster; Newtown Publications; 1997; ISBN 0 9508536 1 5; 216pp/1 x bw Plfep/12 x bw Pl; s/b; Indexed N; Glossary N; Appendices N; Bibliography N; 215 x 136 (8vo); Uncommon
NOTES: In his life story, this prolific military author recounts his war years in 95pp. He signed up in late 1942, being posted to 111 RAC (8pp). He then moved to 144 RAC (8pp) before going to OCTU in 1943. He joined 141 RAC in July 1944 as troop leader of 5 Tp, A Sqn. He was wounded twice in late 1944 and was sent to a Battle Exhaustion Hospital

before being medically downgraded. 45pp on 141 RAC service. There is one chapter commenting on the insubordination episode involving William Douglas Home – refer to books by William Douglas Home listed under 141 RAC.

142nd Regiment, Royal Armoured Corps	142 RAC

RAC service: 08/11/1941 22/01/1945 (Disbanded)
Converted Bns: The Suffolk Regiment
7th Bn = 142 RAC

Regimental publications:
The Suffolk Regimental Gazette
February 1890 to July 1959 (not October 1914 to December 1915 / January 1917 - June 1920) (Variously monthly and three per year)

The Suffolk Regiment (The XIIth Foot)
Its History and Traditions
Not stated PCL
No imprint; No imprint; n.d. [c.1945]; ISBN None; 5pp/Cover illustrations only; Trifold card; Indexed N; Glossary N; Appendices N; Bibliography N; 154 x 128 (16mo); Rare
NOTES: One paragraph mention of 7th Bn, confirming 142 RAC wore the Suffolk badge in their black berets.

The Suffolk Regiment 1928 to 1946
Nicholson, C.M.G., D.S.O., Col W. N. TM; IWM; NAM; RMAS; PCL
Ipswich; The East Anglian Magazine Ltd; n.d. [c.1948]; ISBN None; 374pp/1 x bw PIfep/40 x bw PI/5 x bw SI/2 x clr Mf/10 x bw Mf/1 x clr M/2 x clr M/10 x bw M; h/b / d/j Red cloth; Indexed Y; Glossary Y; Appendices Y; Bibliography N; 235 x 160 (8vo)
NOTES: This regimental history devotes a well detailed single chapter of 44pp with 4 photos to the story of 142 RAC. List of officers as at January 1943 and list of officers killed within chapter. Appendices include list of COs and two short accounts by members of 142 RAC. Honours/Awards.

The Suffolk Regiment
Not stated IWM; RMAS; PCL
London; Malcolm Page Ltd; n.d. [c.1953]; ISBN None; 104pp/1 x bw PIfep/39 x bw PI/5 x bw SI; s/b; Indexed N; Glossary N; Appendices N; Bibliography N; 215 x 138 (8vo); Uncommon
NOTES: 1950s recruiting booklet. No reference to 7th Bn/142 RAC.

The Suffolk Regiment
(The 12th Regiment of Foot)
(Famous Regiments)
Moir, Guthrie; Horrocks, Lt.-Gen. Sir Brian (Ed.) TM; IWM; NAM; RMAS; PCL
London; Leo Cooper Ltd; 1969; ISBN 85052 006 1; 140pp/17 x bw PI/11 x bw SI; h/b / d/j Blue cloth; Indexed N; Glossary N; Appendices N; Bibliography N; 222 x 140 (8vo)
NOTES: 5pp on 142 RAC.

The Suffolk Regiment 1928 -1946
Nicholson, Col W. N.
The East Anglian Magazine Ltd; 1995; See Notes; Uncommon
NOTES: Reprint of 1948 first edition. (Not physically inspected.)

The Suffolk Regiment, 1685 - 1959
Lummis, Eric TM; IWM
Ipswich; The Trustees of the Suffolk Regiment Museum; 1997; ISBN 0 9531942 2 1; 22pp/42 x clr Pl/5 x clr Sl/16 x bw Pl; s/b; Indexed N; Glossary N; Appendices N; Bibliography N; 249 x 249 (4to)
NOTES: One paragraph reference to 142 RAC. Revised edition published 1998.

The Suffolk Regiment 1928 to 1946
Nicholson, C.M.G., D.S.O., Col W. N.
Uckfield; Naval & Military Press Ltd; ISBN 978 1843422464; See Notes; Indexed Y; Glossary Y; Appendices Y; Bibliography N
NOTES: Facsimile reprint by NMP of 1948 first edition, available in s/b and h/b.

143rd Regiment, Royal Armoured Corps — 143 RAC

RAC service:	01/11/1941	01/01/1944 (Suspended animation)
Converted Bns:	The Lancashire Fusiliers	
	1st /5th Bn = 108 RAC, 1st /6th = 109 RAC & 9th Bn = 143 RAC	

Regimental publications:
The Gallipoli Gazette, Regimental Journal of XX The Lancashire Fusiliers
1931 to 1968

Handbook of XX The Lancashire Fusiliers
Surtees, C.B., C.B.E., M.C., Maj-Gen G. IWM; PCL
London; Malcolm Page Ltd; 1952; ISBN None; 184pp/1 x clr Sl/31 x bw Pl/8 x bw SI; s/b; Indexed N; Glossary N; Appendices N; Bibliography Y; 227 x 154 (8vo); Uncommon
NOTES: Regimental recruitment handbook. Single paragraph reference to each of 108/109 and 143 RAC.

A Short History of XX The Lancashire Fusiliers
Surtees, C.B., C.B.E., M.C., Maj-Gen G. IWM; NAM; RMAS
London; Malcolm Page Ltd; 1955; ISBN None; 244pp/2 x clr Sl/27 x bw Pl/13 x bw SI; s/b; Indexed Y; Glossary N; Appendices N; Bibliography Y; 213 x 137 (8vo); Uncommon
NOTES: Updated edition of the 1952 Handbook. Single paragraph reference to each of 108/109 and 143 RAC.

ROYAL ARMOURED CORPS: TA - ROYAL ARMOURED CORPS REGIMENTS

Regiment of the Line
The Story of XX The Lancashire Fusiliers
Ray, Cyril   NAM; RMAS; PCL
London; B. T. Batsford Ltd; 1963; ISBN None; xiii + 194pp/1 x bw SIfep/5 x bw PI/26 x bw SI; h/b / d/j Red cloth; Indexed Y; Glossary N; Appendices N; Bibliography Y; 227 x 154 (8vo)
NOTES: One paragraph reference to RAC regiments.

The Lancashire Fusiliers
(The 20th Regiment of Foot)
(Famous Regiments)
Ray, Cyril; Horrocks, Lt.-Gen. Sir Brian (Ed.)   TM; IWM; RMAS; PCL
London; Leo Cooper Ltd; 1971; ISBN 0 85052 068 1; 135pp/6 x bw PI/19 x bw SI; h/b / d/j Blue cloth; Indexed N; Glossary N; Appendices N; Bibliography N; 222 x 140 (8vo)
NOTES: Single paragraph reference to the RAC regiments. From the title page - 'Abbreviated from *Regiment of the Line* by Cyril Ray, published by Batsford, 1963.'

The History Of Lancashire Fusiliers 1939 - 1945
Hallam, John   IWM; RMAS; PCL
Stroud; Alan Sutton Publishing Ltd; 1993; ISBN 0-7509-0409-7; viii + 232pp/24 x bw PI/4 x bw SI/21 x bw M; h/b / d/j Black cloth; Indexed Y; Glossary N; Appendices Y; Bibliography Y; 255 x 175 (4to)
NOTES: Two paragraphs cover 108/109 and 143 RAC. Honours/Awards.

144th Regiment, Royal Armoured Corps	144 RAC

RAC service: 22/11/1941   01/03/1945*
* Disbanded and renamed 4RTR.
Converted Bns: The East Lancashire Regiment
   8th Bn = 144 RAC

    Regimental publications:
    The East Lancashire Regimental Journal
    Vol. 1, No. 1 Feb 1931 to Vol. 8, No. 5 Sept 1939 (Quarterly) Suspended 1940 – 1944, replaced by
    The East Lancashire Regiment: War Bulletin
    Vol. 1, No. 1 Oct 1944 to Vol. 2, No. 17 Feb 1946 (Monthly), replaced by
    The East Lancashire Regimental Bulletin
    Vol. 3, No. 18 Mar 1946 to Vol. 11, No. 77 Nov 1954 (Monthly), replaced by
    The East Lancashire Regimental Journal
    Vol. 1, No. 1 (new series) Jan 1955 to Vol. 4, No. 16 Dec 1958 (Quarterly), replaced by
    The East Lancashire Regimental Association Journal
    Vol. 1, No. 1 (new series) Mar 1959 to Vol. 7, No. 26 Dec 1965 (Quarterly)
    'The 144 News'
    October 1944 to February 1945 (Daily), re-titled **'The Blue Flash'** upon rechristening to 4RTR March 1945.

Blue Flash
The Story of an Armoured Regiment
Jolly, Alan   TM; IWM; NAM; RMAS; PCL
London; The Solicitors' Law Stationery Society Limited; 1952; ISBN None; xi + 168pp/1 x bw PIfep/11 x bw PI/2 x bw Mf/11 x bw M; h/b / d/j Blue cloth; Indexed Y; Glossary N; Appendices Y; Bibliography N; 233 x 161 (8vo); Rare
NOTES: After a few pages summarising the early history, the book begins with the regiment sailing for Normandy soon after D-Day. Extremely well detailed and informative narrative of the regiment's operations with some well referenced text to maps. Unusually the index lists many men of Trooper, etc. rank. Ends with 15pp on 4RTR, following the renaming of the regiment. Written by one of the regiment's COs. Gale & Polden were to publish originally if 600 copies could be sold. A print run of 600 was deemed too expensive and the book was printed by SLSS Ltd based on the actual orders required and various donations. RoH/Honours/Awards. Came with a loose coloured map *The Campaign in Europe*, 565mm x 265mm.

A Short History of the East Lancashire Regiment
Not stated   NAM; PCL
Preston; T Snape & Co. Ltd; 1952; ISBN None; 23pp/1 x clr SIfep; s/b (card); Indexed N; Glossary N; Appendices N; Bibliography N; 138 x 108 (24mo); Uncommon
NOTES: Incorrect reference to 8th Bn converting immediately to 4RTR, no mention of 144 RAC.

History of the East Lancashire Regiment in War 1939 – 1945
Various   TM; IWM; NAM; RMAS; PCL
Manchester; H Rawson & Co Ltd; 1953; ISBN None; xv + 331pp/1 x bw PIfep/1 x bw SIfep/22 x bw PI/23 x bw Mf/15 x bw M; h/b (d/j - ne) Green cloth; Indexed N; Glossary N; Appendices N; Bibliography N; 245 x 178 (8vo); Uncommon
NOTES: Only 2pp on 8th Bn and bare reference to 144 RAC. Honours/Awards - no battalion distinction. Reprint available from regimental shop.

Turning Points
In a Life With War
The memoirs of Kenneth Macksey
Macksey, Kenneth   TM
Beaminster; Newtown Publications; 1997; ISBN 0 9508536 1 5; 216pp/1 x bw PIfep/12 x bw PI; s/b; Indexed N; Glossary N; Appendices N; Bibliography N; 215 x 136 (8vo); Uncommon
NOTES: In his life story, this prolific military author recounts his war years in 95pp. He signed up in late 1942, being posted to 111 RAC (8pp). He then moved to 144 RAC (8pp) before going to OCTU in 1943. He joined 141 RAC in July 1944 as troop leader of 5 Tp, A Sqn. He was wounded twice in late 1944 and was sent to a Battle Exhaustion Hospital before being medically downgraded. 45pp on 141 RAC service. There is one chapter commenting on the insubordination episode involving William Douglas Home – refer to books by William Douglas Home listed under 141 RAC.

The East Lancashire Regiment 1855 – 1958
Images of England series
Downham, Lt-Col, John TM; PCL
Stroud; Tempus Publishing Limited; 2000; ISBN 0 7524 0000 0; 128pp/1 x bw PIfep/115 x bw PI/3 x bw SI; s/b; Indexed N; Glossary N; Appendices N; Bibliography N; 234 x 165 (8vo)
NOTES: One photograph of 144 RAC, no narrative.

History of the East Lancashire Regiment in War 1939 - 1945
Various
Doncaster; D. P. & G. Military Publishers; 2001; ISBN 1-903972-00-0; viii + 232pp/Illus.; h/b Red cloth; Indexed N; Glossary N; Appendices N; Bibliography N; 215 x 154 (8vo)
NOTES: D. P. & G. facsimile reprint of 1953 first edition. (Not physically inspected.)

145th Regiment, Royal Armoured Corps (Duke of Wellington's)	145 RAC

RAC service: 15/11/1941 17/01/1945 (Disbanded)
Converted Bns: The Duke of Wellington's Regiment (West Riding)
2nd/6th Bn = 114 RAC, 2nd/7th Bn = 115 RAC, 8th Bn = 145 RAC & 9th Bn = 146 RAC

Regimental publications:
The Iron Duke: The Regimental Magazine of The Duke of Wellington's Regiment (West Riding)
Vol. 1, No. 1 May 1925 to current (Quarterly to 1967, then three per year, now twice per year)

The History Of The Duke Of Wellington's Regiment 1919 – 1952
Barclay, C.B.E., D.S.O., Brig. C. N. TM; IWM; NAM; RMAS; PCL
London; William Clowes and Sons Limited; 1953; ISBN None; xxi + 398pp/1 x clr SIfep/26 x bw PI/1 x bw SI/1 x clr Mf/9 x bw Mf/7 x bw M; h/b / d/j Red cloth; Indexed Y; Glossary Y; Appendices Y; Bibliography N; 254 x 196 (4to)
NOTES: Well detailed descriptions of the actions of 145 & 146 RAC. Includes several named references to personnel. Appendices include COs of RAC regiments. 114 RAC = 2pp; 115 RAC = 1pp; 145 RAC = 3 chapters; 146 RAC = 2 chapters. Two photos each of 145 & 146 RAC. RoH by battalion, Honours/Awards.

The Duke Of Wellington's Regiment (West Riding)
Not stated IWM; PCL
London; Malcolm Page Limited; n.d. [c.1956]; ISBN None; 108pp/2 x clr SI/16 x bw PI/1 bw M; s/b; Indexed N; Glossary N; Appendices N; Bibliography N; 215 x 140 (8vo); Uncommon
NOTES: Post Korean War recruiting pamphlet. Passing reference to RAC regiments, including a statement that 2nd/6th Bn and 2nd/7th Bn were infantry only; location of 145 and 146 RAC regiments on maps.

The Duke Of Wellington's Regiment (West Riding)
Not stated IWM; NAM
London; Malcolm Page Limited; n.d. [c.1960]; ISBN None; 96pp/1 x clr SI/17 x bw PI/2 x bw SI/2 x bw M; s/b; Indexed N; Glossary N; Appendices N; Bibliography N; 214 x 138 (8vo); Uncommon
NOTES: Reprint of recruiting booklet.

The Duke Of Wellington's Regiment (West Riding)
(The 33rd/76th Regiment of Foot)
(Famous Regiments)
Lunt, James; Horrocks, Lt.-Gen. Sir Brian (Ed.) TM; IWM; NAM; RMAS; PCL
London; Leo Cooper Ltd; 1971; ISBN 0 85052 067 3; ix + 116pp/1 x bw SIfep/17 x bw PI/7 x bw SI; h/b / d/j Blue cloth; Indexed N; Glossary N; Appendices N; Bibliography N; 222 x 140 (8vo)
NOTES: Brief mention of 145 & 146 RAC including one photograph of 146 RAC. (No mention of 114 RAC/115 RAC.)

A Short History of The Duke Of Wellington's Regiment (West Riding)
Savory, M.B.E., Maj. A. C. S.
No imprint; Reuben Holroyd Ltd (Printers); n.d. [c.1987]; ISBN None; 48pp/1 x clr SIfep/1 x clr PI/3 x clr SI/11 x bw SI/2 x bw M; s/b (card); Indexed N; Glossary N; Appendices N; Bibliography N; 208 x 145 (8vo); Uncommon
NOTES: Regimental booklet, one sentence reference to each of 145 RAC and 146 RAC.

The History Of The Duke Of Wellington's Regiment (West Riding) 1702 - 1992
Brereton, J. M. and Savory, A. C. S. IWM; NAM
Halifax; The Duke of Wellington's Regiment; 1993; ISBN 0 9521552 0 6; x + 446pp/1 x clr PIfep/1 x clr PI/21 x clr SI/65 x bw PI/33 x bw SI/37 x bw M; h/b / d/j Red cloth; Indexed Y; Glossary N; Appendices Y; Bibliography Y; 252 x 196 (4to)
NOTES: A few overview paragraphs on 145 RAC in North Africa and Italy and one on 146 RAC in the Far East.

The Fighting Tykes
The History of the Yorkshire Regiments in the Second World War
Whiting, Charles and Taylor, Eric IWM; NAM; PCL
Barnsley; Leo Cooper; 1993; ISBN 0 85052 3575; xiii + 238pp/59 x bw PI; s/b; Indexed Y; Glossary N; Appendices N; Bibliography Y; 222 x 140 (8vo)
NOTES: One chapter on the Duke of Wellington regiment with 2pp brief reference to 146 RAC plus one photo of a 145 RAC tank.

The Duke Of Wellington's Regiment (West Riding)
1702 - 2002 Fortune Favours The Brave
The Dukes 1702 - 2002
Not stated NAM
Halifax; The Duke of Wellington's Regiment; 2002; ISBN None; 34pp/27 x clr PI/22 x clr SI/91 x bw PI/6 x bw SI/1 x bw M; s/b; Indexed N; Glossary N; Appendices N; Bibliography N; 297 x 210 (4to); Uncommon
NOTES: Tercentenary publication for regiment, one sentence reference to 8th and 9th Bns converting to tanks.

The Fighting Tykes
An Informal History of the Yorkshire Regiments in the Second World War
Whiting, Charles and Taylor, Eric
Barnsley; Pen & Sword Military; 2008; ISBN 978 1 84415 6 450; xiii + 238pp/59 x bw Pl; s/b; Indexed Y; Glossary N; Appendices N; Bibliography Y; 234 x 157 (8vo)
NOTES: Softback reprint of 1993 first edition, same pagination.

The 'Dukes' 1702 – 2006
A concise history and digest of The Duke of Wellington's Regiment (West Riding) with memoirs from the 20th Century
Butterworth, Terry; Flaving, Scott and Harvey, Richard
No imprint; The Duke of Wellington's Regiment Museum and Archive; 2009; ISBN None; 139pp/Fully illustrated; h/b / d/j Red cloth; Indexed N; Glossary N; Appendices N; Bibliography N; 303 x 215 (4to)
NOTES: Updated history published after the amalgamation of The Duke of Wellington's Regiment (West Riding), The Prince of Wales's Own and The Green Howards. Passing reference to the converted battalions, one photograph of 145 RAC.

146th Regiment, Royal Armoured Corps (Duke of Wellington's) — 146 RAC

RAC service:	22/10/1941 Post-war.
Converted Bns:	The Duke of Wellington's Regiment (West Riding) 2nd/6th Bn = 114 RAC, 2nd/7th Bn = 115 RAC, 8th Bn = 145 RAC & 9th Bn = 146 RAC

Regimental publications:
The Iron Duke: The Regimental Magazine of The Duke of Wellington's Regiment (West Riding)
Vol. 1, No. 1 May 1925 to current (Quarterly to 1967, then three per year, now twice per year)

A Short War History of "A" Squadron
146 Regiment Royal Armoured Corps (The Duke of Wellington's) 1940 - 1946
Not stated [See Notes]   NAM
Medan, India; Typ. Varekamp (Printers); 1946; ISBN None; 27pp/24 x bw Pl; s/b (card); Indexed N; Glossary N; Appendices N; Bibliography N; 243 x 160 (8vo); V Rare
NOTES: A souvenir booklet intended for all members of the regiment. Traces the regiment's patchwork history through the Burmese campaign. The author, B. R. Johnston, provided a few notes to the NAM regarding this publication; these notes are pasted to the front cover of the NAM's copy.

The History of The Duke of Wellington's Regiment 1919 - 1952
Barclay, C.B.E., D.S.O., Brig. C. N.   TM; IWM; NAM; RMAS; PCL
London; William Clowes and Sons Limited; 1953; ISBN None; xxi + 398pp/1 x clr SIfep/26 x bw PI/1 x bw SI/1 x clr Mf/9 x bw Mf/7 x bw M; h/b / d/j Red cloth; Indexed Y; Glossary Y; Appendices Y; Bibliography N; 254 x 196 (4to)

NOTES: Well detailed descriptions of the actions of 145 & 146 RAC. Includes several named references to personnel. Appendices include COs of RAC regiments. 114 RAC = 2pp; 115 RAC = 1pp; 145 RAC = 3 chapters; 146 RAC = 2 chapters. Two photos each of 145 & 146 RAC. RoH by battalion, Honours/Awards.

The Duke Of Wellington's Regiment (West Riding)
Not stated IWM; PCL
London; Malcolm Page Limited; n.d. [c.1956]; ISBN None; 108pp/2 x clr SI/16 x bw PI/1 bw M; s/b; Indexed N; Glossary N; Appendices N; Bibliography N; 215 x 140 (8vo); Uncommon
NOTES: Post Korean War recruiting pamphlet. Passing reference to RAC regiments, including a statement that 2nd/6th Bn and 2nd/7th Bn were infantry only; location of 145 and 146 RAC regiments on maps.

The Duke Of Wellington's Regiment (West Riding)
Not stated IWM; NAM
London; Malcolm Page Limited; n.d. [c.1960]; ISBN None; 96pp/1 x clr SI/17 x bw PI/2 x bw SI/2 x bw M; s/b; Indexed N; Glossary N; Appendices N; Bibliography N; 214 x 138 (8vo); Uncommon
NOTES: Reprint of recruiting booklet.

The Duke Of Wellington's Regiment (West Riding)
(The 33rd/76th Regiment of Foot)
(Famous Regiments)
Lunt, James; Horrocks, Lt.-Gen. Sir Brian (Ed.) TM; IWM; NAM; RMAS; PCL
London; Leo Cooper Ltd; 1971; ISBN 0 85052 067 3; ix + 116pp/1 x bw SIfep/17 x bw PI/7 x bw SI; h/b / d/j Blue cloth; Indexed N; Glossary N; Appendices N; Bibliography N; 222 x 140 (8vo)
NOTES: Brief mention of 145 & 146 RAC including one photograph of 146 RAC. (No mention of 114 RAC/115 RAC.)

A Short History of The Duke Of Wellington's Regiment (West Riding)
Savory, M.B.E., Maj. A. C. S.
No imprint; Reuben Holroyd Ltd (Printers); n.d. [c.1987]; ISBN None; 48pp/1 x clr SIfep/1 x clr PI/3 x clr SI/11 x bw SI/2 x bw M; s/b (card); Indexed N; Glossary N; Appendices N; Bibliography N; 208 x 145 (8vo); Uncommon
NOTES: Regimental booklet, one sentence reference to each of 145 RAC and 146 RAC.

The History Of The Duke Of Wellington's Regiment (West Riding) 1702 - 1992
Brereton, J. M. and Savory, A. C. S. IWM; NAM
Halifax; The Duke of Wellington's Regiment; 1993; ISBN 0 9521552 0 6; x + 446pp/1 x clr PIfep/1 x clr PI/21 x clr SI/65 x bw PI/33 x bw SI/37 x bw M; h/b / d/j Red cloth; Indexed Y; Glossary N; Appendices Y; Bibliography Y; 252 x 196 (4to)
NOTES: A few overview paragraphs on 145 RAC in North Africa and Italy and one on 146 RAC in the Far East.

The Fighting Tykes
The History of the Yorkshire Regiments in the Second World War
Whiting, Charles and Taylor, Eric   IWM; NAM; PCL
Barnsley; Leo Cooper; 1993; ISBN 0 85052 3575; xiii + 238pp/59 x bw Pl; s/b; Indexed Y; Glossary N; Appendices N; Bibliography Y; 222 x 140 (8vo)
NOTES: One chapter on the Duke of Wellington regiment with 2pp brief reference to 146 RAC plus one photo of a 145 RAC tank.

The Duke Of Wellington's Regiment (West Riding)
1702 - 2002 Fortune Favours The Brave
The Dukes 1702 - 2002
Not stated   NAM
Halifax; The Duke of Wellington's Regiment; 2002; ISBN None; 34pp/27 x clr Pl/22 x clr Sl/91 x bw Pl/6 x bw Sl/1 x bw M; s/b; Indexed N; Glossary N; Appendices N; Bibliography N; 297 x 210 (4to); Uncommon
NOTES: Tercentenary publication for regiment, one sentence reference to 8th and 9th Bns converting to tanks.

The Fighting Tykes
An Informal History of the Yorkshire Regiments in the Second World War
Whiting, Charles and Taylor, Eric
Barnsley; Pen & Sword Military; 2008; ISBN 978 1 84415 6 450; xiii + 238pp/59 x bw Pl; s/b; Indexed Y; Glossary N; Appendices N; Bibliography Y; 234 x 157 (8vo)
NOTES: Softback reprint of 1993 first edition, same pagination.

The 'Dukes' 1702 - 2006
A concise history and digest of The Duke of Wellington's Regiment (West Riding) with memoirs from the 20th Century
Butterworth, Terry; Flaving, Scott and Harvey, Richard
No imprint; The Duke of Wellington's Regiment Museum and Archive; 2009; ISBN None; 139pp/Fully illustrated; h/b / d/j Red cloth; Indexed N; Glossary N; Appendices N; Bibliography N; 303 x 215 (4to)
NOTES: Updated history published after the amalgamation of The Duke of Wellington's Regiment (West Riding), The Prince of Wales's Own and The Green Howards. Passing reference to the converted battalions.

147th (Hampshire) Regiment, Royal Armoured Corps   147 RAC

RAC service: 01/12/1941   Post-war.
Converted Bns: The Hampshire Regiment
                              10th Bn = 147 RAC & 9th Bn = 157 RAC

Regimental publications:
The Hampshire Regimental Journal
Vol. 1, No. 1 Oct 1905 to Vol. 34, No. 8 Aug 1939 (Monthly) Suspended 1940 – 1945
Vol. 35, No. 1 Feb 1946 to Vol, 35, No. 4 Nov 1946 (Quarterly), replaced by
The Royal Hampshire Regimental Journal
Vol. 36, No. 1 to Vol. 46, No. 4 Nov 1957 (Quarterly)

Regimental History The Royal Hampshire Regiment
Volume Three 1918 - 1954
Daniell, David Scott TM; IWM; NAM; RMAS; PCL
Aldershot; Gale & Polden Limited; 1955; ISBN None; xiii + 294pp/1 x bw PIfep/3 x bw PI/2 x bw Mbds/25 x bw M; h/b / d/j Blue cloth; Indexed Y; Glossary N; Appendices N; Bibliography N; 240 x 166 (8vo)
NOTES: Two pages general information on both regiments' early days plus one chapter on 147 RAC: a 4pp summary of the regiment in NWE. Honours/Awards - not battalion specific.

The Royal Hampshire Regiment
(37th/67th Regiments of Foot)
(Famous Regiments)
Wykes, Alan; Horrocks, Lt.-Gen. Sir Brian (Ed.) TM; IWM; NAM; RMAS; PCL
London; Hamish Hamilton Ltd; 1968; ISBN None; 128pp/18 x bw PI/9 x bw SI; h/b / d/j Yellow cloth; Indexed N; Glossary N; Appendices N; Bibliography N; 222 x 140 (8vo)
NOTES: One sentence referring to 147 RAC and one photograph.

The Royal Hampshire Regiment 1918 - 1954
Daniell, David Scott
Uckfield; Naval & Military Press Ltd; ISBN 978 1845742577; See Notes; Indexed Y; Glossary N; Appendices N; Bibliography N
NOTES: Facsimile reprint by NMP of 1955 first edition, available in s/b and h/b.

148th Regiment, Royal Armoured Corps | 148 RAC

RAC service: 22/11/1941 20/08/1944 (Disbanded)
Converted Bns: The Loyal Regiment (North Lancashire)
5th Bn = 18R, 6th Bn = 2R & 9th Bn = 148 RAC

Regimental publications:
The Lancashire Lad
Started in 1885, break in publication late WWII, resumed September 1947 to present.

A Short History of The Loyal Regiment (North Lancashire)
Not stated NAM; PCL
London; Malcolm Page Limited; n.d. [c.1953]; ISBN None; 60pp/1 x bw PIfep/15 x bw PI; s/b; Indexed N; Glossary N; Appendices N; Bibliography N; 217 x 140 (8vo); Uncommon
NOTES: One paragraph reference to each of 5th, 6th and 9th Bns.

The Loyal Regiment (North Lancashire) 1919-1953
Dean, Capt. C. G. T. IWM; NAM; PCL
Preston; Regimental Headquarters; 1955; ISBN None; xix + 310pp/1 x bw PIfep/23 x bw PI/2 x bw Mbds/9 x bw Mf/9 x bw M; h/b (d/j - ne) Red cloth; Indexed Y; Glossary N; Appendices Y; Bibliography N; 236 x 161 (8vo); Rare

NOTES: Several chapters cover the regiment's armour converted battalions. Two chapters cover the formation of 148 RAC and its short career in NWE. Useful index. Reprinted by DP&G Military Publishers for the regiment with additional material 2003.

A Short History of The Loyal Regiment (North Lancashire)
Not stated IWM
London; Malcolm Page Limited; n.d. [c.1964]; ISBN None; 36pp/1 x bw PIfep/18 x bw PI; s/b; Indexed N; Glossary N; Appendices N; Bibliography N; 217 x 140 (8vo); Uncommon
NOTES: One paragraph reference to each of 5th, 6th and 9th Bns.

The Loyal Regiment
(North Lancashire) (The 47th and 81st Regiments of Foot)
(Famous Regiments)
Langley, Michael; Horrocks, Lt.-Gen. Sir Brian (Ed.) TM; IWM; PCL
London; Leo Cooper Ltd; 1976; ISBN 0 85052 075 4; 118pp/7 x bw PI/11 x bw SI; h/b / d/j Blue cloth; Indexed N; Glossary N; Appendices N; Bibliography N; 222 x 140 (8vo)
NOTES: One paragraph reference to 148 RAC.

Scenes from a One Way Journey
Cooper, Alexander IWM; NAM
Glossop; Senior Publications; 1982; ISBN 903839 91 1; 72pp/1 x bw PIfep/7 x bw PI; s/b (card); Indexed N; Glossary N; Appendices N; Bibliography N; 193 x 143 (12mo); Uncommon
NOTES: The author was serving in 9th Bn, Loyal Regiment when it converted to 148 RAC. He served in Normandy with them until they disbanded, then transferred to 1NY, serving through to the end of the war. The book is a collection of his poetry on his military and civilian experiences.

The Loyal North Lancashire Regiment 1855 - 1970
Images of England series
Bull, Stephen
Stroud; Tempus Publishing Limited; 2002; ISBN 0 7524 2489 0; 128pp/1 x bw PIfep/200 x bw PI/4 x bw SI; s/b; Indexed N; Glossary N; Appendices N; Bibliography N; 235 x 165 (8vo)
NOTES: One sentence narrative reference to 9th Bn/148 RAC, no photographs.

The Loyal Regiment (North Lancashire) 1919-1970
Dean, Capt. C. G. T. (Additional material: Bird, O.B.E., D.L., Col J. A. C. TM
& Maher, M.B.E., Maj. A. J.)
Preston; D. P. & G. Military Publishers; 2003; ISBN 1-903972-31-0; xix + 349pp/1 x bw PIfep/35 x bw PI/2 x bw Mf/15 x bw M; h/b Red cloth; Indexed Y; Glossary N; Appendices Y; Bibliography N; 215 x 154 (8vo)
NOTES: In this expanded edition, the era 1955 - 1970 is dealt with from p.299. RoH/Honours/Awards, RoH discretely lists 2R, 18R & 148 RAC casualties. 26+pp on Recce/RAC regiments.

| 149th Regiment, Royal Armoured Corps | 149 RAC |

RAC service: 22/11/1941 Post-war.
Converted Bns: The King's Own Yorkshire Light Infantry
7th Bn = 149 RAC

Regimental publications:
The Bugle: a monthly journal of The King's Own Yorkshire Light Infantry
Vol. 1, No. 1 Jan 1922 to Vol. 37, No. 3 Sept 1939 (Monthly) Suspended 1940 – 1945
Vol. 38, No. 1 Jan 1946 to Vol. 60, No. 2 Summer 1968 (Monthly)
Officers' news letter
No. 1 - 4 Mar 1941, replaced by
Officers' news
No. 2 – 7 Apr 1941 to No. 29 May 1944 (Irregular), replaced by
Newsletter
No 30 June 1944, replaced by
News sheet
No. 31 July 1944 to No. 44 Oct 1945 (Irregular)

History of The King's Own Yorkshire Light Infantry
Volume IV
A Register of Officers who have served on a Regular Commission in the Regiment since its formation on the 19th December 1755, until the end of the War on 15th August 1945.
Deedes, K.C.B., C.M.G., D.S.O., Gen. Sir Charles P. IWM; PCL
London; Lund Humphries & Co Ltd; 1946; ISBN None; 247pp/1 x bw SIfep; h/b / d/j
Blue cloth; Indexed N; Glossary N; Appendices Y; Bibliography N; 224 x 144 (8vo)
NOTES: Alphabetical list of officers with promotion synopsis, some entries expanded.

A Short History of The King's Own Yorkshire Light Infantry 1755 - 1947
Not stated
Pontefract; The McGowan Press Ltd; 1947; ISBN None; 36pp/1 x bw PIfep/1 x bw PI;
s/b; Indexed N; Glossary N; Appendices N; Bibliography N; 183 x 124 (12mo);
Uncommon
NOTES: One sentence reference to conversion and to disbandment of 149 RAC.

Never Give Up
being Volume V
The History Of The King's Own Yorkshire Light Infantry 1919 - 1942
Hingston, Lt-Col Walter TM; IWM; RMAS; PCL
London; Lund Humphries & Co Ltd; 1950; ISBN None; xvi + 243pp/1 x bw PIfep/1 x bw
PI/24 x bw SI/9 x bw M; h/b / d/j Blue cloth; Indexed Y; Glossary N; Appendices N;
Bibliography N; 224 x 146 (8vo)
NOTES: One paragraph introduction to 149 RAC and to Volume VI where its story will be told.

History Of The King's Own Yorkshire Light Infantry
Volume VI 1939 - 1948
Ellenberger, M.C., M.A., Brig. G. F.   TM; IWM; NAM; RMAS; PCL
Aldershot; Gale & Polden Limited; 1961; ISBN None; xvi + 184pp/7 x bw Mf/21 x bw M; h/b / d/j Blue cloth; Indexed Y; Glossary N; Appendices Y; Bibliography N; 220 x 143 (8vo)
NOTES: The regiment's story is reasonably well covered in a compact two-and-a-half pages. Folding maps are printed on fine tissue paper.

A Short History of The King's Own Yorkshire Light Infantry 1755 - 1965
Huxley, Maj. Colin   NAM
Wakefield; The Wakefield Express Series Ltd; n.d. [1965]; ISBN None; 36pp/1 x bw SIfep/1 x bw Mf; s/b (card); Indexed N; Glossary N; Appendices N; Bibliography N; 186 x 120 (12mo); Uncommon
NOTES: One paragraph reference to 149 RAC.

The King's Own Yorkshire Light Infantry
(The 51st and 105th Regiments of Foot)
(Famous Regiments)
Ellenberger, Brig. G. F.; Horrocks, Lt.-Gen. Sir Brian (Ed.)   TM; IWM; RMAS; PCL
London; Leo Cooper Ltd; 1970; ISBN None; v + 125pp/22 x bw PI/7 x bw SI; h/b / d/j Grey cloth; Indexed N; Glossary N; Appendices N; Bibliography N; 223 x 142 (8vo)
NOTES: No mention of 149 RAC.

The King's Own Yorkshire Light Infantry 1857 - 1968
Images of England series
Johnson, Malcolm K.
Stroud; Tempus Publishing Limited; 2000; ISBN 0 7524 1867 X; 128pp/1 x bw PIfep/216 x bw PI/7 x bw SI; s/b; Indexed N; Glossary N; Appendices N; Bibliography N; 235 x 165 (8vo)
NOTES: One sentence narrative reference and one rare photograph of 149 RAC in India.

150th Regiment, Royal Armoured Corps (York and Lancaster)	150 RAC

RAC service: 22/11/1941   Post-war.
Converted Bns: The York and Lancaster Regiment
                              10th Bn = 150 RAC

Regimental publications:
The Tiger and the Rose: a monthly journal of The York & Lancaster Regiment
Vol. 1, No. 1 (new series) Oct 1920 to Vol. 19, No. 12 Sept 1939 Suspended 1940 – 1945.
Vol. 1, No. 1 (new series) June 1946 to not established – became quarterly.

A Short History of The York & Lancaster Regiment 1758 to 1953
Not stated NAM
Pontefract; E Atkinson & Sons (Printers) Ltd; n.d. [1953]; ISBN None; 16pp/No illus.; s/b (card); Indexed N; Glossary N; Appendices N; Bibliography N; 222 x 142 (8vo); Uncommon
NOTES: One sentence reference to 150 RAC.

The York And Lancaster Regiment 1919-1953
Volume III
Sheffield, Maj. O. F. IWM; RMAS; PCL
Aldershot; Gale & Polden Ltd; 1956; ISBN None; xv + 297pp/5 x bw PIfep/17 x bw PI/1 x bw SI/27 x bw M; h/b (d/j - ne) Red cloth; Indexed Y; Glossary N; Appendices N; Bibliography N; 254 x 186 (4to)
NOTES: One good summary chapter of 15pp and two photos of 150 RAC. List of Honours/Awards to 150 RAC at end of its own chapter.

A Short History of The York & Lancaster Regiment 1758 to 1960
Not stated
Sheffield; Greenup and Thompson Limited (Printers); n.d. [1960]; ISBN None; 20pp/No illus.; s/b (card); Indexed N; Glossary N; Appendices N; Bibliography N; 222 x 142 (8vo); Uncommon
NOTES: Updated version of 1758 - 1953 edition, one paragraph reference to 150 RAC. Also reissued with pasted in typed amendments with date range 1758 -1968 and with 'Amended' hand written on the cover.

The York And Lancaster Regiment
(65th and 84th Regiments of Foot)
(Famous Regiments)
Creighton-Williamson, Donald; Horrocks, Lt.-Gen. Sir TM; IWM; NAM; RMAS; PCL
Brian (Ed.)
London; Leo Cooper Ltd; 1968; ISBN None; 135pp/13 x bw PI/14 x bw SI; h/b / d/j Red cloth; Indexed N; Glossary N; Appendices N; Bibliography N; 222 x 140 (8vo)
NOTES: No reference to 150 RAC.

151st Regiment, Royal Armoured Corps — 151 RAC

RAC service: 01/01/1942 31/12/1943*
* As of 01/01/44, 151 RAC assumed the title of 107 RAC which had been disbanded 31/12/43. See 107 RAC for remaining war service.
Converted Bns: The King's Own Royal Regiment (Lancaster)
  5th Bn = 107RAC & 10th Bn = 151RAC

Regimental publications:
The Lion and the Rose: The King's Own (Royal Lancaster) Regimental Gazette
Vol. 9, No. 1 Jan 1921 to Vol. 47, No. 4 Nov 1959 (Quarterly)

The King's Own
The Story of a Royal Regiment Volume III 1914-1950
Cowper, Col J. M. IWM; NAM; RMAS; PCL
Aldershot; Gale & Polden Ltd; 1957; ISBN None; xv + 527pp/15 x bw PI/1 x bw SI/6 x bw Mf/9 x bw M; h/b (d/j - ne) Blue cloth; Indexed Y; Glossary N; Appendices Y; Bibliography Y; 235 x 161 (8vo)
NOTES: One of the best infantry histories covering those converted to armour. Both regiments receive several entries throughout: 107 RAC approximately 8pp plus one photograph and 151 RAC approximately 1pp. Excellent index. Honours/Awards lists denote battalion of recipient.

The King's Own Royal Regiment
(Lancaster) (the 4th Regiment of Foot)
(Famous Regiments)
Green, Howard; Horrocks, Lt.-Gen. Sir Brian (Ed.) TM; IWM; NAM; RMAS; PCL
London; Leo Cooper Ltd; 1972; ISBN 0 85052 090 8; 143pp/18 x bw PI/14 x bw SI; h/b / d/j Green cloth; Indexed N; Glossary N; Appendices N; Bibliography N; 222 x 140 (8vo)
NOTES: No reference to 151 RAC.

152nd Regiment, Royal Armoured Corps — 152 RAC

RAC service: 01/01/1942   07/1945
Converted Bns: The King's Regiment (Liverpool)
                     11th Bn = 152 RAC

Regimental publications:
The Kingsman: the journal of The King's Regiment (Liverpool)
No. 1 Dec 1927 to No. 23 July 1939 (Half-yearly) Suspended 1940 – 1945
No. 24 July 1946 to No. 47 Oct 1958

The Story of The King's Regiment 1914 - 1948
Burke-Gaffney, M.C., Lt-Col J. J. TM; IWM; RMAS; PCL
Liverpool; Sharpe & Kellet Ltd; 1954; ISBN None; xiii + 203pp/1 x bw PIfep/17 x bw PI/10 x bw M; h/b / d/j Red cloth; Indexed Y; Glossary N; Appendices Y; Bibliography N; 218 x 144 (8vo)
NOTES: Brief two sentence reference to 152 RAC, Errata slip pasted into Contents.

Sutherland's War
Sutherland, Douglas TM; IWM
London; Leo Cooper in association with Secker & Warburg; 1984; ISBN 0-436-50601-7; 184pp/21 x bw SI; h/b / d/j Yellow cloth; Indexed N; Glossary N; Appendices N; Bibliography N; 223 x 143 (8vo)
NOTES: The first half of these memoirs cover the author joining the KOSBs early 1939, going to OCTU in 1940 and being commissioned into the King's Regiment, where he was posted to Brigade HQ to command their reconnaissance unit. Soon after the 11th Bn King's converted, he joined 152 RAC and he provides some interesting detail on the

regiment in a humorous look at his wartime career. 152 RAC underwent a re-
organisation early in 1944 and the author left, serving in other, unspecified, RAC
Churchill regiments in NWE.

'Difficulties be damned'
The King's Regiment 8th, 63rd, 96th
A History of the City Regiment of Manchester and Liverpool
Mileham, Patrick IWM
Not stated; Fleur de Lys Publishing; 2000; ISBN 0 1873907 10-9; 246pp/12 x clr PI/10 x
clr SI/123 x bw PI/20 x bw SI/16 x bw M; h/b / d/j Green cloth; Indexed Y; Glossary N;
Appendices Y; Bibliography Y; 304 x 216 (4to)
NOTES: One sentence, appendix reference only to 152 RAC. 1000 copies published.

153rd Regiment, Royal Armoured Corps — 153 RAC

RAC service:	22/11/1941	24/08/1944 (Disbanded and one sqn absorbed by 107RAC to form its 'C' Sqn)
Converted Bns:	The Essex Regiment 8th Bn = 153 RAC	

Regimental publications:
The Essex Regiment Gazette
Vol. 1, No. 1 (new series) Sept 1926 to Vol. 7, No. 52 Sept 1939 (Quarterly)
Suspended 1940 – 1944, replaced by
The Eagle: the journal of The Essex Regiment
Vol. 8, No. 53 June 1945 to Vol. 17, No. 93 Oct 1958 (Varies)

The Essex Regiment 1929 - 1950
Martin, M.B.E., Col T. A. TM; IWM; NAM; RMAS; PCL
Brentwood; The Essex Regiment Association; 1952; ISBN None; xx + 668pp/11 x clr
SIfep/42 x bw PI/2 x clr Mbds/1 x clr Mf/12 x clr M/2 x bw Mf/22 x bw M; h/b / d/j Red
cloth; Indexed Y; Glossary N; Appendices Y; Bibliography N; 222 x 148 (8vo)
NOTES: Brief summary 8pp on 8th Bn/153 RAC. RoH does not list RAC casualties.
RoH/Honours/Awards.

Memoirs of a Family 1822 - 1944
Young, Robert
Oxford; Robert Young; 1983; ISBN 0 9508991 0 0; vii + 93pp/No illus.; s/b (card);
Indexed N; Glossary N; Appendices N; Bibliography N; 197 x 123 (12mo); Uncommon
NOTES: The author has compiled eight brief chapters from different family members
across 120 years. In his own chapter (24pp), he recounts his first battle in Normandy,
July 1944. Fascinating mature account covering just a few days in action. See also,
author's memoirs, *Before I Forget* covering 153 RAC and 9RTR.

Before I Forget
Young, Robert   IWM
Oxford; Robert Young; 1990; ISBN None; 290pp/No illus.; s/b; Indexed Y; Glossary N; Appendices Y; Bibliography N; 197 x 130 (12mo); Rare
NOTES: The author served as an officer in 8th Bn Essex Regiment, transferring to 153 RAC upon the 8th's conversion. He was OC 2 Tp, B Sqn and when 153 RAC was disbanded the author transferred to 9RTR (taking command of 12 Tp, C Sqn), rather than to the common destination of 107 RAC or 147 RAC. 64pp on his time in tanks. Forthright and occasionally indignant recollections of his wartime experiences. IWM copy rebound. See also, author's previous book *Memoirs of a Family 1822 - 1944*.

154th Regiment, Royal Armoured Corps   154 RAC

RAC service:	01/01/1942	30/07/1943 (Disbanded)
Converted Bns:	The North Staffordshire Regiment (Prince of Wales's)	
	9th Bn = 154 RAC	

Regimental publications:
The Stafford Knot: The Journal of The Staffordshire Regiment (The Prince of Wales's)
No. 1 Aug 1959 to (No. 78 2007 – latest established) (Half-yearly to Oct 1989, then yearly)
Newsletter: The North Staffordshire Regt.
No. 1 May 1946 to No. 5 May 1948 (Irregular)

The North Staffordshire Regiment (The Prince of Wales's)
A Short History 1756 - 1945
Not stated   PCL
Hednesford; A. D. Taylor; n.d. [c.1950]; ISBN None; 20pp/4 x bw Pl/5 x bw SI/6 x bw M; s/b; Indexed N; Glossary N; Appendices N; Bibliography N; 241 x 147 (8vo); Uncommon
NOTES: One passing reference to 9th Bn transferring to the RAC.

The North Staffordshire Regiment (The Prince of Wales's)
A Short History 1756 - 1955
Not stated   PCL
London; Malcolm Page Limited; n.d. [c.1955]; ISBN None; 80pp/21 x bw Pl/4 x bw SI/7 x bw M; s/b; Indexed N; Glossary N; Appendices N; Bibliography N; 215 x 135 (8vo); Uncommon
NOTES: One passing reference to 9th Bn transferring to the RAC.

The North Staffordshire Regiment
(The Prince of Wales's) (The 64th/98th Regiment of Foot)
(Famous Regiments)
Cook, H.; Horrocks, Lt.-Gen. Sir Brian (Ed.)   TM; IWM; NAM; RMAS; PCL
London; Leo Cooper Ltd; 1970; ISBN 0 85052 056 8; iii + 135pp/21 x bw Pl/10 x bw SI; h/b / d/j Brown cloth; Indexed N; Glossary N; Appendices N; Bibliography N; 223 x 141 (8vo)
NOTES: No mention of 9th Bn/154 RAC.

155th Regiment, Royal Armoured Corps	155 RAC

RAC service: 01/01/1942   13/07/1945 (Disbanded)
Converted Bns: The Durham Light Infantry
                        15th Bn = 155 RAC

Regimental publications:
The Regimental Journal of The Durham Light Infantry: incorporating 'The Bugle'
Vol. 1, No. 1 July 1934 to Vol. 3, No. 21 July 1939 (Quarterly) Suspended 1940 – 1945
Vol. 4, No. 22 July 1946 to Vol. 16, No. 107 June 1968 (Quarterly)

The Story of The Durham Light Infantry
Short, Lt E. W.   PCL
Newcastle Upon Tyne; J & P Bealls Ltd; 1946; ISBN None; 32pp/2 x clr SI; s/b; Indexed N; Glossary N; Appendices N; Bibliography N; 183 x 122 (12mo); Uncommon
NOTES: No mention of 155 RAC.

The D.L.I. at War
The History Of The Durham Light Infantry 1939 - 1945
Rissik, David   TM; IWM; RMAS; PCL
Durham; The Depot: The Durham Light Infantry; n.d. [c.1953]; ISBN None; xvi + 352pp/32 x bw Pl/5 x bw Mf/15 x bw M; h/b / d/j Green cloth; Indexed Y; Glossary N; Appendices Y; Bibliography N; 222 x 143 (8vo)
NOTES: Good summary of 155 RAC in 4pp.

Faithful
The Story of The Durham Light Infantry
Ward, S. G. P.   IWM; NAM; RMAS; PCL
Edinburgh; Thomas Nelson & Sons Ltd; n.d. [c.1963]; ISBN None; xx + 574pp/1 x clr SIfep/54 x bw M; h/b / d/j Green cloth; Indexed Y; Glossary N; Appendices N; Bibliography N; 253 x 161 (4to)
NOTES: One paragraph reference to 155 RAC.

The Durham Light Infantry
(The 68th and 106th Regiments of Foot)
(Famous Regiments)
Moore, William; Horrocks, Lt.-Gen. Sir Brian (Ed.)   TM; IWM; NAM; RMAS; PCL
London; Leo Cooper Ltd; 1975; ISBN 0 85052 149 1; xiv + 90pp/20 x bw PI/4 x bw SI; h/b / d/j Green cloth; Indexed N; Glossary N; Appendices Y; Bibliography N; 222 x 140 (8vo)
NOTES: No reference to 15th Bn.

ROYAL ARMOURED CORPS: TA - ROYAL ARMOURED CORPS REGIMENTS 223

Faithful
The Story of The Durham Light Infantry
Ward, S. G. P.
Uckfield; Naval & Military Press Ltd; 2004; ISBN 978 1845741471; See Notes; s/b; Indexed Y; Glossary N; Appendices N; Bibliography N
NOTES: Facsimile reprint by NMP of 1963 first edition, available in s/b.

The D.L.I. at War
The History Of The Durham Light Infantry 1939 - 1945
Rissik, David
Uckfield; Naval & Military Press Ltd; 2004; ISBN 978 1845741440; See Notes; Indexed Y; Glossary N; Appendices Y; Bibliography N
NOTES: Facsimile reprint by NMP of 1953 first edition, available in s/b and h/b.

156th Regiment, Royal Armoured Corps	156 RAC

RAC service: 01/12/1941 31/07/1943 (Disbanded)
Converted Bns: The Highland Light Infantry (City of Glasgow Regiment)
11th Bn = 156 RAC

Regimental publications:
The Highland Light Infantry Chronicle
Vol. 1, No. 1 Jan 1893 to Vol. 54, No. 3 Dec 1958 (Quarterly)

The Highland Light Infantry (City of Glasgow Regiment)
Not stated
London; Malcolm Page Limited; 1953; ISBN None; 84pp; s/b; Indexed N; Glossary N; Appendices N; Bibliography N; Uncommon
NOTES: Not physically inspected.

Proud Heritage
The Story of the Highland Light Infantry
Volume Four The Regular, Territorial and Service Battalions H.L.I. and The H.L.I. of Canada 1919 - 1959
Oatts, D.S.O., Lt-Col L. B. IWM; NAM; RMAS; PCL
Glasgow; The House of Grant Ltd; 1963; ISBN None; xii + 490pp/2 x clr SI/44 x bw PI/1 x bw SI/18 x bw Mf; h/b / d/j Green cloth; Indexed Y; Glossary N; Appendices Y; Bibliography N; 233 x 171 (8vo)
NOTES: Brief two sentence reference to 11th Bn/156 RAC.

The Highland Light Infantry
(The 71st H.L.I. and 74th Highlanders)
(Famous Regiments)
Oatts, L. B.; Horrocks, Lt.-Gen. Sir Brian (Ed.) TM; IWM; NAM; RMAS; PCL
London; Leo Cooper Ltd; 1969; ISBN 85052 008 8; viii + 113pp/15 x bw PI/14 x bw SI; h/b / d/j Brown cloth; Indexed N; Glossary N; Appendices N; Bibliography N; 222 x 141 (8vo)
NOTES: No reference to 11th Bn/156 RAC.

157th Regiment, Royal Armoured Corps — 157 RAC

RAC service: 01/11/1941 30/07/1943 (Disbanded)
Converted Bns: The Hampshire Regiment
10th Bn = 147 RAC & 9th Bn = 157 RAC

Regimental publications:
The Hampshire Regimental Journal
Vol. 1, No. 1 Oct 1905 to Vol. 34, No. 8 Aug 1939 (Monthly) Suspended 1940 – 1945
Vol. 35, No. 1 Feb 1946 to Vol. 35, No. 4 Nov 1946 (Quarterly), replaced by
The Royal Hampshire Regimental Journal
Vol. 36, No. 1 to Vol. 46, No. 4 Nov 1957 (Quarterly)

Regimental History The Royal Hampshire Regiment
Volume Three 1918 – 1954
Daniell, David Scott TM; IWM; NAM; PCL
Aldershot; Gale & Polden Limited; 1955; ISBN None; xiii + 294pp/1 x bw PIfep/3 x bw PI/2 x bw Mbds/25 x bw M; h/b / d/j Blue cloth; Indexed Y; Glossary N; Appendices N; Bibliography N; 240 x 166 (8vo)
NOTES: Two pages general information on both regiments' early days, brief mention of 157 RAC therein. Honours/Awards - not battalion specific.

The Royal Hampshire Regiment 1918 - 1954
Daniell, David Scott
Uckfield; Naval & Military Press Ltd; ISBN 978 1845742577; See Notes; Indexed Y; Glossary N; Appendices N; Bibliography N
NOTES: Facsimile reprint by NMP of 1955 first edition, available in s/b and h/b.

158th Regiment, Royal Armoured Corps — 158 RAC

RAC service: 15/07/1942 01/04/1943 (Revert to inf.)
Converted Bns: The South Wales Borderers
6th Bn = 158 RAC

Regimental publications:
XXIV ('Twenty-fourth'): the journal of The South Wales Borderers
No. 1 May 1932 to No. 75 Mar 1969 (Half-yearly)

History of The South Wales Borderers and the Monmouthshire Regiment 1937 - 1952
Part I
Brett, D.S.O., O.B.E., M.C., Lt-Col G. A. TM; IWM; NAM; RMAS; PCL
Pontypool; Hughes and Son, Ltd; 1953; ISBN None; 132pp/1 x bw PIf/7 x bw PI/5 x bw Mf; h/b Green cloth; Indexed N; Glossary N; Appendices Y; Bibliography N; 220 x 144 (8vo); Uncommon
NOTES: One sentence reference to 158 RAC.

History of The South Wales Borderers and the Monmouthshire Regiment
Part V The 6th Battalion The South Wales Borderers 1940 - 1945
Brett, D.S.O., O.B.E., M.C., Lt-Col G. A. TM; IWM; NAM; RMAS; PCL
Pontypool; Hughes and Son; 1956; ISBN None; 86pp/14 x bw PI/2 x clr Mf/3 x bw M; h/b Green cloth; Indexed N; Glossary N; Appendices Y; Bibliography N; 218 x 143 (8vo); Uncommon
NOTES: Brief summary of 158 RAC in 7pp. RoH.

The South Wales Borderers
(The 24th Regiment of Foot)
(Famous Regiments)
Adams, Jack; Horrocks, Lt.-Gen. Sir Brian (Ed.) TM; IWM; NAM; RMAS; PCL
London; Hamish Hamilton Ltd; 1968; ISBN None; 157pp/10 x bw PI/14 x bw SI; h/b / d/j Blue cloth; Indexed N; Glossary N; Appendices N; Bibliography N; 222 x 141 (8vo)
NOTES: One paragraph reference to 6th Bn transferring to the RAC.

A Short History of The Royal Regiment of Wales (24th/41st Foot)
Not stated [See Notes] NAM
Halesowen; Reliance Printing Works; 1986; ISBN None; 91pp/No illus.; s/b (card); Indexed N; Glossary N; Appendices N; Bibliography N; 213 x 140 (8vo)
NOTES: Summary history produced by the regiment, no reference to 6th Bn converting to tanks. This edition 'Updated Reprint' of 1977 edition.

A History of the Royal Regiment of Wales (24th/41st Foot) 1689-1989
Brereton, J. M. IWM; NAM
Cardiff; Regimental Headquarters, The Royal Regiment of Wales (24th/41st Foot); 1989; ISBN 0 9513397 0 2; xxxi + 512pp/1 x clr SIfep/15 x clr PI/29 x clr SI/60 x bw PI/16x bw SI/49 x bw M; h/b / d/j Green cloth; Indexed Y; Glossary N; Appendices Y; Bibliography N; 252 x 200 (4to)
NOTES: One informative summary page on the brief career of 158 RAC.

The South Wales Borderers (24th Regiment of Foot) 1881 - 1969
Images of Wales series
Everett, Martin TM
Stroud; Tempus Publishing Limited; 1999; ISBN 0 7524 1846 7; 128pp/1 x bw PIfep/218 x bw PI/3 x bw SI; s/b; Indexed N; Glossary N; Appendices N; Bibliography N; 235 x 165 (8vo)
NOTES: One sentence reference to 6th Bn, 158 RAC. Reprinted 2002.

159th Regiment, Royal Armoured Corps (The Gloucestershire Regiment)	159 RAC

RAC service: 15/07/1942 01/04/1943 (Revert to inf.)
Converted Bns: The Gloucestershire Regiment
5th Bn = 43R, 6th Bn = 44RTR & 10th Bn = 159RAC

Regimental publications:
The Back Badge: with which is incorporated the news and accounts of The Gloucestershire Regimental Association
Vol. 1 1932 to Vol. 8 1938 (Annual) Suspended 1939 – 1945
Vol. 1, No. 1 (new series) Dec 1946 to not established (Half-yearly)

Cap of Honour
The Story of The Gloucestershire Regiment (28th/61st Foot) 1694 - 1950
Daniell, David Scott IWM; NAM; RMAS; PCL
London; George G. Harrap & Co Ltd; 1951; ISBN None; 344pp/1 x clr SIfep/3 x clr SI/8 x bw PI/31 x bw SI/2 x bw M; h/b / d/j Blue cloth; Indexed Y; Glossary N; Appendices Y; Bibliography N; 222 x 145 (8vo)
NOTES: 2pp brief summary of 159 RAC. One of the appendices provides an index to the entries for each battalion, including those converted to RTR, Recce and RAC regiments. Reprinted 1953 and revised 1975 and 2005.

Cap of Honour
The Story of The Gloucestershire Regiment (The 28th/61st Foot) 1694 - 1950
Daniell, David Scott RMAS; PCL
London; George G. Harrap & Co Ltd; 1953; ISBN None; 344pp/1 x clr SIfep/3 x clr SI/8 x bw PI/31 x bw SI/2 x bw M; h/b / d/j Blue cloth; Indexed Y; Glossary N; Appendices Y; Bibliography N; 222 x 145 (8vo)
NOTES: Reprint of 1951 first edition.

The Slashers
A New Short History of The Gloucestershire Regiment
Not stated IWM; PCL
Gloucester; John Jennings (Printers) Ltd; 1965; ISBN None; 59pp/1 x clr SIfep/2 x bw PI/11x bw SI; s/b; Indexed N; Glossary N; Appendices Y; Bibliography N; 215 x 138 (8vo); Rare
NOTES: No mention of 10th Bn's transfer to the RAC.

Cap of Honour
The Story of The Gloucestershire Regiment (The 28th/61st Foot) 1694 - 1975
Daniell, David Scott IWM
London; White Lion Publishers Ltd; 1975; ISBN None; 410pp/1 x clr PIfep/4 x clr PI/4 x bw PI/23 x bw SI/2 x bw M; h/b / d/j Yellow cloth; Indexed Y; Glossary N; Appendices Y; Bibliography N; 222 x 144 (8vo)
NOTES: New, second edition with additional material (non-RAC) covering the period to 1975 including the Korean war. Pasted in Errata slip, flyleaf.

Never Feared a Foe of Any Kind
The Glosters, 1694 - 1991
Not stated
Gloucester; John Jennings (Printers) Ltd; 1991; ISBN None; 73pp/1 x clr PI/2 x bw PI/7 x clr SI/5 x bw SI/1 x bw M; s/b; Indexed N; Glossary N; Appendices Y; Bibliography N; 210 x 148 (8vo)
NOTES: 10th Bn mentioned only in infantry context.

Never Feared a Foe of Any Kind
The Glosters, 1694 - 1994
Not stated
Gloucester; John Jennings (Printers) Ltd; 1994; ISBN 978 0 9560391 0 1; See Notes; s/b; Indexed N; Glossary N; Appendices Y; Bibliography N
NOTES: Updated reprint of 1991 first edition. (Not physically inspected.)

From Private to Trooper Back to Private
Coulthard, George (Brum)   IWM; NAM
Bishop Auckland; The Pentland Press Ltd; 1994; ISBN 1 85821 148 4; 247pp/1 x bw PIfep/15 x bw PI; s/b; Indexed N; Glossary N; Appendices N; Bibliography N; 210 x 147 (8vo)
NOTES: The author joined 10th Bn Glosters before they converted to tanks and his narrative, heavily laced with dialogue, is laden with robust army language. Covers the brief period the regiment served in the RAC in 59pp.

Cap of Honour
The 300 Years of The Gloucestershire Regiment
Daniell, David Scott   PCL
Stroud; Sutton Publishing Limited; 2005; ISBN 0-7509-4172-3; xvi + 446pp/2 x clr PI/14 x clr SI/21 x bw PI/36 x bw SI/2 x bw M; h/b / d/j Black cloth; Indexed Y; Glossary N; Appendices Y; Bibliography Y; 240 x 158 (8vo)
NOTES: Third revised edition, covers to 1994, minor editing to first edition content.

160th Regiment, Royal Armoured Corps	160 RAC

RAC service: 15/07/1942   01/04/1943 (Revert to inf.)
Converted Bns: The Royal Sussex Regiment
                  9th Bn = 160 RAC

Regimental publications:
The Roussillon Gazette: a journal of The Royal Sussex Regiment
Vol. 12, No. 1 Jan 1923 to Vol. 37, No. 4 Summer 1966 (Quarterly)

An Outline History of The Royal Sussex Regiment 1701 - 1949
Not stated   PCL
Brighton; The Dolphin Press Ltd; 1949; ISBN None; 23pp/No illus.; s/b; Indexed N; Glossary N; Appendices N; Bibliography N; 189 x 127 (12mo); Uncommon
NOTES: Pocket history, no mention of 160 RAC.

A History of The Royal Sussex Regiment
A History of The Old Belfast Regiment and the Regiment of Sussex 1701 - 1953
Martineau, G. D. IWM; NAM; RMAS; PCL
Chichester; Moore & Tillyer Ltd; 1953; ISBN None; 324pp/13 x bw M; h/b (d/j - ne) Blue cloth; Indexed Y; Glossary N; Appendices N; Bibliography N; 222 x 147 (8vo)
NOTES: Two paragraphs loosely describe 9th Bn's brief conversion to tanks.

An Outline History of The Royal Sussex Regiment 1701 - 1954
Not stated PCL
Chichester; Moore & Tillyer Ltd; 1954; ISBN None; 24pp/No illus.; s/b; Indexed N; Glossary N; Appendices N; Bibliography N; 189 x 127 (12mo); Uncommon
NOTES: Reprint, with minor updates, of 1949 pocket history.

The Royal Sussex Regiment Handbook 1701 - 1955
Not stated
Plymouth; Clarke, Doble & Brendon Ltd; 1955; ISBN None; 36pp/4 x bw Pl/2 x bw Sl; p/b; Indexed N; Glossary N; Appendices N; Bibliography N; 218 x 140 (8vo); Rare
NOTES: Overview handbook for serving soldiers. Single paragraph reference to 9th Bn converting to tanks. Updated version published 1959 - no mention of 9th Bn or 160 RAC.

The Shiny Ninth
9th Battalion The Royal Sussex Regiment 1940 - 1946
Gillings, Murray IWM; NAM
Wittering; The Pinwe Club; 1986; ISBN 0 9511610 0 8; xiii + 176pp/25 x bw Pl/1 x bw SIfep/17 x bw M; s/b; Indexed Y; Glossary N; Appendices Y; Bibliography Y; 209 x 154 (8vo); Uncommon
NOTES: Summary 5pp cover 9th Bn in the role of tanks.

The Shiny Ninth
9th Battalion The Royal Sussex Regiment 1940 - 1946
Gillings, Murray
Wittering; The Pinwe Club; 2001 [Special Edition]; ISBN 0 9511610 0 8; xiii + 176pp + 14pp/25 x bw Pl/1 x bw SIfep/17 x bw M; s/b; Indexed Y; Glossary N; Appendices Y; Bibliography Y; 209 x 154 (8vo) ; Uncommon
NOTES: Updated reprint with a 14pp appendix of new (non-RAC) matter.

161st Regiment, Royal Armoured Corps	*161 RAC*

RAC service: 07/1942 12/10/1943 (Became 161R)
Converted Bns: The Green Howards (Alexandra Princess of Wales's Own Yorkshire Regiment)
12th Bn = 161 RAC then 161R

Regimental publications:
The Green Howards Gazette: A Monthly Chronicle of Alexandra, Princess of Wales's Own (Yorkshire Regiment)
Vol. 5, No. 49 Apr 1897 to not established (at least 1976) (Monthly)

The Story Of The Green Howards 1939-1945
Synge, Capt. W. A. T.   IWM; NAM; RMAS; PCL
Richmond; The Green Howards; 1952; ISBN None; xxviii + 428pp/22 x bw PI/15 x clr Mf; h/b (d/j - ne) Green cloth; Indexed Y; Glossary N; Appendices Y; Bibliography N; 222 x 148 (8vo); Uncommon
NOTES: Sadly, the relevant references to the 12th Bn contain factual errors. Two paragraphs, one incorrectly stating that the 12th converted to 161R, not 161 RAC, in July 1942 and one paragraph implying the replacement squadron for 43R was due to fighting casualties rather than the shipwreck.

The Green Howards
(The 19th Regiment of Foot)
(Famous Regiments)
Powell, Geoffrey   TM; IWM; NAM; RMAS
London; Hamish Hamilton Ltd; 1968; ISBN None; 144pp/13 x bw PI/19 x bw SI; h/b / d/j Blue cloth; Indexed N; Glossary N; Appendices N; Bibliography Y; 221 x 142 (8vo)
NOTES: No reference to 12th Bn.

The Green Howards
(Famous Regiments)
Powell, Geoffrey   IWM; NAM; RMAS
London; Leo Cooper (Martin Secker & Warburg); 1983; ISBN 0-436-37910-4; 150pp/15 x bw PI/19 x bw SI; s/b; Indexed N; Glossary N; Appendices N; Bibliography Y; 221 x 142 (8vo)
NOTES: No reference to 12th Bn. Updated edition with one extra chapter covering 1968 - 1982.

The History Of The Green Howards
Three Hundred Years of Service
Powell, Geoffrey   TM; IWM; NAM; RMAS
London; Arms and Armour Press; 1992; ISBN 1-85409-149-2; 287pp/3 x bw PIfep/5 x clr PI/28 x clr SI/92 x bw PI/9 x bw SI/14 x bw M; h/b / d/j Green cloth; Indexed Y; Glossary Y; Appendices Y; Bibliography Y; 241 x 161 (8vo)
NOTES: No reference to 161 RAC.

It's The Same Brush...
A History of the 12th Battalion Green Howards and its Successors The 161st Regiment Royal Armoured Corps (Green Howards) and The 161st Reconnaissance Regiment Royal Armoured Corps
Sylvester, Fred (Vic)]   NAM
No imprint; No imprint; 1997; ISBN None; 150pp/8 x bw PI/2 x bw SI; s/b; Indexed N; Glossary N; Appendices Y; Bibliography Y; 297 x 210 (4to); Rare
NOTES: The author joined 161 RAC early in 1943 and was one of the men detailed to join 43R in 1944. He recounts the history of 161 RAC/R, units which never fought as regiments, but which supplied one squadron wholesale to replace 43R's losses in the Derrycunihy sinking of June 1944. Full of regimental detail, especially uniform and vehicle notes. Appendices include officer lists for 12th Bn GH and 161 RAC and relevant notes extracted from the Green Howards Gazette. 30pp on 161 RAC, 60pp on 161R. Reproduced dot-matrix format.

The History Of The Green Howards
Three Hundred Years of Service
Powell, Geoffrey and Powell, John RMAS; PCL
Barnsley; Leo Cooper; 2002; ISBN 085052 857 7; 316pp/2 x bw PIfep/5 x clr PI/28 x clr SI/82 x bw PI/7 x bw SI/15 x bw M; h/b / d/j Green cloth; Indexed Y; Glossary N; Appendices Y; Bibliography Y; 240 x 160 (8vo)
NOTES: Revised and enlarged reprint of 1992 first edition. No reference to 161 RAC.

The Green Howards
A History In Photographs 1855 - 2006
Chapman, M.B.E., M.A., Maj. Roger IWM
Scarborough; The Green Howards Regimental Museum in association with Great Northern Publishing; 2006; ISBN 095401412 / 9780954014124; 392pp/1 x bw PIfep/1048 x bw PI; h/b / d/j Black cloth; Indexed N; Glossary N; Appendices Y; Bibliography Y; 240 x 160 (8vo)
NOTES: No narrative mention of 161 RAC, 1 x photograph of officers of 161 RAC in 1942 incorrectly titled as 161R.

162nd Regiment, Royal Armoured Corps — 162 RAC

RAC service: 28/07/1942   20/07/1943 (Disbanded)
Converted Bns: The Queen's Own (Royal West Kent Regiment)
                     9th Bn = 162 RAC

Regimental publications:
The Queen's Own Gazette: a record of the 50th Regimental doings
Vol. 1, No. 1 – 1 Jan 1875 to Vol. 77, No. 2 Feb 1961 (Monthly)

The Queen's Own Royal West Kent Regiment 1920-1950
Chaplin, Lt-Col H. D. TM; IWM; NAM; RMAS
London; Michael Joseph Ltd; 1954; ISBN None; 510pp/1 x clr SIfep/40 x bw PI/1 x bw SI/2 x bw Mbds/7 x bw Mf/20 x bw M; h/b / d/j Blue cloth; Indexed Y; Glossary N; Appendices Y; Bibliography N; 231 x 159 (8vo)
NOTES: Brief 1½pp on 9th Bn/162 RAC. Tucked in errata slip. RoH/Honours/Awards.

The Queen's Own Royal West Kent Regiment
A Short Account of its Origins, Services & Campaigns 1756 - 1956
Chaplin, Lt-Col H. D. IWM; PCL
Maidstone; Kent Messenger; n.d. [c.1956]; ISBN None; 47pp/9 x bw M; s/b; Indexed N; Glossary N; Appendices N; Bibliography N; 215 x 140 (8vo); Uncommon
NOTES: One passing reference to 9th Bn transferring to the RAC.

The Queen's Own Royal West Kent Regiment
The Dirty Half-Hundred (The 50th/97th Regiment of Foot)
(Famous Regiments)
Holloway, Roger; Horrocks, Lt.-Gen. Sir Brian (Ed.) TM; IWM; NAM; RMAS; PCL
London; Leo Cooper Ltd; 1973; ISBN 085052 141 6; 117pp/18 x bw PI/9 x bw SI; h/b / d/j Blue cloth; Indexed N; Glossary N; Appendices Y; Bibliography N; 222 x 141 (8vo)
NOTES: No reference to 9th Bn/162 RAC.

163rd Regiment, Royal Armoured Corps	163 RAC

RAC service: 30/07/1942 01/12/1943 (Revert to inf.)
Converted Bns: The Sherwood Foresters (Nottinghamshire and Derbyshire Regiment)
9th Bn = 112 RAC & 13th Bn = 163 RAC

Regimental publications:
The Sherwood Foresters, Nottinghamshire and Derbyshire Regiment: Regimental Annual
No. 7 1920 to No. 25 1938 (Annual) Suspended 1940 – 1947, replaced by
The Forester: the Regimental Journal of The Sherwood Foresters (Nottinghamshire and Derbyshire Regiment)
Vol. 1, No. 1 Sept 1948 to Vol. 6, No. 9 Jan 1970 (Half-yearly)

The History Of The Sherwood Foresters (Nottinghamshire and Derbyshire Regiment) 1919-1957
Barclay, C.B.E., D.S.O., Brig. C. N. IWM; NAM; RMAS; PCL
London; William Clowes and Sons Limited; 1959; ISBN None; xvi + 182pp/1 x clr SIfep/25 x bw Pl/4 x bw Mf/10 x bw M; h/b (d/j - ne) Red & green cloth; Indexed Y; Glossary N; Appendices Y; Bibliography N; 247 x 183 (8vo)
NOTES: Two paragraphs each on 112 RAC and 163 RAC. Appendices list COs of the regiments.

The Sherwood Foresters Nottinghamshire and Derbyshire Regiment
A Regiment of the Mercian Brigade
Regimental History and Recruiting Handbook
Not stated
London; Malcolm Page Limited; n.d. [c.1962]; ISBN None; 96pp/14 x bw Pl/1 x bw M; s/b; Indexed N; Glossary N; Appendices N; Bibliography N; 215 x 139 (8vo); Uncommon
NOTES: Regimental recruiting handbook, 4pp on WWII, no mention of 163 RAC.

Key to Book Entries
Book Title and Sub-title(s)
Author   Museum Holdings
Place of Publication; Publisher; Date of Publication; ISBN; Pages/Illustrations; Binding; Indexed; Glossary; Appendices; Bibliography; Size (in mm); Availability
NOTES:

Section XI

Corps of Royal Engineers

The Corps of Royal Engineers provided the services of a wide range of specialists for the Army - railways, airfield construction, postal services, pipeline supplies, etc. Those who served in tanks were referred to as Armoured Engineers.

Armoured Engineers appeared mid-way through the war. Although Royal Engineer units were on the strength of armoured divisions from the outset, the progression of tactical doctrine for armoured warfare took time to develop and gain approval for engineers in armoured vehicles. The first armoured vehicles to be provided to engineer units were Bren Gun Carriers toward the end of 1942. The first true armoured vehicle the engineers worked with were the Scorpion flail tanks in the lead-up to the battle of El Alamein, 1942. These were manned by RAC personnel but also had a Royal Engineer sapper to operate the flail mechanism. It would not be until mid-1943, after 79th Armoured Division came into existence, that the Royal Engineers themselves crewed and operated armoured vehicles.

This mid-war point saw an explosion of inventiveness and an enormous increase in the production and development of specialized equipment for the Allied armies - one type of which was known as the 'Funnies'. These specialized tanks were developed, in part, to breach Hitler's Atlantic Wall and enable the Allies to ensure they gained that critical foothold in North-West Europe.

Armoured Engineers utilized many of the specialized tanks; the one they became synonymous with was the A.V.R.E., the Armoured Vehicle Royal Engineer, based on the Churchill tank. As well as the books listed below, the reader may wish to consult 'Section XV - Armoured Divisions' where additional information can be found on the A.V.R.E. and other specialist armour that the engineers utilized.

In addition to the published and privately printed titles listed here, anyone interested in further reading can find many more monographs and deposited memoirs at some of the major libraries, especially the Imperial War Museum.

Corps of Royal Engineers

Corps publications:
The Sapper
Published from 1895 to date.
Currently every two months.

Engineers in the Italian Campaign 1943 - 1945
Bailey, O.B.E., R.E., Lt-Col D. C. TM; IWM; NAM; RE
Not stated; Printing and Stationery Services, C.M.F.; 1945; ISBN None; xiii + 101pp/61 x bw Pl/2 x bw Sl/7 x clr Mf/1 x clr M/2 x bw M; s/b; Indexed N; Glossary N; Appendices N; Bibliography N; 228 x 179 (8vo); Uncommon
NOTES: A review of most aspects of the Royal Engineers' work in Italy, where they provided much of the infrastructure the Army required. Passing reference to Armoured Engineers rather than a combat history of them. Includes reference to 7AD RE, 25 AEB, 1 Scorpion Regt and 101 RTR. Contains a complete OoB for engineers in Italy 1943-45. 2000 printed November 1945.

The Royal Engineers
Sixth Armoured Division
Not stated TM; IWM; RE
Padova; Tipografia Antoniana; 1946; ISBN None; 164pp/45 x bw Pl/13 x bw M; h/b Blue cloth; Indexed N; Glossary Y; Appendices N; Bibliography N; 243 x 171 (8vo); Uncommon
NOTES: This book looks at the work of the Field Park Sqns of 6th Armoured Division's Royal Engineers. Armoured Engineers would have been employed by the division rather than being an integral part of it and do not form part of the narrative. RoH by each sqn. Honours/Awards. Includes 31 tables at rear comprising a War Diary extract from May 1944 to May 1945. Came in a card slip case.

History of the Corps of Royal Engineers
Volume VIII 1938 - 1948
Campaigns in France and Belgium, 1939-40. Norway, Middle East, North West Africa, and Activities in the U.K.
Pakenham-Walsh, C.B., M.C., Maj-Gen. R. P. TM; IWM; NAM; PCL; RE
Chatham; The Institute of Royal Engineers; 1958; ISBN None; xv + 488pp/1 x bw Plfep/1 x clr Sl/7 x bw Mf/12 x bw M; h/b / d/j Red cloth; Indexed Y; Glossary N; Appendices N; Bibliography N; 228 x 152 (8vo); Uncommon
NOTES: This first volume covering WWII lays out an overview of the RE plus a history of their involvement in the first half of the war. Introductory coverage of the Assault Engineers in 6pp, these are dealt with fully in companion Vol IX. For such a large scope and relatively small armoured part of the story the book has a good working index.

History of the Corps of Royal Engineers
Volume IX 1938 - 1948
Campaigns in Sicily and Italy: The War Against Japan: North-West Europe, 1944-45: Minor and Non-Operational Areas: Post-War, 1945-48.
Pakenham-Walsh, C.B., M.C., Maj-Gen. R. P. TM; IWM; NAM; RMAS; PCL; RE
Chatham; The Institute of Royal Engineers; 1958; ISBN None; xviii + 644pp/1 x bw PIfep/49 x bw SI/10 x bw Mf/13 x bw M; h/b / d/j Red cloth; Indexed Y; Glossary N; Appendices N; Bibliography N; 228 x 152 (8vo); Uncommon
NOTES: This volume looks at the second half of the war and the increased use of Armoured Engineers, culminating in their apogee of operations in NWE 1944/45; a third of the book covers all RE activity in NWE. Provides an excellent overview of where and when Armoured Engineers were involved. Although space is limited, the narrative provides some specific operation details.

The Royal Engineers
(Famous Regiments)
Boyd, Derek; Horrocks, Lt.-Gen. Sir Brian (Ed.) PCL; RE
London; Leo Cooper Ltd; 1975; ISBN 0 85052 197 1; xxii + 162pp/1 x bw PIfep/20 x bw PI/16 x bw SI/2 x bw M; h/b / d/j Blue cloth; Indexed N; Glossary N; Appendices Y; Bibliography N; 221 x 141 (8vo)
NOTES: Brief reference to early Flails in the desert, Arks in Italy and a little more on 1st Assault Brigade in NWE.

A Short History of The Royal Engineers
Not stated PCL
Chatham; The Institution of Royal Engineers; 1993; ISBN None; 74pp + 12pp Appdx/6 x clr PI/16 x clr SI/3 x bw SI/1 x bw Mf; s/b; Indexed N; Glossary N; Appendices Y; Bibliography N; 210 x 148 (8vo)
NOTES: 1pp reference to Armoured Engineers.

Follow The Sapper
An Illustrated History of the Corps of Royal Engineers
Napier, Gerald TM; NAM; RMAS; PCL; RE
Chatham; The Institution of Royal Engineers; 2005; ISBN 0-903530-26-0; 251pp/illus. bds/235 x clr PI/1 x clr SIfep/41 x clr SI/180 x bw PI/24 x bw SI/6 x clr M; h/b / d/j Blue cloth; Indexed Y; Glossary N; Appendices N; Bibliography Y; 316 x 250 (Folio)
NOTES: 3pp reference to Armoured Engineers.

A Short History of the Corps of Royal Engineers
Aston, Maj. TM; PCL; RE
Chatham; The Institution of Royal Engineers; 2006; ISBN 0-903530-28-7 / 978-0903530-28-6; 132pp/; s/b; Indexed N; Glossary N; Appendices N; Bibliography N; 210 x 148 (8vo)
NOTES: Updated publication of 1993 short history. Good summary reference to Armoured Engineers in 3pp.

Engineers in the Italian Campaign
Bailey, O.B.E., R.E., Lt-Col D. C.
Not stated; Military Library Research Service Ltd; 2008; ISBN 9781847913401; See Notes; s/b; Indexed N; Glossary N; Appendices N; Bibliography N
NOTES: Facsimile reprint by MLRS Books of 1945 first edition.

5th Armoured Engineer Regiment, R.E. [5 Armd Engr Regt, RE]

5 Armoured Engineer Regiment
H Hour D Day - VE Day
Not stated NAM
No imprint; No imprint; n.d. [c.1945]; ISBN None; 49pp/No illus.; s/b; Indexed N; Glossary N; Appendices N; Bibliography N; 209 x 170 (8vo); Rare
NOTES: No narrative but a Roll of Honour plus 'Rolls of Members Serving on VE Day' for each engineer squadron. RoH/Honours/Awards.

5 Armoured Engineer Regiment
Assault Royal Engineers VE Reunion May 1995
Holmes, James H. TM
No imprint; No imprint ; 1995; ISBN None; 131pp/27 x clr PI/2 x clr SI/68 x bw PI/8 x bw SI/1 x bw M; h/b / d/j Blue paper; Indexed N; Glossary N; Appendices N; Bibliography N; 207 x 150 (8vo); Rare
NOTES: Almost like a collage of memories, this is a curious book put together by an RE veteran. Some of the photos have been photocopied from their source and very poorly printed but overall a fascinating potted collection of Assault Engineer history. Includes 79th Armoured Engineer Squadron RoH.

26th Assault Squadron, R.E. [26 Ass Sqn, RE]

Two Six
A History of 26 Armoured Engineer Squadron
Todd, Capt. P. K. A. RE
Germany; No imprint; 1958; ISBN None; 45pp/No illus.; s/b; Indexed N; Glossary N; Appendices N; Bibliography N; 248 x 201 (8vo); V Rare
NOTES: Privately printed typescript. 13pp summary of the squadron's activities in NWE.

82nd Assault Squadron, R.E. [82 Ass Sqn, RE]

82
North West Europe 1944 - 45
Not stated
No imprint (Hamburg); No imprint (Conrad Kayser - printers); n.d. [1945]; ISBN None; 36pp/Illus. See Notes; s/b; Indexed N; Glossary N; Appendices N; Bibliography N; 128 x 215 (24mo); V Rare
NOTES: With no proper title, sometimes referred to as *Chronicles of 82 Assault Sqn*. Brief summary of events from 6th June 1944, lists of serving officers and ORs, 4pp maps, 20pp of illustrations by Lt B Haward. (Not physically inspected.)

82
North West Europe 1944 - 45
Not stated RE
No imprint; No imprint (J W Parrott, Dover - printers); n.d.; ISBN None; 43pp/26 x bw SI/5 x bw M; s/b; Indexed N; Glossary N; Appendices N; Bibliography N; 198 x 325 (8vo); V Rare
NOTES: Expanded version of booklet above, RoH and serving members lists.

Key to Book Entries
Book Title and Sub-title(s)
Author Museum Holdings
Place of Publication; Publisher; Date of Publication; ISBN; Pages/Illustrations; Binding; Indexed; Glossary; Appendices; Bibliography; Size (in mm); Availability
NOTES:

Section XII

Foot Guards

Britain had a shortage of armoured troops in 1940-41 and what existed was either committed in North Africa or kept in the UK for home defence. In early 1941 the army decided that some existing infantry units needed to be converted to armour and the Brigade of Guards offered a ready-made, well-trained source, albeit initially at variance with their traditional role. Armour was very much in vogue at the time so any natural reticence in adopting tanks was not too difficult to overcome.

The Guards Armoured Division was formed in June 1941 and under the tactical thinking of the time, it consisted of two armoured brigades. 5th Guards Armoured Brigade would remain under the division, whilst 6th Guards Armoured Brigade would become an independent infantry support brigade and change its title to 6th Guards Tank Brigade to reflect that. After training and doctrine had settled, the two brigades would retain their regimental structure from 1943 to the end of the war.

In total, seven armoured battalions of Foot Guards were raised during WWII - raised and disbanded within four years. They were brigaded thus:

5th Guards Armoured Brigade
2nd (Armoured) Battalion, Grenadier Guards
1st (Armoured) Battalion, Coldstream Guards
2nd (Armoured) Battalion, Irish Guards
and as divisional reconnaissance:
2nd (Armoured Reconnaissance) Battalion, Welsh Guards

6th Guards Tank Brigade
4th Tank Battalion, Grenadier Guards
4th Tank Battalion, Coldstream Guards
3rd Tank Battalion, Scots Guards

The armoured Guards retained an infantry connection with respect to their nomenclature - tank units used the term regiment, infantry units the term battalion. The armoured Foot Guards retained 'battalion' instead of adopting 'regiment' but in order to comply with tactical discipline, 'squadron' and 'troop' were adopted within the battalions.

The armoured Guards provided a substantial portion of the forty-one tank regiments which operated in NWE; all seven Guards battalions served there between July 1944 and May 1945. All the battalions reverted to infantry very quickly after hostilities had ceased and on 9 June 1945, the Guards held a 'Farewell to Armour' parade on Rotenburg airfield.

Foot Guards

Regimental publications:
The Household Brigade Magazine
1920 to Spring 1968. (Quarterly)

Fighting With the Guards
Briant, Keith   IWM; NAM; PCL
London; Evans Brothers Limited; 1958; ISBN None; x + 224pp/1 x bw PIfep/26 x bw PI/4 x bw SI; h/b / d/j Blue cloth; Indexed Y; Glossary N; Appendices N; Bibliography Y; 215 x 146 (8vo)
NOTES: Although a general subject book, the armoured Guards regiments receive a well summarised 43pp, mainly of their operations in NWE.

Fighting With the Guards
Cadet Edition
Briant, Keith
London; Evans Brothers Limited; 1960; ISBN None; 191pp/1 x bw PIfep/13 x bw PI/2 x bw SI/2 x bw M; h/b / d/j Blue cloth; Indexed N; Glossary N; Appendices N; Bibliography N; 202 x 135 (8vo)
NOTES: Revised reprint of the 1958 first edition.

The British Foot Guards
A Bibliography
Silverthorne L. C. and Gaskin, W. D.   IWM; NAM; PCL
Cornwallville, NY; Hope Farm Press; 1960; ISBN None; 68pp/No illus.; s/b; Indexed Y; Glossary N; Appendices N; Bibliography Y; 239 x 158 (8vo); V Rare
NOTES: Lists 217 works with descriptions up to its publication date of 1960. Number 2 in the Dornbusch Military Series. 300 copies printed.

The Story of the Guards
Paget, Julian   IWM; NAM; PCL
London; Osprey Publishing Ltd; 1976; ISBN 0 85045 078 0; 304pp/17 x clr PI/12 x clr SI/46 x bw PI/38 x bw SI/11 x bw M; h/b / d/j Blue cloth; Indexed Y; Glossary Y; Appendices N; Bibliography Y; 292 x 218 (4to)
NOTES: A general history of the Household Division (Household Cavalry and Foot Guards) presented in chronological order. Fair summary of armoured Guards in NWE, 19pp on armoured regiments. Index mis-references 4 Gren with 4 Cold Gds and does not indicate these were armoured regiments, likewise 3 Scots Gds. Reprinted 1979.

All the Queen's Men
The Household Cavalry and the Brigade of Guards
Braddon, Russell
London; Hamish Hamilton Ltd; 1977; ISBN 241 89431 X; 288pp/Various clr & bw illus.; h/b / d/j Red/black cloth; Indexed Y; Glossary N; Appendices N; Bibliography N; 252 x 196 (4to)
NOTES: An overview history of the Household Division with a brief 6pp on the HCav and Foot Guards in WWII.

FOOT GUARDS   239

All the Queen's Men
The Household Cavalry and the Brigade of Guards
Braddon, Russell   TM; NAM
Not stated; Book Club Associates; 1977; ISBN None; 288pp/Various clr & bw illus.; h/b / d/j Red/black cloth; Indexed Y; Glossary N; Appendices ; Bibliography N; 250 x 192 (4to)
NOTES: Reprint of 1977 first edition.

The Story of the Guards
Paget, Julian   RMAS; PCL
London; Michael Joseph Limited; 1979; ISBN None; 304pp/17 x clr PI/30 x clr SI/27 x bw PI/39 x bw SI/11 x bw M; h/b / d/j Blue cloth; Indexed Y; Glossary Y; Appendices N; Bibliography Y; 292 x 218 (4to)
NOTES: Hardback reprint of 1976 first edition, same pagination.

Grenadier Guards   GREN GDS

Regimental publications:
The Grenadier Gazette. The Regimental Journal of the Grenadier Guards
No. 1 1978 to current (Annual)

The Grenadier Guards 1939 - 1945
Not stated   IWM; PCL
Aldershot; Gale & Polden Ltd; 1946; ISBN None; viii + 79pp/2 x bw PIfep/38 x bw PI/4 x clr Mf/6 x clr M/1 x bw M; s/b; Indexed N; Glossary N; Appendices N; Bibliography N; 240 x 160 (8vo)
NOTES: Produced as a souvenir history for soldiers of the Grenadiers. A précised account prepared and published whilst Gale & Polden's full two volume set was in preparation. The maps are enhanced by coloured lines indicating the routes of the different battalions; couple of minor date errors.

The Grenadier Guards in the War of 1939 - 1945
Volume I The Campaigns in North West Europe
Forbes, Patrick   TM; IWM; RMAS
Aldershot; Gale & Polden Limited; 1949; ISBN None; xvi + 256pp + xix Index/1 x clr SIfep/19 x bw PI/7 x clr Mf/14 x clr M/2 x bw M; h/b / d/j Blue cloth; Indexed Y; Glossary N; Appendices N; Bibliography N; 248 x 160 (8vo)
NOTES: The early days of the battalions are covered briefly before their operations in NWE are reviewed in detail. There is limited information on the equipment and uniforms used; the narrative is officer-centric. Maps are enhanced by the use of colour denoting the battalion and line style denoting time periods. See Vol. II for the RoH/Honours/Awards and the appendices. Patrick Forbes served in the 4th Tank Bn, Grenadier Gds and also wrote the history of the 6th Guards Tank Brigade. Volume I reuses several sections thereof in reference to the 4th Tank Bn.

The Grenadier Guards in the War of 1939 – 1945
Volume II The Mediterranean Campaigns
Nicholson, M.B.E., Capt. Nigel TM; IWM; NAM; PCL
Aldershot; Gale & Polden Limited; 1949; ISBN None; xi + pp259 to 582 + xix Index/1 x bw PIfep/24 x bw PI/1 x bw SI/7 x clr Mf/5 x clr M/6 x bw M; h/b / d/j Blue cloth; Indexed Y; Glossary N; Appendices Y; Bibliography N; 248 x 160 (8vo)
NOTES: No narrative on the armoured regiments in this volume. Appendices include list of COs plus RoH - highly detailed casualty lists, Honours/Awards.

History of the Grenadier Guards [Abridged] 1656 - 1949
Martin, Capt. F. IWM; NAM; PCL
Aldershot; Gale & Polden Limited; 1951; ISBN None; vi + 66pp/1 x bw PIfep; h/b / d/j Blue cloth; Indexed N; Glossary N; Appendices N; Bibliography N; 186 x 122 (12mo)
NOTES: Published for members of the regiment, 43pp on WWII, 14pp on the armoured battalions.

The Grenadier Guards
Tercentenary Year 1656-1956
A Pictorial Record of the Historic Celebrations of 1956
Not stated RMAS
Ipswich; W. S. Cowell Limited; 1957; ISBN None; 89pp/1 x clr SIfep/1 x clr SI/48 x bw PI/27 x bw SI; h/b Red cloth; Indexed N; Glossary N; Appendices N; Bibliography N; 273 x 217 (4to)
NOTES: Published following the Tercentenary Exhibition held at St James's Palace in 1956. One paragraph on armoured regiments.

The Grenadier Guards
(Famous Regiments)
Whitworth, R. H.; Horrocks, Lt.-Gen. Sir Brian (Ed.) TM; IWM; NAM; PCL
London; Leo Cooper Ltd; 1974; ISBN 0 85052 152 1; 122pp/14 x bw PI/6 x bw SI; h/b / d/j Blue cloth; Indexed N; Glossary N; Appendices Y; Bibliography N; 222 x 140 (8vo)
NOTES: Five pages on 2nd and 4th armoured battalions.

The Grenadier Guards
Osprey Men At Arms Series
Fraser, Gen. Sir David; Additional research by Marrion, R. J. NAM; RMAS; PCL
and Fosten, D. S. V.
London; Osprey Publishing Ltd; 1978; ISBN 0 85045 284 8; 40pp/8 x clr PI/51 x bw PI/12 x bw SI; s/b; Indexed N; Glossary N; Appendices N; Bibliography N; 246 x 183 (8vo)
NOTES: From the Osprey Men-At-Arms series, No. 73, providing an overview of the regiment. 4pp on WWII, brief comment on armoured battalions, one illustration. Reprinted several times.

The British Grenadiers
Three Hundred and Fifty Years of the First Regiment of Foot Guards 1656-2006
Hanning, Henry RMAS; PCL
Barnsley; Pen & Sword Military; 2006; ISBN 1 84415 385 1 / 978 1 84415 385 5; 320pp/109 x clr PI/126 x clr SI/125 x bw PI/35 x bw SI/36 x clr M; h/b / d/j Red cloth; Indexed Y; Glossary N; Appendices Y; Bibliography Y; 278 x 198 (4to)
NOTES: Summary of the regiment in 8pp, references Forbes' Vol. I.

The Grenadier Guards in the War 1939 - 1945
Vol 1 North West Europe
Vol 2 Mediterranean
Forbes, Patrick & Nicholson, Capt. Nigel
Uckfield; Naval & Military Press Ltd; 2010; ISBN 978 1845748760; See Notes; s/b; Indexed Y; Glossary N; Appendices Y; Bibliography N
NOTES: Facsimile reprint by NMP of 1949 first edition, available in s/b.

2nd (Armoured) Battalion, Grenadier Guards	2 GREN GDS

Dates of mechanization: May 1941   June 1945

It's Been a Lot of Fun
An autobiography
Johnston, Brian
London; W. H. Allen & Co. Ltd.; 1974; ISBN 0 491 01471 6; 310pp/36 x bw PI; h/b / d/j Brown cloth; Indexed Y; Glossary N; Appendices N; Bibliography N; 222 x 140 (8vo)
NOTES: The author, a well-known BBC cricket commentator, signed up with the Grenadier Gds in the Officer Cadet Reserve when war broke out. In May 1940 he joined the 2nd Bn, being appointed Transport Officer later that year. Once the battalion became armoured, he became the Technical Adjutant, a role he maintained until the war's end. He gives a generally light-hearted review of his time with the Guards throughout the war but remains informative. (There are many repurposed titles relating to BJ which have not been included here.)

It's Been a Lot of Fun
An autobiography
Johnston, Brian
London; Star Books; 1976; ISBN 0 35239 810 8; See Notes; p/b; Indexed Y; Glossary N; Appendices N; Bibliography N
NOTES: Paperback reprint of 1974 first edition; several reprints. (Not physically inspected.)

Reflect on Things Past
The Memoirs of Lord Carrington
Lord Carrington TM; IWM
London; William Collins Sons & Co. Ltd; 1988; ISBN 0 00 217667 X; x + 406pp/30 x bw PI; h/b / d/j Black cloth; Indexed Y; Glossary N; Appendices N; Bibliography N; 238 x 162 (8vo)

NOTES: The author was commissioned before the war into the Grenadiers, joining the 2nd Bn. Provides an interesting few passages on the merits of converting Britain's premier infantry to tanks. He served as squadron 2 i/c, then OC, through NWE and passes comment on a few selected incidents; 46pp on WWII and 27pp on armoured Grenadiers. Reprinted twice in 1988.

Reflect on Things Past
The Memoirs of Lord Carrington
Lord Carrington
Glasgow; Fontana Paperbacks; 1989; ISBN 0 00 637462 X; viii + 408pp/17 x bw PI; p/b; Indexed Y; Glossary N; Appendices N; Bibliography N; 177 x 110 (12mo)
NOTES: Paperback reprint of 1988 first edition, narrative content has same pagination.

Second Battalion Grenadier Guards 1686 - 1994
A Commemoration of The Models
Russell-Parsons, Maj. D. J. C. and Davies, Lt J. L. NAM
Ipswich; Aldermans (Printers); 1994; ISBN None; 32pp/95 x clr PI/8 x bw PI/4 x clr SI/1x clr M; s/b; Indexed N; Glossary N; Appendices N; Bibliography N; 247 x 185 (8vo)
NOTES: Commemorative booklet produced upon the placing of the Second Battalion into suspended animation. 2pp on WWII, focusing on Arnhem.

Letters Home
1926 - 1945
Johnston, Brian (Johnston, Barry, Ed.)
London; Weidenfeld & Nicolson; 1998; ISBN 0 297 84127 0; xxxi + 383pp/46 x bw PI/1 x bw SI; h/b / d/j Green cloth; Indexed Y; Glossary N; Appendices N; Bibliography N; 240 x 162 (8vo)
NOTES: Brian Johnston wrote to his mother regularly throughout the war; his son has transcribed and compiled many of those letters. The war period is reproduced in 118pp, in tanks 40pp. Generally little direct comment on tanks; those for the period in NWE provide a view into how men in the front line could communicate news back home and how effective the postal system was between home and the front line, for officers at least. Plenty of footnotes to explain comments, names, etc. Includes several personal wartime photographs.

Letters Home
1926 - 1945
Johnston, Brian (Johnston, Barry, Ed.)
London; Orion Books Ltd; 1999; ISBN 0 75282 613 1; xxxi + 384pp/46 x bw PI/1 x bw SI; p/b; Indexed Y; Glossary N; Appendices N; Bibliography N; 197 x 128 (12mo)
NOTES: Paperback reprint of 1998 first edition, same pagination.

Wars and Shadows
Memoirs of General Sir David Fraser
Fraser, General Sir, David TM; NAM
London; Allen Lane The Penguin Press; 2002; ISBN 0-71399-627-7; viii + 328pp/1 x bw PIfep/19 x bw PI/5 x bw SI; h/b / d/j Blue cloth; Indexed Y; Glossary N; Appendices N; Bibliography N; 240 x 160 (8vo)

NOTES: At the start of the war, the author signed up with the Gordon Highlanders. Following interludes with college and the Home Guard he joined the Guards in September 1940. He was commissioned into the 1st Bn but soon transferred to the 2nd Bn, just as they were converting to tanks. He recounts many memories of personalities he met during his service including William Douglas Home, Oliver Leese, Montgomery, Rex Whistler, plus several others. He served in several roles, in No 2 Sqn and HQ Tp and describes many aspects of life and action in NWE, 148pp cover WWII and 99pp in tanks.

Wars and Shadows
Memoirs of General Sir David Fraser
Fraser, General Sir, David
London; Penguin Books; 2003; ISBN 0-14-100859-8; viii + 328pp/1 x bw PIfep/19 x bw PI/5 x bw SI; p/b; Indexed Y; Glossary N; Appendices N; Bibliography N; 197 x 128 (12mo)
NOTES: Paperback reprint of 2002 first edition, same pagination.

4th Tank Battalion, Grenadier Guards* | 4 GREN GDS

* Formed as 4th (Armoured) Battalion, Grenadier Guards.

Dates of mechanization: May 1941   June 1945

A Charmed Life
Grenadier Guards 1936-46
Crosthwaite, D.S.O., E.R.D., Ivor   NAM
Pangbourne; TWM Publishing; 1996; ISBN 07457 5157 1; 127pp/1 x PIfep/4 x bw PI; s/b; Indexed N; Glossary N; Appendices Y; Bibliography N; 204 x 145 (8vo)
NOTES: Several years before the war, the author joined the Supplementary Reserve of the Grenadier Guards, transferring to the 2nd Bn in June 1939. He transferred to the 4th Bn soon after they started conversion to tanks. He recounts his time as a squadron commander in chapter sized recollections. Appendices include notes on No. 3 Sqn officers, awards, organisation of the squadron, and notes on the Churchill tank.

Pawn Shop Dick
Fear, Ray
Stoke on Trent; Ray Fear; 2005; ISBN 978-0-9550218-0-0 / 0-955-0218-0-4; 314pp/1 x bw PIfep/40 x bw PI; s/b; Indexed N; Glossary N; Appendices N; Bibliography N; 210 x 148 (8vo)
NOTES: Brief 15pp cover the author's service with No. 2 Sqn, 4th Bn. Sent to Normandy as a casualty replacement, he was sent back to the Delivery Squadron when discovered to be underage. He returned to the front line in the spring of 1945.

2623520 Gdsm. Kennedy, D. J. 6th Guards Tank Brigade Reminiscences
Kennedy, Guardsman D. J.   TM; IWM
No imprint (Worksop); No imprint (Ryton Typing Service - printers); n.d.; ISBN None; 40pp/9 x bw PI/1 x bw SI; s/b; Indexed N; Glossary N; Appendices N; Bibliography N; 210 x 148 (8vo); Uncommon

NOTES: The author served in No. 3 Sqn, 4th Tank Battalion, Grenadier Guards. The memoirs are a reproduction of the diary he kept covering 1 January 1945 to 28 April 1945.

Coldstream Guards   COLD GDS

Regimental publications:
Coldstream Gazette. The Journal of the Old Coldstreamers' Association
No. 1 1923 to current (Annual), currently
Coldstream Gazette. The Journal of The Coldstream Guards Association

Nulli Secundus
The Record of the Coldstream Guards 1650 - 1950
Marker, D.S.O., Col R. J.; Dawnay, C.B.E, D.S.O., Maj-Gen. A. G. C. & Col Hill, E. R.   IWM
London; William Clowes and Sons Limited; 1950; ISBN None; xii + 91pp/1 x bw Mrbds/5 x bw M; h/b Beige cloth; Indexed N; Glossary N; Appendices Y; Bibliography Y; 189 x 140 (12mo)
NOTES: Brief summary of both armoured regiments within 7pp, 27pp cover WWII. 1939-45 section written by Col E. R. Hill.

The Coldstream Guards 1920 - 1946
Howard, Michael & Sparrow, John   TM; IWM; RMAS; PCL
London; Oxford University Press; 1951; ISBN None; xvii + 593pp/20 x bw M/8 x bw Mf; h/b / d/j Blue cloth; Indexed Y; Glossary Y; Appendices Y; Bibliography N; 258 x 167 (4to)
NOTES: Sparse coverage of formation and early days. The narrative has the useful addition of the date in the margins. It follows the journey of each regiment, modest amount of detail with regard to equipment and uniforms, structure, etc. Comprehensive RoH listed by theatre and battalion, including service number. Appendices include lists of COs, Adjutants, QMs, WOs, Honours/Awards, and a 'Record of Services – Officers' (running to 56pp) listing their service and promotions, OoBs for each battalion at July 1944 and May 1945.

Colours and Customs of the Coldstream Guards
Coldstream Guards
London; Regimental Headquarters, Coldstream Guards; 1951; ISBN None; 43pp/No illus.; h/b Red cloth; Indexed N; Glossary N; Appendices N; Bibliography Y; 165 x 105 (16mo); Uncommon
NOTES: Produced 'for the use of officers only'. No information on armoured regiments but interesting for the social aspects of Guards officers. (Original 1921 with reprints 1931, 1940, 1944, 1951 and 1978.)

The Colonels of the Coldstream Regiment of Foot Guards
Coldstream Guards
No imprint; No imprint; n.d. [c.1955]; ISBN None; 48pp/See Notes; h/b Red cloth; Rare
NOTES: Reproduced typescript biographies of all colonels of the Coldstream Guards listing all their known portraits. (Not physically inspected.)

The Coldstream Guards
Osprey Men At Arms Series
Grant, Charles RMAS; PCL
Reading; Osprey Publishing Ltd; 1971; ISBN 85045 057 8; 40pp/8 x clr Pl/13 x bw PI/30 x bw SI; s/b; Indexed N; Glossary N; Appendices N; Bibliography N; 247 x 184 (8vo)
NOTES: From the Osprey Men-At-Arms series, No. 49, providing an overview of the regiment. Three summary paragraphs on armoured battalions. Reprinted several times.

Second to None
The Coldstream Guards 1650 - 2000
Paget, Julian (Ed.); Chapters individually authoured. TM; IWM; NAM; RMAS; PCL
Barnsley; Leo Cooper; 2000; ISBN 085052 769 4; 350pp/1 x clr PIfep/23 x clr PI/11 x clr SI/127 x bw PI/17 x bw SI/11 x bw M; h/b / d/j Blue cloth; Indexed Y; Glossary N; Appendices N; Bibliography Y; 259 x 193 (4to)
NOTES: Well summarised history of the two regiments within 29pp, 65pp on WWII in total. 1939-45 chapter written by Hugh Boscawen.

1st (Armoured) Battalion, Coldstream Guards — 1 COLD GDS

Dates of mechanization: May 1941   June 1945

1st Armoured Battalion Coldstream Guards
North-West Europe June 1944 - May 1945
Not stated TM
Aldershot; Gale & Polden Ltd; 1946; ISBN None; 44pp/No illus.; s/b (card); Indexed N; Glossary N; Appendices N; Bibliography N; 185 x 123 (12mo); Rare
NOTES: Consists of a reproduction of the unit's newsletter published periodically in NWE. It is a fairly detailed narrative history of the battalion in NWE, without any of the usual domestic newsletter entries.

Armoured Guardsmen
A War Diary June 1944 - April 1945
Boscawen, Robert TM
Barnsley; Leo Cooper; 2001; ISBN 0 85052 748 1; viii + 232pp/33 x bw PI/10 x bw M; h/b / d/j Black cloth; Indexed Y; Glossary Y; Appendices N; Bibliography N; 240 x 157 (8vo)
NOTES: The author joined up in 1941 and, after attending OCTU in the first half of 1942, was commissioned into the Coldstream Guards. In September 1942 he joined No. 2 Sqn, 1st Bn. The memoirs consist of his diary plus explanatory narrative, starting with the journey to Normandy. His original diary finishes at the end of March 1945 where it covers the squadron's experiments in attaching Typhoon rockets to the tanks. He continues the narrative, describing how he was badly burnt when his tank was hit just weeks before the German surrender. Lucid and engaging, this is a particularly informative set of memoirs.

Armoured Guardsmen
A War Diary, June 1944 - April 1945
Boscawen, Robert
Barnsley; Pen & Sword Military; 2010; ISBN 978 1 84884 317 2; viii + 232pp/33 x bw PI/10 x bw M; s/b; Indexed Y; Glossary Y; Appendices N; Bibliography N; 233 x 156 (8vo)
NOTES: Softback reprint of 2001 first edition, same pagination.

4th Tank Battalion, Coldstream Guards* — 4 COLD GDS

* Formed as 4th (Armoured) Battalion, Coldstream Guards.

Dates of mechanization: May 1941   June 1945

The Life of a Boy
Daniel Meinertzhagen 1925 - 1944
Meinertzhagen, Richard   TM
Edinburgh; Oliver and Boyd; 1947; ISBN None; v + 181pp/1 x bw SIfep/6 x bw PI; h/b / d/j Black cloth; Indexed N; Glossary N; Appendices N; Bibliography N; 221 x 147 (8vo); Uncommon
NOTES: The author has created a tribute to his son, Daniel Meinertzhagen, combining his own narrative, letters and diary with DM's letters and diary. DM joined the Guards Training Depot in January 1943 having been selected to join the Coldstream Gds in tanks. A good selection of his diary/letters is reproduced covering the time in training and at Sandhurst. These provide an interesting view into this young man's thoughts and habits as an officer to be. He was commissioned into the Coldstream Guards (he won Sandhurst's Belt of Honour) in November 1943, being assigned to the 4th Bn in January 1944. DM continued to write letters and update his diary up to 1 October 1944, the following day he was killed, aged 19½. Highly recommended.

Memoirs Of An Old Soldier Both On Active Service And In Peace Through The Ranks
Duffield, M.B.E., Captain C. V.
No imprint; No imprint (Purnell S S Ltd, Printers); 1997; ISBN None; 87pp/1 x clr PIfep/60 x bw PI/1 x clr SI/1 x bw SI/1 x bw M; s/b; Indexed N; Glossary N; Appendices N; Bibliography N; 247 x 172 (8vo); Uncommon
NOTES: The author joined the Guards in 1934, serving in the 1st Bn as an instructor at the Guards Depot. He fought in France in 1940 and after returning to England he joined the 4th Bn as Colour Sergeant; early 1944 he became an SSM. He mentions the period of NWE in just two paragraphs. One photograph relating to 4th Tank Bn.

FOOT GUARDS 247

| 3rd Tank Battalion, Scots Guards* | 3 SCOTS GDS |

* Formed as 3rd (Armoured) Battalion, Scots Guards.

Dates of mechanization: May 1941   June 1945

The Scots Guards
Not stated   PCL
London; Crick, Canning & Crick on behalf of The Scots Guards; n.d. [c.1950]; ISBN None; 56pp/27 x bw PI; s/b; Indexed N; Glossary N; Appendices N; Bibliography N; 184 x 122 (12mo); Uncommon
NOTES: Post War recruiting pamphlet. One page of brief information listing the armoured regiment.

The Scots Guards 1919 - 1955
Erskine, David   TM; IWM; NAM; RMAS; PCL
London; William Clowes and Sons Limited; 1956; ISBN None; xx + 624pp/1 x bw PIfep/44 x bw PI/21 x bw Mf/27 x bw M; h/b / d/j Blue cloth; Indexed Y; Glossary N; Appendices Y; Bibliography N; 253 x 162 (4to)
NOTES: Well detailed narrative of the regiment's actions aided by the date running through the margins. The 3rd Bn's entries are easy to follow with page headings and footnotes delineating the relevant pages within chapters. RoH includes Bn, country of death and service number. Appendices include awards listed by Bn, lists of appointments, OoB for officer appointment at start, mid and end of campaign, Nominal Roll of Officers, notes on uniforms, etc.

Scots Guards
Scotland's Own Regiment of Foot Guards
Scots Guards   IWM; NAM
Glasgow; The Paramount Press; 1959; ISBN None; 82pp/1 x clr PIfep/4 x clr PI/38 x bw PI; s/b; Indexed N; Glossary N; Appendices N; Bibliography N; 214 x 136 (8vo); Rare
NOTES: 1950s recruiting booklet. Primarily a pictorial account, passing reference to armoured Guards and one photograph of a Scots Guards Churchill in NWE.

A Short History of the Scots Guards 1642-1962
With Some Notes on the Colours, Badges and Customs of the Regiment
Swinton, Maj. John   PCL
Aldershot; Gale & Polden Ltd; 1963; ISBN None; 44pp/1 x clr SIfep/1 x clr SI/2 x bw PI/35 x bw SI; s/b; Indexed N; Glossary N; Appendices N; Bibliography N; 181 x 120 (12mo)
NOTES: Aimed at new recruits, one sentence reference to 3rd Tank Bn.

The Scots Guards (The 3rd Guards)
(Famous Regiments)
Gooding, Anthony; Horrocks, Lt.-Gen. Sir Brian (Ed.)   TM; IWM; NAM; RMAS; PCL
London; Leo Cooper Ltd; 1969; ISBN 85052 012 6; vi and 149pp/24 x bw PI/6 x bw SI/1 x bw M; h/b / d/j Blue cloth; Indexed N; Glossary N; Appendices N; Bibliography N; 222 x 140 (8vo)
NOTES: 2pp on 3rd Tank Bn.

The Whitelaw Memoirs
Whitelaw, William
London; Aurum Press Ltd; 1989; ISBN 1 85410 028 9; vii + 280pp/27 x bw PI/3 x bw SI; h/b / d/j Red cloth; Indexed Y; Glossary N; Appendices N; Bibliography N; 240 x 162 (8vo)
NOTES: The author was posted to 3rd Bn soon after it formed in 1940 in the role of Transport Officer. Once the battalion converted to tanks, he became the Technical Adjutant. By the time of the landing in France he had become OC S Sqn. Soon after their first action he was promoted to Bn 2 i/c. He recounts his wartime experiences in a very succinct 10pp. Includes two photographs of 3rd Bn officer groups, 1942 and 1943.

The Whitelaw Memoirs
Whitelaw, William
London; Headline; 1990; ISBN 0 7472 3348 9; ix + 370pp/21 x bw PI/3 x bw SI; p/b; Indexed Y; Glossary N; Appendices N; Bibliography N; 176 x 110 (12mo)
NOTES: Paperback reprint of 1989 first edition, different pagination and reduced photograph selection.

350 Glorious Years 1642 - 1992
Kinloch, Wallace and Couser, Ralph (Eds.)
Edinburgh; Lady Haig's Poppy Factory; 1993; ISBN 0 9521598 0 5; 413pp/48 x bw PI/12 x bw SI/8 x bw M; h/b / d/j (cloth - ne); Indexed N; Glossary N; Appendices N; Bibliography N; Uncommon
NOTES: A collection of anecdotes, poems, and reminiscences covering 350 years. Naturally infantry-centric, there are 8pp of armoured Guards' recollections plus 26pp selected from *The Scots Guards 1919 - 1955* by Erskine, q.v. (This edition not physically inspected.)

350 Glorious Years 1642 - 1992
Kinloch, Wallace and Couser, Ralph (Eds.)
Edinburgh; Lady Haig's Poppy Factory; 1993; ISBN 0 9521598 1 3; 413pp/48 x bw PI/12 x bw SI/8 x bw M; s/b; Indexed N; Glossary N; Appendices N; Bibliography N; 247 x 156 (8vo); Uncommon
NOTES: Softback reprint of hardback first edition.

The Whitelaw Memoirs
Whitelaw, William
York; Wilton 65; 1998; ISBN 0 947828 62 1; 280pp/See Notes; s/b
NOTES: Reprint of 1989 first edtion by Wilton 65. (Not physically inspected.)

Reflections 1939-1945
A Scots Guards Officer in Training and War
Farrell, Charles
Bishop Auckland; The Pentland Press Ltd; 2000; ISBN 1-85821-761-X; xii + 161pp/1 x clr PIfep/3 x bw PI/2 x bw M; h/b / d/j Black cloth; Indexed Y; Glossary N; Appendices Y; Bibliography N; 216 x 151 (8vo)
NOTES: The author joined the Scots Gds as a 2nd Lt in October 1939. He variously served with the Ski Bn in 1940, as 2 i/c and OC Left Flank Sqn, and LO with XXX Corps. Following the heavy casualties sustained during the regiment's first engagement he

became a squadron commander. Taking command of S Sqn from Maj. W Whitelaw at the end of July 1944, he commanded it to the end of the war. In these memoirs he aims to counterbalance some of the revisionist works prevalent during the 1990s on the British Army's efficiency. Some fascinating comment on the politics of Guards in tanks and Montgomery's attitudes.

The Scots Guards 1919 – 1955
Erskine, David
Uckfield; Naval & Military Press Ltd; 2001; ISBN 978 1843420613; See Notes; Indexed Y; Glossary N; Appendices Y; Bibliography N
NOTES: Facsimile reprint by NMP of 1956 first edition, available in s/b and h/b.

The Scots Guards
Hendrie, William F. and Smith, Jack   PCL
Stroud; Tempus Publishing Limited; 2002; ISBN 0 7524 2399 1; 128pp/1 x bw PIfep/205 x bw PI/12 x bw SI; s/b; Indexed N; Glossary N; Appendices N; Bibliography N; 234 x 163 (8vo)
NOTES: Pictorial history, poor reference for 3rd Bn, most armour related photos are of Gds AD rather than 3rd Bn SG.

2nd (Armoured) Battalion, Irish Guards   2 IRISH GDS

Dates of mechanization: May 1941   June 1945

Regimental publications:
Irish Guards Association Journal
No. 1 1935 to current (Annual)

The Second Troop
Not stated [See Notes]   IWM
No imprint; No imprint; n.d. [c.1946]; ISBN None; 47pp/5 x bw PI/12 x bw M; s/b (card); Indexed N; Glossary N; Appendices N; Bibliography N; 250 x 186 (4to); V Rare
NOTES: Written by a troop leader of No. 3 Sqn, IG, the author starts these recollections upon re-joining the battalion in Holland 1944 after earlier being wounded. Although entitled The Second Troop, the narrative deals mostly with Third Troop. Very detailed recollections of actions he was involved in, late 1944/1945. Contains detailed lists of 3 Troop at various dates from Nov 1944 to May 1945 including crew lists, plus a list of those who served in 3 Troop at some time. Author is Lt G. N. R. Whitfield.

Hugh Dormer's Diaries
Dormer, Hugh   TM; IWM; NAM
London; Jonathan Cape; 1947; ISBN None; 159pp/1 x bw M; h/b / d/j Red cloth; Indexed N; Glossary N; Appendices N; Bibliography N; 205 x 138 (8vo); Uncommon
NOTES: This book reproduces extracts from the author's diaries starting with his first SOE operation in April 1943. He left the 2nd Bn in the autumn of 1942 to join SOE but returned to the battalion in October 1943. Just under a quarter of the book covers his time with the armoured Guards. In France he was serving in SHQ of No. 2 Sqn; the diary ends with his death in Normandy in July 1944.

History of the Irish Guards in the Second World War
Fitzgerald, M.C., Maj. D. J. L.   IWM; RMAS; PCL
Aldershot; Gale & Polden Ltd; 1949; ISBN None; xv + 615pp/30 x bw PI/2 x bw Mf/20 x bw M; h/b / d/j Brown cloth; Indexed Y; Glossary N; Appendices N; Bibliography N; 220 x 148 (8vo)
NOTES: The narrative is more engaging than many histories, with plenty of quotes and actions with named soldiers. Very little on the early days. For an infantry regiment, the tank battalion is given generous space in this history. Much of the narrative is shared with the 3rd Bn, both battalions fought together in NWE. RoH is by theatre and sub-theatre and then battalion, includes service number. RoH/Honours/Awards.

History of the Irish Guards in the Second World War
Fitzgerald, M.C., Maj. D. J. L.   TM; NAM; RMAS
Aldershot; Gale & Polden Ltd; 1952; ISBN None; xv + 615pp/30 x bw PI/2 x bw Mf/20 x bw M; h/b / d/j Blue cloth; Indexed Y; Glossary N; Appendices N; Bibliography N; 220 x 148 (8vo)
NOTES: Reprint of 1949 first edition.

Irish Guards
Irish Regiment of Foot Guards
Not stated   PCL
Aldershot; Gale & Polden Ltd; n.d. [c.1952]; ISBN None; 4pp/No illus.; Folded sheet; Indexed N; Glossary N; Appendices N; Bibliography N; 215 x 138 (8vo); Uncommon
NOTES: Single folded sheet, brief pocket history. One paragraph mentioning the armoured regiment.

The Micks
the story of the Irish Guards 1900 to 1970
Verney, Peter   IWM; NAM
London; Peter Davies; 1970; ISBN 432 18650 6; xvi + 207pp/14 x bw PI/1 x bw SI/15 x bw M; h/b / d/j Blue cloth; Indexed Y; Glossary N; Appendices N; Bibliography N; 241 x 158 (8vo); Uncommon
NOTES: Draws on Fitzgerald's history and is a naturally abbreviated form of it, 36pp cover the armoured battalion in WWII. 2nd and 3rd Bns' stories are interwoven over these pages.

The Micks
The story of the Irish Guards
Verney, Peter
London; Pan Books Ltd; 1973; ISBN 0 330 23632 6; xvii + 237pp/12 x bw PI/1 x bw SI/15 x bw M; p/b; Indexed Y; Glossary N; Appendices N; Bibliography N; 178 x 112 (12mo); Uncommon
NOTES: Abridged paperback reprint of 1970 first edition.

History of the Irish Guards in the Second World War
Fitzgerald, M.C., Maj. D. J. L.   TM
London; The Irish Guards; 1986; ISBN None; xv + 615pp/21 x bw M; s/b; Indexed Y; Glossary N; Appendices N; Bibliography N; 215 x 138 (8vo)

NOTES: Facsimile reprint of 1949 edition but without photographs. 200pp on 2nd Bn. RoH/Honours/Awards.

War Diary
Dormer, Hugh
Sevenoaks; Fisher Press; 1994; ISBN 1 874037 11 6; 142pp/1 x bw PI/1 x bw SI/3 x bw M; s/b; Indexed N; Glossary N; Appendices N; Bibliography N; 198 x 130 (8vo); Uncommon
NOTES: Softback reprint of *Hugh Dormer's Diaries*, 1947. Contains additional diary entries from an early war naval action in which HD was involved.

Hugh Dormer's Diaries
Dormer, Hugh
Not stated; Richard Netherwood Limited; 1995; ISBN 1-872955-15-0; 159pp/1 x bw M; h/b / d/j Red cloth; Indexed N; Glossary N; Appendices N; Bibliography N; 206 x 140 (8vo)
NOTES: Facsimile reprint of the 1947 first edition on behalf of regiment.

War Diary
Dormer, Hugh
Sevenoaks; Fisher Press; 1998; ISBN 1 874037 11 6; vi + 142pp/1 x bw PI/1 x bw SI/3 x bw M; s/b; Indexed N; Glossary N; Appendices N; Bibliography N; 198 x 130 (8vo)
NOTES: Reprint of 1994 Fisher Press edition with new foreword and preface, different pagination to original publication.

The Armoured Micks 1941 to 1945
Taylor, Capt. Vivian and Faris, Capt. Sandy (Ed.)   TM; IWM; NAM
Not stated; Regimental Headquarters Irish Guards; 1997; ISBN None; vi + 149pp + 21pp unnumbered photo section/97 x bw PI; s/b; Indexed N; Glossary Y; Appendices Y; Bibliography N; 290 x 208 (4to); Rare
NOTES: An introductory history in 8pp, with the remainder of the book given to many reminiscences from members of the regiment. An excellent photo section at the rear of the book. IWM copy rebound.

Irish Guards
The First Hundred Years 1900-2000
Irish Guards   IWM; NAM; RMAS; PCL
Staplehurst; Spellmount Limited; 2000; ISBN 1-86227-069-4; 223pp/122 x clr PI/13 x clr SI/154 x bw PI/8 x bw SI/2 x bw M; h/b / d/j Blue cloth; Indexed Y; Glossary Y; Appendices Y; Bibliography Y; 281 x 226 (4to)
NOTES: A pictorial history. 29pp on WWII with 8pp for 2nd Bn.

The Times of My Life
An Autobiography
Gorman, Sir John   TM
Barnsley; Leo Cooper; 2002; ISBN 0 85052 906 9; viii + 228pp/30 x bw PI; h/b / d/j Green cloth; Indexed Y; Glossary N; Appendices N; Bibliography N; 240 x 160 (4to)

NOTES: The author briefly recounts his childhood before recalling his early army career training to be an officer in the RAC. In Normandy he commanded No. 4 Tp, No. 2 Sqn and, amongst recollections of NWE, describes his famous action wherein he rammed his tank into a King Tiger; a photograph of the result is reproduced. 44pp on WWII. Reprinted 2003. Also published with alternative dust-jacket title - *Always A Mick, The Autobiography of Sir John Gorman*.

2nd (Armoured Reconnaissance) Battalion, Welsh Guards*	4 WELSH GDS

* Formed as 2nd (Armoured) Battalion, Welsh Guards.

Dates of mechanization: May 1941   June 1945

Regimental publications:
Welsh Guards Regimental Magazine
Current (Annual)

Welsh Guards at War
Ellis, C.V.O., C.B.E., D.S.O., M.C., Maj. L. F.   TM; IWM; RMAS; PCL
Aldershot; Gale & Polden Limited; 1946; ISBN None; xiii + 386pp/1 x clr SIfep/58 x bw PI/8 x clr SI/29 x bw SI/4 x clr M/27 x bw M; h/b / d/j Green cloth; Indexed Y; Glossary N; Appendices N; Bibliography N; 220 x 145 (8vo)
NOTES: This history is split into two parts, the first of which provides a summary review of each of the battalions throughout the war. The second part provides a detailed description of each battalion's actions in their theatres of operation, this being NWE for 2nd (Armd Recce) Bn. The 2nd Bn is fully represented throughout this well composed history. Sparse as regards equipment and uniform information. Includes several extracts from the War Diary and named references to officers. At the end of the book is a photo section; opposite each picture page is a full narrative commentary rather than a one-line caption. RoH includes service number but does not differentiate by battalion. Honours/Awards. Reprinted 1989 by NMP and 1990 by London Stamp Exchange.

Welsh Guards
A Short Account of their Achievements
Not stated
Colchester; Benham & Co; 1946; ISBN None; 80pp/See Notes; s/b
NOTES: Not physically inspected.

Wales and the Welsh Guards
Jones-Mortimer, Maj. H.
Cardiff; Western Mail and Echo; 1948; ISBN None; 48pp/See Notes
NOTES: Not physically inspected.

The Work of Rex Whistler
Whistler, Laurence; Fuller, Ronald   NAM
London; B. T. Batsford Ltd; 1960; ISBN None; xxiv + 112 Plates + 122pp/Fully illus.; h/b / d/j Green cloth; Indexed Y; Glossary N; Appendices N; Bibliography Y; 306 x 230 (Folio); Uncommon

FOOT GUARDS 253

NOTES: This book is a catalogue listing 700 pieces of RW's work; no biographical content relating to his war service.

Welsh Guards 1915 - 1965
An Informal Account of the Fifty Years 1915-1965
Not stated IWM; NAM; PCL
Devonport; Hiorns & Miller Ltd; 1965; ISBN None; 164pp/1 x clr SIfep/4 x clr PI/120 x bw PI/2 x clr SI/9 x bw SI; s/b; Indexed N; Glossary N; Appendices N; Bibliography N; 246 x 182 (8vo)
NOTES: Very occasional reference to 2nd Bn.

The Welsh Guards
(Famous Regiments)
Retallack, John; Horrocks, Lt.-Gen. Sir Brian (Ed.) IWM; NAM; RMAS; PCL
London; Frederick Warne (Publishers) Ltd; 1981; ISBN 0 7232 2746 2; 177pp/6 x bw PI/10 x bw SI; h/b / d/j Blue cloth; Indexed Y; Glossary N; Appendices N; Bibliography N; 222 x 140 (8vo)
NOTES: The WG being a young regiment, this summary history is dominated by WWII. 2nd Bn receives a considerable share of the narrative.

The Laughter and the Urn
The Life of Rex Whistler
Whistler, Laurence
London; George Weidenfeld & Nicholson Limited; 1985; ISBN 0 297 78603 2; xiv + 321pp/11 x bw PI/17 x clr SI/25 x bw SI; h/b / d/j Blue cloth; Indexed Y; Glossary N; Appendices N; Bibliography Y; 240 x 162 (8vo)
NOTES: Biography of Rex Whistler by his brother. Contains a few illustrations of RW's paintings/drawings pertinent to the war, including a Medusa based proposal for the Guards Armoured Division. RW joined the WG in 1940 and went on to lead 15 Tp, No. 3 Sqn into action in Normandy. He was killed in the regiment's first action during Operation Goodwood, July 1944. 66pp cover the period of WWII, 47 of these on the WG.

The Laughter and the Urn
The Life of Rex Whistler
Whistler, Laurence
London; George Weidenfeld & Nicholson Limited; 1987; ISBN 0-297-79021-8; xiv + 321pp/11 x bw PI/17 x clr SI/25 x bw SI; s/b; Indexed Y; Glossary N; Appendices N; Bibliography Y; 233 x 154 (8vo)
NOTES: Softback reprint of 1985 first edition, same pagination.

Welsh Guards at War
Ellis, Maj. L. F. NAM; PCL
London; The London Stamp Exchange Ltd (The Military & Naval Book Specialists); 1990; ISBN 0 948130 52 0; xiii + 386pp/1 x clr SIfep/58 x bw PI/8 x clr SI/29 x bw SI/4 x clr M/27 x bw M; h/b / d/j Red cloth; Indexed Y; Glossary N; Appendices N; Bibliography N; 223 x 143 (8vo)
NOTES: Facsimile reprint of 1946 first edition.

Anatomy of a Regiment
Ceremony and Soldiering in the Welsh Guards
Royle, Trevor IWM; NAM; RMAS; PCL
London; Michael Joseph; 1990; ISBN 0 7181 3306 4; xiv + 257pp/24 x bw PI/2 x bw SI; h/b / d/j Blue cloth; Indexed Y; Glossary N; Appendices N; Bibliography N; 240 x 156 (8vo)
NOTES: This is a thematic history – essentially, what is it like to be a Welsh Guardsman? The chapters are organized by subject matter, hence the chronology is per chapter, not through the book. Little on 2nd (Armd Recce) Bn that is not in the *Welsh Guards at War* main history.

Rex Whistler's War 1939 - July 1944
Artist into Tank Commander
Catalogue to the Special Exhibition at the National Army Museum, London 18 May - 18 September 1994
Spencer-Smith, Jenny NAM
London; National Army Museum; 1994; ISBN 0-901721-29-8 (0-901721-31-X 2nd Edn); 180pp/2 x clr PI/1 x bw PIfep/7 x bw PI/40 x clr SI/29 x bw SI/; s/b; Indexed Y; Glossary N; Appendices N; Bibliography Y; 296 x 208 (4to)
NOTES: Catalogue of the NAM's special exhibition presenting RW's artwork from the war period. Full explanatory narrative accompanies the catalogued list of exhibits, themselves fully annotated. Includes some detailed information on the battalion's tank equipment. Two editions published 1994. This book and *In Search of Rex Whistler*, q.v., provide the most informative coverage of RW's military life.

Rex Whistler's War 1939 - July 1944
Artist into Tank Commander
Catalogue to the Special Exhibition at the National Army Museum, London 18 May - 18 September 1994
Spencer-Smith, Jenny
London; Spellmount Publishers Ltd; 1998; ISBN 978-1873376898; See Notes; s/b; Indexed Y; Glossary N; Appendices N; Bibliography Y; Uncommon
NOTES: Revised edition of 1994 first edition by NAM. (Not physically inspected.)

Welsh Guards at War
Ellis, Maj. L. F.
Uckfield; The Naval & Military Press Ltd.; 2001; ISBN 978 1843421634; See Notes; s/b; Indexed Y; Glossary N; Appendices N; Bibliography N
NOTES: Facsimile reprint by NMP of 1946 first edition, available in s/b.

In Search of Rex Whistler
His Life and His Work
Cecil, Hugh & Mirabel
London; Francis Lincoln Limited; 2012; ISBN 978-0-7112-3230-3; 272pp/Fully illus.; h/b / d/j Grey cloth; Indexed Y; Glossary N; Appendices Y; Bibliography Y; 293 x 235 (4to)
NOTES: Beautifully and profusely illustrated biography as befits the artist; 44pp of narrative cover his time as a soldier. This book and the NAM catalogue, q.v., provide the most informative coverage of RW's military life.

Welsh Guards at War
Ellis, Maj. L. F.
Smalldale; MLRS Books; 2013; ISBN 978-1847917850; See Notes
NOTES: Facsimile reprint by MLRS Books of 1946 first edition.

Key to Book Entries
Book Title and Sub-title(s)
Author   Museum Holdings
Place of Publication; Publisher; Date of Publication; ISBN; Pages/Illustrations; Binding; Indexed; Glossary; Appendices; Bibliography; Size (in mm); Availability
NOTES:

Section XIII

Royal Marines

Most of the books listed in this section provide only a nod to the existence of the Royal Marine Armoured Support Group (RMASG), mainly due to the vast range of duties which the Royal Marines carried out in WWII. The work which provides the most detailed and authoritative information is James Ladd's *By Sea, By Land*, the culmination of many years' writing on the history of the Royal Marines.

Their story in tanks is that of only a few weeks on active service. Formed initially as the Royal Marine Support Craft Regiment, they started to train for their role of close artillery support from the summer of 1943. In February 1944 the title was changed to Royal Marine Armoured Support Group and comprised 1st and 2nd Royal Marine Armoured Support Regiments and 5th (Independent) Royal Marine Armoured Support Battery.

Landing on D-Day, the regiments operated mainly Centaur Close Support tanks together with Shermans for the troop leaders. Just over two weeks later the tanks had been disposed of and RMASG was disbanded in September 1944. In early 1945 some Royal Marines were reacquainted with armour upon the formation of the 34th Amphibious Support Regiment, itself on active service for just a couple of months.

Royal Marines

Corps publications:
Globe & Laurel
Published from 1892 to current.
Currently six times a year.

Short History of the Royal Marines
Grover, O.B.E., Col G. W. M.　　　　　　　　　　　　　　　　　　　　IWM; PCL
Aldershot; Gale & Polden Ltd; 1948; ISBN None; 68pp/13 x bw SI/1 x bw Mf; h/b / d/j Blue cloth; Indexed N; Glossary N; Appendices Y; Bibliography N; 182 x 116 (12mo)
NOTES: 18pp on WWII with two paragraphs on the RMASG. Reprinted 1953 and second revised edition published 1959.

The Marines Were There
The Story of the Royal Marines in the Second World War
Lockhart, K.C.M.G., Sir Robert Bruce　　　　　　　　　　　　　　IWM; NAM; PCL
London; Putnam; 1950; ISBN None; 229pp/4 x clr M; h/b / d/j Blue cloth; Indexed Y; Glossary N; Appendices N; Bibliography N; 223 x 145 (8vo)
NOTES: With such a vast range of RM units and actions, this book has the unenviable task of selecting just a few examples. As a result the RMASG has just 1pp on its D-Day activities plus occasional references where they supported other RM units.

The Marines Were There
Lockhart, K.C.M.G., Sir Robert Bruce
London; Hamilton & Co. (Stafford) Ltd (A Panther Book); 1957; ISBN None; 186pp/4 x bw M; p/b; Indexed N; Glossary N; Appendices N; Bibliography N; 180 x 113 (12mo)
NOTES: Paperback reprint of 1950 first edition, different pagination.

A Short History of the Royal Marines
Grover, O.B.E., Col G. W. M.　　　　　　　　　　　　　　　　　　　　　　　PCL
Aldershot; Gale & Polden Ltd; 1959; ISBN None; 98pp/2 x clr SIfep/13 x bw SI/1 x bw Mf; s/b; Indexed N; Glossary N; Appendices Y; Bibliography N; 182 x 111 (12mo); Uncommon
NOTES: Second revised edition of 1948 first edition.

Fighting Marines
Pringle, Patrick　　　　　　　　　　　　　　　　　　　　　　　　　　IWM; NAM; PCL
London; Evans Brothers Limited; 1966; ISBN None; 192pp/18 x bw PI/5 x bw SI/2 x bw M; h/b / d/j Blue cloth; Indexed N; Glossary N; Appendices N; Bibliography N; 208 x 134 (8vo)
NOTES: Brief two paragraph reference to armoured support.

The Royal Marines
(Famous Regiments)
Moulton, Maj-Gen. J. L.; Horrocks, Lt.-Gen. Sir Brian (Ed.)　　　　TM; IWM; NAM
London; Leo Cooper Ltd; 1972; ISBN 0 85052 117 3; x + 100pp/13 x bw PI/10 x bw SI; h/b / d/j Red cloth; Indexed N; Glossary N; Appendices N; Bibliography Y; 222 x 142 (8vo)

NOTES: One informative paragraph on the RMASG's creation. One reference to 34th Royal Marine Amphibian Support Regiment. Reprinted in softback same year of publication.

The Royal Marines
(Famous Regiments)
Moulton, Maj-Gen. J. L.; Horrocks, Lt.-Gen. Sir Brian (Ed.)
London; Leo Cooper Ltd; 1972; ISBN 0 85052 121 1; x + 100pp/13 x bw PI/10 x bw SI; s/b; Indexed N; Glossary N; Appendices N; Bibliography Y; 215 x 136 (8vo)
NOTES: Softback reprint of hardback first edition.

Per Mare Per Terram
A History of the Royal Marines
Smith, Peter C. PCL
St Ives; A Balfour Book (Photo Precision Ltd); 1974; ISBN 0 85944 017 6; 191pp/60 x clr PI/78 x clr SI/1 x bw SI; h/bs/b Blue cloth; Indexed N; Glossary N; Appendices N; Bibliography Y; 242 x 188 (8vo)
NOTES: One sentence reference to RMASG.

The Royal Marines 1919 - 1980
An Authorised History
Ladd, James, D. IWM; NAM; PCL
London; Jane's Publishing Company Limited; 1980; ISBN 0-7106-0011-9; 482pp/98 x bw PI/20 x bw SI/19 x bw M; h/b / d/j Black cloth; Indexed Y; Glossary Y; Appendices Y; Bibliography Y; 248 x 174 (8vo)
NOTES: Comprehensive history of the RMs, 3pp refer to RMASG's activities on D-Day plus 2pp in appendices summarising armoured support formations. Revised and updated as *By Sea, By Land* in 1998, q.v.

Royal Marine Commando
Ladd, James, D. NAM
London; Hamlyn Publishing; 1982; ISBN 0 600 34203 4; 176pp/1 x clr PIfep/13 x clr PI/16 x clr SI/75 x bw PI/31 x bw SI/2 x bw M; h/b / d/j Blue cloth; Indexed Y; Glossary N; Appendices Y; Bibliography Y; 302 x 218 (4to)
NOTES: Brief reference to armoured units. Reprinted in 1982 and 1983, new edition published 1985.

Royal Marine Commando
Ladd, James, D.
London; Hamlyn Publishing; 1985; ISBN 0 600 50036 5; 192pp/1 x clr PIfep/17 x clr PI/16 x clr SI/81 x bw PI/31 x bw SI/2 x bw M; h/b / d/j Illustrated as d/j; Indexed Y; Glossary N; Appendices Y; Bibliography Y; 302 x 218 (4to)
NOTES: New edition of 1982 first edition.

The Royal Marines
A Pictorial History 1664 – 1987
Smith, Peter C. & Oakley, Derek NAM; PCL
Tunbridge Wells; Spellmount Ltd; 1988; ISBN 0-946771-32-4; 256pp/10 x clr PI/15 x clr SI/1 x bw PIfep/290 x bw PI/46 x bw SI; h/b / d/j; Indexed Y; Glossary N; Appendices Y; Bibliography Y; 278 x 204 (4to)
NOTES: A few passing references to RMASG.

The Royal Marines 1939 - 93
Elite Series 57
van der Bijl, Nick IWM; PCL
London; Osprey Publishing Ltd; 1994; ISBN 1 85532 388 5; 64pp/12 x clr SI/56 x bw PI; s/b; Indexed N; Glossary N; Appendices N; Bibliography N; 243 x 180 (8vo)
NOTES: From the Osprey Elite Series, very brief reference to RMASG, one illustration. Reprinted several times.

By Sea, By Land
The Royal Marines 1919 - 1997
The Authorised History
Ladd, James, D. IWM; PCL
London; Harper Collins Publishers; 1998; ISBN 0 00 472366 X; xvii + 606pp/10 x clr PI/33 x bw PI/1 x clr SI/5 x bw SI/19 x bw M; h/b / d/j Black cloth; Indexed Y; Glossary Y; Appendices Y; Bibliography Y; 248 x 174 (8vo)
NOTES: Definitive reference on RMASG, useful index and appendix. 2pp on RMASG's D-Day activities, plus a few paragraphs on the Amphibious Support Regiment. Revised and extensively updated edition of *The Royal Marines 1919 - 1980*, q.v.

The Royal Marines
From Sea Soldiers to a Special Force
Thompson, Julian IWM; NAM; PCL
London; Sidgwick & Jackson; 2000; ISBN 0 283 06315 7; xv + 699pp/49 x bw PI/25 x bw M; h/b / d/j Blue cloth; Indexed Y; Glossary Y; Appendices Y; Bibliography Y; 239 x 158 (8vo)
NOTES: Brief reference to RMASG in 3pp.

A Short History of the Royal Marines 1664 - 2002
Oakley, M.B.E., Capt. Derek; Donald, Maj. Alastair & Bentinck, Maj. Mark NAM; PCL
Portsmouth; The Royal Marines Historical Society; 2002; ISBN 0 9536163 1 2; 144pp/5 x clr PI/39 x clr SI/55 x bw PI/21 x bw SI/1 x bw M; s/b; Indexed N; Glossary N; Appendices Y; Bibliography N; 210 x 147 (8vo)
NOTES: Passing reference to RMASG and Amphibious Support Regiment and one photograph of RMASG Centaur in Normandy. Reprinted 2003 and revised 2004.

A Short History of the Royal Marines 1664 – 2004
Oakley, M.B.E., Capt. Derek; Donald, Maj. Alastair & Bentinck, Maj. Mark　　　IWM; NAM
Portsmouth; The Royal Marines Historical Society; 2004; ISBN 0 9536163 3 9; 160pp/5 x clr PI/57 x bw PI/40 x clr SI/47 x bw SI/2 x bw M; s/b; Indexed N; Glossary N; Appendices Y; Bibliography Y; 210 x 147 (8vo)
NOTES: Second revised edition of 2002 first edition, same coverage of RMASG and Amphibian Support Regiment.

A Short History of the Royal Marines 1664 - 2007
Not stated
Portsmouth; The Royal Marines Historical Society; 2008; ISBN 978 0 9536163 5 0; 160pp/7 x clr PI/57 x bw PI/40 x clr SI/47 x bw SI/2 x bw M; s/b; Indexed N; Glossary N; Appendices Y; Bibliography Y; 210 x 147 (8vo)
NOTES: Third revised edition, same coverage of RMASG and Amphibian Support Regiment.

Key to Book Entries
Book Title and Sub-title(s)
Author　　　　　　　　　　　　　　　　　　　　　　　　　　　　　Museum Holdings
Place of Publication; Publisher; Date of Publication; ISBN; Pages/Illustrations; Binding; Indexed; Glossary; Appendices; Bibliography; Size (in mm); Availability
NOTES:

Section XIV

Armoured Brigades

Brigades are particularly under-represented in published histories. There were thirty-four armoured brigades (excluding dummy brigades) which existed during World War Two, only ten of which are represented here. In part this is due to a lack of personal attachment (the British Army is renowned for its regimental system and allegiance so it naturally follows that regiments have a substantial body of histories) and also to the almost ephemeral nature of higher formations. They are easier to raise and disband, or to rename and repurpose from Army Tank Brigade to Tank Brigade to Armoured Brigade, as did happen to a few.

Some brigades existed for just a few months, some were short-lived vehicles for War Office policy and many existed only to train and did not go into action.

Armoured brigades frequently changed title during the course of the war. Rather than list all the brigades with the majority entered as 'No publications established', only those with entries are listed.

For a particularly useful pocket-book summarising all the brigades with their service dates and compositions, refer to *Datafile British Tanks and Formations 1939-45* by Malcom A. Bellis, details of which are on the next page.

Armoured Brigades

From the Desert to the Baltic
Roberts, C.B., D.S.O., M.C., Maj-Gen. Pip   TM; IWM
London; William Kimber & Co. Limited; 1987; ISBN 0-7183-0639-2; 256pp/30 x bw PI/15 x bw M; h/b / d/j Red cloth; Indexed Y; Glossary Y; Appendices Y; Bibliography N; 240 x 160 (8vo)
NOTES: In December 1940 the author became Brigade Major of 4AB. He provides a few details on the main characters of Bde HQ plus comment on operations late 1940/early 1941. On his time as 22AB CO the author provides technical comment regarding the tanks in use and some of their strengths and weaknesses. He provides quite detailed accounts from his perspective of the battles he was involved in. Led 22AB through the battles of Alam Halfa and El Alamein. Briefer comment on command of 26AB (13pp) and 30AB (1pp). Commands included: 3RTR Jan - Jul 1942; 22AB Jul 1942 - Jan 1943; 26AB Mar 1943 - May 1943; 30AB Aug – Oct 1943; 11AD Dec 1943 - end of war.

Datafile British Tanks and Formations 1939-45
Bellis, Malcolm A.
Crewe; Malcolm A Bellis; n.d. [1980s]; ISBN None; iv + 70pp + v/24 x bw SI; s/b; Indexed Y; Glossary N; Appendices N; Bibliography N; 145 x 208 (24mo); Rare
NOTES: Highly detailed tabular summaries of divisions, brigades and regiments. Shows dates of service, theatres, main tanks employed, insignia and summary tank specifications. There are one or two minor errors but this was pioneering information presentation and would enhance any library.

1st Armoured Brigade   1 ArmdBde

Date raised/disbanded: 14/04/1940*   21/11/1942 (Disbanded)
* Existed pre-war as 1st Light Armoured Brigade.

With the 1st Armoured Brigade in Greece
Waller, Brig. R. P.
No imprint; No imprint; 1945; ISBN None; 18pp/See Notes; Rare
NOTES: Not physically inspected.

4th Armoured Brigade   4 ArmdBde

Date raised/disbanded: 16/02/1940*   Post-war
* Existed pre-war as Heavy Armoured Brigade; 16/02/1940 retitled 4th Heavy Armoured Brigade; 14/04/1940 retitled 4th Armoured Brigade.

The History of Fourth Armoured Brigade
Carver, Brig. R. M. P.   TM; IWM; NAM; PCL
Glückstadt; J. J. Augustin/Gale & Polden; 1945; ISBN None; 46pp/No illus.; s/b; Indexed N; Glossary N; Appendices Y; Bibliography N; 250 x 184 (4to); Uncommon

NOTES: Highly detailed and informative record of the brigade's journey through NA, Italy and NWE.

Monty's Marauders
Black Rat & Red Fox: 4th & 8th Independent Armoured Brigades in WW2
Delaforce, Patrick TM; IWM
Brighton; Tom Donovan Publishing Ltd; 1997; ISBN 1-871085-36-5; 224pp/45 x bw PI/3 x bw SI/30 x bw M; h/b / d/j Black cloth; Indexed Y; Glossary N; Appendices N; Bibliography Y; 240 x 160 (8vo)
NOTES: Follows the history of each brigade chronologically through the war with the emphasis on combat actions. Provides a concentrated history for several of the regiments of each brigade. This author's trademark style is to include a great many quotations from veterans and to reproduce some of their personal photos.

Monty's Marauders
Black Rat & Red Fox: 4th & 8th Independent Armoured Brigades in WW2
Delaforce, Patrick RMAS; PCL
Brighton; Tom Donovan Publishing Ltd; 1998; ISBN 1-871085-41-1; 224pp/47 x bw PI/1 x bw SI/30 x bw M; s/b; Indexed Y; Glossary N; Appendices N; Bibliography Y; 233 x 154 (8vo)
NOTES: Softback reprint of 1997 first edition, same pagination.

Monty's Marauders
Black Rat 4th Armoured Brigade / Red Fox 8th Armoured Brigade
Delaforce, Patrick
London; Chancellor Press; 2000; ISBN 0-75370-351-3; 224pp/46 x bw PI/2 x bw SI/30 x bw M; h/b / d/j Illustrated as d/j; Indexed Y; Glossary N; Appendices N; Bibliography Y; 240 x 158 (8vo)
NOTES: Hardback reprint of 1997 first edition, same pagination. Chancellor's imprint information is incorrect, states first published in 1993 by Alan Sutton. Possible explanation is swapping of imprint information between this book and their reprint of *The Black Bull*, also in 2000.

Monty's Marauders
The 4th & 8th Armoured Brigades in the Second World War
Delaforce, Patrick NAM
Barnsley; Pen & Sword Military; 2008; ISBN 978 1 84415 630 6; 224pp/45 x bw PI/3 x bw SI/30 x bw M; h/b / d/j Black cloth; Indexed Y; Glossary N; Appendices N; Bibliography Y; 240 x 158 (8vo)
NOTES: Reprint of 1997 first edition, same pagination. Imprint information follows Chancellor's error, stating first published date as 1993 rather than 1997.

8th Armoured Brigade	8 ArmdBde

Date raised/disbanded: 01/08/1941*   Post-war
* Existed pre-war as 6th Cavalry Brigade.

The 8th Armoured Brigade 1939 - 1945
Not stated   TM; IWM; NAM; PCL
No imprint; No imprint; 1946; ISBN None; 43pp/24 x clr SI/3 x bw SI/2 x clr Mf; s/b (card); Indexed N; Glossary N; Appendices Y; Bibliography N; 242 x 166 (8vo); Uncommon
NOTES: Commemorative summary history of the brigade and its regiments, split one-third early history and NA and two-thirds NWE. Includes 'Record of Principal Engagements' of the brigade, list of COs, casualties by theatre (and by regiment for NA) and Honours/Awards by theatre. Folding maps pasted to rear cover - one for NA/ME, one for NWE. Issued with a loose compliments slip – 'With the compliments of Brigadier G. E. Prior-Palmer, D.S.O.'

Monty's Marauders
Black Rat & Red Fox: 4th & 8th Independent Armoured Brigades in WW2
Delaforce, Patrick   TM; IWM
Brighton; Tom Donovan Publishing Ltd; 1997; ISBN 1-871085-36-5; 224pp/45 x bw PI/3 x bw SI/30 x bw M; h/b / d/j Black cloth; Indexed Y; Glossary N; Appendices N; Bibliography Y; 240 x 160 (8vo)
NOTES: Follows the history of each brigade chronologically through the war with the emphasis on combat actions. Provides a concentrated history for several of the regiments of each brigade. This author's trademark style is to include a great many quotations from veterans and to reproduce some of their personal photos.

Monty's Marauders
Black Rat & Red Fox: 4th & 8th Independent Armoured Brigades in WW2
Delaforce, Patrick   RMAS; PCL
Brighton; Tom Donovan Publishing Ltd; 1998; ISBN 1-871085-41-1; 224pp/47 x bw PI/1 x bw SI/30 x bw M; s/b; Indexed Y; Glossary N; Appendices N; Bibliography Y; 233 x 154 (8vo)
NOTES: Softback reprint of 1997 first edition, same pagination.

Monty's Marauders
Black Rat 4th Armoured Brigade / Red Fox 8th Armoured Brigade
Delaforce, Patrick
London; Chancellor Press; 2000; ISBN 0-75370-351-3; 224pp/46 x bw PI/2 x bw SI/30 x bw M; h/b / d/j Illustrated as d/j; Indexed Y; Glossary N; Appendices N; Bibliography Y; 240 x 158 (8vo)
NOTES: Hardback reprint of 1997 first edition, same pagination. Chancellor's imprint information is incorrect, states first published in 1993 by Alan Sutton. Possible explanation is swapping of imprint information between this book and their reprint of *The Black Bull*, also in 2000.

Monty's Marauders
The 4th & 8th Armoured Brigades in the Second World War
Delaforce, Patrick NAM
Barnsley; Pen & Sword Military; 2008; ISBN 978 1 84415 630 6; 224pp/45 x bw Pl/3 x bw SI/30 x bw M; h/b / d/j Black cloth; Indexed Y; Glossary N; Appendices N; Bibliography Y; 240 x 158 (8vo)
NOTES: Reprint of 1997 first edition, same pagination. Imprint information follows Chancellor's error, stating first published date as 1993 rather than 1997.

22nd Armoured Brigade — 22 ArmdBde

Date raised/disbanded: 03/09/1939*   Post-war
* Formed initially under the title 22nd Heavy Armoured Brigade; retitled 22nd Armoured Brigade 14/04/1940.

22nd Armoured Brigade 1939 - 1945
Hawkes, R.A., Maj. D. M. NAM
No imprint; No imprint; 1985; ISBN None; 39pp/No illus.; h/b Red cloth; Indexed N; Glossary N; Appendices N; Bibliography N; 301 x 215 (4to); V Rare
NOTES: Privately published, overall history with details of units serving, formations, battles, etc. Includes seven overview War Establishments.

23rd Armoured Brigade — 23 ArmdBde

Date raised/disbanded: 03/09/1939*   Post-war
*As 23rd Army Tank Brigade; retitled 23rd Armoured Brigade 01/11/1940.

23rd Armoured Brigade
Operations in Greece October 15 1944 - January 7 1945
Not stated TM; IWM; NAM
Not stated; HQ, RAC, C.M.F.; 1945; ISBN None; 26pp/4 x bw SI/2 x clr Mf; s/b (card); Indexed N; Glossary N; Appendices N; Bibliography N; 340 x 216 (Folio); Rare
NOTES: 'This account sets out to give an impression of these events as seen from Bde HQ.' Official report prepared by brigade HQ, reproduced typescript, 200 copies printed (A plain typescript copy was also produced excluding the maps - print run unknown.) Includes a breakdown of killed/wounded/POWs. One map is a full copy of GSGS 4457 - MDR641/11435 ATHENS dated Sept. 1944.

Brief History of the 23rd Armoured Brigade 1939 - 1945
Not stated TM; NAM
No imprint; No imprint; 1947; ISBN None; 15pp/No illus.; s/b (card); Indexed N; Glossary N; Appendices N; Bibliography N; 186 x 124 (12mo); Uncommon
NOTES: Chronological summary history intended for members of the brigade, 'all members of the brigade should receive a copy...'

The Valentine in North Africa 1942 - 43
Armour in Action 1
Perrett, Bryan TM; IWM; NAM
London; Ian Allan Ltd; 1972; ISBN 7110 0262 2; 80pp/86 x bw Pl/5 x bw SI/6 x bw M; h/b / d/j Brown cloth; Indexed N; Glossary N; Appendices Y; Bibliography N; 222 x 140 (8vo)
NOTES: Whilst this book deals with the Valentine tank, it is also very much a history of 40, 46 and 50RTR, the Valentine equipped regiments of 23AB in North Africa July 1942 to May 1943. Well written and engaging. Included are many veterans' quotations and the author provides insights into these men in the narrative with asides as to their professions after the war. Well illustrated. Appendices include an overview of the Valentine and a brief history of 23AB.

26th Armoured Brigade — 26 ArmdBde

Date raised/disbanded: 12/10/1940* Post-war
* Formed as 1st Motor Machine Gun Brigade 30/05/1940; retitled 26th Armoured Brigade 12/10/1940.

26th Armoured Brigade Account of Operations May - Nov 1944
Not stated TM
Not stated; Not stated; n.d. [c.1940s]; ISBN None; 30pp/2 x clr Mf; Card folded; Indexed N; Glossary N; Appendices Y; Bibliography N; 342 x 214 (Folio); Rare
NOTES: Official typescript report including personnel and vehicle casualties.

31st Armoured Brigade — 31 ArmdBde

Date raised/disbanded: 15/01/1941* Post-war
* As 31st Army Tank Brigade; retitled 31st Tank Brigade 05/1942; retitled 31st Armoured Brigade 02/02/1945.

Frolics in the Thirty First
Not stated TM
Not stated; Not stated; n.d. [1945]; ISBN None; 36pp/Fully illustrated; h/b Brown cloth; Indexed N; Glossary N; Appendices N; Bibliography N; 176 x 230 (12mo); V Rare
NOTES: Each page, except the last, has one or more humorous cartoons illustrating many of the brigade HQ members. Each page has a two or three stanza humorous poem. Three pages have folded extensions.

34th Armoured Brigade — 34 ArmdBde

Date raised/disbanded: 01/12/1941* Post-war
* As 34th Army Tank Brigade; retitled 34th Tank Brigade 05/1942; retitled 34th Armoured Brigade 17/03/1944.

ARMOURED BRIGADES

The Story of 34 Armoured Brigade
Not stated TM; IWM
Not stated; Not stated; n.d. [1946]; ISBN None; 32pp/1 x bw SI/4 x bw M/1 x clr souvenir M (loose, approx. A1 size); s/b (card); Indexed N; Glossary N; Appendices Y; Bibliography N; 328 x 205 (Folio); Uncommon
NOTES: Brief but highly informative history of the brigade with 12pp on actions in NWE; produced by Brigade HQ for members. Appendices include OoB for UK and NWE, Honours/Awards – by regiment. Large (795mm x 635mm) unbound map included, showing route of the brigade through NWE.

The Story of 34 Armoured Brigade
Not stated
Uckfield; Naval & Military Press Ltd; 2014; ISBN 978 1783311019; 32pp/1 x bw SI/4 x bw M/1 x clr M; s/b; Indexed N; Glossary N; Appendices Y; Bibliography N; 297 x 210 (4to)
NOTES: Facsimile reprint by NMP of first edition, available in s/b.

35th Armoured Brigade — 35 ArmdBde

Date raised/disbanded: 01/12/1941*   Post-war
* As 35th Army Tank Brigade; retitled 35th Tank Brigade 12/08/1942; retitled 35th Armoured Brigade 14/07/1945.

Brigade publications:
The Black Beret*
No. 1 July 1944 to No. 12 June 1945 plus Special Number 8 May 1945 (Monthly)
Vol. 2, No. 1 July 1945 to Vol. 2, No. 6 Farewell Number Dec 1945 (Monthly)
*issues often entitled simply as **Black Beret**.

No histories established.

1st Assault Brigade, RE* — [1 Ass Bde RE]

*23/04/1945 retitled 1st Armoured Engineer Brigade, RE.

Date raised/disbanded: 26/11/1943   Post-war

A.R.E
The Story of the 1st Assault Brigade Royal Engineers 1943 - 1945
Not stated TM; NAM; RE
No imprint; No imprint ; 1945; ISBN None; 78pp/7 x bw Pl/11 x clr SI/7 x bw SI/1 x clr Mfep/2 x clr Mf/16 x clr M; h/b / d/j Blue cloth; Indexed N; Glossary N; Appendices Y; Bibliography N; 230 x 199 (8vo); Uncommon
NOTES: Well detailed and highly informative history of Armoured Engineers in NWE. Honours/Awards. Includes OoB for D-Day and VE-Day.

Cracking Hitler's Atlantic Wall
The 1st Assault Brigade Royal Engineers on D-Day
Anderson Jr, Richard C. TM
Mechanicsburg; Stackpole Books; 2010; ISBN 978-0-8117-0589-9; 266pp/168 x bw Pl/7 x bw SI/20 x bw M; h/b / d/j Blue paper; Indexed Y; Glossary N; Appendices N; Bibliography Y; 259 x 206 (4to)
NOTES: Although strictly outside the scope of titles included, being a US publication, it would be remiss to exclude this first class, exceptionally well detailed, study of 1st Armoured Engineer Brigade landing on D-Day. Includes OoBs and casualty statistics for each landing. RoH for D-Day.

6th Guards Armoured Brigade — 6 Gds ArmdBde

Date raised/disbanded: 15/09/1941* 16/06/45 (Reverted to inf.)
* Changed to 6th Guards Tank Brigade 15/01/1943, then back to 6GdsAB 02/02/1945.

6th Guards Tank Brigade
The Story of Guardsmen in Churchill Tanks
Forbes, Patrick TM; IWM; NAM; PCL
London; Sampson Low, Marston & Co Ltd; n.d.; ISBN None; xii + 244pp/1 x clr SI fep/29 x bw PI/29 x bw SI/1 x clr Mbds/13 x clr M/1 x bw M; h/b / d/j Blue cloth; Indexed Y; Glossary Y; Appendices Y; Bibliography N; 252 x 160 (4to)
NOTES: Expansive and capable history with thorough detail following the brigade across NWE. Extremely well detailed set of appendices include: RoH by battalion including OR service number, awards by battalion, OoBs and a list of all tank names for each battalion.

2623520 Gdsm. Kennedy, D. J. 6th Guards Tank Brigade Reminiscences
Kennedy, Guardsman D. J. TM; IWM
No imprint (Worksop); No imprint (Ryton Typing Service - printers); n.d.; ISBN None; 40pp/9 x bw PI/1 x bw SI; s/b; Indexed N; Glossary N; Appendices N; Bibliography N; 210 x 148 (8vo); Uncommon
NOTES: The author served in No. 3 Sqn, 4th Tank Battalion, Grenadier Guards. The memoirs are a reproduction of the diary he kept covering 1 January 1945 to 28 April 1945.

6th Guards Tank Brigade
The Story of Guardsmen in Churchill Tanks
Forbes, Patrick
Uckfield; Naval & Military Press Ltd; ISBN 9781845749705; See Notes; s/b
NOTES: Facsimile reprint by NMP of first edition, available in s/b.

Key to Book Entries
Book Title and Sub-title(s)
Author Museum Holdings
Place of Publication; Publisher; Date of Publication; ISBN; Pages/Illustrations; Binding; Indexed; Glossary; Appendices; Bibliography; Size (in mm); Availability
NOTES:

Section XV

Armoured Divisions

Britain's first armoured divisions were the pre-war 'Mobile Division' and the 'Mobile Division (Egypt) and Abbassia District'. The former became the 1st Armoured Division and the latter evolved into the famous 7th Armoured Division – the Desert Rats.

Expansion started quickly after war broke out, four armoured divisions being formed between December 1939 and December 1940. Equipment may have been sparse to start with but the key element was to get men trained. In total, Britain created eleven armoured divisions, the last being the 79th Armoured Division in October 1942.

Although eight armoured divisions saw active service, only five receive varying degrees of attention in published histories. They are: 6th Armoured Division, 7th Armoured Division, 11th Armoured Division, 79th Armoured Division, and the Guards Armoured Division.

The 7AD naturally receives the limelight; it fought from the early days of the North African campaign, through Tunisia, Italy and ended the war in North West Europe. 11AD and 79AD are well represented due to fighting in NWE but also in the case of 79AD because it operated Hobart's Funnies, the specialized tanks designed to overcome many of the obstacles of Hitler's' Atlantic Wall.

The 6AD and the GdsAD receive less coverage. 6AD fought in Italy, a campaign which has received far less attention than Normandy and NWE. The Guards Armoured Division's coverage is also sparse, perhaps because it came from Britain's premier infantry and returned there immediately the war ended.

Of the 1st, 2nd, 8th, 9th, 10th, and 42nd Armoured Divisions there is little record. As a result of either limited active service, or none at all, there are no histories directly telling their story, only reference to them within other works.

Armoured Divisions

Datafile British Tanks and Formations 1939-45
Bellis, Malcolm A.
Crewe; Malcolm A Bellis; n.d. [1980s]; ISBN None; iv + 70pp + v/24 x bw SI; s/b; Indexed Y; Glossary N; Appendices N; Bibliography N; 145 x 208 (24mo); Rare
NOTES: Highly detailed tabular summaries of divisions, brigades and regiments. Shows dates of service, theatres, main tanks employed, insignia and summary tank specifications. There are one or two minor errors but this was pioneering information presentation and would enhance any library.

Datafile 2 Divisions of the British Army 1939 - 1945
Bellis, Malcolm A.
Crewe; Malcolm A Bellis; 2000; ISBN 0-9529693-1-9; iv + 45pp + xx/68 x bw SI; s/b; Indexed Y; Glossary N; Appendices Y; Bibliography N; 211 x 148 (8vo); Uncommon
NOTES: Simple text listing of each division with its constituent brigades and regiments, plus précised organization and insignia.

British Armoured Divisions and Their Commanders, 1939 - 1945
Doherty, Richard TM; RMAS
Barnsley; Pen & Sword Military; 2013; ISBN 978-1-84884-838-2; xxxi + 270pp/32 x bw PI/3 x bw SI/20 x bw M; h/b / d/j Black Cloth; Indexed Y; Glossary N; Appendices Y; Bibliography Y; 240 x 160 (8vo)
NOTES: Provides a study of the operations in which British armoured divisions took part, together with a 10pp appendix providing single paragraph mini-biographies of British armoured commanders. Appendices also include OoBs of all the armoured divisions.

1st Armoured Division — 1 ArmdDiv

Date raised/disbanded: Spring 1938   11/01/1945

Divisional publications:
The Rhino. The Magazine of the First Armoured Division
Vol. 1 No. 1 July 1947 and Vol. 1 No. 2 August 1947 (Monthly – but only two produced)

Outline History of First Armoured Division to July 1946
Not stated
No imprint; No imprint; n.d. [1946]; ISBN None; 13pp/2 x bw M; s/b; Indexed N; Glossary N; Appendices N; Bibliography N; 212 x 138 (8vo); Rare
NOTES: Written upon the renumbering of 6AD to 1AD in 1946, this short booklet provides a summary of both 1st and 6th Armoured Divisions - 5pp each.

Raymond Briggs and the Western Desert
Edwards, A. C. IWM
Chelmsford; Shergold and Company(Printers); n.d. [c.1990s]; ISBN None; 16pp/16 x bw PI; s/b (card); Indexed N; Glossary N; Appendices N; Bibliography N; 254 x 202 (4to); Rare
NOTES: Précis essay of Raymond Brigg's career in the desert 1941 - 1943.

2nd Armoured Division — 2 ArmdDiv

Date raised/disbanded: 15/12/1939   10/05/1941

No publications established.

6th Armoured Division — 6 ArmdDiv

Date raised/disbanded: 12/09/1940   Post-war.

Divisional publication:
The Sheffield Daily News
Full run not established but published in 1944 up to 30 October.

Prepare To Move
With the 6th Armoured Division in Africa & Italy
Beckett, Frank TM; IWM
Grimsby; Frank and Eileen Beckett; 1994; ISBN 0 9520897 0 X; xiv + 300pp/202 x bw PI/16 x bw SI/8 x bw M; h/b / d/j Black cloth; Indexed N; Glossary Y; Appendices N; Bibliography N; 215 x 153 (8vo)
NOTES: The author served in the Honourable Artillery Company, the 12th Regiment of which served with 6AD. He has written a generalised story of the campaigns 6AD took part in. Where it does focus, the attention is with the artillery rather than the tanks. The author has also written his memoirs of serving with 12th HAC Regt, RHA in 6AD under the title *Algiers to Austria with the First and Eighth Armies*, self-published in 1986. Refer to *Mailed Fist* by Ken Ford for the history of 6AD.

Prepare To Move
With the 6th Armoured Division in Africa & Italy
Beckett, Frank NAM
Grimsby; Frank and Eileen Beckett; 1994; ISBN 0 9520897 1 8; xiv + 300pp/202 x bw PI/16 x bw SI/8 x bw M; s/b; Indexed N; Glossary Y; Appendices N; Bibliography N; 209 x 149 (8vo)
NOTES: Softback reprint of hardback first edition, same pagination.

Mailed Fist
6th Armoured Division at War, 1940 – 1945
Ford, Ken PCL
Stroud; Sutton Publishing Limited; 2005; ISBN 0-7509-3515-4; x + 213pp/30 x bw Pl/10 x bw M; h/b / d/j Black cloth; Indexed Y; Glossary N; Appendices Y; Bibliography Y; 240 x 160 (8vo)
NOTES: A history of the division from formation to the war's end. Several veterans are quoted throughout supporting the narrative which is quite well detailed. The journey of the division is extensively covered, the structure and detail of the division only briefly referred to. OoB.

7th Armoured Division — 7 ArmdDiv

Date raised/disbanded: 16/02/1940* Post-war.
* As 7th Armoured Division - previously Armoured Division (Egypt)

Divisional publications:
Jerboa
No. 1 16 May 1940 to unknown. Roneo style sheet(s) produced during 1940.
The Jerboa Journal
No. 1 11 June 1944 to No. 330 8 May 1945 (Daily)

A Short History Of The Seventh Armoured Division
October 1938 - May 1943
Carver, Lt-Col R. M. P. TM; IWM; NAM
'In the field'; The Printing and Stationery Services, M.E.F.; 1943; ISBN None; iii + 43pp/2 x clr Mf/1 x bw Mf; s/b; Indexed N; Glossary N; Appendices N; Bibliography N; 254 x 203 (4to)
NOTES: Written by the author 'in the field', this history takes the unusual step of marking the war's mid-point with a divisional history so far. Well detailed with regard to the division's composition, commanders and route. The style lies between full narrative and expanded war diary. Includes several OoBs at various dates.

A Short History Of The 7th Armoured Division
June 1943 - July 1945
Lindsay, Capt. Martin & Johnston, Capt. M. E. TM; IWM; NAM; RMAS; RE
'In the field'; Printing and Stationery Service; 1945; ISBN None; iii + 171pp/92 x bw Pl/11 x clr Mf; h/b Grey cloth; Indexed N; Glossary N; Appendices N; Bibliography N; 228 x 152 (8vo)
NOTES: The Italian campaign occupies 16pp and the invasion of Europe occupies the remainder of the book. The history follows the division's route in quite some detail. However, to limit the scope and time spent researching and in order to publish before the end of 1945, the authors deliberately chose not to mention individuals; only very senior personnel get named. 15,000 printed November 1945 'before demobilisation claims too many of the veteran "Desert Rats".' Despite the quantity produced, examples with intact spines are particularly rare. The eleven maps are loose in a rear pocket and came with a paper retaining loop.

The Desert Rats
The History of the 7th Armoured Division 1938 to 1945
Verney, D.S.O., M.V.O., Maj-Gen. G. L. TM; IWM; NAM; RE
London; Hutchinson & Co. (Publishers) Ltd.; 1954; ISBN None; 312pp/1 x bw PIfep/21 x bw PI/2 x clr Mbds/18 x bw M; h/b / d/j Black cloth; Indexed Y; Glossary N; Appendices Y; Bibliography Y; 235 x 160 (8vo)
NOTES: This history represents the first incremental improvement to the telling of the story of probably the most famous armoured division. With the passing of time and the publication of many memoirs, the author had the opportunity to improve upon wartime publications. Well written narrative makes a good job of condensing the full war history of the division into one volume. The chapters are conveniently subtitled and include the applicable date range. Appendices include OoBs at significant stages during the war, senior officer positions, and a brief history of the Jerboa divisional symbol. Published October 1954, itself reprinted in same month and in December 1954.

The Desert Rats
The History of the 7th Armoured Division 1938 to 1945
Verney, D.S.O., M.V.O., Maj-Gen. G. L.
London; Hutchinson & Co. (Publishers) Ltd.; 1955; ISBN None; See Notes; h/b / d/j Black cloth; Indexed Y; Glossary N; Appendices Y; Bibliography Y
NOTES: Hardback reprint of 1954 first edition. (Not physically inspected.)

Take These Men
Joly, Cyril TM; IWM; RE
London; Constable and Company Ltd; 1955; ISBN None; 357pp/2 x bw Mf; h/b / d/j Red cloth; Indexed N; Glossary N; Appendices N; Bibliography N; 193 x 135 (12mo)
NOTES: All the characters are fictitious but the detailed actions are based on real events. By writing this as a novel, the author is able to explore insightful topics in the narrative, from simple daily matters such as why scarves were adopted in the desert, to deeper meaningful thoughts about the comradeship of a tank crew. A renowned classic of tank warfare in the desert; evocative of the ebb and flow of the desert campaign. His front line experience of desert warfare (serving with 2RTR and 3RTR) is the basis of the narrative up to autumn 1942 when he became a brigade major. The book ends with a précis of the movements from El Alamein to Tunisia. Second impression printed same month, 1955.

Take These Men
The campaign of the Desert Rats from 1940 to 1943
Joly, Cyril NAM
Harmondsworth; Penguin Books Ltd; 1956; ISBN None; 315pp/2 x bw M; p/b; Indexed N; Glossary N; Appendices N; Bibliography N; 180 x 110 (12mo)
NOTES: Paperback reprint of 1955 first edition, different pagination, 'complete and unabridged'.

The Desert Rats
The History of the 7th Armoured Division 1938 – 1945
Verney, Maj-Gen. G. L.
Not stated; Arrow Books; 1957; ISBN None; 320pp/22 x bw PI/20x bw M; p/b; Indexed N; Glossary N; Appendices Y; Bibliography Y; 180 x 112 (12mo)
NOTES: Paperback reprint of 1954 first edition, different pagination.

The Desert Rats
(A Sentinel Book)
Holden, Matthew TM
London; Wayland (Publishers) Ltd; 1973; ISBN 85340 217 5; 96pp/1 x bw PIfep/51 x bw PI/1 x bw SI/14 x bw M; h/b / d/j Red cloth; Indexed Y; Glossary Y; Appendices N; Bibliography Y; 242 x 200 (8vo); Uncommon
NOTES: Simple overview, 'classroom' style.

Desert Rats at War 1 - North Africa
Forty, George TM
Shepperton; Ian Allan Ltd; 1975; ISBN 0 7110 0661 X; 192pp/1 x bw PIfep/1 x bw SIfep/4 x clr PI/3 x clr SI/237 x bw PI/10 x bw SI/7 x bw M; h/b / d/j Red cloth; Indexed N; Glossary N; Appendices N; Bibliography Y; 298 x 220 (4to)
NOTES: Pictorial history with accompanying narrative including personal anecdotes. The two volumes split naturally between the Mediterranean and NWE. Although they are not detailed histories, they do provide a wide range of photographs from all elements of the division. Chapter dealing specifically with tanks is 18pp. (A single volume edition was created for the US market.) (Republished June 2014 as a revised and updated single softback volume, q.v.)

Desert Rats at War 1 - North Africa
Forty, George IWM; NAM; RE
Abingdon; Purnell Book Services Limited; 1975; ISBN None; 192pp/1 x bw PIfep/1 x bw SIfep/4 x clr PI/3 x clr SI/237 x bw PI/10 x bw SI/7 x bw M; h/b / d/j Red cloth; Indexed N; Glossary N; Appendices N; Bibliography Y; 298 x 220 (4to)
NOTES: Book Club Edition reprint of first edition, same pagination.

Desert Rats at War 2 - Europe
Forty, George TM; NAM; RMAS
Shepperton; Ian Allan Ltd; 1977; ISBN 0 7110 07330; 160pp/2 x bw PIfep/209 x bw PI/9 x bw SI/8 x bw M; h/b / d/j Black cloth; Indexed N; Glossary N; Appendices N; Bibliography Y; 298 x 220 (4to)
NOTES: Volume Two spans the departure from NA through to the end in Europe, again with many personal anecdotes and a good selection of photographs. (A single volume edition was created for the US market.) (Republished June 2014 as a revised and updated single softback volume, q.v.)

Desert Rats at War 2 – Europe
Forty, George   IWM; NAM; RE
London; Purnell Book Services Limited; 1977; ISBN None; 160pp/2 x bw PIfep/209 x bw PI/9 x bw SI/8 x bw M; h/b / d/j Black cloth; Indexed N; Glossary N; Appendices N; Bibliography Y; 298 x 220 (4to)
NOTES: Book Club Edition reprint of first edition, same pagination.

British 7th Armoured Division 1940 - 1945
Osprey Vanguard 1
Sandars, John   TM; NAM; RMAS
London; Osprey Publishing Ltd; 1977; ISBN 0 85045 281 3; 40pp/5 x clr SI/28 x bw PI/2 x bw M/8 x bw WET; s/b; Indexed N; Glossary N; Appendices N; Bibliography N; 246 x 183 (8vo)
NOTES: From the Osprey Vanguard series providing an overview of the division. Extremely well illustrated including the series' familiar 8pp colour illustrations. Seven OoBs, including one in the illustrations section. Reprinted several times.

Take These Men
Echoes of War
Joly, Cyril
London; Buchan & Enright, Publishers, Limited; 1985; ISBN 0-907675-40-9; x + 357pp/No illus.; p/b; Indexed N; Glossary N; Appendices N; Bibliography N; 215 x 134 (8vo); Uncommon
NOTES: Paperback reprint of 1955 first edition, same pagination.

The Desert Rats
The 7th Armoured Division in World War II
Verney, DSO, MVO, Maj-Gen. G. L.
London; Greenhill Books; 1990; ISBN 1-85367-063-4; 312pp/22 x bw PI/20 x bw M; h/b / d/j Green cloth; Indexed Y; Glossary N; Appendices Y; Bibliography Y; 145 x 221 (24mo)
NOTES: Reprint of 1954 first edition with new introduction by General Sir John Hackett. Reprinted 2002 in s/b.

The Desert Rats
7th Armoured Division 1940-1945
Neillands, Robin   TM; IWM; NAM; PCL
London; George Weidenfeld & Nicholson Limited; 1991; ISBN 0 297 81191 6; xvi + 284pp/16 x bw PI/15 x bw M; h/b / d/j Black cloth; Indexed Y; Glossary N; Appendices N; Bibliography Y; 239 x 164 (8vo)
NOTES: The author acknowledges the lack of histories with accounts from Other Ranks and this is the first history of the division to include such. He has utilised many interviews and quotations from the men, balancing the strategic and the moment. As such this represents the next stage in the telling of the division's story and is a useful complement to Verney's *The Desert Rats*, q.v. (See also Delaforce's *Churchill's Desert Rats*.) Includes six OoBs for various stages of the war.

Churchill's Desert Rats
From Normandy to Berlin with the 7th Armoured Division
Delaforce, Patrick   TM; IWM; NAM
Stroud; Alan Sutton Publishing Ltd; 1994; ISBN 0-7509-0529-8; viii + 200pp/52 x bw PI/1 x bw SI/11 x bw M; h/b / d/j Black cloth; Indexed Y; Glossary N; Appendices N; Bibliography N; 240 x 163 (8vo)
NOTES: The author's association with the period (he served with 13RHA in 11AD) and obvious passion show through in his lively narrative. Employs a greater density of veteran quotations than Neillands and as such is potentially the better complement to Verney. The index is useful for listing veteran's names but there are no units listed.

Churchill's Desert Rats
From Normandy to Berlin with the 7th Armoured Division
Delaforce, Patrick
Stroud; Alan Sutton Publishing Ltd; 1994; ISBN 0-7509-0625-1; viii + 200pp/52 x bw PI/1 x bw SI/11 x bw M; s/b; Indexed Y; Glossary N; Appendices N; Bibliography N; 233 x 153 (8vo)
NOTES: Softback reprint of first edition, same pagination.

The Desert Rats
7th Armoured Division 1940-1945
Neillands, Robin
London; Orion Books Ltd; 1995; ISBN 0 75280 298 4; xvi + 284pp/16 x bw PI/15 x bw M; p/b; Indexed Y; Glossary N; Appendices N; Bibliography Y; 197 x 129 (12mo)
NOTES: Paperback reprint of 1991 first edition, same pagination.

Churchill's Desert Rats
From Normandy to Berlin with the 7th Armoured Division
Delaforce, Patrick
London; Chancellor Press; 1999; ISBN 0 75373 264 9; viii + 200pp/52 x bw PI/1 x bw SI/11 x bw M; h/b / d/j Illustrated as d/j; Indexed Y; Glossary N; Appendices N; Bibliography N; 240 x 159 (8vo)
NOTES: Hardback reprint of 1994 first edition, same pagination; itself reprinted 2001.

The Desert Rats
A Pictorial History of the Western Desert Campaign
Jones, Kevin
London; Caxton Editions; 2001; ISBN 1 84067 157 2; 184pp/1 x bw PIfep/81 x bw PI/2 x bw M; h/b / d/j Illustrated as d/j; Indexed N; Glossary N; Appendices N; Bibliography N; 294 x 205 (4to)
NOTES: A collection of IWM photographs, many printed full or double page with accompanying narrative overview.

A Short History Of The 7th Armoured Division
June 1943 - July 1945
Lindsay, Capt. Martin & Johnston, Capt. M. E.
Doncaster; D. P. & G. Military Publishers; 2001; ISBN 1-903972-09-4; iii + 171pp/Illus.; h/b Grey cloth; Indexed N; Glossary N; Appendices N; Bibliography N; 215 x 154 (8vo)
NOTES: D. P. & G. facsimile reprint of 1945 first edition. (Not physically inspected.)

The Desert Rats
The History of the 7th Armoured Division 1938 - 1945
Verney, Maj-Gen. G. L.
London; Greenhill Books; 2002; ISBN 1-85367-521-0; 312pp/22 x bw PI/20 x bw M; s/b; Indexed Y; Glossary N; Appendices Y; Bibliography Y
NOTES: Softback reprint of Greenhill's 1990 hardback edition.

Churchill's Desert Rats 2
7th Armoured Division in North Africa, Burma, Sicily and Italy
Delaforce, Patrick   TM; PCL
Stroud; Sutton Publishing Limited; 2002; ISBN 0 7509 2929 4 / 978 0 7509 2929 5; viii + 216pp/51 x bw PI/1 x bw SI/31 x bw M; h/b / d/j Black cloth; Indexed Y; Glossary N; Appendices Y; Bibliography Y; 240 x 159 (8vo)
NOTES: The prequel to the author's first book on the Desert Rats. Follows the same style, again with a particularly good selection of veteran supplied photographs and anecdotes. Includes two chapters on 7AB's (7H & 2RTR) operations after it left 7AD, in the Far East and Iraq, Syria and Italy, 42pp.

Churchill's Desert Rats
From Normandy to Berlin with the 7th Armoured Division
Delaforce, Patrick
Stroud; Sutton Publishing Limited; 2003; ISBN 0 7509 3198 1; ix + 229pp/31 x bw PI/3 x bw M; p/b; Indexed Y; Glossary N; Appendices N; Bibliography N; 198 x 127 (8vo)
NOTES: Reprint of 1994 first edition, different pagination and reduced illustration content.

7th Armoured Division
The 'Desert Rats' (Spearhead # 14)
Forty, George   TM
Hersham; Ian Allan Ltd; 2003; ISBN 0 7110 2988 1; 96pp/17 x clr PI/1 x bw PIfep/94 x bw PI/3 x bw SI/15 x bw M; s/b; Indexed Y; Glossary N; Appendices N; Bibliography Y; 248 x 185 (8vo)
NOTES: A useful compact study of the division with a good selection of photographs including many private ones. In addition to the history, there are chapters on uniforms and insignia (a selection of modern living history uniform displays in colour) and mini-biographies of senior officers.

Desert Rats
From El Alamein to Basra: The Inside Story of a Military Legend
Parker, John   TM; PCL
London; Headline Book Publishing; 2004; ISBN 0 7553 1288 0; vii + 376pp/40 x bw PI/1 x bw M; h/b / d/j Cream cloth; Indexed Y; Glossary N; Appendices Y; Bibliography N; 240 x 159 (8vo)
NOTES: This history of the 7AD adopts a campaign level approach rather than detailed descriptions of the battles and engagements of the division itself. There are some veterans' anecdotes. The three final chapters bring the story of the Desert Rats up to date with an overview of their involvement in the two Gulf wars of 1991 and 2003. Appendix comprises seven OoBs throughout the war plus one each for 1991 and 2003.

Desert Rats
From El Alamein to Basra: The Inside Story of a Military Legend
Parker, John
London; Headline Book Publishing; 2005; ISBN 0 7553 1289 9; ix + 472pp/41 x bw Pl/1 x bw M; p/b; Indexed Y; Glossary N; Appendices Y; Bibliography N; 177 x 111 (12mo)
NOTES: Paperback reprint of 2004 first edition, different pagination.

Desert Rats
From El Alamein to Basra: The Inside Story of a Military Legend
Parker, John
London; Bounty Books; 2005; ISBN 9780753712955 / 0 7537 1295 4; vii + 376pp/40 x bw Pl/1 x bw M; h/b / d/j Illustrated as d/j; Indexed Y; Glossary N; Appendices Y; Bibliography N; 240 x 159 (8vo)
NOTES: Hardback reprint of 2004 first edition, same pagination, itself reprinted 2006.

The Desert Rats
7th Armoured Division 1940-1945
Neillands, Robin
London; Aurum Press Limited; 2005; ISBN 1 84513 115 0; xvi + 284pp/15 x bw M; p/b; Indexed Y; Glossary N; Appendices N; Bibliography Y; 197 x 129 (12mo)
NOTES: Paperback reprint of 1991 first edition, same pagination but no photograph selection.

A Short History Of The 7th Armoured Division
June 1943 - July 1945
Lindsay, Capt. Martin & Johnston, Capt. M. E.
Smalldale; MLRS Books; 2005; ISBN 978-1-84791-219-0; See Notes; Indexed N; Glossary N; Appendices N; Bibliography N
NOTES: Facsimile reprint by MLRS Books of 1945 first edition.

Churchill's Desert Rats
In North Africa, Burma, Sicily and Italy
7th Armoured Division's Campaigns 1940 - 1943
Delaforce, Patrick PCL
Barnsley; Pen & Sword Military; 2009; ISBN 978 1 84884 039 3; x + 216pp/51 x bw Pl/1 x bw M; h/b / d/j Black cloth; Indexed Y; Glossary N; Appendices Y; Bibliography Y; 239 x 162 (8vo)
NOTES: Hardback reprint of *Desert Rats 2*, q.v., from 2002, addition of Foreword by Maj-Gen. Cordingley, same main pagination.

The Desert Rats Scrapbook
Cairo to Berlin 1940 - 1945
Fogg, Roger
Stroud; Spellmount; 2010; ISBN 978 0 7524 5575 4; 192pp/148 x bw Pl/42 x bw Sl; s/b; Indexed Y; Glossary N; Appendices N; Bibliography Y; 246 x 172 (8vo)
NOTES: This book is a compilation of photographs and anecdotes from two Desert Rats compiled by the son of one of them. One served in Tac. HQ and the photographs are largely his, the other served in 1RTR as a tank driver. Also photographed are many items

of ephemera these two soldiers collected across their five years of war. A good picture reference with accompanying narrative and veterans' letters and recollections.

Churchill's Desert Rats in North-West Europe
From Normandy to Berlin
Delaforce, Patrick
Barnsley; Pen & Sword Military; 2010; ISBN 978 184884 111 6; viii + 200pp /52 x bw Pl/1 x bw Sl/11 x bw M; h/b / d/j Black cloth; Indexed Y; Glossary N; Appendices N; Bibliography N; 240 x 160 (8vo)
NOTES: Hardback, retitled, reprint of 1994 *Churchill's Desert Rats, From Normandy to Berlin with the 7th Armoured Division*, q.v., same pagination.

A Desert Rat Entertains
Hall, Jenny
Brighton; Pen Press; 2013; ISBN 978-1-78003-654-0; xviii + 196pp/1 x bw PIfep/4 x clr Pl/69 x bw Pl/6 x bw M; s/b; Indexed N; Glossary N; Appendices N; Bibliography N; 216 x 140 (8vo)
NOTES: The author's father, Ray Harris, served in HQ Sqn, 7AD but was also a forces' entertainer. He performed with and produced 'The Jerboa Strollers' and later performed with ENSA. Reproductions of many of RH's letters to Doreen Sellman conducting their romance which led to their wartime marriage. RH served with 7AD from late 1940 through to demobilisation in December 1945. Provides an interesting insight into the importance of entertainment and morale, and also of the nature of maintaining a wartime relationship almost entirely through correspondence.

Desert Rats At War
North Africa. Italy. Northwest Europe
Forty, George
Not stated; Air Sea Media Services; 2014; ISBN 978-0-9576915-2-0; 224pp/1 x bw PIfep/46 x clr Pl/215 x bw Pl/6 x bw Sl/21 x clr M; s/b; Indexed N; Glossary N; Appendices N; Bibliography Y; 240 x 186 (8vo)
NOTES: Originally published in two volumes, *Desert Rats at War 1 - North Africa*, and *2 - Europe*, q.q.v. Substantially revised and updated layout with text condensed.

8th Armoured Division	8 ArmdDiv

Date raised/disbanded: 04/11/1940   01/01/1943

No publications established.

9th Armoured Division — 9 ArmdDiv

Date raised/disbanded: 01/12/1940   31/07/1944

A Full Life
Horrocks, K.C.B., K.B.E., D.S.O., M.C., LL.D. (Hon.), Sir Brian
London; Collins; 1960; ISBN None; 320pp/1 x bw PIfep/29 x bw PI/10 x bw M; h/b / d/j Black cloth; Indexed Y; Glossary N; Appendices N; Bibliography N; 215 x 148 (8vo)
NOTES: The author commanded 9AD from March to August 1942, passing comment in 3pp on this topic. Reprinted in year of publication and 1961.

A Full Life
Horrocks, K.C.B., K.B.E., D.S.O., M.C., LL.D. (Hon.), Sir Brian   IWM; NAM
London; Leo Cooper Ltd; 1974; ISBN 0 85052 144 0; 342pp/1 x bw PIfep/29 x bw PI/10 x bw M; h/b / d/j Red cloth; Indexed Y; Glossary N; Appendices N; Bibliography N; 223 x 143 (8vo)
NOTES: Hardback reprint of 1960 first edition, revised and extended; 192pp on WWII.

10th Armoured Division — 10 ArmdDiv

Date raised/disbanded: 23/07/1941   15/06/1944

Divisional publications:
Div
No. 1 Feb 1943 to No. 9 20 Apr 1943

No publications established.

11th Armoured Division — 11 ArmdDiv

Date raised/disbanded: 09/03/1941   Post-war.

Divisional publication:
The Bulletin
No. 1 17 July 1944 to No. 295 8 May 1945 (Daily) Replaced by
The Bulletin: 11th Armoured Division
No. 1 15 Sept 1951 to not established

Taurus Pursuant
A History of 11th Armoured Division
Not stated [See Notes]   TM; NAM; RMAS; RE
Not stated; Printing & Stationery Service; 1946; ISBN None; vi + 118pp + 44pp Appxs/15 x bw PI/27 x bw SI/2 x clr Mbds/20 x clr Mf; h/b / d/j Blue leather; Indexed N; Glossary N; Appendices Y; Bibliography N; 235 x 156 (8vo)

NOTES: The author served in Divisional HQ and tells the story of the division throughout the NWE campaign. After a few pages summarising the formation and equipment up to 1944, this history starts with the invasion of France, June 1944. The narrative focuses on the division's route with reference to the brigade and its regiments, rather than detailed descriptions of any actions. Well executed overall history although it does not provide much detail with regard to equipment, uniforms and personnel. RoH for most units of the division, including location. Spine prone to damage, especially head and tail. 15,000 copies printed March 1946. Author "E.W.I.P." is Edgar W. I. Palamountain.

From the Desert to the Baltic
Roberts, C.B., D.S.O., M.C., Maj-Gen. Pip   TM; IWM
London; William Kimber & Co. Limited; 1987; ISBN 0-7183-0639-2; 256pp/30 x bw PI/15 x bw M; h/b / d/j Red cloth; Indexed Y; Glossary Y; Appendices Y; Bibliography N; 240 x 160 (8vo)
NOTES: The author was one of Britain's most able tank commanders. From a senior position in 4AB, late 1940, he rose through brigade commands until given command of 11AD in December 1943. He briefly recounts acting as a new broom before providing a flowing summary of 11AD's operations, together with his own commentary on certain situations – 92pp. Commands included: 3RTR Jan - Jul 1942; 22AB Jul 1942 - Jan 1943; 26AB Mar 1943 - May 1943; 30AB Aug – Oct 1943; 11AD Dec 1943 - end of war.

The Charge of the Bull
A History of the 11th British Armoured Division in Normandy 1944
Brisset, Jean   TM; IWM; RMAS; RE
Norwich; Bates Books; 1989; ISBN 0 9512349 0 0; iii + 344pp/1 x bw PIfep/127 x bw PI/2 x bw SI/9 x bw M; h/b / d/j Red leatherette; Indexed Y; Glossary N; Appendices Y; Bibliography Y; 216 x 155 (8vo)
NOTES: The author was a teenager living in Normandy during the war and has written the story of the division in Normandy; a brief summary chapter describes its path thereafter. The book was first published in French under the title *La Charge du Taureau* in 1975 and has been translated by a British serviceman. The narrative interweaves the recollections of British soldiers and French civilians and is well delineated with frequent topic headings. 2000 copies printed.

The Black Bull
From Normandy to the Baltic with the 11th Armoured Division
Delaforce, Patrick   IWM; RMAS
Stroud; Alan Sutton Publishing Ltd; 1993; ISBN 0-7509-0406-2; iv + 252pp/44 x bw PI/17 x bw M; h/b / d/j Black cloth; Indexed N; Glossary N; Appendices N; Bibliography N; 240 x 158 (8vo)
NOTES: Patrick Delaforce served in 11AD as a Forward Observation Officer in 13th Royal Horse Artillery. He has collated the memoirs and photographs of a number of the men who fought within the division and employed them to enhance a fine narrative, making this the prime history of 11AD. This is his first armour related book and he subsequently wrote six more titles which are listed within this bibliography.

The Black Bull
From Normandy to the Baltic with the 11th Armoured Division
Delaforce, Patrick
Stroud; Alan Sutton Publishing Ltd; 1993; ISBN 0-7509-0407-0; iv + 252pp/44 x bw PI/17 x bw M; s/b; Indexed N; Glossary N; Appendices N; Bibliography N; 232 x 153 (8vo)
NOTES: Softback reprint of original hardback, same pagination. 'Special Forces Edition' (Note - a 1994 edition appears on many web listings, this is incorrect and may be attributable to an anomaly in the ISBN submission.)

The Black Bull
From Normandy to the Baltic with the 11th Armoured Division
Delaforce, Patrick NAM
London; Chancellor Press; 2000; ISBN 0-7537-0350-5; iv + 252pp/44 x bw PI/17 x bw M; h/b / d/j Illustrated as d/j; Indexed N; Glossary N; Appendices N; Bibliography N; 240 x 158 (8vo)
NOTES: Hardback reprint of 1993 first edition, same pagination. Chancellor's imprint information is incorrect, states first published in 1997 by Tom Donovan. Possible explanation is swapping of imprint information between this book and their reprint of *Monty's Marauders*, q.v., also in 2000.

The Black Bull
From Normandy to the Baltic with the 11th Armoured Division
Delaforce, Patrick
Stroud; Sutton Publishing Limited; 2002; ISBN 0 7509 3183 3; viii + 280pp/33 x bw PI/1 x bw Mfep/2 x bw M; p/b; Indexed N; Glossary N; Appendices N; Bibliography N; 196 x 125 (12mo)
NOTES: Paperback reprint of 1993 first edition, different pagination, central illustration section instead of in-line with narrative.

Taurus Pursuant
A History Of The 11th Armoured Division
Not stated
Smalldale; MLRS Books; 2006; ISBN 978-1-905696-38-3; See Notes
NOTES: Facsimile reprint by MLRS Books of 1946 first edition.

The Black Bull
From Normandy to the Baltic with the 11th Armoured Division
Delaforce, Patrick
Barnsley; Pen & Sword Military; 2010; ISBN 978 184884 228 1; iv + 252pp/44 x bw PI/17 x bw M; h/b / d/j Black cloth; Indexed N; Glossary N; Appendices N; Bibliography N; 240 x 160 (8vo)
NOTES: Hardback reprint of 1993 first edition, same pagination.

42nd Armoured Division — 42 ArmdDiv

Date raised/disbanded: 01/11/1941   17/10/1943

No publications established.

79th Armoured Division — 79 ArmdDiv

Date raised/disbanded: 14/08/1942   Post-war.

Divisional publication:
The Bull's Head
First issue 28/08/1944 to 30/08/1945 (Daily)
Typewritten single sheet, double sided

The Story of 79th Armoured Division
October 1942 - June 1945
Not stated [See Notes]   TM; IWM; NAM; RE
Hamburg; No imprint; 1945; ISBN None; 314pp/257 x bw Pl/1 x bw SIfep/6 x bw SI/2 x clr Mbds/38 x clr Mf/4 x clr M; h/b / d/j Cream cloth; Indexed Y; Glossary N; Appendices Y; Bibliography N; 211 x 155 (8vo)
NOTES: A tour-de-force history with many tables of OoBs, dispositions, detailed action maps, etc., printed July 1945, only two months after VE Day. The actions are highly detailed and full of named references. Appendix includes a list of senior officers in each brigade, a diary of major events and some general statistics. Some copies still have the 'Restricted' sticker on the title page and/or dust jacket. The book's status was changed to unrestricted in 1954 by the War Office. (From letter held with copy at PCL.) A large version (620mm x 200mm) of the colour illustrated map printed on the boards/end-papers was issued separately in a card tube, almost invariably no longer accompanying the book. Author is Maj. John Borthwick who served in Division HQ from July 1943.

79th Armoured Division Final Report
Not stated   TM; IWM; NAM; RE
Germany; Printing and Stationery Services 21 Army Group; 1945; ISBN None; ix + 312pp + to xvii Index/64 x bw Pl/121 x bw SI; h/b Red cloth; Indexed Y; Glossary N; Appendices Y; Bibliography N; 336 x 212 (Folio); V Rare
NOTES: Highly detailed and fully illustrated report on the operations and equipment of the division. Describes the vehicles used, the WE for each type of regiment, DD, Crocodile, Buffalo, etc. and their employment in action. Printed August 1945, 200 copies. Appendices include many technical drawings of modified fittings for Funnies. Reprinted by MLRS Books. (There is also a two volume 1951 publication entitled *Final Report of the Specialised Armour Establishment (Royal Armoured Corps)* which is a post war record of the SAE only.)

The Characteristics and Tactical Employment of Specialised Armour
Staff, 79 Armd Div
Not stated; Not stated; n.d. [c.1947]; ISBN None; 158pp/44 x bw PI/13 x bw SI; s/b (card); Indexed Y; Glossary N; Appendices Y; Bibliography N; 330 x 205 (Folio); V Rare
NOTES: Reproduced typescript of a report into the use of Funnies. In six parts covering Flamethrowers, Flails, AVREs, Specialised Armour, DD Tanks & LVTs. Includes WE tables for each type of Funnies. 120 copies printed. Reprinted by MLRS Books.

79th Armoured Division Hobo's Funnies
(Profile Book 3)
Duncan, Nigel TM; IWM; RMAS; RE
Windsor; Profile Publications Limited; 1972; ISBN 85383 082 7; 70pp/96 x bw PI/1 x clr SI/8 x clr M; h/b Illustrated paper; Indexed N; Glossary N; Appendices N; Bibliography N; 245 x 188 (8vo); Uncommon
NOTES: The author commanded 30AB of 79AD and has produced a classic work which is still invaluable to the 79AD student. OoBs.

The Funnies
A history, with scale plans, of the 79th Armoured Division
Futter, Geoffrey W. TM; RMAS
Hemel Hempstead; Model & Allied Publications Ltd; 1974; ISBN 0 85242 405 1; ix + 131pp/97 x bw PI/59 x bw SI; s/b; Indexed Y; Glossary N; Appendices N; Bibliography N; 245 x 188 (8vo); Uncommon
NOTES: Expanded from the author's articles in *Military Modelling* magazine published in the early 1970s, this book contains many excellent 1/76 scale plans of Funnies used by 79AD plus background detail about them.

Vanguard of Victory
The 79th Armoured Division
Fletcher, David TM; NAM; RMAS; PCL
London; Her Majesty's Stationery Office; 1984; ISBN 0 11 290422 X; 88pp/135 x bw PI/12 x bw SI/3 x bw M; s/b; Indexed Y; Glossary Y; Appendices N; Bibliography N; 275 x 218 (4to); Uncommon
NOTES: Written to complement the existing histories of the division, this book takes advantage of The Tank Museum's extensive photographic archive to tell the story through that collection.

Churchill's Secret Weapons
The Story of Hobart's Funnies
Delaforce, Patrick TM; IWM
London; Robert Hale Limited; 1998; ISBN 0 7090 6237 0; 256pp/17 x bw PI/16 x bw SI/18 x bw M; h/b / d/j Blue cloth; Indexed Y; Glossary Y; Appendices N; Bibliography Y; 222 x 142 (8vo)
NOTES: Starting with a background to some of the fantastical inventions Britain devised before and during the early part of the war, the author also provides background character sketches to some of the important figures involved in the development of the Funnies. The remainder deals with the invasion of Europe. Well detailed narrative

describes the landings on D-Day with particular emphasis on the Funnies, the AVREs, Crabs and DD tanks and continues in the same vein for 79AD's subsequent actions.

Churchill's Secret Weapons
The Story of Hobart's Funnies
Delaforce, Patrick
London; Robert Hale Limited; 2000; ISBN 0 7090 6722 4; 256pp/17 x bw PI/16 x bw SI/18 x bw M; s/b; Indexed Y; Glossary Y; Appendices N; Bibliography Y; 216 x 139 (8vo)
NOTES: Softback reprint of 1998 first edition, same pagination.

Innovation in the Face of Adversity: Major-General Sir Percy Hobart and the 79th Armoured Division (British)
Daniels, Maj. M. J.
Smalldale; MLRS Books; 2003; ISBN 978-1-84791-046-2; viii + 105pp/16 x bw PI/3 x bw SI/2 x bw M; s/b; Indexed N; Glossary Y; Appendices Y; Bibliography Y; 254 x 189 (4to)
NOTES: Reprint by MLRS Books of the author's thesis toward the degree, Master of Military Art and Science - Military History for the US Army. Very useful summary of 79AD and its equipment. Each major vehicle type is profiled, aspects of training are studied and American attitudes and use of 'Funnies' reviewed. Accessible thesis. TM has a copy of the original published dissertation.

The Story Of 79 Armoured Division
Not stated
Smalldale; MLRS Books; 2005; ISBN 978-1-84791-251-0; See Notes
NOTES: Facsimile reprint by MLRS Books of 1945 first edition.

The Characteristics and Tactical Employment of Specialised Armour
Staff, 79 Armd Div
Smalldale; MLRS Books; 2005; ISBN 978-1-84791-239-8; See Notes
NOTES: Facsimile reprint by MLRS Books of 1947 first edition.

Final Report of 79th Armoured Division
Staff, 79 Armd Div
Smalldale; MLRS Books; 2006; ISBN 978-1-905696-27-7; See Notes
NOTES: Facsimile reprint by MLRS Books of 1945 first edition.

Churchill's Secret Weapons
The Story of Hobart's Funnies
Delaforce, Patrick
Barnsley; Pen & Sword Military; 2006; ISBN 1 84415 344 4; 256pp/17 x bw PI/16 x bw SI/18 x bw M; h/b / d/j Black cloth; Indexed Y; Glossary Y; Appendices N; Bibliography Y; 240 x 161 (8vo)
NOTES: Hardback reprint of 1998 first edition, same pagination.

Churchill's Secret Weapons
The Story of Hobart's Funnies
Delaforce, Patrick
Barnsley; Pen & Sword Military; 2007; ISBN 1 84415 464 5; 256pp/17 x bw Pl/16 x bw SI/18 x bw M; s/b; Indexed Y; Glossary Y; Appendices N; Bibliography Y; 233 x 155 (8vo)
NOTES: Softback reprint of 2006 hardback, same pagination.

Hobart's 79th Armoured Division At War
Invention, Innovation & Inspiration
Doherty, Richard TM; RMAS
Barnsley; Pen & Sword Military; 2011; ISBN 978-1-84884-398-1; xxii + 233pp/36 x bw Pl/10 x bw M; h/b / d/j Black cloth; Indexed Y; Glossary N; Appendices Y; Bibliography Y; 240 x 161 (8vo)
NOTES: Looks in detail at all the major, and some of the minor, actions involving units of 79AD. Includes an extensive bibliography. Particularly useful for recording the awards issued to men of 79AD units.

Guards Armoured Division — Gds ArmdDiv

Date raised/disbanded: 15/09/1941 12/06/1945*
* Re-organised as Guards Division.

Divisional publication:
The News Guardian – no publication details established

Guards Armoured Division
"Farewell To Armour" Parade
Rotenburg Airfield Germany 9 June 1945
Not stated TM
Not stated; (Lührs & Röver); 1945; ISBN None; 5pp/No illus.; s/b (card); Indexed N; Glossary N; Appendices N; Bibliography N; 209 x 148 (8vo); Uncommon
NOTES: Programme of events for the parade plus a one page summary of GdsAD 1941 to 1945.

The Guards Armoured Division 1941 - 1945
Captain The Earl of Rosse & Verney, D.S.O., M.V.O., Maj-Gen. G. L. (Collab.) NAM
London; Collins; 1952; ISBN None; 296pp/12 x bw M; s/b; Indexed N; Glossary Y; Appendices Y; Bibliography Y; 210 x 142 (8vo)
NOTES: Copy seen at NAM, possibly a unique pre-press copy since it lists Illustrations and Index but neither is present.

The Guards Armoured Division
A Short History
Verney, D.S.O., M.V.O., Maj-Gen. G. L. TM; IWM; NAM
London; Hutchinson & Co. (Publishers) Ltd.; 1955; ISBN None; 184pp/2 x clr Mbds/10 x bw M; h/b / d/j Red cloth; Indexed Y; Glossary N; Appendices Y; Bibliography Y; 219 x 143 (8vo)

NOTES: This history begins with an informative section on the division's formation and training. The narrative is conveniently divided with headings and dates and provides a useful overview history following the division's route and story. The armoured battalions being one element, they share a portion of the narrative. No illustrations. Amongst appendices: OoBs for June 1944 and a list of senior officers of the division and its brigades.

The Story Of The Guards Armoured Division
Captain The Earl of Rosse, M.B.E. & Hill, D.S.O., Col E. R. TM; IWM; NAM; RE
London; Geoffrey Bles Ltd; 1956; ISBN None; 320pp/1 x bw PIfep/11 x bw PI/2 x bw Mf/3 x bw M; h/b / d/j Red cloth; Indexed Y; Glossary N; Appendices Y; Bibliography N; 222 x 147 (8vo)
NOTES: Solid divisional history, more detailed than the *Short History* published just the year before. One brief chapter deals with the division leading up to the invasion of France. Appendices include OoBs for 1 July 1942, 6 June 1944, 3 September 1944, and 5 May 1945. Two printings in 1956.

British Guards Armoured Division 1941 - 45
Osprey Vanguard 9
Sandars, John TM; IWM; NAM; PCL
London; Osprey Publishing Ltd; 1979; ISBN 0 85045 313 5; 40pp/5 x clr SI/29 x bw PI/1 x bw M/9 x bw WET; s/b; Indexed N; Glossary N; Appendices N; Bibliography N; 247 x 183 (8vo)
NOTES: From the Osprey Vanguard series, No. 9, providing an overview of the division. Extremely well illustrated including the series' familiar 8pp colour illustrations. Reprinted several times.

A Guards' General
The Memoirs of Major General Sir Allan Adair B.T., G.C.V.O., C.B., D.S.O., M.C., J.P., D.L.
Adair, Maj-Gen. Allan; Lindsay, F. R. Hist. S., Oliver (Ed.) IWM; RMAS
London; Hamish Hamilton Ltd; 1986; ISBN 0-241-11947-2; ix + 214pp/21 x bw PI/7 x bw M; h/b / d/j Grey cloth; Indexed Y; Glossary N; Appendices N; Bibliography Y; 240 x 159 (8vo)
NOTES: The author started the war as 2 i/c of 3rd Bn, Grenadier Guards and his career with armour started in May 1941 with the announcement of the formation of the GdsAD. At the time he commanded 30th Gds Bde which was then re-titled 6th GdsAB. Later, in September 1942, he became the divisional commander. His recollections focus on the major actions GdsAD was involved in from Operation Goodwood to the crossing of the German frontier. A rare set of memoirs from an armoured divisional commander, demonstrating how close high level officers can come to injury or death. Armoured career occupies 54pp of the 77pp covering WWII. Second edition printed 1987.

A Guards' General
The Memoirs of Major General Sir Allan Adair B.T., G.C.V.O., C.B., D.S.O., M.C., J.P., D.L.
Adair, Maj-Gen. Allan; Lindsay, F. R. Hist. S., Oliver (Ed.)
London; Hamish Hamilton Ltd; 1987; ISBN 0-241-11947-2; ix + 214pp/21 x bw PI/7 x bw M; h/b / d/j Grey cloth; Indexed Y; Glossary N; Appendices N; Bibliography Y; 240 x 159 (8vo)
NOTES: Reprint of first 1986 edition, same pagination.

Oliver Leese
Ryder, Rowland IWM; NAM
London; Hamish Hamilton Ltd; 1987; ISBN 0-241-12024-1; xii + 308pp/16 x bw PI/1 x bw SI/4 x bw M; h/b / d/j Brown cloth; Indexed Y; Glossary N; Appendices Y; Bibliography Y; 240 x 162 (8vo)
NOTES: Oliver Leese commanded 1st Bn Cold. Gds in 1936 and in 1941 became the CO of the Guards Armoured Division; later commanded 30 Corps in the Middle East and commanded an Army Group in Burma in 1944. Only 4pp on Gds AD.

The Story Of The Guards Armoured Division
Captain The Earl of Rosse & Hill, D.S.O., Col E. R.
Smalldale; MLRS Books; 2006; ISBN 978-1-905973-73-6; See Notes
NOTES: Facsimile reprint by MLRS Books of 1956 first edition.

Key to Book Entries
Book Title and Sub-title(s)
Author Museum Holdings
Place of Publication; Publisher; Date of Publication; ISBN; Pages/Illustrations; Binding; Indexed; Glossary; Appendices; Bibliography; Size (in mm); Availability
NOTES:

Section XVI

Miscellaneous

This section contains those titles which fall outside the regimental, brigade, and other categories, and which provide more generalised information on Britain's armoured forces in World War Two. It includes several that were produced obviously with an eye to boosting mid-war morale.

The British people had few victories to read about in the first two years of the war. France 1940, the desert retreats in 1941 and Singapore 1942 were amongst the striking reverses. Only with the major victory at El Alamein in October 1942 was there the opportunity to recognise that the tide had turned. Some of these books were in production during that period of uncertainty and were published as Britain's armies were just starting to produce solid victories.

Also listed are other bibliographies, all of which provided inspiration for the production of this book. Few military enthusiasts of this period would consider their library complete without a copy of Arthur White's work - *A Bibliography of Regimental Histories of the British Army*, first published in the 1960s. Until the late 2000s this received just one update, produced by The London Stamp Exchange in 1988. Victor Sutcliffe worked with the Army Museums' Ogilby Trust to produce an online version of White's book, which lists several thousand titles across the subject of the British Army. To bring the printed subject up-to-date, he published his two-part bibliography in 2007 and 2008. It was Victor Sutcliffe's next-generation improvement to White's which provided the spark for this bibliography to expand on the armoured formations of World War Two.

Miscellaneous

A Brief History of The Royal Tank Corps
Woolnough, L.C.P., F. G.
Aldershot; Gale & Polden Ltd; 1925; ISBN None; 41pp/4 x sepia PI/1 x bw SI/3 x bw M, 1 x bw Mf; s/b; Indexed N; Glossary N; Appendices N; Bibliography N; 190 x 125 (12mo); Rare
Notes: Although outside the period scope of this bibliography, all six ediitons are listed for completeness. Produced as a summary history of the Corps aimed at recruits as their textbook. Pasted in errata paragraph p5 and errata slips p17, 21, 24 & 36. Includes list of current units, 'Deeds which won the VC', and a summary of total awards gained.

A Short History of The Royal Tank Corps
Not stated TM
Aldershot; Gale & Polden Ltd; 1930; ISBN None; ix + 112pp/1 x bw PIfep/1 x bw PI/5 x bw SI; s/b; Indexed N; Glossary N; Appendices Y; Bibliography N; 190 x 125 (12mo); Rare
Notes: Expanded second edition of the 1925 first edition, bringing operations in the 1920s up-to-date. Dated tabular list of units with their location 1916 - 1929. Also available in h/b.

A Short History of The Royal Tank Corps
Not stated TM
Aldershot; Gale & Polden Ltd; 1934; ISBN None; xii + 134pp/1 x bw PIfep/4 x bw PI/9 x bw SI; s/b; Indexed N; Glossary N; Appendices Y; Bibliography N; 190 x 125 (12mo); Rare
Notes: Third Edition, expanded and corrected version of second edition.

A Short History of The Royal Tank Corps
Not stated TM
Aldershot; Gale & Polden Ltd; 1936; ISBN None; xii + 139pp/1 x bw PIfep/4 x bw PI/9 x bw SI; s/b; Indexed N; Glossary N; Appendices Y; Bibliography N; 190 x 125 (12mo); Rare
Notes: Fourth Edition, reprint with minor updates of third edition.

A Short History of The Royal Tank Corps
Not stated
Aldershot; Gale & Polden Ltd; 1938; ISBN None; xii + 168pp/1 x bw PIfep/4 x bw PI/9 x bw SI/2 x bw M; s/b; Indexed N; Glossary N; Appendices Y; Bibliography N; 190 x 125 (12mo); Uncommon
Notes: Fifth Edition, further expansion to bring the history up-to-date and now with an index. (Sixth and final edition, q.v., published 1945.)

Standing Orders of the 51st Light Training Regiment RAC
Not stated TM
Aldershot; Gale & Polden Limited; 1940; ISBN None; 64pp/28 x bw SI; h/b Blue cloth; Indexed N; Glossary N; Appendices N; Bibliography N; 183 x 126 (12mo); Rare
NOTES: Standard set of military standing orders. Interesting set of illustrations showing the RAC cap badges at the beginning of the war.

Tanks Advance!
Beckles, Gordon TM; IWM; NAM
London; Cassell and Company Limited; 1942; ISBN None; 128pp/48 x bw PI/3 x bw SI; h/b / d/j Red cloth; Indexed N; Glossary N; Appendices Y; Bibliography N; 191 x 128 (12mo)
NOTES: An example of mid-war morale boosting propaganda, telling the story of our tanks through the nom de plume characters of O'Reilly and Ginger Jones plus some real-life quotations. Also tells some of the story of tank production.

The Royal Armoured Corps
Murland, Capt. J. R. W. TM; IWM; NAM; PCL
London; Methuen & Co Ltd; 1943; ISBN None; viii + 106pp/11 x bw PI; h/b / d/j Red cloth; Indexed Y; Glossary N; Appendices Y; Bibliography Y; 188 x 129 (12mo)
NOTES: Written in July 1942, the scope is therefore the first three years of the RAC and ends mid-war. Because it was written so early in the war, there is only a single brief chapter on WWII. The bulk of the book provides a very readable account of tanks and formations from WWI up to this point. Includes RAC lineage charts in the appendices. A second reprint was published in 1943.

With Pennants Flying
The Immortal Deeds of The Royal Armoured Corps
Masters, David TM; IWM; NAM; PCL
London; Eyre & Spottiswoode; 1943; ISBN None; 200pp/1 x bw PIfep/10 x bw PI; h/b / d/j Brown cloth; Indexed Y; Glossary N; Appendices N; Bibliography N; 220 x 145 (8vo)
NOTES: The author has selected certain battles from early to mid-war and told their story through the RTR at Sidi Barrani, the Hussars cavalry at Sollum, etc. He has also focused on the Matilda equipped regiments, using them to convey the struggle of British forces in the first years of the war. There are several reminiscences from R. Farran of 3H who wrote *Winged Dagger*, q.v. Despite being written during the war the propaganda tone is kept to a modest level.

Tanks and Tank Folk
Kennington, Eric TM; IWM
London; Country Life Ltd; 1943; ISBN None; 32pp/1 x bw PI/3 x clr SI/19 x bw SI; s/b; Indexed N; Glossary N; Appendices N; Bibliography N; 259 x 208 (4to)
NOTES: Six pages of text followed by sketches by Eric Kennington. Production costs were funded by Vauxhall Motors Limited and proceeds went to three charities.

Training Handbook of the 55th Training Regiment R.A.C.
Martell, E. D. (Ed.)
London; Officer Commanding the 55th Training Regiment; 1943; ISBN None; 256pp/6 x bw PI/80 x bw SI/1 x bw M; s/b; Indexed Y; Glossary Y; Appendices N; Bibliography Y; 166 x 107 (16mo); Rare
NOTES: A collection of training material compiled from military training pamphlets and other documents. An interesting view into the range of topics taught to tank recruits.

With Pennants Flying
The Immortal Deeds of The Royal Armoured Corps
Masters, David
1945; ISBN None; See Notes; Rare
NOTES: Second, revised edition of 1943 first edition. (Not physically inspected.)

The First Official Account of the Royal Armoured Corps
Through Mud & Blood to the Green Fields Beyond
Owen, Frank & Atkins, H. W.   TM; NAM; PCL
London; His Majesty's Stationery Office; 1945; ISBN none; 72pp/73 x bw PI/3 x bw SI+/6 x clr M/1 x bw M; s/b; Indexed N; Glossary N; Appendices N; Bibliography N; 227 x 178 (8vo)
NOTES: Commemorative publication, fully illustrated. The booklet goes through the training received by each crew member, officer training, types of regiment, the desert war, and a few recollections of fighting to give a very stiff official review of the RAC to the end of the desert war. Written in August 1944, it was not published until 1945 and so cuts short the wartime history of the RAC. Cover illustrations by Eric Kennington, inside covers show most of the RAC regiment cap badges including all the infantry regiments that converted to RAC regiments. (Note: not all these regiments wore their parent badge, some wore the RAC badge.) No doubt removed as a souvenir, the cover is often missing, leading to the impression of a different edition - refer to Illustrations 27 and 28. Interesting note at the end, 'There are many men and women in the Forces who would welcome a chance of reading this book. If you hand it in to the nearest Post Office, it will go to them.' PCL copies rebound.

A Short History of The Royal Tank Corps
Not stated   TM; NAM
Aldershot; Gale & Polden Ltd; 1945; ISBN None; xii + 168pp/1 x bw PIfep/4 x bw PI/9 x bw SI/2 x bw M; s/b; Indexed Y; Glossary N; Appendices Y; Bibliography N; 190 x 125 (12mo); Uncommon
Notes: Sixth Edition, reprint of fifth edition, not updated for WWII. The editor is John E. Cairnes, Adjutant at Bovington and later CO of 50RTR.

Armoured Operations in Italy
From May 1944 to January 1945
Collenette, Maj. D. A.   TM; IWM; NAM; RE
Italy; Allied Force HQ; 1945; ISBN None; 90pp/7 x bw PI/1 x clr SI/10 x bw SI/11 x clr Mf/1 x bw M; s/b; Indexed Y; Glossary N; Appendices Y; Bibliography N; 322 x 204 (Folio); Rare
NOTES: The book presents eleven actions involving armour with the following regiments: 3H, 7H, 2RTR, 6RTR, 51RTR, 46R, and 142RAC. Introduction by Maj-Gen. H. L. Birks. Tipped in Errata slip. 10 sketch illustrations by Capt. E. G. Manning. 750 copies printed. Also facsimile reprinted by MLRS Books, 2009.

The Life and Letters of Paul Fisher
Artist. Scientist. Soldier.
With reproductions from a selection of original drawings by Paul Fisher.
Various IWM; NAM
West Drayton; Bastien Brothers; 1945; ISBN None; 42pp/20 x bw SI; h/b / d/j Brown cloth; Indexed N; Glossary N; Appendices N; Bibliography N; 260 x 187 (4to); Rare
NOTES: Paul Fisher served in 256 Forward Delivery Squadron, RAC. The book contains reproductions of some of his sketches (nine related to his war service), a brief biographical account, tributes from friends and colleagues, and some of his letters, pre-war and wartime.

The Italian Campaign 3 Sep 1943 - 2 May 1945
Royal Armoured Corps
No imprint TM; IWM; NAM
No imprint; No imprint; n.d. [1945]; ISBN None; 99pp/1 x sepia PI/43 x sepia SI/1 x bw M; s/b; Indexed N; Glossary N; Appendices N; Bibliography N; 305 x 405 (4to)
NOTES: Commemorative publication which includes reproductions of 43 of Eric Manning's sketches made during the campaign. These include several commanding officers of brigades in Italy. Includes a full listing of all the RAC regiments that took part in the Italian campaign.

Our Armoured Forces
Martel, K.C.B., K.B.E., D.S.O., M.C., Giffard le Q., Lt-Gen. Sir TM; IWM; NAM
London; Faber and Faber Limited; 1945; ISBN None; 406pp/2 x bw Mf/15 x bw M; h/b / d/j Black cloth; Indexed Y; Glossary Y; Appendices Y; Bibliography N; 222 x 140 (8vo)
NOTES: A study of the strategy and theory of Britain's armoured forces and policies by this expert author, together with his own thoughts on the subject.

To the Stars...
A Tribute to the Junior Officers of the Royal Armoured Corps
Mabyn Ross, Peter TM; IWM; NAM
Bovington; RAC Publications; n.d. [1946]; ISBN None; 96pp/3 x bw PIfep/19 x bw SI; h/b / d/j Red cloth; Indexed N; Glossary N; Appendices N; Bibliography N; 222 x 142 (8vo); Uncommon
NOTES: The book goes through, in reasonable detail, the training and courses of an RAC officer cadet. It also provides some brief early information on the Inns of Court regiment. Also by author - *All Valiant Dust*, see 3RTR listing.

With Pennants Flying
The Immortal Deeds of the Royal Armoured Corps
Masters, David
London; John Spencer & Co. (Publishers) Ltd; 1957; ISBN None; 159pp/No illus.; p/b; Indexed N; Glossary N; Appendices N; Bibliography N; 181 x 120 (12mo); Uncommon
NOTES: Badger Books abridged edition, chapters XI and XVII dropped from the original 1943 publication.

Orders of Battle
United Kingdom and Colonial Formations and Units in the Second World War 1939 - 1945
Volume I
Joslen, Lieut-Col, H. F. TM; IWM; NAM; RMAS; PCL; RE
London; Her Majesty's Stationery Office; 1960; ISBN None; xii + 404pp/No illus.; h/b / d/j Red cloth; Indexed N; Glossary Y; Appendices Y; Bibliography N; 340 x 212 (Folio); Uncommon
NOTES: Immense reference work, still a benchmark today. Vol. I holds information relating to armoured units, containing the compositions of the armoured divisions and brigades and their regiments. Extremely useful for establishing where formations served, for how long and under which senior formation; also includes basic WEs for divisions and brigades. 3 x gatefold pages. 5000 copies published. Republished in 1964 and 1974 and facsimile single volume reprints 1990 and 2003, q.q.v.

Orders of Battle
United Kingdom and Colonial Formations and Units in the Second World War 1939 - 1945
Volume II
Joslen, Lieut-Col, H. F. TM; IWM; NAM; RMAS; PCL; RE
London; Her Majesty's Stationery Office; 1960; ISBN None; x + 224pp/No illus.; h/b / d/j Red cloth; Indexed Y; Glossary Y; Appendices N; Bibliography N; 340 x 212 (Folio); Uncommon
NOTES: Vol II contains OoBs for El Alamein and the Normandy landings, pagination runs p405 - p628, 1 x gatefold page. References to Phantom and IoC are in this volume. 5000 copies published.

A Bibliography of Regimental Histories of the British Army
White, I.S.O., M.M., F. R. Hist. S., Arthur S. (Compiler) TM; IWM; NAM
London; The Society for Army Historical Research; 1965; ISBN None; viii + 265pp/No illus.; h/b / d/j Green cloth; Indexed Y; Glossary N; Appendices Y; Bibliography N; 253 x 194 (4to)
NOTES: Collated by the MoD's Librarian, Arthur White, it was published largely in response to the quantity of works published after WWI and WWII. Remained the prime source until Victor Sutcliffe's *Regiments of the British Army* published in the late 2000s. Excludes memoirs and journals. (The copy with the NAM has typed additional entries pasted in.)

Short Histories of the Regiments of the Royal Armoured Corps
Not stated TM
Wareham; RAC Tank Museum; n.d. [c.1970]; ISBN None; 61pp/19 x bw SI; s/b; Indexed N; Glossary N; Appendices N; Bibliography N; 202 x 148 (8vo)
NOTES: Tank Museum publication providing summary histories of the regiments of the RAC up to c. 1970. Each regiment has two to three pages with, generally, one WWII paragraph therein.

The Valentine in North Africa 1942 - 43
Armour in Action 1
Perrett, Bryan   TM; IWM; NAM
London; Ian Allan Ltd; 1972; ISBN 7110 0262 2; 80pp/86 x bw PI/5 x bw SI/6 x bw M; h/b / d/j Brown cloth; Indexed N; Glossary N; Appendices Y; Bibliography N; 222 x 140 (8vo)
NOTES: Whilst this book deals with the Valentine tank, it is also very much a history of 40, 46 and 50RTR, the Valentine equipped regiments of 23AB in North Africa July 1942 to May 1943. Well written and engaging. Included are many veterans' quotations and the author provides insights into these men in the narrative with asides as to their professions after the war. Well illustrated. Appendices include an overview of the Valentine and a brief history of 23AB.

The Matilda
Armour in Action 2
Perrett, Bryan   TM; IWM
London; Ian Allan Ltd; 1972; ISBN 0 7110 0405 6; 112pp/96 x bw PI/12 x bw SI/11 x bw M; h/b / d/j Green cloth; Indexed N; Glossary N; Appendices Y; Bibliography N; 222 x 140 (8vo)
NOTES: Following the same format as the author's sister title on the Valentine. This book covers 4RTR and 7RTR in France 1940, 4RTR, 7RTR, 42RTR and 44RTR in North Africa and 4RTR in Eritrea. Includes several veterans' quotations and is well illustrated.

The Churchill
Armour in Action 4
Perrett, Bryan   TM; IWM
London; Ian Allan Ltd; 1974; ISBN 0 7110 0533 8; 148pp/66 x bw PI/11 x bw SI/12 x bw M; h/b / d/j Brown cloth; Indexed N; Glossary N; Appendices N; Bibliography N; 222 x 140 (8vo)
NOTES: Follows the pattern of the author's books on the Valentine and Matilda. Tells the story of the Churchill through example actions of NIH and 51RTR in Tunisia; NIH, 51RTR and 145RAC in Italy; and 7RTR, 9RTR, 107RAC, 141RAC, 147RAC, 153RAC, 4GrenGds, 4ColdGds and 3ScotsGds in NWE. Good reference for some of the more obscure actions where Churchills were employed.

Through Mud and Blood
Infantry/Tank Operations in World War II
Perrett, Bryan   TM; IWM; NAM
London; Robert Hale & Company; 1975; ISBN 0 7091 4822 4; 272pp/31 x bw PI/1 x bw SI/30 x bw M; h/b / d/j Black cloth; Indexed Y; Glossary N; Appendices Y; Bibliography Y; 222 x 142 (8vo)
NOTES: Here the author combines his three previous books on the infantry tanks, Matilda, Valentine and Churchill, re-using much but also adding some new material. Includes some new recollections from veterans. Predominantly the same photographic selection but again some new, particularly illustrating NWE. All four infantry tank books by this author should be referenced to cover the subject because they all bring something discrete. Appendices include technical summaries of the infantry tanks and 'Other Peoples 'I' Tanks.'

Tank Tracks to Rangoon
Perrett, Bryan TM; IWM; NAM
London; Robert Hale Limited; 1978; ISBN 0 7091 6481 5; xiv + 255pp/30 x bw Pl/14 x bw M; h/b / d/j Red cloth; Indexed Y; Glossary N; Appendices Y; Bibliography Y; 222 x 142 (8vo)
NOTES: The author opens with a review of the Japanese soldier and his weapons, an essential forward to the story of fighting in Burma. The following regiments have some of their actions detailed to a greater or lesser degree: 3DG, 7H, 25D, 2RTR, 116RAC, 146RAC, 149RAC, and 150RAC. Also contains a good deal of information on the actions of the Indian armoured regiments. Appendices include comment on Japanese armour and technical information on Allied tanks.

A History of the Royal Armoured Corps and its Predecessors 1914 - 1975
Macksey, M.C., Maj. (Retd), Kenneth TM; IWM; NAM; RMAS
Beaminster; Newtown Publications; 1983; ISBN 0-950853-60-7; 229pp/8 x bw SIfep/30 x bw PI/3 x bw SI/13 x bw M; h/b / d/j Red cloth; Indexed Y; Glossary N; Appendices Y; Bibliography Y; 234 x 155 (8vo)
NOTES: An excellent volume to refer to for a history of the Royal Armoured Corps, balancing the extent of early tank history against the wartime and post-war history.

Regimental Journals and Other Serial Publications of the British Army 1660 - 1981
An Annotated Bibliography in Four Volumes
Lake, Frederick H. (Compiler) IWM
London; Ministry of Defence Whitehall Library; 1985; ISBN None; 1180pp in 4 vols plus Index volume published later; h/b Blue cloth; Indexed Y; Glossary N; Appendices N; Bibliography N; 298 x 210 (4to)
NOTES: A monumental work listing as many regimental, corps, command, etc. journals as the author could find, to form the basis for his Library Association thesis. Four copies deposited at: Library Association x 2, MOD Whitehall Library London x 1, Author x 1.

Regimental Journals and Other Serial Publications of the British Army 1660 - 1981
An Annotated Bibliography in Four Volumes
Lake, Frederick H. (Compiler) IWM; NAM; RMAS; PCL
London; Ministry of Defence Whitehall Library; 1987; ISBN None; Vol 1 - 322pp / Vol 2 - 328pp / Vol 3 - 293pp / Vol 4 - 116pp / Index - 177pp/Vol 2 & 3 and Vol 4 & Index bound together; h/b Red cloth & biscuit canvas; Indexed Y; Glossary N; Appendices N; Bibliography N; 241 x 190 (8vo)
NOTES: Reduced size Library Editions deposited at: AMOT copy 1A / IWM copy 1B / MOD Whitehall Library, London copy 1C / National Army Museum copy 1D / Institute of Historical Research copy 1E / PCL copy 1F (Missing) / RMAS copy 1G.

A Bibliography of Regimental Histories of the British Army
White, I.S.O., M.M., F. R. Hist. S., Arthur S. (Compiler) TM; NAM
London; The London Stamp Exchange Ltd; 1988; ISBN 0 948130 61 X; viii + 317pp/No illus.; h/b / d/j Green cloth; Indexed Y; Glossary N; Appendices Y; Bibliography N; 246 x 170 (8vo)
NOTES: Facsimile reprint plus an addendum covering works previously omitted and bringing the list up to date.

MISCELLANEOUS 297

Orders of Battle
Second World War 1939 - 1945
Joslen, Lieut-Col, H. F. NAM; PCL
London; The London Stamp Exchange Ltd; 1990; ISBN 0 948130 03 2; xii + 628pp/No illus.; h/b / d/j Black cloth; Indexed Y; Glossary Y; Appendices Y; Bibliography N; 305 x 258 (Quarto); Uncommon
NOTES: Facsimile reprint of 1960 editions in one volume with new introduction.

Tank Tracks to Rangoon
Perrett, Bryan NAM
London; Robert Hale Limited; 1992; ISBN 0 7090 4749 5; xiv + 255pp/12 x bw Pl/14 x bw M; s/b; Indexed Y; Glossary N; Appendices Y; Bibliography Y; 205 x 137 (8vo)
NOTES: Reprint of 1978 first edition, same pagination, reduced photo selection.

A Bibliography of Regimental Histories of the British Army
White, I.S.O., M.M., F. R. Hist. S., Arthur S. (Compiler)
Dallington; The Naval & Military Press Ltd; 1992; ISBN 1 897632 25 8; viii + 331pp/No illus.; h/b / d/j Green cloth; Indexed Y; Glossary N; Appendices Y; Bibliography N; 246 x 171 (8vo)
NOTES: NMP facsimile reprint plus an addendum covering works up to the early 1990s.

Orders of Battle
Second World War 1939 - 1945
Joslen, Lieut-Col, H. F.
Uckfield; Naval & Military Press Limited; 2003; ISBN 978-1843424741; xii + 628pp/No illus.; s/b; Indexed Y; Glossary Y; Appendices Y; Bibliography N
NOTES: Facsimile reprint by NMP of 1990 edition, available in s/b. (Not physically inspected.)

Regiments of the British Army
A handbook with book lists. Part 1 - Infantry
Sutcliffe, Victor
East Rudham; Mulberry Coach House Books; 2007; ISBN 978-0-9556364-0-0; viii + 505pp/No illus.; h/b Blue cloth; Indexed Y; Glossary N; Appendices N; Bibliography N; 222 x 142 (8vo)
NOTES: In addition to the bibliographical entries, the author has also added background notes on the regiments including regimental titles, mottoes, and dress distinctions for many. Excludes memoirs and journals.

Regiments of the British Army
A handbook with book lists. Part 2 - Cavalry and Armour
Sutcliffe, Victor TM
East Rudham; Mulberry Coach House Books; 2008; ISBN 978-0-9556364-1-7; viii + 283pp/No illus.; h/b Blue cloth; Indexed Y; Glossary N; Appendices N; Bibliography N; 222 x 142 (8vo)
NOTES: Second volume dealing with armour related regiments. Loose errata sheet. Excludes memoirs and journals. Part 3 - Artillery was not formally published.

Armoured Operations in Italy
From May 1944 to January 1945
Birks, Maj. H. L.
Smalldale; MLRS Books; 2009; ISBN 978-1847914002; See Notes
NOTES: Facsimile reprint by MLRS Books of 1945 first edition.

Tank Tracks to Rangoon
The Story of British Armour in Burma
Perrett, Bryan
Barnsley; Pen and Sword Aviation; 2014; ISBN 978-1-78383-115-9; xiv + 255pp/12 x bw Pl/14 x bw M; s/b; Indexed Y; Glossary N; Appendices Y; Bibliography Y; 234 x 156 (8vo)
NOTES: Pen and Sword reprint of 1978 first edition. (Not physically inspected.)

Key to Book Entries
Book Title and Sub-title(s)
Author   Museum Holdings
Place of Publication; Publisher; Date of Publication; ISBN; Pages/Illustrations; Binding; Indexed; Glossary; Appendices; Bibliography; Size (in mm); Availability
NOTES:

Appendix A

Theatres of Operations

Unit	France	NA	Italy	FE	NWE	UK
1 HCR	N	Y†	Y	N	Y	Y
2 HCR	N	N	N	N	Y	Y
KDG •	N	Y	Y***	N	N	Y
BAYS •	Y	Y†	Y	N	N	Y
3 DG •	N	N	N	Y	N	N
4/7 DG •	Y	N	N	N	Y‡	Y
5 DG •	Y	N	N	N	Y	Y
ROYALS	N	Y†	Y	N	Y	Y
GREYS	N	Y†	Y	N	Y	Y
3 H •	N	Y**†	Y	N	N	Y
4 H •	N	Y*†	Y	N	N	Y
7 H •	N	Y	Y	Y	N	N
8 H •	N	Y†	N	N	Y	Y
9 L •	Y	Y†	Y	N	N	Y
10 H •	Y	Y†	Y	N	N	Y
11 H •	N	Y†	Y	N	Y	Y
12 L •	Y	Y†	Y	N	N	Y
13/18 H •	Y	N	N	N	Y‡	Y
14/20 H •	N	Y	Y	N	N	N
15/19 H •	Y	N	N	N	Y	Y
16/5 L •	N	Y	Y	N	N	Y
17/21 L •	N	Y	Y	N	N	Y
22 DGNS	N	N	N	N	Y‡	Y
23 H	N	N	N	N	Y	Y
24 L	N	N	N	N	Y‡	Y
25 DGNS	N	N	N	Y	N	N
26 H	N	N	N	Y	N	N
27 L	N	Y	Y	N	N	Y
1 R Tks •	N	Y†	Y	N	Y	Y
2 R Tks •	Y	Y	Y	Y	N	Y
3 R Tks •	Y	Y*†	N	N	Y	Y
4 R Tks •	Y	Y	N	N	Y	Y
5 R Tks •	Y	Y†	Y	N	Y	Y
6 R Tks •	N	Y	Y	N	N	N
7 R Tks •	Y	Y**	N	N	Y	Y

Unit	France	NA	Italy	FE	NWE	UK
8 R Tks •	N	Y†	Y	N	N	Y
9 R Tks	N	N	N	N	Y	Y
10 R Tks	N	N	N	N	N	Y
11 R Tks	N	Y	N	N	Y	Y
12 R Tks	N	Y	Y	N	N	Y
1 Recce Regt	N	Y	Y	N	N	Y
2 Recce Regt	N	N	N	Y	N	Y
3 Recce Regt	N	N	N	N	Y‡	Y
4 Recce Regt	N	Y	Y***	N	N	Y
5 Recce Regt	N	N	Y	Y	Y	Y
15 Recce Regt	N	N	N	N	Y	Y
18 Recce Regt	N	N	N	Y	N	Y
38 Recce Regt	N	N	N	N	N	Y
43 Recce Regt	N	N	N	N	Y	Y
44 Recce Regt	N	Y†	Y	N	N	Y
45 Recce Regt	N	N	N	Y	N	Y
46 Recce Regt	N	Y	Y***	N	N	Y
49 Recce Regt	N	N	N	N	Y	Y
50 Recce Regt	N	Y	N	N	N	Y
51 Recce Regt	N	Y†	N	N	N	Y
52 Recce Regt	N	N	N	N	Y	Y
53 Recce Regt	N	N	N	N	Y	Y
54 Recce Regt	N	N	N	N	N	Y
56 Recce Regt	N	Y	Y	N	N	Y
59 Recce Regt	N	N	N	N	Y	Y
61 Recce Regt	N	N	N	N	Y‡	Y
161 Recce Regt	N	N	N	N	N	Y
1 Abn Recce Sqn	N	N	Y	N	Y	Y
6 Abn Recce Regt	N	N	Y	N	Y‡	Y
PHANTOM	Y	Y*	Y	N	Y‡	Y
NIH^	N	Y	Y	N	N	Y
R WILTS YEO	N	Y†	Y	N	N	Y
WARWICK YEO	N	Y†	Y	N	N	Y
YORKS H	N	Y	N	N	N	Y
NOTTS YEO	N	Y†	N	N	Y‡	Y
STAFFS YEO	N	Y†	N	N	Y‡	Y
CHESHIRE YEO	N	Y	N	N	N	Y
YORKS DGNS	N	Y†	N	N	N	Y
N SOMERSET YEO	N	Y	N	N	N	Y
1 DERBY YEO •	N	Y	Y	N	N	Y
2 DERBY YEO	N	Y†	N	N	Y	Y
1 RGH •	N	N	N	N	N	Y
2 RGH	N	Y	N	N	N	Y
1 LOTHIANS •	Y	N	N	N	Y	Y

APPENDIX A – THEATRES OF OPERATIONS

Unit	France	NA	Italy	FE	NWE	UK
2 LOTHIANS	N	N	Y	N	N	Y
1 FF YEO •	Y	N	N	N	Y	Y
2 FF YEO	N	N	N	N	Y	Y
W DGNS •	N	N	N	N	Y‡	Y
SHARPSHOOTERS 3 CLY •	N	Y	Y	N	Y	Y
SHARPSHOOTERS 4 CLY	N	Y†	Y	N	Y	Y
1 N YEO •	N	N	N	N	Y	Y
2 N YEO	N	N	N	N	Y	Y
1 E RIDING YEO •	Y	N	N	N	Y‡	Y
2 E RIDING YEO	N	N	N	N	N	Y
INNS OF COURT	N	N	N	N	Y‡	Y
40 R Tks •	N	Y†	Y***	N	N	Y
41 R Tks •	N	Y†	N	N	N	Y
42 R Tks •	N	Y†	N	N	Y	Y
43 R Tks •	N	N	N	Y	N	Y
44 R Tks •	N	Y†	Y	N	Y	Y
45 R Tks •	N	Y†	N	N	N	Y
46 R Tks	N	Y†	Y***	N	N	Y
47 R Tks	N	Y†	N	N	N	Y
48 R Tks	N	Y	Y	N	N	Y
49 R Tks	N	N	N	N	Y	Y
50 R Tks	N	Y†	Y***	N	N	Y
51 R Tks	N	Y	Y	N	N	Y
107 RAC	N	N	N	N	Y	Y
108 RAC	N	N	N	N	N	Y
109 RAC	N	N	N	N	N	Y
110 RAC	N	N	N	N	N	Y
111 RAC	N	N	N	N	N	Y
112 RAC	N	N	N	N	N	Y
113 RAC	N	N	N	N	N	Y
114 RAC	N	N	N	N	N	Y
115 RAC	N	N	N	N	N	Y
116 RAC	N	N	N	Y	N	N
141 RAC	N	N	N	N	Y‡	Y
142 RAC	N	Y	Y	N	N	Y
143 RAC	N	N	N	N	N	Y
144 RAC	N	N	N	N	Y	Y
145 RAC	N	Y	Y	N	N	Y
146 RAC	N	N	N	Y	N	N
147 RAC	N	N	N	N	Y	Y
148 RAC	N	N	N	N	Y	Y
149 RAC	N	N	N	Y	N	N

Unit	France	NA	Italy	FE	NWE	UK
150 RAC	N	N	N	Y	N	N
151 RAC	N	N	N	N	N	Y
152 RAC	N	N	N	N	N	Y
153 RAC	N	N	N	N	Y	Y
154 RAC	N	N	N	N	N	Y
155 RAC	N	N	N	N	N	Y
156 RAC	N	N	N	N	N	Y
157 RAC	N	N	N	N	N	Y
158 RAC	N	N	N	Y	N	Y
159 RAC	N	N	N	Y	N	Y
160 RAC	N	N	N	Y	N	Y
161 RAC	N	N	N	N	N	Y
162 RAC	N	N	N	N	N	Y
163 RAC	N	N	N	Y	N	N
2 GREN GDS	N	N	N	N	Y	Y
4 GREN GDS	N	N	N	N	Y	Y
1 COLDM GDS	N	N	N	N	Y	Y
4 COLDM GDS	N	N	N	N	Y	Y
3 SG	N	N	N	N	Y	Y
2 IG	N	N	N	N	Y	Y
2 WG	N	N	N	N	Y	Y

^ **NIH** is listed here in accordance with the Army List. However, the regiment was brigaded above 12RTR in 21TB at the end of 1944. 12RTR was a war-raised but regular regiment. Without a definitive answer to this anomaly, the NIH is listed between the Reconnaissance Corps and the Yeomanry, with reference to 1944 Army Lists.

• Regiments in the Royal Armoured Corps upon its creation in April 1939.

This chart notes a regiment's presence in that theatre, it did not necessarily fight in that theatre.

France   France 1940.
NA   North Africa/Greece/Palestine/etc.
     * Also operated in Greece 1941.
     ** Also operated on Crete 1941.
     † Took part in the battle of El Alamein; with armour. (4H and 8H operated as a composite regiment – 4/8H.)
Italy   Sicily/Italy/Greece.
     *** Also operated in Greece 1944/45.
FE   Far East, India/Burma.
NWE   North West Europe, Normandy to Germany.
     ‡ Took part in the landings on D-Day 6th June 1944. (3R and 61R supplied Contact Detachments for D-Day)
UK   United Kingdom.

Appendix B

Regiments Operating Funnies

Unit	Prime 'Funnie'	Secondary 'Funnies'	Brigade
4/7 DG	DD	-	27AB
13/18 H	DD	-	27AB
22 DGNS	Crab	-	30AB
4 R Tks	Buffalo	-	33AB
7 R Tks	Crocodile	-	31AB
11 R Tks	CDL	Buffalo	1TB
42 R Tks	CDL	-	1TB
43 R Tks	Experimental regiment. May 1945 – CDL.		(79AD)
44 R Tks	DD	-	4AB
49 R Tks	CDL	Kangaroo (as 49APC Regt)	1TB/35TB
44 R Tks	DD	-	4AB
49 R Tks	CDL	Kangaroo (as 49APC Regt)	1TB/35TB
STAFFS YEO	DD	-	(79AD)
1 LOTHIANS	Crab	-	30AB
1 FF YEO	Crocodile	-	31AB
W DGNS	Crab	-	30AB
1 N YEO	Buffalo	-	33AB
E RIDING YEO	DD	Buffalo	27AB/33AB
141 RAC	Crocodile	-	31AB
152 RAC	CDL	-	35TB
155 RAC	CDL	-	35TB
5 Ass Regt RE	AVRE	-	1 Ass Bde RE
6 Ass Regt RE	AVRE	-	1 Ass Bde RE
42 Ass Regt RE	AVRE	-	1 Ass Bde RE

This chart provides an overview of the main types of 'Funnies' employed by the regiments serving in the 79AD and attached brigades during the war.

AVRE   Armoured Vehicle Royal Engineers: engineers' support tanks.
Buffalo   LVT – Landing Vehicle Tracked – amphibious cargo carrier.
CDL   Canal Defence Light: high powered search light.
Crab   Mine clearing flail tanks.
Crocodile   Flame-throwing tanks.
DD   Duplex Drive: swimming tanks.
Kangaroo   Armoured Personnel Carrier.

Appendix C

Cavalry and RTR Regimental Titles Post-war

From the end of World War Two to the present day, the army has undergone several contractions as economic and political pressures have dictated. The natural need to move from a wartime to a peacetime army meant that dozens of regiments were placed in suspended animation or disbanded. All of the infantry raised RAC regiments were disbanded fairly quickly or reverted to the infantry role.

Within a year of the war's end the Reconnaissance Corps ceased to exist, its role effectively taken by Yeomanry units in the post-war Royal Armoured Corps and the Yeomanry became ever more distilled into squadrons or troops of larger units. The result was a tank arm managed solely by the RAC rather than several diverse branches during the war.

As this book was being written, the latest contraction was announced in the form of Army 2020. The 9th/12th Royal Lancers (Prince of Wales's) and The Queens Royal Lancers will be amalgamated to form The Royal Lancers and the 1st and 2nd Royal Tank Regiments will be merged to become a single regiment - The Royal Tank Regiment. The Royal Tank Regiment held its first parade on 2 August 2014 and The Royal Lancers are due to be formed on 1 May 2015.

The following table provides a quick reference to the post war amalgamations and mergers of the cavalry and RTR regiments. Some regiments take the opportunity to publish an updated history upon these amalgamations/mergers and naturally adopt their new regimental title. This chart will help the reader identify which regiments formed the newly titled one.

WWII Title	Amalgamations and Mergers		
1st Household Cavalry Regiment			1993 – The Household Cavalry Regiment & The Household Cavalry Mounted Regiment
2nd Household Cavalry Regiment		1969 – The Blues and Royals (Royal Horse Guards and 1st Dragoons)	1993 – The Household Cavalry Regiment & The Household Cavalry Mounted Regiment
1st King's Dragoon Guards	1959 – 1st The Queen's Dragoon Guards		

APPENDIX C – CAVALRY AND RTR REGIMENTAL TITLES POST-WAR

WWII Title	Amalgamations and Mergers			
The Queen's Bays (2nd Dragoon Guards)	1959 – 1st The Queen's Dragoon Guards			
3rd Carabiniers (Prince of Wales's Dragoon Guards)		1971 – The Royal Scots Dragoon Guards (Carabiniers and Greys)		
4th/7th Royal Dragoon Guards				1992 – The Royal Dragoon Guards
5th Inniskilling Dragoon Guards				1992 – The Royal Dragoon Guards
1st The Royal Dragoons	1961 - The Royal Dragoons (1st Dragoons)	1969 – The Blues and Royals (Royal Horse Guards and 1st Dragoons)		1992 – The Household Cavalry Regiment & The Household Cavalry Mounted Regiment
The Royal Scots Greys (2nd Dragoons)		1971 – The Royal Scots Dragoon Guards (Carabiniers and Greys)		
3rd The King's Own Hussars	1958 – The Queen's Own Hussars			1993 - The Queen's Royal Hussars (The Queen's Own and Irish)
4th Queen's Own Hussars	1958 – The Queen's Royal Irish Hussars			1993 - The Queen's Royal Hussars (The Queen's Own and Irish)
7th Queen's Own Hussars	1958 – The Queen's Own Hussars			1993 - The Queen's Royal Hussars (The Queen's Own and Irish)
8th King's Royal Irish Hussars	1958 – The Queen's Royal Irish Hussars			1993 - The Queen's Royal Hussars (The Queen's Own and Irish)
9th Queen's Royal Lancers	1960 – 9th/12th Royal Lancers (Prince of Wales's)			2015 – The Royal Lancers

WWII Title	Amalgamations and Mergers		
10th Royal Hussars (Prince of Wales's Own)	1969 - The Royal Hussars (Prince of Wales's Own)		1992 - The King's Royal Hussars
11th Hussars (Prince Albert's Own)	1969 - The Royal Hussars (Prince of Wales's Own)		1992 - The King's Royal Hussars
12th Royal Lancers (Prince of Wales's)	1960 – 9th/12th Royal Lancers (Prince of Wales's)		2015 – The Royal Lancers
13th/18th Royal Hussars (Queen Mary's Own)			1992 – The Light Dragoons
14th/20th Kings Hussars			1992 - The King's Royal Hussars
15th/19th The King's Royal Hussars			1992 – The Light Dragoons
16th/5th Lancers	1954 – 16th/5th The Queen's Royal Lancers	1993 – The Queen's Royal Lancers	2015 – The Royal Lancers
17th/21st Lancers		1993 – The Queen's Royal Lancers	2015 – The Royal Lancers
1st Royal Tank Regiment			2014 – The Royal Tank Regiment
2nd Royal Tank Regiment			2014 - Disbanded
3rd Royal Tank Regiment		1992 – 2nd Royal Tank Regiment	
4th Royal Tank Regiment		1992 – 1st Royal Tank Regiment	
5th Royal Tank Regiment		1969 - Disbanded	
6th Royal Tank Regiment	1959 – 3rd Royal Tank Regiment		
7th Royal Tank Regiment	1959 - 4th Royal Tank Regiment		
8th Royal Tank Regiment	1960 – 5th Royal Tank Regiment		

Index of Authors

A

Adair, Maj-Gen. Allan, 287, 288
Adams, Jack, 225
Addyman, Ronald, 180, 185
Allen, W. D., 163, 164
Anderson Jr, Richard C., 268
Anderson, Ray, 178
Andrews, Capt. K. S., 98
Ansell, Col Sir Mike, 155
Antonio, D. G., 156
Aston, Maj., 234
Astor, Michael, 125
Athawes, Peter D., 135
Atkins, H. W., 292

B

Bailey, O.B.E., R.E., Lt-Col D. C., 233, 235
Baker, M.C., Capt. Peter, 124
Baker, Paul, 137
Baker, Peter, 123
Barclay, C.B.E., D.S.O., Brig. C. N., 63, 104, 177, 182, 195, 197, 198, 209, 211, 231
Barker, A. J., 196
Barlett, Capt. W. J. C. (Contr.), 98
Batchellor, F. H. Dr, 115
Baynes, John, 17
Beale, Peter, 96, 97
Beckett, Frank, 271
Beckles, Gordon, 291
Beddington C.B.E., Maj-Gen. W. R., 21, 23
Belfield, Eversley, 19, 22
Bellamy, Bill, 46, 47
Bellis, M. A., 134
Bellis, Malcolm A., 262, 270
Bentinck, Maj. Mark, 259, 260
Bird, O.B.E., D.L., Col J. A. C., 103, 108
Bird, S/Sgt D., 152
Birks, Maj. H. L., 298

Birt, Raymond, 67
Bishop, M.C., Geoffrey S. C., 70
Bishop, Tim, 55
Blacker, 'Monkey', 29, 69
Blacker, Gen. Sir Cecil, 30, 31, 70
Blacklock, Michael, 36
Blaxland, Gregory, 203
Boardman, Capt. C. J., 30
Bolitho, Hector, 39
Booth, Tony, 183
Boscawen, Robert, 245, 246
Boyd, Derek, 234
Boyd, Neil, 40
Boynton, Sir John, 105
Braddon, Russell, 13, 238, 239
Brander, Michael, 49
Brereton, J. M., 27, 44, 197, 199, 210, 212, 225
Brett, D.S.O., O.B.E., M.C., Lt-Col G. A., 224, 225
Brett-Smith, Richard, 52
Briant, Keith, 238
Bright, O.B.E., Joan (Ed.), 48
Brisset, Jean, 281
Brookes, Jack, 58
Brown, M.C., Lt-Col A. G., 178
Buckledee, Harry, 52, 53
Bull, Stephen, 103, 107, 215
Bullock, Richard (Ed.), 159
Burke-Gaffney, M.C., Lt-Col J. J., 219
Burton, Brian, 154
Butler, M.C., Capt. K .F., 60
Butterworth, Terry, 198, 199, 211, 213

C

Calvey, Robert W., 112
Carmichael, Ian, 67, 68
Carrington, Lord, 241, 242
Carver, Brig. R. M. P., 262
Carver, Lt-Col R. M. P., 35, 37, 272
Cawston, R. F. H., 163
Cawston, Roy, 162

Cazenove, H. De L., 165
Cecil, Hugh & Mirabel, 254
Chadwick, 14483488, Sgt K., 79, 80
Chadwick, Kenneth, 75
Chadwick, M.C., Captain Tom, 38
Chamberlain, Tim, 106
Chaplin, Lt-Col H. D., 230
Chapman, M.B.E., M.A., Maj. Roger, 119, 230
Charrington, Richard, 49, 55
Christopherson, DSO, MC, TD, Stanley, 145, 146
Clarke, C.B., C.B.E., Brig. Dudley, 51
Clifford, Rollo, 152
Close, Major Bill, 84, 85, 86
Cloudsley-Thompson, J. L., 164
Collenette, Maj. D. A., 292
Connolly, M., 25
Connolly, M. L., 25
Conradi, Peter J., 129
Coogan, Chris, 147
Cook, Edmund, M.B.E., 182
Cook, H., 221
Cook, Helen & Bill, 150
Cooper, Alexander, 166, 215
Cooper, Derek, 16
Coulthard, George (Brum), 227
Courage, D.S.O., Maj. G., 61
Couser, Ralph (Ed.), 248
Cowper, Col J. M., 187, 219
Creighton-Williamson, Donald, 218
Crisp, Robert, 81, 82, 83
Crocker, Vincent A., 50
Cropper, Andy, 71, 141
Crosthwaite, D.S.O., E.R.D., Ivor, 243
Cundall, Charles B., 56

D

Dallas, Ron, 153
Daniell, David Scott, 109, 110, 111, 214, 224, 226, 227
Daniels, Maj. M. J., 285
Davies, Lt J. L., 242
Davies, Peter, 170
d'Avigdor-Goldsmith, Maj. J. A., 26
Davy, C. B., C. B. E., D. S. O., Brig. G. M. O., 44, 45

Dawnay, C.B.E, D.S.O., Maj-Gen. A. G. C., 244
Dawnay, D.S.O., Brig. D., 49
de la Falaise, Henry, 53
de Rusett, Alan, 115
Dean, Capt. C. G. T., 102, 103, 106, 108, 214, 215
Deedes, K.C.B., C.M.G., D.S.O., Gen. Sir Charles P., 216
Delaforce, Patrick, 78, 79, 80, 85, 86, 263, 264, 265, 276, 277, 278, 279, 281, 282, 284, 285, 286
Dodwell, K. C. E., 178
Doherty, Richard, 101, 132, 270, 286
Dolby, Eddie, 94
Donald, Maj. Alastair, 259, 260
Dormer, Hugh, 249, 251
Douglas Home, William, 202, 204
Douglas, Keith, 137, 138, 139, 140, 141, 142, 143, 145
Downham, Lt-Col, John, 209
Dowsett, Ken C., 117
Drew, Brig. Dinham, 90
Duffield, M.B.E., Captain C. V., 246
Duncan, Nigel, 284
Dunn, Kate (Ed.), 128
Dyas, O.B.E., Patrick, 164
Dyson, Stephen W., 189

E

Eastwood, Stuart, 189
Edwards, A. C., 271
Ellenberger, Brig. G. F., 217
Ellis, Maj. L. F., 252, 253, 254, 255
Ellison, V. C., 170
Elstob, Peter, 81, 82
Erskine, David, 247, 249
Evans, Roger, 29, 31
Everett, Martin, 225
Ewing, Ken, 143

F

Fairley, John, 120
Fallon, Dr, James A., 27, 57, 146, 170
Faris, Capt. Sandy (Ed.), 251
Farran, Roy, 38, 40
Farrell, Charles, 248

INDEX OF AUTHORS

Fear, Ray, 243
ffrench Blake, D.S.O., Lt-Col R. L. V., 64
ffrench Blake, R. L. V., 65
Field, Roger, 154
Fielden, Philip, 34
Fisher, John, 163
Fitzgeorge-Parker, Tim, 50, 149
Fitzgerald, M.C., Maj. D. J. L., 250
Fitzroy, Olivia, 45
Flaving, Scott, 198, 199, 211, 213
Fletcher, David, 284
Flint, Keith, 121, 122, 123
Fogg, Roger, 278
Foley, John, 187, 188
Forbes, Patrick, 239, 241, 268
Ford, Ken, 272
Forty, George, 75, 76, 78, 84, 91, 92, 94, 179, 274, 275, 277
Forty, George (Ed.), 78, 85, 90, 91, 94, 179
Foster Hall, M.C., Brigadier E., 202
Foster, Philip, 142
Fox, The Rev. Colin (Ed.), 104
Francis, Julian, 41
Fraser, G. S. (Eds.), 138, 139
Fraser, General Sir David, 240, 242, 243
Fraser, W. G. P., 21
Freer, Arthur F., 25
Fuller, Ronald, 252
Fullick, Roy, 46, 47
Futter, Geoffrey W., 284

G

Gardiner, Andrew S., 154
Gardiner, Gilbert Alec, 20
Garnett, Jack (Ed.), 90
Gaskin, W. D., 238
Gell, Harry, 163, 175
German, David, 147
Gethyn-Jones M.B.E., T.D., M.A., F.S.A., Canon J. Eric, 110
Giffard le Q., Lt-Gen. Sir, 293
Gillings, Murray, 228
Goddard, Fred, 80
Goodinge, Anthony, 247
Gordon-Creed, Geoffrey, 154
Gorman, Sir John, 251
Graham, Andrew, 160

Graham, Desmond, 139, 140, 145
Graham, Desmond (Ed.), 139, 140, 142, 143
Grant, Charles, 36, 245
Green, Howard, 188, 219
Greenwood, Barry (Ed.), 96
Greenwood, Richard Trevor, 96, 97
Grimond, Jo, 157
Grounds, Tom, 71, 72
Grover, O.B.E., Col G. W. M., 257
Groves J., 109
Gudgin, Peter, 95, 181

H

Haig, Major The Earl, OBE, DL, ARSA, 37
Hall, J. C. (Eds.), 138, 139
Hall, Roger, 176
Hallam, John, 191, 192, 207
Halsted, O.B.E., J. Michael G., 22
Hamilton, M.C., Stuart, 95
Hamilton, Stephen D., 184
Hammerton, Ian C., 68
Hamond, Robert, 107
Hanning, Henry, 241
Hanwell, Maj. W., 48
Harclerode, Peter, 122
Harvey, Richard, 170, 198, 199, 211, 213
Hatton TD, Major, D. M., 173
Hawkes, R.A., Maj. D. M., 265
Hayter, Peter, 78, 149
Heathcoat-Amory, Roderick, 34
Hendrie, William F., 249
Hennessey, Patrick, 57
Heseltine, Richard, 41
Hildyard, Myles, 144, 145
Hill, Col E. R., 244
Hill, D.S.O., Col E. R., 287, 288
Hill, Peter, 165
Hills, M.C., Stuart, 144
Hills, R. J. T., 14, 16, 34, 124
Hingston, Lt-Col Walter, 216
Hislop, John, 125
Hobson, C. H., 25
Hodges, John Henderson, 41
Holden, Matthew, 274
Holland, James (Ed.), 145, 146

Holloway, Roger, 230
Holmes, James H., 235
Honniball, F. E., 178
Hopkinson, C.B., D.S.O., O.B.E., M.C.,
  Maj-Gen G. C., 178
Horrocks, K.C.B., K.B.E., D.S.O., M.C.,
  LL.D. (Hon.), Sir Brian, 280
Horrocks, Lt.-Gen. Sir Brian (Ed.), 14,
  16, 34, 36, 44, 49, 52, 63, 75, 103,
  104, 107, 113, 188, 191, 192, 196,
  200, 205, 207, 210, 212, 214, 215,
  217, 218, 219, 221, 222, 223, 225,
  230, 234, 240, 247, 253, 257, 258
Howard Jones, Maj. S (Ed.), 98
Howard, Michael, 244
Howard, Roy, 117
Huett, Denis, 92
Hughes, Ted (Ed.), 138
Hunt, Donald F., 131
Hutchings, Maj. B. L. B., 19, 20
Huw-Williams, Capt. N., 158, 159
Huxley, Maj. Colin, 217

J

Jarvis, Robert B., 28, 58, 144, 147, 170
Johnson, Malcolm K., 217
Johnston, Barry, Ed., 242
Johnston, Brian, 241, 242
Johnston, Capt. M. E., 272, 276, 278
Jolly, Alan, 87, 208
Joly, Cyril, 273, 275
Jones, Keith, 168
Jones, Kevin, 276
Jones, M.B.E., Capt. A. J., 151
Jones-Mortimer, Maj. H., 252
Joslen, Lieut-Col, H. F., 294, 297

K

Kemp, R.N. (Retd), Lt-Cmdr P. K., 146
Kemsley, Capt. W., 105, 106
Kennard, George, 42
Kennedy, Guardsman D. J., 243, 268
Kennington, Eric, 291
Kinloch, Wallace (Ed.), 248
Knappett, Frank, 151
Knight, O.B.E., Col C. R. B., 202
Knight, R. G., 77

Koolwyk, Jos van, 110

L

Ladd, James, D., 258, 259
Lake, Frederick H. (Compiler), 296
Langdon, M.C., Maj. John, 85
Langley, Michael, 103, 107, 215
Lawrence, Vic, 165
Lawson, Capt. C. C. P., 158, 159
Lawson, John, 52
Leakey, Rea, 78, 84, 85, 91, 94, 179
Legard, Maj. C. P. D., 29
Leppard, Ernie, 143
Lewis, Iolo, 85, 152
Liddell Hart, Capt. B. H., 74
Lindsay, Capt. Martin, 272, 276, 278
Lindsay, F.R. Hist. S., Oliver (Ed.), 287,
  288
Lindsay, T. M., 138, 141, 143
Littlewood, Pete, 127
Lockhart, K.C.M.G., Sir Robert Bruce,
  257
Lummis, Eric, 206
Lunt, James, 63, 210, 212
Lynton, Mark, 84

M

Mabyn Ross, Peter, 172, 293
MacDonald, Maj. N. P., 175
Mace, Paul, 169
Macksey, Kenneth, 74, 75, 194, 204,
  208
Macksey, M.C., Maj. (Retd), Kenneth,
  296
Macksey, Maj. K., 75
Maher, M.B.E., Maj. A. J., 103, 108
Mallinson, Allan, 57, 58, 59, 62
Manby, T. G., 149
Mann KCVO, Rt Revd Michael, 20
Mann, Michael, 20, 23
Mark, Sir Robert, 126
Marker, D.S.O., Col R. J., 244
Martel, K.C.B., K.B.E., D.S.O., M.C., 293
Martell, E. D. (Ed.), 291
Martin, Capt. F., 240
Martin, Lt G. W., 156
Martin, M.B.E., Col T. A., 220

Martineau, G. D., 228
Masters, David, 291, 292, 293
Mather, M.C., Carol, 128
Maugham, Robin, 161, 162
Maxse, A. J. (Ed.), 16
Maxwell, Lt-Col J. P., 76
May, Col Ralph, 189, 193
Mayhew, Christopher, 127
Mayman, Doug, 62
McCorquodale, O.B.E., Col D., 19, 20
McEwen Charlish, M., 101
McGregor, Duncan, 77
McMahon, Capt. T., 152
McQueen Sgt, 114
Meakin, W.O.1 D., 14
Meek, Leslie A., 114
Meinertzhagen, Richard, 246
Merewood, Jack, 23
Mileham, P. J. R., 134, 135
Mileham, Patrick, 194, 220
Miles, Wilfrid, 200, 201
Miller, C.B., C.B.E., D.S.O., p.s.c., Maj-Gen. Charles H., 56
Miller, J. F. (Peter), 93
Moir, Guthrie, 205
Mollo, Boris, 160
Moore, William, 83, 222
Morgan, Maj. I. E., 25
Morgan, Paul, 152
Morland, Carole, 71, 79
Morris, G. A., 83
Morris, Geoffrey, 184
Mortimer, Denzil, 161
Moulton, Maj-Gen. J. L., 257, 258
Murland, Capt. J. R. W., 291
Murray, Maj. J. S. F., 61

N

Nairn, John, 113
Napier, Gerald, 234
Napier, Richard, 46
Neave, Julius, 58
Neillands, Robin, 275, 276, 278
Neville, Capt. R. F., 166
Newton, Cecil, 27, 28
Newton, E.T. (John), 117
Newton, Sgt M., 76

Nicholson, C.M.G., D.S.O., Col W. N., 205, 206
Nicholson, Capt. Nigel, 240, 241
Nicholson, Col W. N., 206
Nisbett, Gordon, 102
Niven, David, 125, 127

O

Oakley, Derek, 259, 260
Oatts, D.S.O., Lt-Col L. B., 24, 59, 223
Oatts, L. B., 223
O'Connor, Gary, 15
Onslow, K.B.E., M.C., T.D., The Earl of, 162, 164
Orde, R., 16
Osborne, Keith, 52, 53, 151, 173
Owen, Frank, 292

P

Packer, Cole, 109
Paget, Julian, 13, 238, 239
Paget, Julian (Ed.), 245
Pakenham-Walsh, C.B., M.C., Maj-Gen. R. P., 233, 234
Parker, John, 277, 278
Parlour, Andy & Sue, 128
Partington, S.V. (Ed.), 97
Peacock, Basil, 104, 113
Perrett, Bryan, 60, 266, 295, 296, 297, 298
Pharo-Tomlin, John, 60
Pierson, Brig. H. T., 42, 45
Pilborough, J., 29, 30
Pile, Frederick, 77
Pitman, Maj. Stuart, 153
Pitt Rivers, J. A., 33
Pitt, T.D., Lt-Col P. W., 135, 136
Platt, D.S.O., O.B.E., Brig. J. R. I., 136
Podmore, M.B.E., T.D., Maj. A. J., 179
Pollock, John, 22
Pope, M.C., Maj. Michael, 131
Powell, Geoffrey, 118, 119, 229, 230
Powell, John, 119, 230
Prescot, H. K. (Ed.), 148
Price, D.S.O., M.C., Lt-Col K. J., 42, 47
Prince, Lt-Col A. R. (Ed.), 105
Pringle, Patrick, 257

Pyman, G.B.E., K.C.B., D.S.O., M.A., Gen. Sir Harold, 82

Q

Queen, Harry, 29

R

Ramsbottom, Harry, 163
Rankin, Eric, 155
Ray, Cyril, 190, 191, 192, 207
Reddish, Arthur, 141, 142, 143
Redgrave, Roy, 15
Reetham, Edwin, 106
Reid, M.B.E., M.C., D.L., Miles, 126
Retallack, John, 253
Rhoderick-Jones, Brig. R. J., 42, 45
Richardson, Sue (Ed.), 176
Riesco, Capt. M. R., 105, 106
Rissik, David, 222, 223
Roach, Peter, 76
Roberts, C.B., D.S.O., M.C., Maj-Gen. Pip, 83, 262, 281
Rocksavage, M.C., The Earl of, 33
Rose, John, 115
Ross, Peter, 83
Rosse, Captain The Earl of, 286, 287, 288
Rossiter, Keith, 98
Royle, Trevor, 201, 254
Russell-Parsons, Maj. D. J. C., 242
Rutter, S.Q.M.S. H. W., 59
Ryder, Rowland, 288

S

Samm, Allan A., 121
Sandars, John, 275, 287
Sandes, D.S.O., M.C., R.E. (Retd), Lt-Col E. W. C., 196
Sankey, Martin L. H., 159
Savory, A. C. S., 197, 199, 210, 212
Scammell, William, 140
Scott Daniell, David, 42
Scott Dickins, Maj. G. L., 25
Scott, Anthony, 109
Scull, M.M., L. V., 183

Seaman, Peter, 67
Sellar, R. J. B., 157
Senior, M.C., Colonel Victor J., 176, 184
Senior, Sgt Anthony J., 40
Shand, Bruce, 54
Shand, Bruce (Ed.), 55
Sharpe, Phil, 112
Shears, Philip J, 192
Sheffield, Maj. O. F., 218
Shilleto, Carl, 115
Short, Lt E. W., 222
Silverthorne L. C., 238
Siminson, John, 55
Simpson, Gordon R., 156
Sinclair-Stevenson, Christopher, 200
Skinner, RAChD., Rvd Leslie, 140, 142
Smiley, David, 15
Smith, J. G., 204
Smith, Jack, 249
Smith, Norman, 90
Smith, Peter C., 258, 259
Sparrow, John, 244
Spencer-Nairn, M. A., 147, 158
Spencer-Smith, Jenny, 254
Sprot, M.C., Lt-Col Aidan, 37
Stammer, Olive Wood (Ed.), 126
Stephenson, Lt J. R., 114
Stewart, M.C., Capt. P. F., 54
Stiebel, H. A. J., 65
Stirling, Maj. J. P. D., 26, 27
Stone, Brian, 89
Strawson, C.B., O.B.E., Maj-Gen. J. M., 42, 45
Strawson, John, 43
Sumner, Ian, 169
Surtees, C.B., C.B.E., M.C., Maj-Gen G., 190, 191, 206
Sutcliffe, Victor, 297
Sutherland, Douglas, 193, 219
Swift, Sydney Fox, 31
Swinton, Maj. John, 247
Sylvester, Fred, 110, 111, 119, 229
Synge, Capt. W. A. T., 118, 229

T

Talbot, G. A. L. C. (Ed.), 60
Tamplin, Maj. R. L. C., 64
Taylor Firth, J. N., 176, 180

INDEX OF AUTHORS

Taylor, Capt. Vivian, 251
Taylor, Eric, 169, 210, 211, 213
Taylor, Jeremy, 100
Taylor, Jeremy (Ed.), 109
Taylor, Les, 167
Tee, Ronald A., 117
Tetley, Lt-Col, T.D., J. N., 179
Thomason, G. G., 181
Thompson, E. P., 124
Thompson, Julian, 259
Thompson, Ralph, 61
Thompson, T. J., 124
Thorogood, George Grant, 178
Todd, Capt. P. K. A., 235
Tout, Ken, 166, 167, 168
Treloar, G., 57

U

Underhill, Maj. D. F., 146, 147
Upton, Lt-Col P. K., 52
Upton, Peter, 50
Urban, Mark, 92, 93

V

van der Bijl, Nick, 259
Vaux, Peter, 89
Verdin, O.B.E., T.D., Lt-Col Sir Richard, 148
Verney, D.S.O., M.V.O., Maj-Gen. G. L., 273, 275, 286
Verney, D.S.O., M.V.O., Maj-Gen. G. L. (Collab.), 286
Verney, Maj-Gen. G. L., 274, 277
Verney, Peter, 250

W

Walker, Murray, 37, 38
Waller, Brig. R. P, 262
Waller, John (Eds), 138, 139
Wallington, R. S. J., 43
Ward, Ken, 78
Ward, S. G. P., 222, 223

Wardrop, Jake, 90, 91
Warner, Philip, 126, 128
Watney, John, 123
Watson, J. N. P., 13, 16, 34
Watt, Jock, 86
Whistler, Laurence, 252, 253
White, I.S.O., M.M., F. R. Hist. S., Arthur S. (Compiler), 294, 296, 297
Whitehead, Robert, 178
Whitelaw, William, 248
White-Spunner, Harvey, 14, 35
Whitfield, Maj. T. D. W., 114, 115
Whiting, Charles, 169, 210, 211, 213
Whitworth, R. H., 240
Williams, Hugh, 128
Williams, Margaret, 128
Williams, R. W. S., 94
Willis, Leonard, 70
Wilson, Andrew, 203, 204
Wilson, CBE, MC, DL, MA, FRGS, Major-General Dare, 104
Wilson, Edward, 91
Wilson, Maurice, 98
Wilson, Roy, 169
Windrow, Martin (Ed.), 101
Wood, Stephen, 25, 36
Woods, M.B.E., M.C., M.A., Maj-Gen. H. G., 30
Woods, Rex, 89
Woolley, J. F., 177
Woolnough, L.C.P., F. G., 290
Woolward, W. A., 155
Woozley, Maj. A. D., 19, 20
Worsthorne, Peregrine, 127
Wykes, Alan, 214
Wylly, C.B., Col H. C., 194
Wyndham M.C., Col the Hon. Humphrey, 14

Y

Young, Lachlan B., 156
Young, Robert, 96, 220, 221
Yule, C.S.M Andrew, 107

T.F.P. 101 C3 9/14

ADDENDA

The following publications were established just as this book was going to print. These two titles relate to **Section X – TA - Royal Armoured Corps Regiments**. Refer to p206, p224, and p228 for each regiment's listing.

143rd Regiment, Royal Armoured Corps	143 RAC

157th Regiment, Royal Armoured Corps	157 RAC

Through The Mill And Beyond
An Autobiography with Linton Mitchell
English, Arthur
London; Mildmay Books Limited; 1986; ISBN 1-8699450-1-8; 172pp/Illustrations; h/b / d/j Blue cloth; Indexed Y; Glossary N; Appendices N; Bibliography N
NOTES: The author, a well-known British comedian, joined 9th Bn, Hampshires prior to their conversion to 157 RAC. In 1943, after 157 RAC disbanded, he transferred to 143 RAC and following their disbandment at the end of 1943, he went to Lulworth Gunnery Ranges as an instructor. He served with 2nd Armoured Replacement Group in NWE and later fought as a tank commander although he does not expand on this nor specify the regiment. Military service covered in 8pp with only passing reference to tank regiments. (Not physically inspected.)

Through The Mill And Beyond
An Autobiography with Linton Mitchell
English, Arthur
Basingstoke; The Basingstoke Press (75) Ltd; 1989; ISBN 0-9514492-0-6; 183pp/Illustrations; s/b; Indexed Y; Glossary N; Appendices N; Bibliography N; 210 x 135 (8vo)
NOTES: Softback reprint of hardback first edition with additional few pages of update.

161st Regiment, Royal Armoured Corps	161 RAC

The History Of The Green Howards
A Series of Short Lectures
Not stated
Aldershot; Gale & Polden Ltd; 1954; ISBN None; 56pp/1 x clr SI/1 x bw M; s/b (card); Indexed N; Glossary N; Appendices Y; Bibliography N; 180 x 117 (12mo); Uncommon
NOTES: Pocket history for recruits, aimed at telling the stories behind the regiment's battle honours. 8pp on WWII, no reference to 12th Bn.

September 2014